L. F.

ESSAYS ON CLASSICAL LITERATURE

Views and Controversies about Classical Antiquity
General Editor: M. I. Finley

ESSAYS ON CLASSICAL LITERATURE

Selected from ARION
with an introduction by
NIALL RUDD
*Professor of Latin
in the University of Liverpool*

HEFFER / *Cambridge*
BARNES & NOBLE BOOKS / *New York*
(division of Harper & Row Publishers, Inc.)

This volume first published in 1972
by W. Heffer & Sons Limited
Cambridge, England

Heffer ISBN 0 85270 042 3
Barnes & Noble ISBN 389–04608–6

Photographically reprinted in Great Britain
by William Clowes & Sons, Limited,
London, Beccles and Colchester

CONTENTS

*The pagination of the present volume
is given in square brackets*

[v]

WHEN THESE ESSAYS HAD BEEN BROUGHT TOGETHER MY ORIGINAL plan was to confine the introduction to a few words about the principle of selection and arrangement. It was then suggested, however, that something more was called for—some kind of survey which would assess the present situation in the study of classical literature. If taken seriously such a task would demand an erudition and perspective which I cannot claim to have. What follows is meant rather as an impressionistic sketch outlining the main trends and features. Nevertheless, I have frequently referred to scholars by name. This may look like mere affectation, but it seemed the only way to prevent the essay from becoming completely vague and superficial.

As a start it may be helpful to look back and ask what works were commonly consulted by the pre-war undergraduate.[1] If he was taking his finals in 1939 he had no doubt read Bowra on the *Iliad* and Woodhouse on the *Odyssey*, and he might have known something about Allen, Bassett and Scott. For elegy and lyric he would go to Bowra, for Aeschylus to Weir Smyth and perhaps Miss Matthaei, and for Sophocles to Webster and the introduction to Sheppard's *Oedipus*. He would rely mainly on Murray for Euripides, though he might consult Appleton or Thomson. Other approaches to tragedy were available in the books of Norwood, Pickard-Cambridge, and F. L. Lucas. For comedy there was Norwood's general study and also Murray's *Aristophanes*. (Cornford was regarded with suspicion.) For new comedy and the Alexandrian poets the student would probably use Loeb's translations of Legrand and Couat. In addition to these works one thinks of Stanford's books on metaphor and ambiguity; a few collections of essays like those of Butcher and Mackail; and the literary histories of Sinclair and Rose. There was a notable deficiency in the area of Greek fiction, but as the novelists did not form part of the university syllabus nobody worried.[2]

On the Latin side, in addition to the literary histories of Sellar, Rose and Wight Duff, and collections of essays by Conway, Wright, and a few others, there was one book on Terence (Norwood), two on Plautus (Norwood and Westaway), two on Lucretius (Masson and Sikes), two and a half on Catullus (Wheeler, Havelock, and part of Frank), two and a half on Horace (D'Alton, Campbell, and the second part of Frank), and five on Virgil (Glover, Prescott, Frank, de Witt, Rand). There were also books on special aspects of Virgil, e.g. those by Bailey, Warde Fowler, Drew and Crump. Except, however, for Day's genetic inquiry, the student had nothing on the elegists; and apart from Butler nothing on the silver age poets. Mendell and Lucas had written on Seneca, but as far as I can recall no help was available on Cicero as a literary artist, or on Livy and Tacitus,[3] or on Petronius and Apuleius.

The reader will want to add other titles (I have made no systematic check). But allowing for some omissions the list remains rather short, and some of the gaps on the Latin side are embarrassingly obvious. Moreover, a large proportion of this work was devoted to problems of biography and literary history or else to the discussion of general ideas removed from their context. That, of course, was entirely legitimate, but it did mean that there was less than might have been expected in the way of comparison, analysis and appreciation. Finally, however excellent some of these books may be (and a number are undeniably excellent), their *total* does not reflect the strength of English classical scholarship in the previous fifty years.

That strength lay elsewhere. At the beginning of the period came the great Victorian commentaries—Leaf, Jebb, Munro, Ellis, Tyrrell and Purser, Mayor. The tradition was continued in the numerous commentaries large and small which came from the university presses, and in the admirable red Macmillan series. In America before 1914 the same type of scholarship was represented by men like Gildersleeve, Morris, Merrill, and Shorey. Many of these editors were sound textual critics who could describe a problem clearly and then make a judicious choice from a number of variants and conjectures. A few had the originality of genius. One thinks immediately of Housman, and then perhaps of Headlam. But many others made notable advances in restoring and explaining texts—Pearson, Lindsay, Postgate and Palmer are just a few of the names that come to mind. Such men have few equals today.

The preoccupations of editors and commentators were reflected in the journals of the period. The index to *Classical Review*, volumes I–LXIV, lists nineteen notes or articles on Catullus. Of these, eight concern his manuscripts; only two could be termed 'literary', and one of these turns out to be an article on Virgil's minor poems. Other entries show the same philological emphasis. A piece of work like Higham's essay on Ovid (1934) was very exceptional. No index is available for the *Classical Quarterly*, but in a quick glance through the thirty-odd pre-war volumes I noticed about fifteen articles on literature, that is about one article in every four numbers. *Greece and Rome* did print a more generous amount of literary material—at least one item per number, and this was no doubt of considerable value to pupils in their last two years at school. But with a few exceptions the articles were too brief and elementary for under-graduates or interested laymen.

It would be wrong, however, to imply that the British classic was trained solely in editorial skills. One other skill received almost equal attention, namely that of composition. This is no place to argue about the merits of prose- and verse-writing, but it is certainly true that in the curriculum of that time, when a student was rarely required to write literary criticism, composi-tion was virtually the only exercise that gave scope for creative activity. Not only did it demand a wide active vocabulary in Greek and Latin, it also required a close familiarity with the style and idiom of individual authors. The standard of expertise attained by the professionals can still be seen in such volumes as *Cambridge Compositions* and *Dublin Translations*, and it is not hard to understand why Tyrrell said of a similar collection that it contained more evidence of genuine scholarship than all the washing-lists of Thothnes that ever came out of Egypt.

If one thinks of classical graduates who are now in their seventies, it is not hard to see what type of mind this training produced. First, such men often retain an impressive store of facts. From early years they learned to cultivate what might be called a substantive memory, i.e. a memory for things in them-selves, as distinct from a procedural memory, which records only where and how a particular fact can be ascertained. Secondly, they will tend to assume that in a given context a word or phrase has a single meaning which can be discovered and demonstrated by logical argument; for them ambiguity is a sign of sloppy thinking if not of actual deceit. This tough-minded approach was developed long ago in grappling with philology (and later, history and philosophy), and it stood them in good stead in office, boardroom, and study during their working careers. To master a large array of facts, to order them and decide what is relevant, to reach a conclusion by deductive reasoning and then report one's findings in brief and lucid language—these are virtues of scholarship, and that is why Bacon said 'the general counsels, and the plots and marshalling of affairs, come best from those that are learned'.

Last of all, it is humiliating to think of the amount of classical poetry which such men have by heart. No doubt they spent weary hours acquiring it, and such effort is now, as we know, not encouraged. But in return they still possess after fifty years a mental anthology of Homer, Virgil and Horace, along with pas-sages of Shakespeare, the Romantics, Macaulay, Tennyson, and many others. By 'mental anthology' I do not mean anything external or mechanical. In many cases the poetry which the older classical man remembers is part of his spiritual being. Without it he would not be what he is. With it he is in a real sense the embodiment of a cultural tradition.

[ix]

I hope enough has been said to show that the old system, which was still vigorous in the twenties, was worthy of high respect. What those men did they did extremely well, and it is up to those who are now *nel mezzo del cammin* to ensure that as much as possible of that scholarly rigour is maintained.

Nevertheless, it must be conceded that, from about 1930 on, certain limitations were becoming apparent in the approach to classical literature, and by 1950 there was real cause for dissatisfaction. This was not primarily due to a lack of explanatory notes. True, some of the major authors had gone without a commentary for a very long time (we still await something new on the *Iliad* and Juvenal), but in most cases the older works could be brought reasonably up to date by a competent teacher. In other areas new and helpful commentaries *had* appeared (some of them, like those of Fraenkel and Gow, monumental works of scholarship). What the student now required was some indication of why the lines on the page before him were supposed to constitute a work of art. With very few exceptions (e.g. Dodds and Stanford) the editors gave no assistance.[4] This might have been justified had there been a large body of critical literature available, but this was not the case. Or perhaps I should say that what *was* available was only partly what one wanted.

This may sound very ungrateful. After all, several distinguished books had appeared since 1939. Readers of tragedy were particularly fortunate in having the help of Kitto, Murray, Bowra, and Winnington-Ingram. As for Latin studies, Rose, Jackson Knight and Cruttwell (in descending order of clarity) had written on Virgil; and Wilkinson had produced his scholarly and elegant account of Horace's characteristics as a lyric poet.[5] Nevertheless, in spite of what these works supplied, the student of 1950 was aware of certain deficiencies, partly of matter, partly of method, in the study of ancient literature.

First (though not most important), it was extraordinarily hard to get help with, and sometimes even to find out about, those passages which had been suppressed by Victorian prudery. I can remember being mildly surprised at the brevity of Horace, *Sat.* I.2, until I came to Gow's laconic warning: 'The last 110 lines of this Satire are not read.' Of English editors only the despised Macleane had the courage to print and comment on Juvenal 2 and 9. There was no commentary on the *Ars Amatoria*, and in reading the Loeb Martial one found that, although the obscene poems had been translated, the language chosen for the purpose was for some reason Italian. Naturally where there was neither translation nor commentary it was useless to expect criticism.

Secondly, although the cruder ideas about the nature of originality were now on the wane, it was not easy to obtain any notion of the various ways in which tradition was creatively employed. Terence's 'contamination' of new comedy, Virgil's allusions to Homer and Ennius, Ovid's use of Nicander, the elegists' treatment of common themes, Persius's adaptations of Horace, Petronius's parody of Greek romance—these are all different procedures, and they can only be appreciated by setting numerous passages side by side and asking why a given phrase or episode was taken over, how it has been changed, and how it functions in its new context. Studies of this kind were rare in 1950, and even now a good deal remains to be done.

Thirdly, in what had been written about the ideas and religion and style of the major authors the method, more often than not, had been that of abstraction and synthesis. Now it may well be that such a method is necessary if one is aiming at a comprehensive survey; but in that case neither the ideas nor the religion nor the style can be studied in a single poem; still less can they all be seen working there together. Obviously single poems vary enormously in length and complexity. With epic and tragedy one is obliged to examine selected passages (a scene, an episode, or a chorus). But the same problem does not exist in the case of shorter poems, and there relatively little had been done. In Virgil's *Eclogues*, for instance, great subtlety and learning had been expended on the site of the poet's farm, the eviction-question, the use of allegory, and the identity of the marvellous child. But, to put it rather crudely, would these studies have been substantially different had Virgil written in prose? There was, then, some substance in the complaint that not enough attention had been given to poems as artistic units.[6]

Fourthly, the relation of history and biography to literary criticism had not been very fully considered. One thinks of all those commentaries and handbooks which give an outline of the poet's life and times, and then after a few words of paraphrase or eulogy leave the reader to his own devices. A more positive illustration of the same confusion was the assumption that details of a biographical kind could be inferred quite freely from a poet's work. Writing about Propertius, Sellar tells us that 'his extreme paleness and the slightness of his figure were the signs of a constitution unfitting, or at least disinclining him for any of the more manly amusements of youth'.[7] Our concern for the sickly lad is relieved by the discovery that the statement rests entirely on

> nec iam pallorem totiens mirabere nostrum
> aut cur sim toto corpore nullus ego   (1.5.21–22)

—a conventional picture of the woebegone lover.

Fifthly, in general reading one often encountered judgements which appeared to be the outcome of great erudition, insight and maturity—and perhaps indeed they were; unfortunately they were seldom supported by any kind of evidence or argument. 'The central heart of [Sophocles'] poetry', says Mackail, 'is found, I think, in the other two plays of the lesser selection. The *Aias* is unequalled for splendour and elevation, the *Electra* for brilliance and elasticity.'[8] T. E. Page in the introduction to his commentary on the *Odes* (p. xx) tells us that 'the characteristics of the *Odes* are (1) their wonderful charm of rhythm, and (2) their perfect literary finish'. Neither scholar offers adequate illustration; which is disappointing—it would have been interesting to learn more about the elastic *Electra*.

These pronouncements and many others like them, which seemed designed to impress rather than instruct, served in the end only to exasperate the reader. One can therefore understand the excitement with which students read the opening words of Kitto's preface: 'A book on Greek Tragedy may be a work of historical scholarship or of literary criticism; this book professes to be a work of criticism. Criticism is of two kinds: the critic may tell the reader what he so beautifully thinks about it all, or he may try to explain the form in which the literature is written. This book attempts the latter task.' The questions Kitto asked were just the ones which we wanted to see discussed (even if we had never thought of them), and his provocative style was immensely refreshing. Some of his views are doubtless open to attack, but it is no accident that Kitto is one of the very few classical critics with a wide general audience.

The discontent felt in 1950 therefore implied a wish to learn about ancient poetry as poetry; to see what remained when background, biography, sources, and paraphrasable content had all been ascertained. There was an eagerness to compare, analyse and interpret—to do all the things that English critics had been doing for twenty years. The tools were at hand; but first one had to find them, and then try to learn how to use them. That was to take another decade.

All this poses an interesting question. Why was it that when Richards, Spurgeon, Wilson Knight and others had been known for so long, when *Scrutiny* was nearing the end of its run, and when the volume of criticism by and about Pound and Eliot was formidably large, classical scholars should on the whole have had so little to say about such phenomena as structure, texture, and tone? I do not pretend to know the full answer, but some of the truth may be contained in the following points. First, the number of people interested in applying the new techniques to Greek and Latin was smaller than might be assumed. In the British universities the men who lectured on Sophocles and Virgil might be expert philologists or highly qualified in history or philosophy. On the whole they were not especially interested in literary criticism, and some of them despised it.

As most of these scholars came from Oxford or Cambridge their interests reflected the strengths of those two institutions.

Some very able Oxford men have been known to say that the structure of Mods and Greats signified that literature (by which they meant classical philology) was useful mainly as a propae-deutic to the more serious disciplines of history and philosophy. An outsider is afraid to laugh at a remark like that. It is safer simply to ask whether literary criticism had much chance to develop in a system where philology itself had a subordinate role.[9]

At Cambridge the situation was different. In Part II of the Tripos it was possible to take special papers in literature. One of these, however, was devoted to traditional scholarly topics and the other to textual criticism. Here one should mention the influence of Housman, which was doubly potent in that one could hardly brand the author of *A Shropshire Lad* and *The Name and Nature of Poetry* as an insensitive philistine—unless one possessed the ardour and confidence of Ezra Pound.[10]

And so the classical student with an interest in literature had to seek help from outside his own discipline. Unfortunately when he listened to some of the leading English critics what he heard was discouraging. He was told that the common result of a classical training was 'to incapacitate from contact with litera-ture for life'.[11] He had understood that Milton was a poet worth reading, and that Homer and Virgil were indispensable keys for comprehending him. Now he learned that Milton had been dis-lodged. Shelley was also out of favour, and so was Tennyson.

What, in fact, had happened to the kind of public which enjoyed Tennyson? It had been warned off; it had been treated to sneers, threats and enigmas. It had been told so often that it had no status and no business in the sacred wood, and it had found the business actually being transacted there so remote from its ordinary apprehension, that it had turned away, in indifference, or disgust, or despair.

The language in that last paragraph may perhaps be thought rather too powerful. But then it isn't mine. It comes from Profes-sor Graham Hough.[12] Whether or not things were quite that bad, enough has been said, I hope, to show that in 1950 the classic did not find it easy to join in the common pursuit.

In North America the situation had developed along different lines.[13] There literary scholarship had never been so subordinate as in England. If once again we recall the position in 1950 we find that a number of books had recently appeared by such men as H. Fraenkel, Solmsen, Carpenter, Norwood and Grube. In addition, there had always been a fair proportion of literary material in the journals, of which there were at least half a dozen (not counting university publications). As a result, anyone working on, let us say, Horatian satire in the 1950s was helped and challenged by Hendrickson, Ullman, Fiske, Frank, and W. S. Anderson. These men had no counterparts in England. Or again, let us imagine four students looking for assistance on Aesop, Chariton, Petronius, and Apuleius. They would all have ended up at the same source—B. E. Perry. As for Homer, the brilliant researches of Milman Parry, which began to appear in the 1930s, are still being assimilated and assessed.[14]

Because of this continuous tradition of literary inquiry, the effects of English criticism were felt rather more quickly. Earlier examples may be found, but one suspects that the influence began to appear when Elder wrote about Catullus, Knox about the imagery of *Aeneid* Book II, Goheen about the *Antigone*, and Helmbold about the *Oedipus Rex*.[15] After that quite a lot of work was published, especially on Catullus, Horace, and Propertius, much of it showing the influence of Brooks, Wimsatt, Wellek, and Warren. Writers now did their best to examine the poems as autonomous entities, and this procedure (employed by Richards in 1929) was defended for classical readers by Cherniss and Allen.[16]

Another healthy sign was the growing number of good translations. The 1950s saw the appearance of Lattimore's *Iliad*, the Chicago translations of Greek tragedy, and the *Metamorphoses* of Humphries, Watts, and Gregory. These are some examples of works which met the demands of large classes of students throughout the continent and did much to make the educated public aware of the importance of ancient literature. Perhaps surprisingly, Classics in Translation programmes also served the cause of literary criticism. For at the prospect of meeting a group of fifty or more students—all literate and some highly intelligent —the scholar had to decide what the universal and enduring elements in Homer and Virgil really were. There was no use in discussing Arcado-Cyprian or the authenticity of the Appendix. Nor in time of trouble could one fall back on translating the text. Admittedly the literary approach had its own dangers, but one could always remember that Matthew Arnold's thin green volume, which Housman so much admired, was a series of lectures on translation.

So much for the happier aspects of the scene. But *nihil est ab omni/parte beatum*. One grim question cannot be avoided: 'What texts and commentaries were produced in the United States or Canada between 1915 and 1965?' For texts one thinks of Perry's *Aesopica*, Blake's Chariton, Clausen's Persius and Juvenal, and perhaps the Harvard Servius (though it hardly comes into our categories). There must be others, but it is not a long list. Commentaries are hardly more numerous—Pease's *Aeneid* IV, Leonard and Smith's Lucretius, and, on a much smaller scale, Hammond's *Menaechmi* and *Miles Gloriosus*. One assumes that this dismal situation has some connexion with the decline of language-teaching in the high schools, which is itself a complex cultural phenomenon. Its relevance to our present

[xiv]

topic lies in the fact that when literary criticism is not based on a reasonably sound knowledge of the language, and when it is not controlled by logic and common sense (as the traditional commentaries were), it is liable to become fanciful and pretentious. This sounds very obvious, but anyone who has been connected with a North American classical journal and has seen some of the material submitted will concede that the point is sometimes forgotten.

If we broke off here it might seem as if there was a gulf as wide as the Atlantic between Britain ('sound, conservative, philological') and North America ('lively, literary, occasionally unsteady'). But that would be a very crude and misleading dichotomy, and so it is worth mentioning some of the factors which bring the two areas together. First, in Britain there has been a noticeable movement in favour of literary criticism from within the secondary schools, which has found expression through JACT, *Didaskalos*, the *Greece and Rome* surveys, and Balme and Warman's *Aestimanda*. In various centres school-teachers and lecturers are getting together to study literary texts and the ways in which they can be interpreted to classes. At Cambridge dons and graduate students meet to discuss papers on practical criticism. Essays appear in the *Proceedings of the Virgil Society* and in the Dudley and Dorey series. Scholars like R. G. Austin and R. D. Williams incorporate far more literary material into their commentaries than was done by Page or Sidgwick; they are also willing to use their erudition as a basis for lively literary articles. The same is true of E. J. Kenney and R. G. M. Nisbet.[17] Others, like H. A. Mason, John Jones, and M. R. Ridley, whose special interest lies in English literature, are willing to bring their wider experience to bear on the classical authors. New translations (Lee's *Amores*, Sullivan's Petronius, and others) are appearing which will delight the general reader and benefit the student —especially if he is taking a course on literature in translation. Finally, reputable Latinists are now writing more books of a literary kind e.g. Camps and Wilkinson on Virgil, West on Horace and Lucretius, Walsh on Petronius, and G. W. Williams on the Roman poets. These developments are all welcome, and there is no reason why they should have any injurious effect on the fundamental scholarly skills, which are still guaranteed by the prestige of the Oxford, Cambridge and London professors.

In North America during the last twenty years or so there has been a steady output of scholarly work owing nothing to what is loosely referred to as the new criticism. One thinks of Highet on the classical tradition. Duckworth on Roman comedy, and Grube on the Greek and Roman critics. There have also been several books in which the new insights have been assimilated and combined with traditional learning—e.g. Kirkwood on Sophocles, Conacher on Euripides, Otis on Virgil. In one particular area—that of Homeric studies—a great deal of linguistic work has been done, e.g. by Lord, Notopoulos, Kirk, and Adam Parry. Here nothing subjective or loosely argued is allowed to pass. Finally, it is hard to imagine that with Clausen, Goold, and Shackleton Bailey in the States, and Young and Huxley in Canada, the art of editing will not begin to recover lost ground.

And so to the present collection. The idea took shape in discussions between the general editor of this series and J. P. Sullivan. It was decided that all the contributions should come from ARION, partly for administrative convenience, partly because that journal was to a large extent the outcome of the worries and aspirations described above. This decision in no way implied that ARION was the only periodical publishing literary work. But to collect a dozen essays, related only by the tie of literary interest, would have been a difficult and rather pointless undertaking; some further limitation was necessary. It was also decided that the editor should be someone who shared ARION's general aims, without having any association with its board and without necessarily approving of everything which that journal had published.

After taking on this role I had to make some decisions of a negative kind: nothing later than Volume VI, no translations, no excerpts, nothing which was not directly related to classical literature, and (regrettably) nothing from Autolycus. Then one looked for variety and balance. It seemed best that there should be three sections—one on Greek, one on Latin, and one on the classical tradition. Finally, an attempt was made, though without complete success, to acknowledge the main genres. Of the resulting arrangement the reader must judge. If he finds that the emphasis is perhaps rather on continuity than on novelty I shall not complain. In such cases it is hard to produce 'an easy commerce of the old and the new', and only a hardened optimist will hope to set 'the complete consort dancing together'. At any rate it is the individual essays that matter, and here the only important question is 'Do they promote an intelligent appreciation of classical literature?' I believe they do.

It remains only to thank the contributors for allowing their work to be reprinted (and the Macmillan Company, New York, for permission to include Robert Fitzgerald's introduction to Virgil's *Aeneid*), Miss Duell and Miss Anderson of ARION for dealing with the preliminary correspondence, and Mr Collieson and his colleagues in Heffers for bringing out the finished product.

NOTES

1. I shall be speaking throughout only of works written in English, and I use 'literature' in the narrow sense of poetry and fiction. History and philosophy are excluded, as are books on ancient criticism and on the theatre (as distinct from drama).

2. To be more specific: there were two very helpful works—R. M. Rattenbury's paper in *New Chapters in Greek Literature*, Third Series (1933), and M. Braun, *History and Romance in Graeco-Oriental Literature* (1938). Neither scholar was primarily concerned with literary criticism. For that one had to go to S. L. Wolf, *The Greek Romances in Elizabethan Prose Fiction* (New York 1912 and 1961). It is significant that Wolf was an English Literature scholar and an American.

3. The raw material for a literary study of Tacitus was to be found in Furneaux's introduction.

4. The policy was later made explicit by H. J. Rose in the preface to his commentary on Aeschylus (p. 1): 'Of aesthetic criticism the reader will find little or none. This is deliberate. Aesthetic criticism, unless it is very good indeed, is apt to be dull and to tell a reasonably intelligent student of literature nothing which he cannot see for himself.'

5. Here only British scholars are mentioned. Below something will be said of the situation in North America. Unfortunately space prevents any reference to work done in Australia, New Zealand, and South Africa.

6. At the end of his book on Virgil, Brooks Otis says, 'In general I have gained far more from recent Virgilian scholarship in French and German than from that in English or Italian' (413). An exception is made in favour of R. S. Conway.

7. W. Y. Sellar, *The Roman Poets of the Augustan Age*, p. 281.

8. J. W. Mackail, *Lectures on Greek Poetry*, p. 68. These lectures were reprinted in 1926.

9. This has now ceased to be true.

10. Cf. the essay entitled 'Mr. Housman at Little Bethel'.

11. F. R. Leavis, *Education and the University*[2] (1948), 134.

12. Graham Hough, *Image and Experience* (1960), 26.

13. 'North America' is used to include the United States and Canada.

14. See *Yale Classical Studies* 20 (1966), and *The Language and Background of Homer*, edited by G. S. Kirk in the present series.

15. J. P. Elder, *Harvard Studies in Classical Philology* 60 (1951) 101–36.
B. W. Knox, *American Journal of Philology* 71 (1950) 379–400.
R. F. Goheen, *The Imagery of Sophocles' Antigone* (1951).
W. C. Helmbold, *American Journal of Philology* 72 (1951) 293–300.

16. The essays of both scholars were republished in *Critical Essays on Roman Literature*, Vol. I, ed. J. P. Sullivan (1962).

17. Eg. R. G. Austin's inaugural lecture, *Some English Translations of Virgil* (1956); R. D. Williams on *Aeneid* Book VI in *Greece and Rome* 11 (1964) 48–63; E. J. Kenney on Juvenal, *Latomus* 22 (1963) 704–20; R. G. M. Nisbet on Persius, *Critical Essays on Roman Literature*, Vol. II, ed. J. P. Sullivan (1963) 39–71.

NOTES ON CONTRIBUTORS

WILLIAM ARROWSMITH: PH.D. Princeton, M.A. Oxford. Professor of Classics and University Professor in Arts and Letters, University of Texas. He is well known as a translator, essayist and critic, and is associated with several literary journals, including *Hudson Review, Mosaic,* and *Delos.*

D. S. CARNE-ROSS: M.A., English Language and Literature, Oxford. Professor of Comparative Literature, University of Texas. He has written extensively on classical and Italian subjects in *The Times Literary Supplement,* the *New York Review of Books,* ARION, and elsewhere. Now editor of *Delos,* a journal specializing in translation.

HENRY EBEL: PH.D. Columbia. He has taught at Wesleyan, Fordham, and the City University of New York. At present he is preparing a study of Apuleius.

ROBERT FITZGERALD: Widely known for his translations of Greek drama and also for his version of the *Odyssey* (1961). He has had a distinguished career both as a journalist (*New York Herald Tribune* and *Time*) and as a poet (*A Wreath for the Sea* [1943] and *In the Rose of Time* [1956]). Recently he has edited the poetry and short prose of James Agee.

THOMAS GOULD: PH.D. Cornell. Professor of Classics and Philosophy, University of Texas. He has held visiting appointments at St Andrews, Cambridge, and Yale. His published works include a book entitled *Platonic Love* (1963) and a translation of Sophocles' *Oedipus Rex* with introduction and commentary.

C. J. HERINGTON: A graduate of Oxford, Professor Herington was at Manchester and Toronto before moving to Texas, where he is now Chairman of the Classics department. In addition to articles and reviews, he has written a book entitled *Athena Parthenos and Athena Polias* (1955). He is now preparing a translation of Aeschylus' *Prometheus Vinctus* with commentary.

RICHMOND LATTIMORE: Has achieved an international reputation in more than one field. His scholarly work began with *Themes in Greek and Latin Epitaphs* (1942); his translations of Homer and Greek tragedy have won wide acclaim; and he is a poet in his own right. His degrees include an Oxford B.A. and a PH.D. from Illinois. He is Professor of Greek at Bryn Mawr.

H. A. MASON: M.A. Oxford and Cambridge. From 1947 to 1953 an editor of *Scrutiny*, now an editor of *The Cambridge Quarterly*. He has written the following books: *Humanism and Poetry in the Early Tudor Period* (1959 and 1966), *Love and Death in Shakespeare* (1970) and *Introducing Homer's Iliad* (1970). His essay on Juvenal ('Is Juvenal a Classic?'), which originally appeared in ARION, was reprinted in *Critical Essays on Roman Literature*, ed. J. P. Sullivan (1963).

KENNETH QUINN: Read Classics at Cambridge, where he became a Fellow of St John's College. Held appointments at Melbourne and Otago before moving to Toronto, where he is now a Professor of Classics. The titles of his books are: *The Catullan Revolution* (1959), *Latin Explorations* (1963), *Virgil's Aeneid: A Critical Description* (1968).

NIALL RUDD: PH.D. Trinity College Dublin; a Professor at Toronto until 1968, when he moved to Liverpool. In addition to articles and reviews, has published *The Satires of Horace* (1966).

J. P. SULLIVAN: M.A. Cambridge; Fellow and Tutor in Classics, Lincoln College, Oxford; Professor of Classics at Texas 1963–9; now Faculty Professor of Arts and Letters at Buffalo. His books include *Ezra Pound and Propertius* (1965) and *The Satyricon: A Literary Study* (1968).

DOUGLAS YOUNG: M.A., D.LITT. (St Andrews); has held appointments at Aberdeen, St Andrews, and Minnesota; now a Professor of Classics at McMaster University. Besides editing Theognis for Teubner (1961), Dr Young has published numerous papers on Greek literature, and also collections of verse, translations, and a travel book, *Chasing an Ancient Greek* (1950). He is now working on the manuscripts of Aeschylus' *Septem Contra Thebas*.

AESCHYLUS: THE LAST PHASE

C. J. Herington

THE STARTING-POINT OF THIS article[1] is a fact which now seems to me almost certain: that Aeschylus' *Suppliants*-tetralogy, *Oresteia*, and *Prometheia*—in that order—form a compact group of works at the very end of the poet's career. I accept (as I think most people now do) the implication of the papyrus-hypothesis that the *Suppliants*-tetralogy must date from 466 B.C. or later, perhaps 463[2]. It has always been known, beyond doubt, that the *Oresteia* was produced in Spring 458. And lastly I am convinced by a number of arguments of varying type, produced over the last fifty years, that the *Prometheia* must have been written after the *Oresteia* if it was written by Aeschylus at all (which I firmly believe).[3] The *Prometheus* must in that case belong to the last two years of Aeschylus' life: between 458 and his death in Sicily, 456/5.

These datings mean that we still have, in whole or part, a very high proportion of the tetralogies that Aeschylus actually composed in his last ten years, or perhaps even in his last seven. It could be that they represent *all* the tetralogies which he composed in this time; but even if that is not so, there is hardly space for more than one other tetralogy in the period, or two at the outside. Now my belief is that they are not merely chronologically a compact group, but that they are so artistically as well. Even more: that in these last three surviving works Aeschylus created a new art-form, something that differs *in kind* from any work that was staged under the name of tragedy, either his own or anybody else's, before or after that final decade of his life. A consequence of this will be that the three surviving examples of what I think of as a unique art-form can be used, more than is generally recognized, to explain each other; and that, in particular, the *Prometheus* begins to make more sense than it did.

That, in outline, is the position whose meaning and consequences are to be discussed in this paper. But I feel it necessary, first, to step right back and ask a question of method. There seem to be some artists whose works gain little or nothing in meaning through being dated at a specific point in the maker's life, and grouped with the other works of the same period. This sort of artist engineers internally-consistent structures that are independent of himself: the façade is raised, is checked for symmetry and mechanical stress in all directions—and the little architect steps

from behind it with a wave of the hand and wanders off anywhere, leaving behind him a thing made. With such work (I
think, heretically perhaps, of the plays of Sophocles and the odes
of Horace) dating and grouping seem to be largely antiquarian
labor. But there exists another sort of artist, whose work, and
whose relationship to the work, are altogether different. Not long
ago a large exhibition of Picasso's works toured the northern parts
of America, showing some of us (at least) for the first time a
really representative selection of his paintings and drawings, in
chronological order. The first impression of an innocent observer,
after walking through the galleries from one end to the other,
was: an exhibition by seven or eight different men, practising
seven or eight different arts. What it actually was, of course, was
an exhibition by an individual who many times, under the stress
of a new technical idea or of something he had seen in the world,
ruthlessly and abruptly threw overboard his previous achievement, and tried again. That drawing of a rampant Minotaur in
Room VII really did not have a lot to do with that painting of a
serene woman's face under a broad-brimmed hat in Room I. Each,
in its own way, gave proof of a treasury of skill and experience.
But the woman breathed the air and the style of Paris in the early
nineteen-hundreds, the Minotaur had crept out of the labyrinth of
the Spanish Civil War. Fully to come to grips with the monster,
you had to realize that he was only a study, a fragment of a
greater experience; you had to move to the canvases on the wall
around him and even, in imagination, to Spain and to the war
itself.

Now although the point is not mathematically provable, I
believe that most people who have spent any reasonable time on
Aeschylus will have felt that they are having to do with this second
sort of artist. As a citizen and as a poet he lives in an age of crisis.
Classical society—or, if you like, modern society—is being born out
of archaism. Correspondingly, tragedy is being born out of song.
We cannot at any stage of Aeschylus' life say that tragedy is;
we can only say that it is becoming. Aeschylus' thought, and the
technique to match his thought, are dynamic and evolutionary,
receptive always to what is new. Such a poet as that might begin
his career with a two-dimensional imagination like a Persian
carpet,[4] close-woven with archaic centaurs, hippocamps and
horsecocks; he might end it with a mind fixed on the profound
space that is opened by the coming of philosophy. If that was in
fact so, then the grouping of the plays by date would be an
unavoidable stage towards understanding.

On these assumptions I again turn to the main position: that
the *Suppliants*-tetralogy, the *Oresteia*, and the *Prometheia* (to
which I shall refer from now on as "the late group," for short)
were composed in that order during Aeschylus' last ten or seven
years, and that they represent most, if not all, of a phase in the

tragic art which is sharply set off from anything discernible before or after.

The first step must be to survey the tragedies which lie on either side of the late group, chronologically speaking. Before 466 B.C. Aeschylus had already been composing for well over thirty years—a good working lifetime in itself. During that time the only two fixed dates and fixed points, so far as present knowledge goes, are the production of the *Persians* in 472, and that of the *Seven Against Thebes* in 467. Now, wildly different as these two tragedies are, thematically and musically, they yet imply the same cosmic background, and the same view of the human situation and human destiny. The cosmos here is—by comparison with what is to come in the late group—almost a comfortable one; in the sense that, however grim it is, however frightful the choices to be made within it, at least the roots of things remain the same. The archaic powers, both those in heaven and those below the earth reign each unquestioned in their own spheres; in the *Seven*, infernal Furies and Olympian Apollo conspire towards the downfall of the house of Oedipus.[5] And in this universe the laws, though harsh, are not blind, nor purely deterministic. Catastrophe, when it comes, is doubly motivated: something said or done in the past (an oracle, a family curse) preordains it externally, but it is only triggered off by something internal, something in the man himself. The two types of motivation are not, indeed, equally stressed in each play. In the *Persians* the disaster due to Xerxes' pride is already known when the ghost of Darius suddenly produces an oracle (otherwise unrecorded, either in history or in the actual play) which has foretold the downfall of the Persian army (*Persians*, 739–44, 801); conversely, in the *Seven*, it is the inner rage of Eteocles—long ago destined to destruction by the Curse—that is held back from the audience until comparatively late (653 ff.). But in both plays the dual motivation of catastrophe is there for all to see. I would stress that it is not, of course, just a superficial matter of plot-mechanics; it involves, in itself, a subtle and not yet quite disproved view of human nature and destiny.

So much for the two tragedies that survive from the period before the Aeschylean late group. Paradoxically, but I believe truly, it must now be observed that their closest relatives, in some important respects, are to be found not in that late group, but in the earlier surviving plays of Sophocles: the *Ajax*, the *Antigone*, and the *Oedipus Tyrannus*, which were produced within the twenty years or so following Aeschylus' death. For those three Sophoclean plays fundamentally imply for dramatic purposes the same cosmos, and are constructed round the same double motivation, as the *Persians* and the *Seven*. In saying this, of course, I am not forgetting the great differences between the plays, and between the poets; each play has its individual soul, as it were, which at the moment I am not trying to approach. But behind

[3]

all the differences I seem to see the same frame of reference, within which the drama is built. That is true, also, of yet another tragedy written down in the same period as the earlier Sophoclean plays, probably in the forties of the fifth century: the prose tragedy of Croesus, King of Lydia, which stands at the opening of Herodotus' History.[6] Here, in fact, the two motivations which converge towards the downfall of the hero are emphasized almost too clearly—the oracle which foredooms the end of Gyges' dynasty in the fifth generation (I. 13, 91), and the recklessness which springs from within Croesus himself.

So far as our evidence goes, then (and there seems just enough of it to exclude the possibility that we are being deluded by the accidents of preservation), tragic writing both before and in the generation after the Aeschylean late group, for all its variety in detail, moves against the background of the same universe. If there is any rift in that universe, it is between man and the unseen powers; whose laws he may challenge or misread, just as he may misread his own nature. In any of those events he, the individual, is due for destruction; but the universe itself remains as it was before, static, undivided. I repeat that the variety of movement against that cosmic background is immense, even to judge from the extant plays. And we should certainly have some shocks if the sands were to open up and yield some of the more eccentric lost tragedies of which the fragments now allow us only glimpses —Jason and the Argonauts rolling drunk on the stage in Aeschylus' *Kabeiroi*; the sword doubling back against the invulnerable flesh when the Aeschylean Ajax tries to commit suicide;[7] or the Aeschylean Priam literally weighing Hector's body in the scales against gold.[8] But there is nothing in the fragments to indicate that such plays, too, did not move within the frame of this unified, archaic universe.

It will at once be clear that the Aeschylean late group— *Suppliants*-tetralogy, *Oresteia*, *Prometheia*—will not fit into that frame at all; that from this point of view it forms a completely separate enclave in the known history of Greek tragedy before *c*. 440 B.C., or rather of all Greek tragedy. But, although that is to my mind the most striking of the features that link the three works together, I do not think it is the only one, either in detail or on the grand scale. Of the many others, there are four which seem to be of special significance: the technique of trilogy-composition; the involvement of Gods in human feuds; the comic (in the technical sense of *Old Comic*) element; and the intrusion of contemporary philosophical speculation. I shall look at these in turn, with just one remark by way of preface. Throughout this article, but especially here, I am obliged to pass over many controversies and doubts as to points of detail, simply in order to keep the outlines clear at all. But I hope that this is not for lack of

[4]

careful consideration, both of the basic evidence and of much of the controversy about it.

Probably the most striking feature is the first of those mentioned: the technique of putting together a tragic trilogy. The Aeschylean late group shows an odd, unbalanced relationship between the three plays which constitute the trilogy on the one hand, and the traditional myth which contributes its subject-matter on the other. The complete *Oresteia* is the simplest example. Its trilogic form can be symbolized as *A, A, B*: two responding plays to begin with and the third wild, non-responding. The *Agamemnon* and *Choephori* not only respond to each other in movement—murder and counter-murder—but they are also grouped together by the fact that the basic story in both, and even the characters, are in conformity with the traditional myth already known (in outline at least) a century before Aeschylus, and in part known to Homer too. (Again I should emphasize that I am not trying to touch the soul of these plays, nor forgetting that Aeschylus slants the traditional story in ways all his own. Here I am trying to view the grand overall movement, as if through the eyes of the designer as he makes his first outline, sketch-block on knee.) But the *third* member of the *Oresteia*, the *Eumenides*, has a totally different character and movement from the first two; and all the evidence which we have so far, both internal and external, suggests that its plot was freely invented by Aeschylus *ad hoc*, to resolve the issues raised, through the medium of the traditional story, in the first two plays. The only traditional legendary element visible in the *Eumenides* is, probably, the purification of Orestes at Delphi—and my own reading of the play suggests that even this element is not so much re-used by Aeschylus as perverted. Instead of a proof of Apollo's ultimate healing and reconciling power (as which it was surely intended by its inventors) it has become, in the context of this play, a proof of Apollo's inefficacy; instead of a pious and harmonious finale to Orestes-story it now serves merely as a horrific *proagon*, in which the two parties to the coming cosmic *agon* are first alternately paraded and then confronted.

The same curious principle of trilogic composition seems to have applied in the remaining two trilogies of the late group. Appallingly fragmentary as the *Suppliants*-trilogy and the *Prometheia* now are, there are still more solid reasons than one might think for this belief. To take the *Prometheia*: the basic story here, that Prometheus was bound by Zeus and later released by Herakles, is standard in Greek mythical accounts from Hesiod (*Theogony* 521ff.) until the end of the ancient world (and beyond the end). But there is no such universal agreement as to what happened *after* the release. Hesiod says nothing on the point, and if we look to the many later ancient versions of the Prometheus-story we find the wildest diversity. Now Aeschylus' *Prometheus*

Bound and *Prometheus Unbound,* for all their deliberate re-handling and censoring of Hesiod's story, were fundamentally based on that story, and presupposed a knowledge of it in their audience. In fact, we know enough of the two of them to be sure that between them they covered approximately the same legendary area as the Hesiodic version, the boundary being drawn between the two antithetic parts: the binding and the releasing (compare the murder and counter-murder in the *Agamemnon* and *Choephori*). It is a necessary inference from these facts that the third play of the trilogy—which I believe, in common with the majority of those who have considered the problem, to have once existed, and to have been entitled the *Prometheus Pyrphoros* —abandoned Hesiod entirely. And it is a likely inference, since no important pre-Aeschylean source for the Prometheus story other than Hesiod is known, that it must have contained a freely invented synthesis of the antithesis set up in the first two plays.

Finally, the evidence about the earliest of the Aeschylean late group, the *Suppliants*-trilogy, strongly suggests the same pattern. All versions of the legend of the Danaid girls, at all dates, agree on the basic story: the escape of the girls and their father from Egypt to Argos, chased by their cousins; their eventual unwilling marriage; and those 49 murders on the wedding-night. But there is no fixed tradition at all as to what happened after that night; thenceforward there are as many versions as there are tellers.[9] What is known of Aeschylus' *Suppliants*-trilogy suggests, beyond reasonable doubt, that the first two of its plays, the *Suppliants* and the *Aigyptioi,* between them contained the two responding movements that are found in the universal tradition—the enforced flight, the enforced union. The third and last play of the trilogy, the *Danaides,* evidently opened[10] with the discovery of the massacre in the wedding-chamber, on the dawn after the wedding. But the most important fragment from this play (125 Mette; one of the most famous passages of Aeschylean poetry in its own right) indicates that it, too, subsequently ran wild, like the *Eumenides* and the *Prometheus Pyrphoros.* The speaker is the goddess Aphrodite herself, who has, it must be noticed, no business in any other recorded dénouement of the Danaid legend. And she is speaking, not about the *human* sexual relationship, with which the earlier two plays of the trilogy were concerned, but about the love which unites the Earth and Sky in the spring rains:

> "Now the pure Heaven yearns to pierce the Earth;
> now Earth is taken with longing for her marriage.
> The rains showering from the mating Sky
> fill her with life, and she gives birth, for man,
> to flocks of sheep and to the lifegiving wheat.
> And from that liquid exultation springs,
> perfect, the time of trees. In this I share."

[6]

It seems certain from these lines that a deity has materialized in person on the stage in the *Danaides,* presumably to take one side or the other in the human feud. And it further seems likely from their mutilated context (preserved on a papyrus[11]) that Aphrodite's speech dealt *at length* with the question of the relationship between male and female right across the cosmos, including vegetable and animal fertility as well as the primal marriage between Earth and sky. This development, of course, would closely associate the ending of the *Suppliants*-trilogy with that of the *Oresteia*; where we can still observe in detail how one of the human motifs of the *Agamemnon* and *Choephori,* the relative roles of man and woman, is raised to cosmic importance in the *Eumenides.* In the latter play, as we all know, the male Olympian powers are ranged on one side, the female pre-Olympians on the other; holding the balance is the sexually ambiguous figure, Athena (daughter who has no mother, earth-deity and Olympian deity, woman in hoplite-armor); and an issue that becomes of increasing importance as the play marches to its climax is the fertility of Athenian crops, cattle and women.

To summarize: the principle of trilogic composition that appears to obtain in the Aeschylean late group means that the first two members of a trilogy follow the outline of the traditional legend and have responding movement, while the third is largely free invention, designed to synthesize the antitheses set up in the former two. It is useless to look for such a principle of composition in anything that was written after Aeschylus' death, because of course the practice of composing connected trilogies was then almost entirely abandoned (there are only three recorded instances later than 456 B.C., and no details survive of these). But we do possess one example of a connected trilogy from immediately *before* Aeschylus' late group, the Theban trilogy of 467 B.C., and the comparison is startling. Here there survives only the last of the three plays, the *Seven Against Thebes,* but the titles of the two plays that stood before in the trilogy, the *Laius* and the *Oedipus,* are known, and are revealing enough for the contents. The third member of *this* trilogy—which, as already mentioned, is played out against the background of a still undivided archaic cosmos—comes to its grim end in accordance with the universal legendary tradition, with the annihilation of the princely brothers, Eteocles and Polyneices, at each others' hands. In the *Seven* there seems to be very little rehandling of the basic legend, except to make it slightly more ghastly than the versions known to Pindar earlier and Herodotus later by causing the princes to die without issue. Here the Gods do not materialize on the stage; they do not take sides in the human feud, nor are their relationships in any way affected by it; far from being divided, they join hands to bring about the disaster on the mortal plane. In fact, in the Theban trilogy Aeschylus retains both the archaic cosmos and the archaic story, dramatizing the saga right to the end.

A word should be said here about the tetralogies of Aeschylus that are represented only by fragments, and by no surviving plays. Not one can be precisely dated, but the vast majority must certainly belong to the thirty-year period before the late group; as we have seen, there is simply not room for more than a minute fraction of them in the years from 466 onwards. What little can be seen of these lost works—and it must be admitted that it *is* little—implies the trilogic technique of the Theban trilogy rather than that of the late group; dramatization, that is, of the ancient saga to the end, not free invention and synthesis in the third play. This is almost certainly true of one of the most deplorable losses from ancient poetry as a whole, Aeschylus' trilogy on Achilles;[12] the final tragedy in that, the *"Phrygians or Ransoming of Hector"* followed the outlines, at least, of the twenty-fourth book of the *Iliad*. And the trilogies on Ajax and on Odysseus respectively, though no-one would dare to speak dogmatically about their contents, would seem to suit a straight treatment of the heroic saga, rather than the A, A, B movement of the late group.

Trilogy-technique, then, is one major feature which certainly links together the three works of the late group, and at the same time sets them sharply off from the immediately preceding Theban trilogy, if not perhaps also (though this is obviously far more speculative) from some other earlier trilogies. A second such feature has already entered this argument, and I need not add much to it here: this is the *involvement of the Gods* as partisans in the issues of the trilogy, and the concomitant split, not just on the human level, but in the cosmos itself. This happened very probably in the last play of the *Suppliants*-trilogy (we recall the speech of Aphrodite), and certainly at the end of the *Oresteia*. The *Prometheia* evidently contains this same feature, but gives an amazing twist to the pattern; for here the trilogy opens instantly with the involvement of the Gods and the cosmic split, and the humans, except the semi-human Io and (in the *Unbound*) Herakles, are kept off the stage altogether, at least in the first two plays. There is a distinct possibility, however, that the humans came back in the third play, the *Pyrphoros*; many enquirers have guessed, and with some sound reasons, that this play may have culminated in the founding of the Athenian torch-races in honor of Prometheus. If that is so, there will have been in the *Prometheia* a sort of inversion of the process seen in the *Suppliants*-trilogy and the *Oresteia* (where the problem climbed up through the human level to the divine), but the strong family resemblance is still there.

A third feature common to the late group must be stated at this time with dogmatic brevity;[13] it is the appearance in these trilogies of the forms and techniques of Old Comedy—an art which became a respectable form only in the last twenty years of Aeschylus' life. If I am right in my belief that the whole structure of the *Eumenides* is largely explainable in the light of the Old Comic convention, and that there are distinct traces of the same convention in the *Suppliants* and *Prometheus*, then this is at least further proof that Aeschylus' art was receptive, even in his comparatively advanced old age, to what was *new*: to what was new outside tragedy, as well as within it. But there is one likeness to Old Comedy (at least as we know it from Aristophanes' earlier plays thirty years later) that goes deeper than mere formal considerations. I think we are all agreed, unless we are theorists of the medieval school, that a play need not end in physical catastrophe in order to merit the name of 'tragedy.' And yet what other Athenian plays, outside the *Oresteia*, end in positive outbursts of *joy*, in a triumphal torch-procession, and with benedictions on the land for the fertility of its crops and its women? Practically the whole of the final song of the Eumenides consists in such benedictions, with the loud refrain 'Rejoice,' χαίρετε!

⟨χαίρετε,⟩ χαίρετ᾽ ἐν αἰσιμίαισι πλούτου.
    χαίρετ᾽ ἀστικὸς λεώς, . . .
"Rejoice, rejoice in your just shares of wealth!
People of the city, rejoice!"   (*Eum.* 996f.).
χαίρετε, χαίρετε δ᾽ αὖθις, ἔπη διπλοίζω,
    πάντες οἱ κατὰ πτόλιν, . . .
"Rejoice, again rejoice, our cry redoubles:
all who in the city live!"   (*Eum.* 1014f.).
In fact, that sort of benediction is only heard once elsewhere in Aeschylus, in the *Suppliants* of all plays (625ff.); while for *dramatic finales* which contain such benedictions, and a torchlight procession, and the redoubled cry 'Rejoice!', we have to turn to a comedian, Aristophanes. The end of the *Peace*, for instance, combines all three (1317ff.):

"We must carry torches . . . and pray the Gods to give wealth to the Greeks, and that we may all alike raise much barley and much wine, and eat figs, and that our women may bear us children . . ."

And then, in the final words of the *Peace* (1355ff.):

ὦ χαίρετε χαίρετ᾽ ἄν-
δρες, κἂν ξυνέπησθέ μοι
    πλακοῦντας ἔδεσθε.
"Rejoice, rejoice, people, and if
you follow me you'll have cakes to eat!"

The *Oresteia*, I think beyond doubt, *ended* in what the spectators could at once see was the manner of Old Comedy—though of course transposed into a nobler key. In estimating what this means we must not forget that Comedy, down till near the end of the fifth century, was much closer to its origins in actual

[9]

popular religious cult than Athenian tragedy was at any stage
where we have knowledge of it. Paradoxically, to the conservative
religious or pious spectator, an Old Comedy was probably a more
serious act than tragedy itself; in that not only by its origins, but
by its costumes and the very form of many of its jokes, it concerned the most ancient and urgent of human needs—the reproduction of crops, of animals, and of the race itself. Aeschylus, it
seems to me, so modelled the end of the *Oresteia* that it would
appeal to that primeval religious feeling too, besides appealing
to the more modern type of mentality among his audience; to the
old tribal consciousness as well as to the New Learning in that
hectically changing community which was the Athens of his last
years.

It would be a bold man—certainly a bolder man than I am
—who flatly asserted that the finales of the *Suppliants*-trilogy and
of the *Prometheia* must have shared the Old Comic character of
the *Eumenides*. Yet three considerations certainly point strongly
in that direction. First, few who consider the extant material will
doubt that those two trilogies must have ended in harmony, in a
synthesis of the antitheses expounded in their first two plays.
Second, the great *Danaides* fragment, quoted and discussed
above, shows that the last play of the *Suppliants*-trilogy moved
into the same ambit—fertility—as the *Eumenides* does; a subject
which otherwise is the province of comedy, not tragedy. Third,
one notes with great interest the theory already mentioned, that
the *Prometheus Pyrphoros* culminated with the founding of the
Promethean torch-races. Torchlight at the end of the play, with
its symbolism of triumph and marriage, would again link the
Prometheia to the *Oresteia*, and at the same time distinguish the
pair of them from any other Attic drama whatsoever *except Old
Comedy*; where torches appear towards the end more commonly
than not, and in which three of the eleven extant finales actually
consist of torchlight processions.

The last characteristic feature of the late group which I am
going to speak of can be dealt with more briefly because the
individual facts involved have long been recognized. There is a
number of passages in the plays of Aeschylus which are so close
to doctrines known to have been under discussion by contemporary pre-Socratic philosophers that mere coincidence seems
ruled out. What is not so early recognized, but is (I believe) true,
is that all the reasonably certain instances of this sort of allusion
are found in the plays of the late group.[14] They are not specially
obtrusive in their dramatic contexts, but if one reflects on them
as a whole they add up to a certainty: that in his last years
Aeschylus was, at least, *aware* of the philosophical movements
that were gathering in strength across the Greek world (especially in Sicily, which Aeschylus knew well in the last two decades
of his life, and where, in fact, he died)—a rising hurricane which,

[10]

by the end of the following generation, was to have swept away the structure of archaic thought and religion. How much does that awareness have to do with the new shape and new tendencies of the late trilogies? Are the late trilogies a sort of response by an enquiring, but still essentially religious late-archaic mind, to the coming of philosophy?

The answer to that may become clearer a little later. Meanwhile, to sum up on what has been said so far, I suggested at the beginning of this paper, first, that these three trilogies stood close together chronologically. That belief was reached in the first instance from external and technical considerations, but I hope that what has been said since may reinforce it; thematically too, and compositionally, they seem to belong together. Second, I suggested that they were in fact so different from anything called "tragedy" before or after them that they practically constitute an art-form of their own, a very short-lived art-form that flourished, at the outside, for a decade, and was never revived. One of the trilogies concerned does not even *begin* like a conventional tragedy; the stock complaint, and a well-justified complaint, about the *Suppliants* is that it is not "tragic." And while the *Oresteia* may seem to begin like tragedy of the older type—the *Agamemnon* in many ways reads like a maturer draft of the *Persians*[15]—it is, taken as a whole, almost a denial of tragedy. To seek a name for the new form would be pointless; "tragicomedy," which might have served, is already in use for something quite different. But one may look for a parallel to it, and I do not think it too fanciful to find that parallel centuries later and in a sphere far from Athens: in Dante's Comedy. Dante, by the way, would have called the *Oresteia* too a "comedy" without hesitation, if we can trust the views put forward about his own work in the letter to Can Grande: *a principio horribilis et fetida quia Infernus; in fine prospera, desiderabilis et grata, quia Paradisus . . . et sic patet quare comedia dicitur.*[16] But perhaps it is better not to quibble over names; I see more than a superficial likeness between the *things*, between Dante's Hell, Purgatory and Paradise and Aeschylus' *Agamemnon, Choephori* and *Eumenides*. In both the tripartite works there is a similar movement, a gradual climb from torment, through testing, into the light. Indeed, if Headlam's and Thomson's ideas about the Orphic symbolism of the *Oresteia* are anything like correct, there is not only a likeness but—at a vast distance—a historical connection. For there exists a certain underground current of mystical belief which flows for ever, calmly ignoring frontiers and religions.

But to come back to that troubled decade, 466–456 B.C. Another of the suggestions made at the beginning of this paper was that once these three trilogies were firmly grasped as being a unique group, produced within a short period under a single

[11]

impulse, they would throw considerable light on each other, and especially on the *Prometheus*. It will be worth while to end by outlining the way in which the grouping might help towards the understanding of that most problematic of all the characters in Aeschylus: Zeus.

The great argument here for the last century or more has been, of course, that the tyrant-Zeus of the *Prometheus* will not fit—that he is irreconcilable with the sublime Zeus known elsewhere in Aeschylus' work. Does he really not fit? The question is worth reconsidering.

Through the series *Suppliants*-trilogy, *Oresteia*, *Prometheia*, I trace two new and ever more urgent preoccupations, which I believe, must explain each other. A preoccupation with the split in the cosmos; and a preoccupation with the possibility that Zeus may emerge from the chaos as the ultimate authority, παναίτιος, πανεργέτας, all-responsible, all-worker (to quote the Chorus of the *Agamemnon*, 1486). I think we need have little hesitation about the significance of the ·cosmic split in these late trilogies. When archaic man runs head-on into classical free enquiry, when a tradition of static authoritarianism in politics and religion finally comes face to face with classical democracy (and it happens that the emergence of full-blown democracy, both in Athens and in Sicily, coincides very closely with the last ten years of Aeschylus' life)—when these confrontations occur all at once, the world will in fact seem to split; from the microcosm of the mind, through the state, to the divine macrocosm itself. It is almost a matter of indifference at which of those levels you think of the cleavage. Though Aeschylus (characteristically) chooses in these plays to show it primarily in its aspect of cosmic cleavage, one might think that the struggle in the *Eumenides* makes almost equal sense if you take it as the struggle between the Olympian *ego* and the infernal *id*, or, more prosaically, as that between liberal and conservative. Certainly, for our time as well as for that of Aeschylus, it seems to mean more than a momentary disturbance among fading pagan gods. It is a deadly feud from which not one of us is free.

    Aeschylus, it is true, did not have so gloomy an opinion, for in these same plays, as a possible healer of the cleavage, stands Zeus. Lately an assault has been launched against the idea, so popular in the nineteenth and early twentieth centuries, that Aeschylus was the founder of a new and sublime Zeus-monotheism, and it has been held instead that all the difficulties can be swept away by assuming that his Zeus is quite primitive (that is the word used) throughout; no more developed than the Zeus of the epic poets.[17] I am coming to wonder whether this assault does not go too far and simplify too much. It has done valuable work by questioning some hardened prejudices. But even apart from the difficult question of its method (the rigidly positivist interpreta-

[12]

*for 'cleavage'] *read* 'division'

tion of Aeschylus' language gives me pause, because poets of all people, almost by definition, do not and cannot use words positivistically), do its results perfectly fit the phenomena?

There is, indeed, a primitive Aeschylean Zeus, no advance on the Zeus of Homer and Hesiod (or, come to that, on the woman- and boy-chasing Zeus who appears on early fifth-century vase-paintings), but I suspect that he belongs to the dramas of the phases earlier than 466 B.C. This is the Zeus who is cursorily mentioned, with no special emphasis, in the *Persians* and the *Seven*; perhaps the fully anthropomorphic Zeus who was actually brought on the stage—on the only occasion we know of in fifth-century Attic tragedy—in Aeschylus' *Psychostasia*; certainly the Zeus who mated with a cow-formed Europa in the play called *Kares ē Europe*, and who is roundly abused by Danae (whom he has seduced in the golden rain) in the satyric *Diktyoulkoi* (lines 774–84). But Aeschylus certainly knows of at least one other Zeus, who has nothing to do with Homer or Hesiod, or any writer earlier than his own day: the Zeus of that stupendous couplet from the lost *Heliades (The Daughters of the Sun)*: "Zeus is Aither, Zeus is earth, Zeus is heaven; Zeus is all, and whatever is beyond the all."—

Ζεύς ἐστιν αἰθήρ, Ζεὺς δὲ γῆ, Ζεὺς δ᾽ οὐρανός,
Ζεύς τοι τὰ πάντα χὤτι τῶνδ᾽ ὑπέρτερον·

(Fragment 70 Nauck, 105 Mette.)

The dramatic context of these words is unknown, and the play to which they belong is undated. But even as they stand, even if the play should be rediscovered and it should prove that they were qualified or denied in the next line, they surely constitute complete proof that the poet's mind was at least open to more than the epic and archaic view about Zeus. For a brief and shattering moment they let us glimpse a universe in which the orthodox polytheism and anthropomorphism simply cannot exist—in that respect strikingly similar to the universe implied in the writings of Aeschylus' senior contemporary Xenophanes (whom, so far as dates and known movements go, he could quite well have met at the court of Hieron in Sicily).

If, to Aeschylus, the concept "Zeus" was as malleable as the *Heliades* fragment suggests, there now seems nothing to forbid the conjecture that in these last three trilogies we see a series of experiments, not only with the idea of a cosmic split, but with the idea of Zeus as the possible answer to the new and chaotic condition of heaven and earth. The experiments will be open-minded and honest, though there will underlie them a basic faith, inherited from archaism, in the simple power of the archaic supreme god. In the process of the experiments, Zeus will gradually and naturally move nearer to the centre. The same critic who has assaulted the concept of a sublime Aeschylean Zeus has also objected to the idea (likewise popular in the nineteenth and earlier twentieth centuries) of an "evolving" Zeus, which is often brought in to solve our problems. I think he is justified, and I have learned from him not to believe in an evolving Zeus, either. But I do believe, as the whole of this paper has suggested, in an evolving Aeschylus. From that point of view I take a final look at the late group of trilogies.

The *Suppliants* was always famed for its majestic and moving Zeus-hymns.[18] And even in the days, not so long ago, when the play was commonly dated in the 490's or 480's B.C., they were customarily compared with the equally splendid Zeus-hymn of *Agamemnon* 160–183, Ζεύς, ὅστις ποτ' ἐστίν, . . . ("Zeus, whoever he may be . . .")–without anyone's feeling much embarrassment, apparently, about the almost total absence of such august language from what would then have to be the intervening plays, the *Persians* and the *Seven*. Now that the *Suppliants* seems to be brought down within perhaps as little as five years of the *Agamemnon*, that difficulty, at least, vanishes. But what is still perhaps not enough noticed is that in both these trilogies the Zeus-hymns occur fairly early in the first play, and are placed, of course, in the mouth of the chorus. One would naturally incline to take them within rather than outside their dramatic context: as intuitive hopes by the helpless girls and the old men respectively, rather than, at that stage, as definite statements by the poet. And in fact, in the *Oresteia* we have to wait very long indeed before that intuitive hope is justified. Not only does unnatural murder have to be done, but the universe has to be parted in two, with Apollo and the Furies (and behind them, offstage, Zeus and the Fates respectively) as opposing partisans. And during the middle section of the *Eumenides* we are to have visions of a universe from which all authority has gone, leaving only that mindless and pitiless chaos across which Euripides, later on, was to move consciously all his life. (But that was after the philosophic revolution was complete.) It is only at the very end of the *Oresteia* that the gash is healed, and the original intuitions fulfilled; but it has been touch and go. We cannot know about Zeus's part in the later stages of the *Suppliants*-trilogy, for obvious reasons. The immense importance, however, that is attached to him in the extant play, suggests that he must have been heavily involved at the end also. And the *Danaides*-fragment makes it almost certain that the cosmic cleavage was there.

In almost every way, even down to minor technical and metrical details, the *Prometheia* takes a stride beyond the *Oresteia*. Here the trilogy *begins* on the cosmic level, instead of rising to it from humanity, and *begins* with a total cleavage on that level. And here Zeus, instead of being kept on the periphery of the actual struggle—instead of being the remote object of human hopes—has moved into the eye of the storm. If there was to be anything beyond the *Oresteia*, it probably had to be this. The two preoccupations, with the cosmic split and with Zeus, fuse into one, and the last question is being asked: can the archaic god survive as a viable force in the new world? We only see, now, one side of the debate, not the response. But this much seems likely. In the *Prometheus Bound* Aeschylus fearlessly and honestly shows, through the eyes of Io and Prometheus, a picture of the archaic power-god which is not really too exaggerated a caricature of the Zeus known to Homer and Hesiod, except that it has taken on political overtones. It apparently includes even Zeus the se-ducer, the Zeus of the *Europe* and *Diktyoulkoi*, here shown at his worst with Io. There are hints, however, both in the proph-ecies of the *Bound* and in the fragments of the *Unbound* itself, that in that second play a different aspect of Zeus began to be uncovered: the Zeus who freed the Titans, who at least did not prevent the coming of Prometheus' savior Herakles, who—almost unbelievably—*pitied*,[19] and who in the end came to terms with the intellectual, the σοφιστής, Prometheus.[20]

Anything said about the final synthesis in the last play of the *Prometheia* is bound to be a guess, but here is one. Those who have claimed that the Zeus of the *Prometheia* is irreconcilable with the Zeus of Aeschylus' other works have always pointed to the great Zeus-hymns near the beginning of the *Suppliants* and the *Agamemnon,* and the absence of anything of the sort in the *Prometheia.* The guess is that when the Day of Judgment comes and all vanished Greek literature is unrolled before us, we shall find that missing Zeus-hymn—in the finale of the last play of the *Prometheia,* the *Pyrphoros.* And that it will be a hymn of joy.[21]

NOTES

[1] Originally given as a lecture at the University of Texas, and here printed substantially as it was delivered. Its main purpose was to ex-plore on a larger scale some ideas about the development of Aeschylus' art which the author briefly put forward in the introduction to an article on Aeschylus and Old Comedy: *TAPhA* 94 (1963) 113ff.

[2] A convenient publication, translation and discussion of this papyrus is that by H. Lloyd-Jones in his Appendix to H. W. Smyth's *Aeschylus,* Volume II (second edition, 1957), 595f.

[3] This controversial subject is much too large to be treated here. The writer hopes to discuss it in detail at a later date; for some—but only some—of the strong metrical and stylistic arguments for placing the *Prometheia* later than the *Oresteia,* he would refer provisionally to the works cited in *CR* 14 (1964) 239f. Some—but again only some—the-matic and compositional arguments that lead to the same result will emerge later in this article.

[4] Compare Aristophanes, *Frogs* 938.

[5] This point is well made by F. Solmsen in *TAPhA* 68 (1937) 204.

6 Herodotus I, chapters 6–91, *passim*. If Professor D. Page is right, this Herodotean story will have been based itself on an early fifth-century tragedy or group of tragedies by an older contemporary of Aeschylus; see *A New Chapter in the History of Greek Tragedy* (Cambridge 1951), with some startling evidence in support, *TCPhS* no. 186 (NS 8; 1962). In that case we should have the record of *three* tragic works, earlier than the Aeschylean late group, which presupposed the undivided cosmos discussed here. But it is right to add that Page's theory, excellently argued as it is, still faces certain difficulties, and does not yet seem to be generally accepted.

7 Aeschylus, *Threissai*, Fragment 292 in Mette's collection of the fragments.

8 Aeschylus, *Phryges e Hektoros Lytra*, Fragment 254 in Mette.

9 The ancient versions of the Danaid story are surveyed, for example, by J. Vürtheim, in *Aischylos' Schutzflehende* (Amsterdam 1928) 10ff.

10 Evidence: Fragment 124 in Mette (43 Nauck, Murray). Although the exact reading of this fragment is in dispute, its general drift and reference seem fairly certain.

11 *Oxyrhynchus Papyri*, Volume 20 (1952), 21f.; reprinted by Mette as Fragment 125. The tiny fragments of the nineteen lines which preceded those translated in my text here contain one, possibly two, references to *cattle* (lines 2, 6); and perhaps references to *the mating of cattle* (line 2, as restored by Mette) and to *parturition* (line 7).

12 It probably consisted of the tragedies *Myrmidones, Nereides* and *Phryges e Hektoros Lytra*; see Mette's collection of the fragments, pp. 70–92.

13 For the detailed arguments (as I see them) I refer to the article mentioned above, in the first note. Some new considerations are added here.

14 Summarily: (1) *Suppliants* 556ff. implies a theory of the risings of the Nile otherwise attributed to Aeschylus' younger contemporary Anaxagoras (Anaxagoras, Fragment A42; cf. J. Vürtheim, *Aischylos' Schutzflehende*, 79ff.). (2) *Danaides*, Fragment 125 Mette, seems closely related to passages in Empedocles (Empedocles, Fragments B71–73; cf. *Phoenix* 17 [1963], 195n.). (3) Apollo's "biology" in *Eumenides* 658ff. abruptly introduces almost the sole Athenian reference to a problem known to have been under discussion by six non-Athenian philosophers and medical men in the middle years of the fifth century (evidence collected by A. Perretti in *Parola del Passato* 11 [1956] 241ff.). (4) *Prometheus* 88ff. (allusion to the Four Elements, and perhaps to Empedoclean thinking? Compare, e.g., *Phoenix* 17 [1963], 180ff.). (5) *Prometheus*, 459f., on the excellence of arithmetic (evidently a Pythagorean notion; cf. G. Thomson, note on lines 475f. in his edition of the play).

15 Noticed at least as early as 1663 by Stanley (quoted by E. Fraenkel in his edition of the *Agamemnon*, I, p. 43), and often since.

[16]

16 Paragraph 10, ed. Arnaldo Monte, *Le Lettere di Dante* (Milan 1921).

17 H. Lloyd-Jones, "Zeus in Aeschylus," *JHS* 76 (1956) 55ff.; compare D. Page in his and J. D. Denniston's edition of the *Agamemnon* (Oxford 1957), xixff.

18 *Suppliants,* 86–103, 524–599.

19 *Prometheus Unbound,* Fragment 326 Mette (199 Nauck, Murray).

20 *Prometheus Bound,* 186–192.

21 See also *Phoenix* 17 (1963) 236–243, where some reasons are put forward for suspecting, not only that such a hymn once existed, but that echoes of it may still be heard in the solemn finale of Aristophanes' *Birds.*

Richmond Lattimore

Phaedra, the wife of theseus, fell in love with Hippolytus, who was Theseus' son by an earlier liaison with an Amazon woman. This love was communicated to Hippolytus, who rejected it. Phaedra then killed herself and left a note which said that Hippolytus had attacked her. Theseus believed that this was true. He banished his son from the country, and also prayed to Poseidon, asking him to kill Hippolytus. As the young man was departing a monstrous bull came out of the sea and made his horses bolt. Hippolytus was dragged to his death, but before he died Artemis revealed the truth, and father and son were reconciled. Hippolytus was worshiped as a hero or a young god after his death.

This is the simple outline of the story out of which Sophocles made a tragedy, and Euripides made two, one of which has survived. The story has been retold, imitated, or adapted by Seneca, Racine, d'Annunzio, O'Neill, Jeffers, and doubtless many others. If we isolate what seems to be the center of the plot, that is, the temptation of a young man by the wife of a man to whom he owes loyalty, his refusal, the calumny of the wife against him which is believed, then the story appears as a particular instance of what we might call a pattern story which (like the story of the foundling or of brother and sister lost and reunited) has numerous independent variants and seems to be one of those forms of fiction which grow naturally out of men's minds and human experience. The best known parallel outside of Greek is the story in *Genesis* (39) where the nameless wife of Potiphar, Joseph's patron, begged Joseph to make love to her, and when he would not she said he had tried to force her and caused him to be thrown into prison. But there are plenty of parallels in the Greek. Homer tells of Bellerophon who at the court of Proetus was solicited by his host's wife, and when he refused her she told her husband of Bellerophon's designs on her, and Proetus, unwilling to kill his guest with his own hands, sent him to a friend abroad carrying, in a sealed letter, instructions for his own death (Il. 6.145–211). Homer calls the wife of Proetus Antaea, but others knew her as Sthenoboea, and Euripides wrote a tragedy, now lost, which went by that name and used that story. Then there was Astydameia, sometimes called Hippolyta, the wife of Acastus, who when Peleus was the king's suppliant and guest tried to seduce him and when he refused reversed the story in the customary way so that Acastus, believing, stole Peleus' sword and left him alone on the mountain to be killed by wild beasts,

* or by centaurs (*Nem.* 5). Pindar told this story and Euripides may have used it in his lost *Peleus.* Not to go on too long, there was also Tennes, son of Cycnus, traduced like Hippolytus by his amorous stepmother, and put in a box by his father and set adrift at sea (Paus. 10.14.2). Euripides seems to have written a play called *Tennes.*

We emerge, then, with the story of the young man traduced as a pattern of Greek tragedy, or that legendary material out of which the Greeks made their tragedies, and to this pattern the story of Hippolytus, Phaedra, and Theseus belongs. Sometimes the most striking dramatic effects are wrought when the familiar modes of fiction are made to yield unfamiliar results. In *King Lear* we have a familiar figure of coldness disguised as love and love disguised as coldness. *Of course* it is going to be the cool-spoken Cordelia who loves Lear, and the truth must come out and they must be reconciled, and so they are—but *too late* to do any good, and the happy ending proper to such a morality is mocked and mutilated. *Oedipus* is the foundling-story, at the end of which the lost child will be recognized and find his own home and people. You will find out who you are and who your parents are, says Teiresias to Oedipus, and you will wish you never had (Sophocles, *Oed. Tyr.* 413–428). It is the perversion of this blithe type of romance, so happily illustrated in *The Winter's Tale* and *The Importance of Being Earnest,* that gives Oedipus its gruesome and ironic force. To the surprise of the story itself, now grown familiar, is added the surprise of making this story come out the way such stories ought not to come out.

And something like this has happened to *Hippolytus,* both in the story given to Euripides, which does not go quite the way of the pattern story, and in what Euripides did with the story he was given.

Joseph was thrown into prison, but that was where he began those prophetic exercises which brought him to power and made him a great man. When Bellerophon reached his destination, the king who was requested to murder him passed him on, sending him out on deadly errands, and Bellerophon disappointed him and killed monster after monster until he ended with the hand of the princess and half the kingdom. Chiron rescued Peleus who went on to become a hero and a potent king and married the daughter of the sea. The traduced hero like the foundling meets his trials on the way to success, and emerges triumphant because the gods look after their own darlings. But they did not look after Hippolytus. He died.

And what of the lady in the case? Bellerophon in some versions, not the earliest, returned to murder Stheneboea, and Peleus, also in later versions only, butchered Hippolyta for her sins. Are these later embroideries which aim to balance the reward of the virtuous with the punishment of the wicked? We do not know. The

[20]

---

* for 'centaurs (*Nem.* 5). Pindar'] *read* 'centaurs. Pindar (*Nem.* 5)'

false temptress seems early to be not much more than a prop to push the hero off on his brilliant way, not interesting in herself, and her subsequent fate is a matter of indifference. Only in our Hippolytus story does she kill herself.

And these two facts, that the hero does not come through and that the lady buys belief at the price of her own life, change the action of the play from romance to tragedy, and, because action and character are interdependent, they change the characters too.

Phaedra is the easiest, so let us begin with her. She is far more than the mere stock character who sends the hero off to his perils and glories. We can dismiss the wife of Potiphar, though Thomas Mann did not, and say we know all about *her*, but we cannot do that with Euripides' heroines, Phaedra or, if we had that play, Stheneboea. Euripides, as we know, wrote an earlier version, which seems to have given offence, for, says the critic who wrote the preliminary notice in our manuscripts, what was improper and shocking in the first play has been corrected in this one. What gave offence was, for one thing, a scene in which Phaedra made her proposition to Hippolytus in person, but we may choose to suppose that this was not all, that the entire character of Phaedra which supported this action and made it credible, provoked distaste and lost him the prize. Here he has set about to rehabilitate Phaedra, or to make his audience sympathize with her, and whether or not he has succeeded will be a question each reader or listener will have to decide for himself. Let us see, at least, what he has done.

First, Aphrodite herself speaks the prologue, and announces the outcome of the play, the *that* of it not the *how*, and explains that *she* has made Phaedra fall in love with Hippolytus, that Phaedra is keeping it secret and like to die, but she is a necessary instrument for the young man's punishment. We can think what we like about Aphrodite and what she meant to Euripides and we shall have to come back to all that later, but for the dramatic purpose of the prologue we must suspend belief, admit Aphrodite ✻ is what she says she is and that what she tells us is so, and therefore Phaedra, resisting love, is beaten from the start. Second, Euripides seems to have gone out of his way to emphasize her youth. She is not a mature woman or a hardened campaigner. The nurse talks to her as if she were a baby. She could be older than Hippolytus, but, since Greek girls often married at 14 or less, she could easily be younger and still have two children. Euripides is content to make us see her as young. (This is of course a shading in sympathy, an aesthetic point, not a moral one, since an eighteen-year-old stepmother who acts like Phaedra is morally no better than a thirty-eight year old, merely, to some, less repulsive). Also, she is sick, in body as in mind. *Nosos* is her keyword, for she has been starving herself for days, meaning to die before she can have what she wants or not have it. Weakened

[21]

in every way, she lets the nurse extract, first her secret, then permission to go and do what she can (charms, witchcraft, persuasion?) with Hippolytus; she does not, as in the earlier play, go to him herself.

All this is a mere jumble of data about Phaedra, as stated by Euripides, not, I would repeat, to justify the defamation and instigated murder of a young man by a stepmother who has tried to seduce him, so much as to show that the stepmother who did this was not a monster. Sufficient reason would be that monsters make dull theatre. It takes us somewhat farther, though, if we ask just how much she intended to do to punish Hippolytus, and in what belief.

When Phaedra let the nurse go off on her errand, vaguely described as 'to make everybody happy', Phaedra stayed behind while the chorus sang in sympathy, until she overheard the outburst of the young man against the nurse's proposition. We do not know how this scene was staged. Hippolytus and the nurse may have spoken loudly from behind the backdrop, unseen, while Phaedra listened at the door, or more probably the pair burst out through the door, violently talking, while Phaedra huddled away in shame. Did she and Hippolytus ever look each other in the face, did she leave the stage while he was still talking? We do not know, but however this scene was meant, written, and staged, Phaedra had cause for fear. The nurse had sworn Hippolytus to silence before she said anything to him. Now he hinted that he might break that silence. 'Do not, my child, disown your sworn oath', said the nurse, and Hippolytus answered in the famous line which Euripides' tormentors never allowed him to forget, 'My tongue swore, but my heart remains unsworn' (611–12). Hippolytus paid for that piece of sophistry with his life. For he did not, later, when accused by his father of the rape of the dead Phaedra, tell the truth, even in the most trying circumstances (if he had told the truth he would not have been believed), though he was not above throwing out a couple of good broad hints. What he meant or is meant to have meant is, I think, merely, 'You have trapped me with a technicality and I can say nothing, and it is not fair' but he (and Euripides) could not resist putting it in a more pointed and terrifying way. If he meant 'you can't hold me with an oath like this' then, before he was through with his too long speech, he saw that honor was going to make him keep his promise (656–60). 'I see my duty, madam, and that saves you. If I were not caught by oaths sworn to the gods, which I must not break, I could not have kept it from my father. Now, since I must, I shall stay out of this house while Theseus remains abroad, and I will shut my mouth and say nothing.' This he means and this he does. Whether Phaedra heard this last or was listening, or not, it was said too late; the first fatal sentence made her sure that Hippolytus would break his

oath, and her thoughts are plain as she speaks to the nurse
(688–93). 'Now I must think and think quickly. That creature
in his rage will tell his father of the wrong *you* made me do, and
he will tell grandfather Pittheus all about it and make the whole
country ring with scandalous stories. Damn you, go away.' This
to the nurse; she begs the other women to keep her secret, and
they swear by Artemis to do so. Now she will kill herself but so
doing she will hurt Hippolytus too. There follows the scene where
her body is discovered, with the suicide note.

Her motives are complex, but they do not cancel each other.
Foremost, of course, is sheer rage at the self-satisfied young man
who has not only turned her down when she was not sure she was
offering herself at all but insulted the whole world of women as
well. But that is not all. She is a foreign princess, from Crete; her
people will be sneered at by these Athenians and Troezenians.
Her boys will be disinherited as of a suspect mother, and this
bastard, by-blow of an early affair of her husband, will inherit
the throne and mock them all. She has been made a fool of; well,
she will make a fool of him. Does she foresee his death? Probably
not; she says not a word of it. This does not excuse her much.
Every playgoer knew that Theseus was of the old line of heroes,
honorable and just but terrible in his just angers, the sort of man
to strike Hippolytus dead on the spot if he believed Phaedra's
story. And Phaedra means that he shall believe it.

Such, then, is Phaedra: treacherous, mean, even murderous under
provocation. And yet not, in the end, treacherous, mean or murderous. So Euripides means us to understand, for he has made
her three bitterest enemies pay tribute to her honor. Aphrodite
says in the beginning (47): 'Phaedra is honorable, but there is
no hope for her'. Hippolytus says in his defence—limited by oath
(1032–35):

> Whether, in fear of something, she took her own life,
> I do not know, and am not allowed to say more.
> She could not quite be virtuous, and yet she was.
> So we, who could be virtuous, have been ill used.

Artemis speaks to Theseus (1300–01) of 'your wife's mad passion, or, somehow, her nobility'. The hint of an unresolved puzzle
about Phaedra lurks throughout; drama does not have to be finished off in a precise arrangement of logically coherent contrasts,
so long as we believe. Phaedra acted dishonorably because of her
own nature yet acted against her own nature, which was honorable. Can we resolve further?

Perhaps. With her secret out, Phaedra turned to the women
about her, confiding (377–423, much abridged):

> I think that lives go wrong not because people
> decide to go wrong; no, rather look at it like this:

[24]

we understand the better way and recognize it
but do not work it out. . . .
Now I, when I found I felt as I did
I tried first to keep silent and cover my sickness up.
Then next, I determined to be strong
and by force of will to overcome my stupid weakness.
Third and last, when I was making no headway
against love, I decided I had to die.
For I hope, when I do well, that it is plain to all,
and when I do shame, that I shall not have the world to
                                                    witness.
So, dear friends, I must die,
because I must never be known to have shamed my husband
and my children, so they may flourish, free to say and do
what they please in glorious Athens; or, if not, it will not be
their mother's fault.

Taking these lines or some of them as the true index of
Phaedra's nature, some critics have very reasonably concluded
that she is, indeed, no villainess, but a rather pitiful little Athenian
wife who is concerned beyond anything else with respectability
and putting the best face on things. From four of the lines above
this conclusion is certainly just but it is a final conclusion only if
the lines are fully *in character,* and I am not sure they are.
We remember that when Phaedra first appears she is feverish
and delirious, answers no questions but babbles of woods and
waters and her longing for these. Then, recovering, she speaks
reasonably in answer to the nurse's questioning but is still overwrought, fiercely reticent and ashamed. Once the admission is
torn from her, she embarks on the long discourse (58 lines)
which I abridged above, explaining in language mostly cool and
even, her experience and the reasons for her attitude and purposes. Now it is a sort of dramatic trope or habit of structure (for
Euripides and Sophocles) in this period to present, early in the
drama, the heroine first strongly emotional and wrought upon
and heard in lyric or anapaestic verse: then, in temperate blank
verse annotating or explaining her emotion of the previous scene
in a long speech, whose burden might be summarized thus:
'Women and friends, I am sorry to have made such an exhibit of
myself before you, but I have reasons to be so overwrought. Listen
and I will tell you' (*Medea: Alcestis,* modified: returned to in
Helen: Sophocles, *Electra, Trachiniae*). Part of the speaker's bear-
ing here is the generalization of this particular case—this is the
sort of thing we women have to put up with, say Deianeira and
Medea—a resultant flattening of the heroine's individual features.
Deianeira and Medea speak about the routine of courtship and
marriage, but their own experience has been anything but routine, and the effect for Medea is that she temporarily loses her

[25]

vital character of barbarous Colchian witch or minor goddess
fetched by her own magic from the end of the world, to enact the
lines of Woman or Everywoman (*Medea* 248–49). 'Men say of *us*
that we sit safe at home and live a life secure, while they carry
the spear and fight.' These lines seem not part of the heroine
Medea, but rather Euripides on women; and so 'I think we understand the better way but do not work it out'—this does not show
so much what Phaedra was like, but rather represents the poet
taking issue with Socrates' proposition that virtue is knowledge
and nobody does wrong when he knows better. It is hard to draw
the line, and this speech of Phaedra's is by no means all out of
character: mixed with the generalizing moralities are outbursts
that come from inside the living person, as (413–18):

> I hate those women, virtuous by reputation,
> whose secret lives are full of guilt;
> o queen and mistress, Aphrodite of the waters,
> how can they look those whom they sleep with in the face,
> how can they not shiver at the darkness which has been
> accessory; how not fear the walls of the rooms, that they
> may speak?

This is Phaedra indeed, but she is concerned with more than
the conventions of respectability. Still, it is not all of Phaedra.
After all, she was not a typical young Athenian wife of good
family, but a princess from Crete, a Dorian or at least a non-Athenian, and so raised, perhaps, by standards which would be most
unconventional in Athens. This other side comes out in Phaedra's
first scene, where her fevered murmurings are answered by the
nurse (198–238):

> —Lift my weight, straighten my head.
> I am weak, dear friends. My strength is unstrung.
> Hold me up, my maids, by the firm curve
> of my arms. The veil is a weight. Take it away.
> Let my hair stream free on my shoulders.
>
> —There child. Stop tossing about
> so crossly.
> Keep still, be brave, and the sickness
> will not trouble you so.
> Mortals always have pain and suffering.
>
> —If I could only lean and drink
> from a running spring clear water!
> Or in the trees, in the long meadow
> grass, lie down and rest.
>
> —Hush dear, what are you saying?
> There are people here. Don't speak
> so loud. You're almost raving.

[26]

—Take me away from here, to the hills.
I want to go to the forest, to the pines
where the hunting hounds
shadow the spotted deer. Oh gods
how I long to hallo the dogs on
and hold close along my blond blown curls
the northern spear, barbed weapon, poise it
and make my cast.

—Dear dear this is wild. What does it mean?
What has riding to hounds to do with you?
This craving for spring water, what is it?
Here by the walls is a fresh bank
and a spring. We can get you a drink from there.

—Artemis, queen of the sea, lady
of lakes, of riding and the thunder of hoof beats,
how I long to be where you are, in the plains,
riding blood horses, breaking them.

—More madness, crazy words, why?
Just now your longing was for hill country, the chase,
and now again for the sand flats, beyond
the breakers, and horses to ride.
Here is a puzzle for diviners. Who knows
what god rides you on a wild rein,
dear child, and stampedes your reason?

Phaedra longs for the woods and the sands, the strenuous life
which in fact Hippolytus leads, and critics who have dealt with
this scene from the ancient annotator on down have concluded
that she longs for this life and these places because she longs for
Hippolytus. The implication, if you leave it at that, as the critics
constantly do, is that this is all that the lines mean, that this most
vivid and imaginative scene in the play contrives no more than a
disguise for a love which, intense as it is, is of a quite ordinary
sort. I wish to avoid assaults on straw men but when or if this
interpretation is held, it is wrong. A character in drama who is
not deliberately playing the hypocrite—and Phaedra with her conventional manners burned away by fever is speaking from the
bare mind—should be heard as one who speaks the truth. Here
she says not one word about Hippolytus, does not long for him
to be brought away from his forests and into her bedchamber.
There is not a line of sex in the scene. She really does wish she
could run and ride; she is not a usual Athenian matron. I have
thought Euripides means to characterize her as a girl from Crete,
and he does frequently though not consistently emphasize na-
tional characteristics. It is important that Medea is not a Greek
wife. She is from Colchis, not that Euripides knew much about
Colchis or knew it accurately, but the point is that she is a wild

[27]

barbarian lost and fighting among Greeks, and then again when
the purpose serves she will speak not as a barbarian at all but
merely as a wife forlorn in an unfair convention of marriage.
Phaedra speaking of marriage does not speak as a Cretan but
Phaedra longing to run and ride may be doing so. Spartan girls,
unlike Athenians, were brought up to a tradition of athletic sports
and athletic costumes, and one Euripidean character wonders,
affronted, whether girls who showed their legs like that and
wrestled with the boys could ever be virtuous even if they wanted
to be (*Andromache* 595–600). Euripides, well aware of the
Spartan customs, may also have known and taken for granted
that his audience would know that Crete was Dorian, that Spartan
institutions were much like the Cretan and said by some to have
been imported to Sparta from Crete. If that is so, Phaedra is not
only a foreigner but a foreigner misunderstood, one dwelling in
a country strange to her ways, a displaced person in a predicament congenial to Euripides' invention. It is true that she is attended by a figure who properly belongs only in Athens or in
one of the cities Euripides would have thought of as conventionally Greek, the nurse, who in Athens looked after a girl when
she was a baby and a child and followed her to her new home
when she married. This character is then out of place, but Medea
(as does Deianeira) has such a nurse too, more incongruous for
a Colchian princess than a Cretan one. Euripides is rather careless in these matters. The play's the thing; and for the play's
purposes Phaedra here needs someone to misunderstand her,
which this nurse does to perfection with 'if you're thirsty, I can
find you a drink of water, why go all the way to the woods?'

I do not insist on the Cretan coloring. Euripides may not mean
us to assume that she was trained to be an athlete and to roam
the wilderness. What I do insist on is that she craves to do so.
If we put together the following speech with this one, the careful
and conscious account of her malady with the uninhibited bab-
bling of delirium caused by that malady, then we see Phaedra
and her two lives: the one she has got, fretful and brooding,
pampered, sedentary, confined between walls; and the one she
wants, free, wild, galloping headlong through the woods and over
the sand and flinging herself down to drink without a cup from
running streams. Why does she love Hippolytus? People fall in
love with the wrong people, or the right ones, principally for
their own sake, or Euripides would say because Aphrodite makes
them, but if we need more reasons, then it is as true to say that
Phaedra loves Hippolytus because he lives and stands for the
wild and innocent and strenuous life which she wants and cannot have, and is thought crazy for wanting it, as to say that she
longs for wild places because they suggest Hippolytus and if she
were there she might be with him.

Which brings us to that young man. The play falls into two

halves: the first is the tragedy of Phaedra, the second is the tragedy of Hippolytus. But they are interdependent and neither is complete without the other.

Remembering our pattern story, we will see at once what is the indispensable characteristic of the young hero. He must be virtuous. Hippolytus fills the bill. He is virtuous with a muscular, somewhat belligerent, and utterly self-righteous virtue which makes his critics wonder how in spite of all Phaedra could love him, since we cannot, though we give him full marks.

Agreeing as I do in general with this opinion, I do not wish any more than others to leave it at that. The Prig's Tragedy is not as moving a subject as Euripides wished to make or, somehow, did make, the subject of his play. I do not think the poet, then, intended to create the at times repellent character (at least to modern tastes) which he has created. He failed then in part, but only I think in part, and we can still ask what he was trying to do and how far he succeeded in doing it.

Hippolytus repels us through the starchy rhetoric and phony arguments he uses in his defence before Theseus; in the scene with the nurse because he not only spurns Phaedra but insults her, and because of her all women, wishing they, or sex, could be dispensed with entirely; in the scene of his destruction reported by the messenger, when, dragged and battered and in agony and terror, he cannot even call for help without saying (1242): 'Who will come and rescue *me, the best of all men?*' In the Theseus scene he has been accused, accurately, of addressing his father as if he were a public meeting. Well, but his father *is* a public meeting. This is the one person in the world who can break him or save him. The evidence against him is damning, and he is debarred by oath and his own honor from speaking the truth, thus forced back on those arguments from probability which may impress an audience of dilettantes but convince nobody. So he, and the chorus, and we, all knowing the truth, can only watch, helpless, the inevitable drive of Theseus' rage. Euripides' dramaturgy has formed a bitter, breathless scene, but his execution has spoiled it a little because, as so often, he is under the spell of his own virtuosity and does not know where to stop, so the 'plain unschooled speech' comes out too obviously varnished. In his protest to the nurse he makes himself ridiculous by his wish that we could deposit money in the temples and buy the seed of children there instead of having to make them as we do. The poet has hurt his hero by forcing him to speak for the poet's own fustian fancy. But under it all lies the strong desperate mood of the play, the wish for the impossible voiced at one time or another by every character in it except Aphrodite (who is having her way). Only one figure of this mood is the Prig's progress, the wish, even the demand, that everybody else in the world shall be as good as he thinks he is. This spoils it somewhat, but even under the disastrous 'me, the best of men' we feel a sense of outrage which Hippolytus would be inhuman not to feel. Everything is unfair, and he knows it. Unfairness is the inverse of the impossible wish.

Bastard son of an Amazon forced by Theseus, Hippolytus stood queerly among the Athenian nobles, neither quite Athenian nor quite a noble, but naturally noble, reflecting some of fifth century Greece's wistful admiration of the noble savage, the blissfully uncomplicated barbarian. Only in part: he must also be, no savage, but accomplished in every way, the star of Athens. Out of his strange position Hippolytus has found his way to a life that suited him completely, one utterly immersed in athletics and hunting, blissfully uncomplex, modestly useful, free from society except for the company of a few friends and free from the love of women except for Artemis. Like Ion in the beginning of *Ion* we find him a truly happy young man who has so far escaped all responsibility and is placidly doing only what he wants most to do. 'I only hope I can live all my life as I have begun it' (87) are his last words as he deposits his wreath to Artemis. Of course, it does *not* last: the world catches up with him and wrecks his peace.

Racine in his version found all this well enough, but felt that such a character was too philosophical and his sufferings would arouse indignation rather than pity; therefore he, Racine, has presumed to give him an amiable weakness, through his sweetheart, Aricie. Now if Aricie represents Diana of Aricia and Diana is Artemis, I think Racine was right in a way he probably did not suspect, for surely Hippolytus was in love with Artemis. I do not mean that Artemis represents, actually is, the life he loves, for this is true, but that is not what I mean by love. Rather in the full sense Hippolytus loves Artemis as a woman, the voice and fragrance and presence of her and her invisible companionship, which is all that is given him and all that he asks or hopes for. But now he must be entangled with a woman of flesh and blood, the one woman in the world he cannot have and who must not have him, but *also*, and here is the irony, though he does not want her, the nearest thing to Artemis this side of paradise, a woman who could have shared his favorite pleasures and kept him company as well as simply keeping his house. *Medea* gave us one mode of tragedy in marriage, two hostile natures fastened together by accidents of love and need but each inwardly disliking and despising the other. *Hippolytus* conversely gives two ideally suited natures forced apart by circumstance. Or at least, that is one way to put it. The terms are too romantic for fifth century Athens and the interpretation goes beyond Euripides, but the materials for this interpretation were all put by Euripides in his play.

Circumstances, I said, keep these two apart, but it is more than circumstance (*Tyche*) which forces them into hatred and mutual death, it is the whole way of the world and the nature of the world of which their own natures are a part. This way, which one might call love, is here enacted by two goddesses, Aphrodite and Artemis. It is part of the whole structure of the play that these, again, who are here so different and opposed, are elsewhere so often confused, because they are two aspects and faces of the same goddess who is only the eternal constantly recurring figure of the lovely and beloved young woman, variable as Plato's Heavenly Aphrodite and Vulgar Aphrodite, or Sacred and Profane Love. Critics have complained that Euripides is not clear in his concepts, that Aphrodite in particular is both an immortal person with a human personality, vain and silly and spiteful, and also an impersonal force, the whole reproductive process and urge of nature. This doubtless, I think, is exactly what Euripides meant. One knows very well that floods, blizzards and hurricanes have no personality, that we cannot reason with them and so it is useless to be angry with them and at the same time we cannot when caught help seeing them as maliciously and spitefully aiming at *us*. Here Aphrodite appears not in a theological tract but as a person in a play. She is still divine and we know what she stands for. Artemis is not so clear. She represents, I think, something which the Greeks never isolated and defined, must have felt but did not articulately understand, the sheer pleasure of straining muscles until they ache and running until breath goes (even Pindar commiserates his wrestlers for 'toil', congratulates them on success which redeems it and makes it worth while); and Artemis is other things too, the green woods themselves, and lonely places, the harsh and sterile side of pleasure. But also she too is a person in a play: one who cannot stop Aphrodite but resents her and will get her own back, who pities Phaedra and scolds Theseus and then forgives him, who rewards Hippolytus' devotion with the disinterested shadow of love.

Between the two they wreck everything. Things as they are go wrong. Everything is unfair. We can think of Yeats' lines:

And God-appointed Berkeley, that proved all things a dream,
That this pragmatical, preposterous pig of a world, its farrow
that so solid seem,
Must vanish on the instant if the mind but change its theme.

The mood of hate for the world despite or because of love for its individual people is very strong in this play, expressed in the constant wish for impossibilities, the sense of outrage, the longing for escape. 'My own horses, whom I fed' (1240, 1355–56) complains Hippolytus: or to Zeus (1363–67): 'I was the most pious man on earth and you've killed me. Why?' 'Why do you not go hide in the hells of the earth for shame,' says Artemis to Theseus,

'or take wings like a bird and fly away in the air, to escape?'
(1290–93) It doesn't make sense, of course: Artemis merely
speaks the insistent mood of the drama, and as she does so reminds us of Theseus' line when he discovered Phaedra dead
(828): 'You were gone suddenly out of my hands, like a bird'.
So too the women of the chorus, involved only as spectators, long
to turn into birds and escape to the ends of the ocean, the inac-
cessible cliffs and the sea caves.

That the world is more wrong than right is the statement of
pessimism, and Euripides often seems to be a pessimist, but to
summarize this play as such a statement would be wrong. This
is a particular action done by particular people. Other actions
which follow the pattern story of the young man traduced see
these same gods or others like them guiding their hero through to
the end where the falsified truth is made plain again and the
injuries of accidents made good. Euripides wrote some of these
actions as plays, but that did not make him an optimist. Here
the pattern story ends badly and the gods must see that everything is done for the worst. Theseus in his first rage and before
Hippolytus appeared cursed his son to death, then forgot it or
did not believe Poseidon's promise meant anything; and was
content with a sentence of exile, but Poseidon heard and, though
he did not like to, carried out the sentence. But though the gods
control the springs of action they do not move puppets. Phaedra
and Hippolytus are caught in circumstances, but their own nature
is part of these circumstances, in Phaedra the vanity and lust
which, for all her good qualities, answers Aphrodite, in Hippolytus the chilly and selfish righteousness, or maybe nothing worse
than immaturity, which answers Artemis. Nor again is drama,
however realistic, a mere piece of reality of such and such dimen-
sions transposed, in full, into words and action. There is no room
in this play for a full Theseus, only enough to fill the stock part
of outraged father and headlong angry king; and so too the gods
of the *Hippolytus* appear not as full theological studies but only
as characters in the play sufficient to their part in realizing the
action. That, and to establish the play as a solemn progress at the
beginning, in Aphrodite's stiffly formal prologue: and to fasten it
to its base in the cult of contemporary life, in Artemis' farewell
(1423–30):

> For you, dear wretch, to atone for your injuries
> I shall give you high honors in the city
> of Trozen: for girls unwedded, near their marriage time
> shall cut their hair short in your memory. You shall have
> the tribute of their tears through time forevermore.
> There will be music made and songs of you, to make
> the virgins think of you, and Phaedra's love
> for you shall not be forgotten and a thing of silence.

NEVER BLOTTED A LINE?
FORMULA AND PREMEDITATION IN HOMER AND HESIOD

Douglas Young

Finding formulas, which used to be a prime duty of diplomats and chemists, for over thirty years now has been an increasingly absorbing avocation of literary students, since the late Professor Milman Parry of Harvard extended his inquiries from formulas in Homer to comparable phenomena in heroic songs uttered by illiterate Serbo-Croats. After Milman Parry's lamented early death, his collaborator Professor Albert B. Lord, also of Harvard, added to Parry's recordings of Serb material, and developed further Parry's theories about the composition and transmission of what they term "oral poetry." Another leader in what may be called the "Parryite" School of comparativists is Professor James A. Notopoulos. They are grouped as a trio by Professor Cedric H. Whitman, of Harvard, in *Homer and the Heroic Tradition* (1958), when he writes: "Clearly, my chief points of departure are the works of Milman Parry, Albert Lord, and James Notopoulos, the men who have done the most, by far, for the all-important doctrine of oral composition."

My purpose here is to adduce some evidence from Celtic, French, English, and Russian material, either produced by illiterates or characterized by formulas, or both, to suggest certain grave caveats about the so-called "all-important doctrine of oral composition." Dr. Nora K. Chadwick, of Cambridge, has kindly encouraged me to pursue the lines of thinking here set forth; and I am particularly obliged to my St. Andrews colleagues Kenneth J. Dover, Ian G. Kidd, and Christopher J. Carter for detailed discussions of earlier drafts. They are not to be taken as each agreeing with all my propositions. More generally I am indebted, as we all must be, to the writings of Geoffrey S. Kirk, Sir Maurice Bowra, and Albert B. Lord, who expound "Parryism" with individual variations of insight—for instance, recently, in the chapters

* Dr. Young's article is based on lectures given in the Universities of Toronto and Glasgow, and part of the material appeared in an abbreviated form in the *Minnesota Review* 5 (1965) 65–75.

by Bowra and Lord in the Wace-Stubbings *Companion to Homer* (1962). But, as the most generally useful text for discussion, I would here cite the well-known orthodox Harvard formulation of Parryite doctrine, as it is currently fashionable to apply it in fields other than Greek or Serbo-Croatian, by Professor Francis P. Magoun, Jr., of Harvard, who wrote in *Speculum* 28 (1953) 446–63, an article, "Oral Formulaic Character of Anglo-Saxon Narrative Poetry," in which he states thus the Parryite orthodoxy. (For convenience of reference I insert Arabic numerals to mark off some of his propositions.) Magoun writes:

> In the course of the last quarter-century much has been discovered about the techniques employed by unlettered singers in their composition of narrative verse. (1) Whereas a lettered poet of any time and place, composing (as he does and must) with the aid of writing materials and with deliberation, creates his own language as he proceeds, (2) the unlettered singer, ordinarily composing rapidly and extempore before a live audience, must and does call upon ready-made language, upon a vast reservoir of formulas filling just measures of verse. (3) These formulas develop over a long period of time; they are the creation of countless generations of singers, and can express all the ideas a singer will need in order to tell his story, itself usually traditional. . . . First in connection with Homeric language, later as a result of field work in Yugoslavia, Parry, aided by Lord, demonstrated that (4) the characteristic feature of all orally composed poetry is its totally formulaic character. From this a second point emerged, namely, that (5) the recurrence in a given poem of an appreciable number of formulas or formulaic phrases brands the latter [Magoun means "the given poem"] as oral, just as a lack of such repetitions marks a poem as composed in a lettered tradition. (6) Oral poetry, it may safely be said, is composed entirely of formulas, large and small, while lettered poetry is never formulaic, though lettered poets occasionally consciously repeat themselves, or quote verbatim from other poets, in order to produce a specific rhetorical or literary effect.

[34]

Finally, it is clear that (7) an oral poem until written down has not and cannot have a fixed text . . . ; its text, like the text of an orally circulating anecdote, will vary in greater or lesser degree with each telling. (8) The oral singer does not memorize either the songs of singers from whom he learns nor later does he memorize, in our sense of the word, songs of his own making.

Let us consider first Magoun's proposition 4, where I capitalize for emphasis: "The characteristic feature of ALL orally composed poetry is its TOTALLY formulaic character." Then let us take note of some statistics offered by another Parryite authority, James A. Notopoulos, in his paper "Homer, Hesiod, and the Achaean Heritage of Oral Poetry" in *Hesperia* 29 (1960) 177–97. Notopoulos calculates that, in the 2,380 hexameters of the extant Hesiodic works that he considers genuine, there are 527 repetitions of lines or phrases. He concludes:

> It follows that 23 percent of the Hesiodic corpus consists of repetitions of lines or phrases found in other parts of Hesiod's poems. This compares with 33 percent in the case of Homer, for out of 27,853 [*N.B.* On my count this should be 27,803, in the Oxford text] verses in Homer, 9,253 are repeated or contain repeated phrases. . . . This proportion of 23 percent and 33 percent respectively, a phenomenon found nowhere in subsequent Greek or Latin poetry, is the litmus test of the oral style.

Pray observe, now, the flagrant disagreement between the two Parryites. Magoun says (4): "The characteristic feature of all orally composed poetry is its TOTALLY formulaic character." Notopoulos finds Hesiod is only 23 percent formulaic, which means that Hesiod must be 77 percent non-formulaic, and therefore presumably not "orally composed"; and Homer, with ten times the number of verses that Hesiod now has, is only 33 percent formulaic, and, one must conclude, 67 percent non-formulaic and non-oral.

Albert B. Lord, in *The Singer of Tales* (1960), page 12, remarks: "Although often referred to, the oral theory of

Milman Parry is at best vaguely understood." Indeed his Harvard colleague Magoun would appear to have over-looked the important distinction between a *formula* and a *formulaic expression*. Parry defined *formula* as "a group of words which is regularly employed under the same metrical conditions to express a given essential idea" (*Harvard Studies in Classical Philology* 41 [1930] 80), while Lord defines *formulaic expression* as "a line or half line constructed on the pattern of the formulas" (*Singer* p. 4). Parry exempli-fies *formula* by the line: ἦμος δ'ἠριγένεια φάνη ῥοδοδάκτυλος Ἠώς, "but when early-born rose-fingered Dawn appeared." To illustrate the much more flexible category of expressions "constructed on the pattern of the formulas," Parry refers (p. 85) to "a group of phrases which all express between the beginning of the verse and the trochaic caesura of the third foot, in words which are much alike, the idea 'but when he (we, they) had done so and so'." Parry's examples include: αὐτὰρ ἐπεὶ δείπνησε, αὐτὰρ ἐπεί ῥ'ἔσσαντο, αὐτὰρ ἐπειδὴ ζέσσεν, αὐτὰρ ἐπὴν ἔλθητε, meaning "but after he dined," "but after they dressed," "but after it boiled," "but whenever you have come." Parry says these expressions are "words which are much alike." How much alike do you find the Greek expres-sions translated as "he dined," "they dressed," "it boiled," "you have come"? Parry's flexible category of expressions "constructed on the patterns of the formulas" is so flexible as to be useless for classification. But the Parryites since Parry's death have tended to amplify the role they assign to such ex-pressions "constructed on the pattern of the formulas." Lord terms them "formulaic expressions," and Notopoulos calls them "formulae by analogy." In this category of "formulae by analogy" the avant-garde Parryites put word-groups classified on the basis of metrical shape or syntactical struc-ture. Thus any word-group consisting of a verb and its object is a "formula by analogy," e.g., "John likes horses," "John loves Susie," "John wants dollars." Another formula by analogy would be a word-group occupying a given metrical area, say, from the caesura to the end of the verse. By the same reasoning, every word-group occupying a whole hex-ameter must be a formula by analogy. On this basis Hesiod will be not merely 23 percent formulaic as containing 527 repetitions of lines or phrases in his 2,380 hexameters, but 100 percent formulaic *by analogy*. So will Apollonius of

[36]

Rhodes and Tryphiodorus. To my mind this watering down of the meaning of *formula* is to be resisted. H_2O is a formula, and H_2SO_4 is a different formula. FE 3–2276 is not a formula in the same sense; it is a telephone number, and irrelevant to chemistry. Certainly let us study formulas in Homer or in Nonnos, that is to say, word-groups repeated identically, (or, if you like, with case inflections varying with the syntax of their contexts). But let us waste no time on Lord's "formulaic expressions" and Notopoulos' "formulae by analogy."

Suppose, then, that we quantify word-groups repeated identically—in prose they are usually called clichés, or even bromides, but, to sound scientific, let us term them "formulas" —and suppose we accept Notopoulos' figures, then 33 percent of Homer's two extant epics consists of repeated lines and phrases, and 23 percent of Hesiod's *Theogony* and his *Works and Days*. With these statistics in mind let us look at an Anglo-Saxon poet known to have been literate, Cynewulf.

H.M. and N.K. Chadwick, in *The Growth of Literature* (I, 478), comment on the religious poems containing the name of the author, Cynewulf, in runic acrostics, that: "This may probably be taken to mean that the author himself committed his poems to writing." His syntax, they say, "suggests a date not earlier than the ninth century, when acrostics were popular on the Continent." The Anglo-Saxons had imported the runic alphabet with them into England from the Continent, where it was not recent in the fourth century A.D. (p.476). Magoun himself states (p.457, n.22), on the authority of Mr. Robert E. Diamond, that "20 percent of the 5,194 verses (i.e., 2,598 numbered typographic lines of the editions) in the signed poems of Cynewulf are repeated in the signed poems themselves." Magoun admits (p. 460) that "Cynewulf was surely a lettered person, else how could he have conceived a plan to assure mention of his name in prayers by means of runic signatures which depend on a knowledge of spelling and reading for their efficacy?" Magoun then ties himself into absurd knots trying to reconcile Cynewulf's literacy with the 20 percent of formulas in his verses, which, according to the Parryite dogmas, ought to prove him an "oral poet." We recall Magoun's proposition 5: "The recurrence in a given poem of an appreciable number of formulas or formulaic phrases brands the latter [=

[37]

"the given poem"] as oral, just as a lack of such repetitions marks a poem as composed in a lettered tradition." The first half of Magoun's proposition is disproved by the work of the literate Cynewulf; the second half can be readily disproved by examination of the poetry of the illiterate Scots Gaelic poet Duncan Macintyre.

Two centuries ago worldwide attention was drawn to Scots Gaelic literature during the controversy aroused by James Macpherson's publication of what purported to be English translations of epics by "Ossian" (Oisein). His six-book *Fingal* (1762) and eight-book *Temora* (1763) appear to have used some traditional Gaelic ballads, but were mainly the products of his own imagination, adapting also Irish, Latin, Greek, Biblical, and English elements. Macpherson's *succès de scandale* gave an impetus to the collection of genuine Gaelic poems and stories, which had begun already before the 1760s, and to the gathering of what was supposed to be "folk poetry" in many other languages. Indeed, the Ossianic controversy greatly promoted Homeric studies, though often in misguided directions, from which they have not yet fully recovered. In the middle of the controversy there came from the press the first edition (1768) of poems by the most popular of the Scots Gaelic poets, Donnchadh Bàn Macantsaoir, known in English as Duncan Macintyre. In his long life (1724–1812) he never learned to read or to write, except that he managed to sign his name on receipts for pay, after he had got a sinecure employment in the Edinburgh City Militia. For most of his life he was a game warden on the mountainous borders of Argyll and Perthshire. As most recently edited by Angus Macleod (Edinburgh 1952), the works of this illiterate gamekeeper run to some 6,003 lines, more than the *Argonautica* epic of Apollonius of Rhodes. This was all mentally composed and orally dictated by the illiterate poet. Macintyre's longest single poem consists of 554 lines, of beautifully melodious Gaelic, in a complicated stanza system, with elaborate assonantal schemes. It is called *Moladh Beinn Dóbhrain (Praise of Ben Doran)*, and must have been premeditated by the illiterate poet in the course of his gamekeeping perambulations of the beloved mountain. It is far more highly wrought than anything yet recorded from illiterate Serbo-Croats: more highly wrought, indeed, than any passage of Homer or Hesiod. Yet the poem was

[38]

wholly made up in the unlettered author's head, and then dictated to the Rev. Donald MacNicol, Minister of Lismore.

In regard to the Parryite theory that illiterate "oral" poets extemporize rapidly before live audiences, it is notable that Macintyre dictated to the Rev. MacNicol an abusive poem about a tailor, arising out of a quarrel fourteen years earlier. The minister at first refused to write it down; but the poet insisted, because it was his answer to a Rabelaisian lampoon by the tailor. Clearly the gamekeeper had carried this around in his head for fourteen years, perfected and prefabricated for publication *via* dictation. Even were it true that illiterate Serb poets do not premeditate, but merely improvise, that would be no proof that Homer and Hesiod were mere improvisers, for the illiterate Duncan Macintyre proves that unlettered authors can premeditate and memorize their own compositions, even to the average length of a book of Homer. Further, on the crucial question of formulas, it is to be noted that Macintyre's 554-line *Praise of Ben Doran* is not characterized by formulas. Personally, I am not a Celtic scholar, though I have read and translated many hundreds of lines of Gaelic verse: therefore, after I began to suspect that Macintyre's poetry is not formulaic, as Parryites preach that all poetry by illiterates must be, I applied to the School of Scottish Studies in the University of Edinburgh, where scholars have been studying material collected, with tape recorders and otherwise, from poets and tradition-bearers of the Gaelic-speaking areas. Here is the considered opinion given to me, in a letter from Mr. John MacInnes (30 April 1962): "There is, in Scottish Gaelic poetry, concrete, positive evidence that oral composers do compose without using formulaic expressions at all." Mr. MacInnes goes on to discuss the Gaelic court poets, who, as he states, "were highly literate." He finds that "a much better case could be made for describing their verse as formulaic."

In the light of the above, comparativists will take a new look at Magoun's dictum 6: "Oral poetry, it may safely be said, is composed entirely of formulas, large and small, while lettered poetry is never formulaic. . . ." Before plunging further into Celtic twilight, I would draw attention to what can be learned from French *chansons de geste* regarding Magoun's proposition 3, that "formulas develop over a long period of time; they are the creation of countless generations of singers. . . ." Here we are greatly helped by the controversy aroused by Jean Rychner's book, *La chanson de geste: Essai sur l'art épique des jongleurs* (Geneva-Lille 1955). In this a Neuchâtel professor attempted to apply Parryite theories to French medieval narrative poetry, and inspired a certain following. But adverse criticism rapidly overtook the French-writing Parryites. Coryphaeus of anti-Parryites is the Liège professor Maurice Delbouille, who issued in 1959 a paper called "Les chansons de geste et le livre," in the volume *La technique littéraire des chansons de geste*. There Delbouille deals, *inter alia*, with the arguments of Rychner and other Parryites about the formulas used for episodes of battle. Delbouille's detailed study shows (354ff) that some repeated half-lines could have belonged to a current repertory of clichés, but the greatest number of the formulas in any particular *chanson de geste*, e.g., the *Pélerinage de Charlemagne à Jérusalem* or the *Rainouart*, are peculiar to it, and were probably created by its author. This is borne out by a study of the formulary technique of the three oldest *chansons de geste* by Jeanne Wathelet-Willem, in the *Mélanges . . . Delbouille* (Gembloux 1964, II, 705–27). In these works, known for short as *Roland, Guillaume*, and *Gormont*, formulas do occur, but Mlle. Wathelet-Willem finds them more flexible and less stereotyped than might have been expected. She finds only a few of the formulas common to all three of the texts. Each poem shows individual preferences in repeating phrases, a fact all the more remarkable because the phrases studied are those relating to horses, armor, and ways of hitting people, a large part of the stock in trade of the genre. Further, the poets of these *chansons de geste* tend to repeat a formula a certain number of times and then abandon it for some other formula. She argues that the proportion of formulas does not support the thesis that the earliest authors of *chansons de geste* used formulas as prefabricated half-lines to help them to improvise.

In fact, the whole theory about improvisation in regard to the *chansons de geste* looks to me to be baseless. They were written by literate *trouvères*, often clerics who knew Latin. The Latin novel *Apollonius of Tyre* is the source for one of the *chansons de geste*, *Jourdain de Blaye*. All the historical material in the *Chanson de Roland*, written around 1100 A.D., concerning a battle that occurred on 15 August 778, is contained in a single page of Einhard's *Vita Karoli Magni,* itself written in 829 A.D. It is plausibly argued that the *chanson de geste* developed from a secularization of a narrative song form used for lives of saints. *Trouvères* wrote them for *jongleurs* to memorize and perform, or for domestic chaplains of grandees to read aloud for postprandial entertainments in baronial halls or ladies' boudoirs. Certainly they were destined for oral performance to audiences, not for silent reading; but that applies equally to such works as Virgil's *Aeneid,* or Lucan's *Pharsalia,* by literate authors, or Shakespeare's *Hamlet.* Works designed primarily for an individual reader's silent reading are a late product of the literate phases of poetical traditions.

A well-liked *chanson de geste* might go through quite a long evolution, just as plays of Shakespeare have gone through different editions for theatrical productions. Garrick's eighteenth-century promptbook for *Hamlet* was substantially different from those used by such producers today as Sir Tyrone Guthrie or Sir Laurence Olivier. Thus we find the *Chanson de Roland* rejuvenated in a rhymed version. One recalls how the Carian Pigres, when Greek elegiacs came into fashion, attempted to rejuvenate Homer's *Iliad* by interpolating a pentameter after each hexameter. The cycle of the *Gestes de Guillaume* was subjected to three successive *remaniements,* which have been studied by Mlle. Madeleine Tyssens in the *Mélanges . . . Delbouille.* A point she makes is that the extant manuscripts fall into groups traceable to distinct copying workshops, which produced luxury editions of collections of *chansons de geste* for the libraries of *grands seigneurs.*

This reminds one that the Homeridai, the family of Homer, on the island of Chios, had in their possession in Plato's time (cf. *Phaedrus* 228b) what he calls ἀπόθετα ἔπη, "unpublished verses or poems or epics." It is conceivable that they possessed even in the fourth century copies of the *Iliad* and the *Odyssey* and other works in the handwriting of their ancestor Homer, if he personally wrote works down, or the original copies made from his dictation, if and when he may be supposed to have dictated (say if and when he had gone blind). Indeed, author's holographs or original texts from dictation may have existed in various drafts in the possession of the Homeridai, just as Wagner's operas exist in various

[41]

drafts. The ἀπόθετα ἔπη of Homer might have their Wagnerian equivalent in Wagner's less important and little-demanded operas, like *Die Feen* and *Das Liebesverbot*. When the Athenians sought an authentic text of Homer to control rhapsodic performances at the Panathenaia, it would be natural for Solon or Peisistratos to secure a copy from the Homeridai on Chios, doubtless for a suitable *douceur*. When the great library of the Museum at Alexandria was founded in the earlier part of the third century B.C., the Ptolemies and their librarians were zealous in assembling texts of Homer, some of which were official state copies from Marseilles, Sinope, Argos, and elsewhere. It is presumable that they secured a copy of the Athenian official Panathenaic text, just as they got the official Athenian text of the great Attic tragedians. It may be this Panathenaic text which eventually, from about 150 B.C., dominated the book trade, as evidenced by extant papyri.

Many of the variants in the text of Homer attested from "state editions" or from private owners' copies consist merely of repetitions, perhaps out of context, of verses which appear elsewhere in Homer. But a fair number of variants are substantially different phrasings, at least some of which may derive from different drafts by the author at different times, rather than from the errors and caprices of copyists and editors. This proposition holds good not only for the major epics, but also for the long *Hymn to Apollo*, which is ascribed to Homer by Thucydides and Aristophanes. Herodotus already had been skeptical about attributions of works to Homer, and abjudicated from Homer an epic entitled *Kypria* (2, 117). A.B. Lord remarks: "Herodotus, of course, is less critical than Thucydides" (*apud* Wace-Stubbings, p.214, n.75). Assuming that Thucydides ascribed to Homer the *Hymn to Apollo* after due skeptical consideration, then great interest attaches to the fact that his quotations present variants from the text found in the direct manuscript tradition of the Homeric Hymns; and they look, almost all of them, extremely like author's variants (and first thoughts, at that) rather than copyists' or quoters' mistakes.

I am emphasizing at this point my inclination to entertain seriously the proposition that the Homeric texts, formulas and all, have come to us from the beginning in writing. A purely written tradition seems to be presumable also for another set of narrative poems that present formulas, namely the Middle English Romances, of the "Matter of England" group, illuminatingly studied by Professor Albert C. Baugh, in his article, "Improvisation in the Middle English Romance" (*Proceedings of the American Philosophical Society* 103 [1959] 418–54). These poems are: *King Horn, Havelok, Beves of Hampton, Guy of Warwick, Richard the Lion-Hearted,* and *Athelstan.* Professor Baugh remarks that the Middle English romances are honeycombed with stock phrases and verbal clichés, often trite and at times seemingly forced; but he quotes (p.420) George Saintsbury's reminder that "repetition, stock phrases, identity of scheme and form, which are apt to be felt as disagreeable in reading, are far less irksome, and even have a certain attraction, in matter orally delivered." I concur, too, in his quotation from J.S.P. Tatlock (p.421) that "the well-tried phrase for what is usual leaves the full sharpness of the attention for what is fresh," and that Layamon's auditors "found a pleasure in the repetition . . . as we feel in recognizing a recurring *motif* in music."

In Middle English rhymed romances many of the formulas are of obvious convenience to a writer faced with the requirement of rhyming, and the largest number of formulas occur at the rhymed ends of lines. But, says Baugh (p.422), "the formula . . . is also useful in furnishing a ready-made opening for the verse, a general-purpose approach to the main predicate." He also finds that "at times a couplet assumes the character of a formula, at least within a single romance"; and he suggests that "instances of such repeated couplets . . . may be due to *the habit of the individual poet.*" Now note that this is precisely what Mlle. Wathelet-Willem found in the three oldest French *chansons de geste* which she studied. Only a few of the formulas are common to all three texts; each *chanson* shows individual preferences in repeating phrases.

The Middle English romances of the Matter of England group have, of course, their stock themes: for example, on Baugh's analysis, there are 49 stock themes relating to fighting. Another feature is what Baugh terms the "predictable complement":

Certain statements seem to call up automatically in the mind of the poet or reciter a conventional way of completing the thought. It is as though he were subject to a kind of conditioned reflex. Generally the statement and its predictable complement form a couplet, and this feature of the composition is the result of the fact that the couplet is the basic unit of most English romances, even the stanzaic romances. . . . Such complements occur not only where rime words are *not* easy to find, but in cases where there is a considerable range of choice [428].

For instance, there are in English many rhymes for *knight*, but only three of them occur frequently, "with such frequency as to suggest that the narrator tends to fall into a few conventional thought patterns." Baugh notices also (p.430) that "another type of predictable complement involves association of ideas, with great variety of rimes." He then poses the question:

Are we to believe that those English romances which meet the test of formulaic and thematic elements were composed in the act of oral delivery as are heroic poems of Jugoslavia? In its full form I do not see how such a conclusion can be accepted [431].

He proceeds to emphasize the fact that

many of the Middle English romances are translations, or else adaptations, of French poems . . . the similarities are often such as to leave little doubt that the English poet was following his source with reasonable fidelity, such fidelity as to suggest that the source lay open in a manuscript before him. . . .

Beves of Hampton . . . contains a considerable number of verbal clichés. If we could assume that the minstrel in reciting the story was also partially composing it as he went along, many of these clichés would qualify as formulaic elements. But there can be little doubt that we have to do here with a translation, an English rendering of a French text. There are several specific references in the Cambridge manuscript to the French source, and they are confirmed by other evidence [431].

The English version is based on the Anglo-Norman; it is a

free paraphrase, but "follows the French text so closely as to leave no doubt of the relationship, and there are verbal correspondences which are conclusive." Baugh concludes (p.432) that "oral composition would be conceivable only on the assumption that he [the composer of the English version] was truly bilingual, and could have sung or recited the story in French as well as English." Baugh finds it "equally possible to show the close dependence of *Guy of Warwick* upon the French." On the other hand, Baugh contends that imperfect memory, supplemented by oral improvisation, may account for some variants in parts of the manuscript tradition of romances.

In view of the Wathelet-Willem conclusion from the three oldest French *chansons de geste*, one must note particularly Baugh's proposition (p.439) that: "Each poet or minstrel has to a certain extent *his own favorite formulas* and his own way of treating a theme, as would be expected; but many of these formulas and themes are the common property both of poets who compose in writing and (as I believe) of minstrels" (I italicize). Baugh records also his opinion that the Parry theory about "oral improvisation" by illiterates "probably attaches too little importance to memory."

In Middle English romances, then, some of which are demonstrably derived by translation from French, we find that some formulas are common to several poets, but other formulas are peculiar to individual poets; and that those formulas which are common are shared both by literates and by illiterates.

Glancing for a moment somewhat further back into English literature, one may note that in the Anglo-Saxon poets many formulas are *kennings,* that is to say decorative and allusive phrases, such as "the whale's path," meaning the sea, or "the storm of swords," meaning the battle. Long ago, in 1909, J.W. Rankin proved that many such kennings were virtually translated from Latin poets and prose writers (*apud* Jackson J. Campbell, *Speculum* 35 [1960] 87 n.3). Most Anglo-Saxon poetry extant seems to have been composed by literate men of more or less learning. Their verses contain many clichés or formulas, not because their composers were illiterate improvisers—they were not such—but because the composers and their public liked clichés or formulas, as eighteenth-century audiences liked the flourishes and grace

[45]

notes of contemporary musicians. In the 30,000 or so lines of Anglo-Saxon poetry extant, only one poem is demonstrably by an illiterate poet, namely the 18-line hymn of Caedmon, and he was certainly not an improviser. The little hymn consists almost entirely of formulas, but it is merely a versified doxology based on the liturgy that was familiar, through many hearings, to Caedmon, a pious farmhand on the lands of the abbey of Whitby. All Caedmon did was to accommodate liturgical clichés to the Anglo-Saxon alliterated and accentual verse measure. The Venerable Bede tells us how the religious would read out passages of Scripture to Caedmon, who would then meditate on them overnight, "quasi mundum animal ruminando"—chewing the cud like a cow. In the morning he would regurgitate his Biblical material duly versified, and the religious would write it down. Homer too may have drawn on some liturgical formulas. For instance, it is curious that his repeated phrase for Zeus, ἐρίγδουπος πόσις Ἥρης, "thundering husband of Hera," occurs only in the contexts of prayers and curses (J.B. Hainsworth, *JHS* 78 [1958] 71).

Now what is the position regarding Homer and the Serbo-Croatian material adduced by Parry to try to prove his theory about Homer? Here it is important to note that Parry's thoughts were still evolving up to his untimely death in December 1935; and that some of his provisional generalizations have been upset by his pupil Lord's further work on the Serbo-Croatian material collected by Parry and himself.

Milman Parry started by publishing in 1928 a Paris doctoral thesis, *L' épithète traditionelle dans Homère*, in which he examined those repeated phrases, or formulas, in the *Iliad* and the *Odyssey*, that are made up of a noun and one or more fixed epithets, of the type: πόδας ὠκὺς Ἀχιλλεύς ("swift-footed Achilles"), θεὰ γλαυκῶπις Ἀθήνη ("the bright-eyed, gray-eyed, or owl-eyed goddess Athene"). In that thesis, and another work issued in 1928, *Les formules et la métrique d'Homère*, Parry argued that these recurrent groups of nouns with fixed epithets existed to facilitate a poet's composition of verses with a noble tone, a grand style. The epic poets had created the formulaic technique, Parry then thought, for two simultaneous purposes: (1) to express proper ideas suitably, and (2) to diminish the difficulties of making up hexameters. There is probably a great deal of force in the first motive

assigned, and a certain amount of force in the second supposed purpose. In 1928 Parry also studied in detail the recurrence of formulas, and evaluated, with more precision than
anyone previously, what has come to be called "the thrift of
formulas." This means that the poet, or poets, of the Homeric
epics has, or have, a noun-epithet formula to meet every
recurring need, and there is usually only one such formula
for a given section of the hexameter, say the "paroemiac"
section from the feminine caesura of the third foot to the end
of the verse; and, Parry reckoned, there are never more than
two applicable to the same personality, e.g., βοῶπις πότνια
Ἥρη ("the cow-eyed [or cow-faced] goddess Hera") and
θεὰ λευκώλενος Ἥρη ("the pale-forearmed goddess Hera").

In 1928, it should be stressed, Parry had not yet proposed
the theory that the high frequency of formulas in Homer,
and the thrift of formulas, had any connection with the possibility that Homer was an illiterate improviser. But in the
next year, 1929, a Czech scholar, Mathias Murko, who was
well known in the Paris circle of A. Meillet, which Parry fre-
quented, published a book called *La poésie populaire épique
en Yougoslavie au début du XXe siècle*. Murko there discussed the apparently improvised and extemporary verse-
making by illiterate Serbo-Croatian poet-singers, with their
production of narrative poems that varied in content and
phrasing from one performance to another. It was from reading Murko's book that Parry came to entertain his theory that
Homer's formulas existed to help an illiterate improvising
poet by giving him a traditional repertory of ready-made
phrases out of which he could extemporize hexameters without a metrical breakdown. Parry then went off to Yugoslavia,
with heroic zeal. Mobilizing various illiterate singers of heroic songs, and plying them with suitable beverages, he collected nearly 13,000 texts of South Slavic lore of various
kinds, by different methods, largely on phonograph discs. As
Lord remarks (*Singer*, 3), Parry's work on the formulaic
epithets in the *Iliad* and the *Odyssey*

> had convinced him that the poems of Homer were tra-
> ditional epics, and he soon came to realize that they must
> be oral compositions. He therefore set himself the task
> of proving, incontrovertibly if it were possible, the oral

[47]

∘ character of the poem, and to that end he turned to the study of the Yugoslav epics.

But has the study of the Yugoslav material proved what Parry expected? Consider particularly Magoun's proposition 3: "These formulas develop over a long period of time; they are the creation of countless generations of singers. . . ." In *Harvard Studies in Classical Philology* 41 (1930) 73, Parry referred back to his Paris doctoral thesis of 1928 as having proved

> that the technique of the use of the noun-epithet formulas is worked out to so fine a point that it could be only for the smallest part due to any one man. . . . The poet— or poets—of the Homeric poems has—or have—a noun-epithet formula to meet every regularly recurring need. And, what is equally striking, there is usually only one such formula. An artifice of composition of this variety and of this thrift must have called for the long efforts of many poets who all sought the best and easiest way of telling the same kind of stories in the same verse-form.

Now see how Lord's detailed studies of Serbo-Croatian material have exploded Parry's *a priori* theorizing about a common stock of traditional formulas developed by generations of poets. Lord found, for example, that a particular singer, Salih Ugljanin, in some 9,000 lines, had only one formula to express a given idea under one set of metrical conditions, but that in the same district (Novi Pazar) other singers had other formulas for the same idea. Lord therefore concludes:

> The thriftiness which we find in individual singers, and not in districts or traditions, is an important argument for the unity of the Homeric poems. Homer's thriftiness finds its parallel in the individual Yugoslav singer, but not in the collected songs of a number of different singers.

Homeric Unitarians will certainly relish this result of research in the Serbo-Croatian field.

It might be found, on inquiry, that the Serbo-Croatian singer Salih Ugljanin himself invented some of his favorite

[48]

∘for 'poem'] *read* 'poems'

formulas, which are not found in the effusions of other poets in his district. There is certainly evidence to suggest that Homer himself invented many of the formulas he used. I refer to a paper by Professor M.W.M. Pope, of Capetown, "The Parry-Lord Theory of Homeric Composition," in the South African periodical *Acta Classica* 6 (1963) 1–21. Pope there studied the repeated phrases in the similes of the *Iliad*, and reckoned that there are 184 similes, totaling 665 lines, with 379 different noun-epithet combinations. Of these 379 noun-epithet combinations in the Iliadic similes, 53 can be termed formulas. Of these 53 formulas, about half, namely 27, also appear in the *Iliad* outside the similes, and all but two of those 27 are found in the *Odyssey* also. They include expressions like φίλος υἱός ("dear son"), νήπια τέκνα ("infant children"), χλωρὸν δέος ("green fear"), κρατερὸν μένος ("powerful force"), ὀξέϊ χαλκῶι ("with sharp bronze"), which could indeed be traditional formulas of poetic diction, but equally could be habitual phrases of everyday conversation in prose. At any rate, no more than 27 of the 379 noun-epithet combinations in the *Iliad* similes are likely to be traditional formulas. Homer may have invented the other 26 formulas himself when writing his similes. In sum, the 53 formulas, traditional or original to Homer, make up only 15 percent of the noun-epithet combinations in the *Iliad* similes; all the rest, 85 percent of the total, are likely to be Homer's original and individual phrases. Pope's investigation therefore is somewhat disconcerting to those who swallow Magoun's proposition 6, "Oral poetry, it may safely be said, is composed entirely of formulas, large and small," and at the same time swallow Parry's theory that Homer was an "oral poet."

I wish to take next some Celtic testimony regarding another Parryite contention, Magoun's proposition 7, that "an oral poem, until written down, has not and cannot have a fixed text," and his proposition 8, "The oral singer does not memorize either songs of singers from whom he learns, nor later does he memorize, in our sense of the word, songs of his own making." On the matter of illiterate performers' having fixed texts a good deal of field work has been done in the Gaelic-speaking areas of Scotland and Ireland, about which a useful survey is in Professor Duncan McMillan's article, "A propos de traditions orales," in *Cahiers de Civilisation Médiévale* 3 (1960) 67–71, with a "bibliographie d'initiation."

In some areas there is still an immense repertory of prose narratives and songs, including legendary material, some of it of the type called "Ossianic." Shepherds, crofters, and fishermen who have this material in mind take themselves seriously, and are locally respected, as authentic holders of venerable traditions. Most of them are not readers, and the older ones are usually almost totally analphabetic for practical purposes.

My late friend Calum Maclean took tape recordings from an octogenarian crofter on the island of Benbecula, Angus McMillan, who had in his head more than seventy tales lasting at least one hour each, and some novels lasting seven to nine hours, one of them running to 58,000 words, which is nearly as long as Homer's *Odyssey,* and twice as long as the *Chanson de Roland.* Angus McMillan could talk for eight hours at a stretch, almost without a pause. On the nearby island of Barra, Roderick MacNeil is reported to have told tales every winter night for fifteen years without ever repeating himself. On the Scottish mainland, in Lochaber, John Macdonald recorded over 600 tales, each of them a comparatively short story complete in itself. An Irish taleteller recorded over half a million words of tales he knew. A curious case is that in South Uist, where there was a noted teller of tales named Duncan Macdonald, whose repertory was never taken down complete before he died. Accordingly his son, not himself a teller of tales, remembered and wrote down over 1,500 pages of texts which he had heard from his father; then he got tired and stopped. These Gaelic taletellers in Scotland and Ireland appear not to have had mnemotechnical systems, and to have taken no trouble to work up their repertories. They seem to have assimilated the lore, rather than learned it in our ordinary sense of learning by "swotting-up." Old Angus McMillan of Benbecula claimed that he needed to hear a story only once and then retell it himself only once, in order to have it fixed in his mind definitely forever.

On this fixation of the text, many Gaelic witnesses assert that a text is assimilated in its totality and in all its details. It is not just the main lines that are remembered and then redeveloped in a new telling. A good test of this took place in 1953 at an International Celtic Congress, when the members of the Congress were handed copies of a 50-minute tale that

had been recorded in 1950 by Duncan Macdonald of South
Uist. Duncan Macdonald re-performed it in 1953 *verbatim,*
while the Celtologists sat and checked that he did so. The
same man had previously recorded the same tale in 1944. A
Dutch scholar, Miss Maartje Draak, therefore sat down to
compare the 1944 recording with the 1950 recording, and
gave her conclusions in an article in *Fabula* 1 (1957) 47–58.
She found only the following discrepancies between Macdonald's two recordings six years apart: he had in one phrase
altered an epithet applied to the hero; he had changed some
interjections and conjunctions; he had altered some synonyms; he had varied the order of words slightly sometimes;
he had two or three mere lapses in utterance, and only a very
few substantial variants in his 50-minute story told at intervals of six years. Furthermore, Macdonald's version of 1944
and 1950 and 1953 agreed well with a version of the same
tale that had been taken down from dictation so long ago as
1817, a century and a quarter earlier. J. Rychner, in his book
La chanson de geste . . . (p.33), mentions a Russian *bylina*
collected in almost identical terms from the same singer at
40 years' interval. Thus the Gaels may not be unique in fidelity to a fixed text. Gaelic taletellers of repute reject with
indignation any suggestion that they improvise.

The Celtic evidence, then, seems, to show that the concept
of a fixed text is not incompatible with illiteracy. It appears
also that Scots and Irish taletellers have had a traditional
practice of organizing competitions among themselves; and
that in preparation for competition men would practice their
repertories while out plowing their fields or herding their
animals. This brings me to the Parryite Magoun's proposition
2: "The unlettered singer, ordinarily composing rapidly and
extempore before a live audience, must and does call upon
ready-made language, upon a vast reservoir of formulas. . . ."
This does not sound at all applicable to the Gaelic gamekeeper Duncan Macintyre, meditating his 554-line poem,
Praise of Ben Doran, while marching around with his beloved gun in his hand. He must have premeditated it, without formulas, till he got it to his liking, and then dictated it to
the Rev. MacNicol for the edition of 1768. In later editions
(1790 and 1804) Macintyre ordered deletion of some bits
that had failed to please him after the lapse of years; but no

doubt he could still have recited it, either in the longer or the shorter form.

Moreover, even with the Serbo-Croatian poets, among whom a considerable degree of variation from recital to recital seems to be well attested, one detects also large elements of premeditation. Of the vast mass of material housed at Harvard, there have been published so far only the two volumes of *Serbocroatian Heroic Songs,* "collected by Milman Parry, edited and translated by Albert Bates Lord" (Cambridge [Mass.] 1954). One finds there nothing like an epic, but merely 32 pieces by five poets of Novi Pazar, with an average length of 786 decasyllabic lines. The longest Serbian heroic song so far published by Parry and Lord is 1,811 lines, equivalent in syllables to 1,207 Homeric hexameters, equal to about two books of the *Iliad.* The first volume of the Parry-Lord publication presents some thirty pages of reports of talks with poet-singers, in which Parry put to them scores of questions. Parry was proud of his questionnaires, but they seem not to have included the crucial question that would have tested his theory about Homer: "Why do you use so many repeated word-groups? Is it as a safeguard against metrical breakdown while you are improvising?" However, from Lord's *Singer of Tales* we pick up a clue (p.22) when he remarks: "Others have a formulaic phrase of general character addressed to the audience which they use to mark time, like Suljo Fortić with his *Sad da vidiš, moji sokolovi,* "Now you should have seen it, my falcons." But (says Lord) these devices have to be used sparingly, because the audience will not tolerate too many of them." I conclude that Parry erred in thinking that formulas came into existence primarily as metrical devices against breakdown in improvisation, for even the comparatively unsophisticated Serb audiences resent them if so used. Another point to note is that many of the Serbian formulas are curses, of the type "May your bones rot!", "May their flesh never rest!" According to the Parryites, these curses are uttered by an improvising bard while trying to think out some more trochaic decasyllables. It would be curious to hear the reply if some Parryite with his tape recorder asked a Serbo-Croatian singer, "How many verses can you extemporize in your mind while pronouncing the formula *May their bones rot!*'?" My own suspicion is that the Serb

curses are merely stylistic ornaments, like Homer's "But
when early-born rose-fingered Dawn appeared."

Moreover, consider the testimony of Šečo Kolić, quoted by
Lord (*Singer,* 21). As a boy he used to tend sheep alone on
the mountain by day. In the evenings, in his village, he listened to men singing to the *gusle,* or one-stringed violin. Next
day, again with his sheep, he would sing the song from memory, as the singer had sung it. However, said Kolić, "I didn't
sing among the men until I had perfected the song, but only
among the young fellows in my circle." Here, then, is an illiterate Serbo-Croatian poet with the concept of a perfected
text, and the habit of rehearsing to himself or a small circle
of his age group. How can Parryites claim that such an illiterate is an improviser? *Webster's New International Dic-
tionary* (2nd ed., 1959) defines the verb *improvise,* in its in-
transitive use, thus: "to produce or render extemporaneous
compositions, especially in verse or in music, without previous preparation; hence, to do anything offhand." It is
grossly false to say that Kolić produced extemporaneous compositions without previous preparation.

The factor of time is much stressed by Lord, who writes
(*Singer,* 22): "The literate poet has leisure to compose at
any rate he pleases. The oral poet must keep singing. His
composition, by its very nature, must be rapid." In *A Companion to Homer* (ed. A.J.B. Wace and F.H. Stubbings
[1962] 184) Lord avers that the "oral poet" "must compose
as he sings, at sometimes breakneck speed." But one wonders
why on earth Šečo Kolić must have kept singing, at breakneck or any other speed, while herding his sheep alone on
the mountain. He had all day and every day to premeditate
and perfect a song, till he got it exactly to his mind, just as
the Gaelic gamekeeper Macintyre premeditated and perfected his 554-line poem on Ben Doran.

It may, nonetheless, be true that Serbo-Croatian poets so
far recorded premeditate imperfectly. They seem to be mostly
poorish poets, belonging to an inferior culture in a decayed
stage; and nothing produced by them bears the slightest resemblance to the quality of the works of Homer and Hesiod.
It is also grossly misleading to call their heroic songs "epics,"
as Lord and others have done. Lord argues (*Singer,* 6): "*Epic*
is sometimes taken to mean simply a long poem in 'high
style.' Yet a very great number of the poems which interest us

in this book are comparatively short; length, in fact, is not a criterion of epic poetry." Lord's assertion must be resolutely denied. Length is a major criterion of epic poetry. The *Iliad* has 15,693 lines in the Oxford text, the *Odyssey* 12,110; the *Aeneid*, still unfinished, 9,896; Nonnos' *Dionysiaca* 21,287. Milton's *Paradise Lost* has 10,558 lines, and its appendix, *Paradise Regained*, 2,070. Apollonius' *Argonautica*, with four books totaling 5,835 hexameters, is a miniature epic, with the frequent Alexandrian taste for the highly ornamented miniature. So far the longest Serbo-Croatian heroic song published by Parry and Lord is of 1,811 lines, equivalent in syllables to 1,207 Homeric hexameters, say two books of the *Iliad*. The Serbian heroic songs are not epics, and they cannot be compared in scale, any more than in quality, with the epics of Homer.

It is curious that Lord claims that "we know from the Yugoslav material that the oral singer can compose unified songs as long as the *Iliad* or *Odyssey* without any difficulty" (*Companion to Homer*, 195). No such unified song as long as the *Iliad* has been published. The longest Yugoslav metrical effort so far recorded appears to be the still unpublished *Wedding of Smailagić Meho*, which would equal only two-thirds of the *Odyssey*, and was certainly not composed "without any difficulty," if we believe Sir Maurice Bowra's account of it in *Heroic Poetry* (1952) 351. It was composed by a sixty-year-old illiterate butcher at Bijelo Polje, one Avdo Medyedovitch, who was somehow stimulated—perhaps one might say commissioned—by Milman Parry to the effort. And a difficult effort it was. Bowra states:

> He would sing for about two hours in the morning and for another two hours in the afternoon, resting for five or ten minutes every half-hour. To sing a long song took him two weeks, with a week's rest in between to recover his voice.

Now it is grossly erroneous to claim that a long poem so composed is composed "without any difficulty." It is obvious that it was an extraordinary effort for a totally abnormal audience, namely Milman Parry's phonograph; and that no Serbo-Croatian audience would ever have been available for a production scheduled for two hours in the morning and two hours in the evening of the first and third weeks of a three-week period.

Bowra tells us further that Medyedovitch "seems to have composed the poem as he went on. No doubt he formed certain plans in his head, and was helped in the execution of them by the formulaic elements which belong to his art and appear abundantly in his poems." That is to say, Medyedovitch premeditated his long poem with a lot of clichés in it, like the literate Anglo-Saxon Cynewulf, who premeditated poems with a 20-percent quota of clichés, but unlike the illiterate Duncan Macintyre, who premeditated much better poetry without clichés. Medyedovitch would also be unlike the truly classic example of an "oral poet," the blind Milton, premeditating and dictating an epic without a significantly high proportion of repeated word-groups.

Medyedovitch, all the same, is certainly a performer worth studying. Lord, in *Serbocroatian Heroic Songs* (I, 16), calls him a "singer of tales who could produce songs as long as the *Iliad* and the *Odyssey*," and promises to print two versions, separated by fifteen years, of his 12,000-line song, *The Wedding of Smailagić Meho*. Bowra states that "it is an epic constructed on a well-conceived plan, ànd not a series of separate lays joined together by superficial transitions. The bard in this case could not read or write, and seems to have composed the poem as he went on. . . ." Let us recall that Medyedovitch paused for five or ten minutes in every half hour of his two-hour sessions of recital, both morning and evening for the days of two separate weeks, with an interval of a week, and it will be clear that in his high proportion of pauses and intervals Medyedovitch could be bringing back to memory portions of a work already premeditated. One may doubt whether he was truly improvising, that is to say, composing extemporaneously without previous preparation. Lord asserts (*Singer*, 13): "For the oral poet the moment of composition is the performance. . . . An oral poem is not composed *for* but *in* performance." As well might one say that a dinner is composed when it is served on the table. Every housewife knows differently. Medyedovitch is likely to have been rather in the position of a cook who prepares a series of dishes and puts them in an oven, in this instance his memory, and then brings them out as the occasion demands.

With Medyedovitch, and some other illiterate Serbo-

Croatians whom Parry prompted to record long poems, Bowra notes that

> the impulse to compose a long poem came from outside, in Parry's request for it. But once he had been asked for it, the poet had no great difficulty in providing it. The psychological process of composition must remain a mystery, but at least we know that the poets were able, by following a routine of recitation and pauses, to produce poems as long as the *Odyssey*. This is a fundamental fact of first importance. . . .
>
> A similar art of composition on a large scale can be found among the Uzbeks. The bard Pulkan (1874–1941), who was a simple shepherd by origin and never learned to read or write, was not only the author of some seventy different poems, most of some length, but composed one, called *Kiron-Khan,* which has more than 20,000 lines. Unfortunately the text is not available, and we are unable to see what its methods of construction are. Since the normal length of an Uzbek poem is about 3000–4000 lines, this shows how a bard can extend himself when he feels called upon to do so. More is known about another long Uzbek poem, the *Alpamys* of Fazil, which has about 14,000 lines. . . . The poem is one of many on Alpamys, and nine other versions are known in Uzbek. None of these is on anything like the same scale, and Fazil shows how a bard who has enough inventive power can extend a story to a large scale without making it look at all inflated. Part of his gift lies in the speeches which he gives to his characters, and which abound in eloquence and dramatic strength [354].

Eloquence and dramatic strength are among the chief distinctions of Homer, whose skill in dramatic characterization is praised by Aristotle in his *Poetics* (iv.12). Like Fazil, Homer very properly varied his narrative with plenty of speeches. Indeed, Homer carried this so far that many books read almost like plays.

Reverting to the problem of premeditation, with a view to perfecting a poem, and extemporaneous composition, or true improvisation, it may be that one should not make too hard and fast a separation, having regard to the ways in which the

[56]

human mind, and especially the subconscious layers of the mind, may work. Mark Twain is said to have remarked that "nobody can do a decent improvisation in less than three hours." By that he presumably meant especially improvisation of public speeches. Bowra has some helpful remarks on a celebrated character connected with Wadham College, Oxford, namely F.E. Smith, first Earl of Birkenhead (*Memories* [1966] 138f):

> He spoke with effortless fluency, but always with a literary flavour, which was even more marked when he made a speech. Then the famous voice rolled out the majestic periods. . . . I never saw him use a note or hesitate for a word, and, though often enough at a speech at a college dinner there was no need for him to make much preparation, I suspect that he made some, and that he had the full shape of a speech in his head before he delivered it.

In other words, the apparently extemporary effusion had been premeditated, at least to a large extent.

Incidentally, like the Yugoslav singers who delight in distilled hard liquor, *rakija*—Murko (p.18) notes that beer and wine had adverse effects on their voices!—"Birkenhead drank [writes Bowra] what seemed to be a great deal, especially brandy, but it had no perceptible effect on his words. He remained equally coherent through the evening." Maybe indeed the effect of the alcohol, with Birkenhead and the Yugoslav singers, was simply to liberate the utterance that had been prefabricated on some level of the consciousness, to serve it to the table from the oven where it had been kept warm after being cooked.

In view of Murko's phonograph recordings, since 1912, and those of Parry and Lord a generation later, we must admit that recent Yugoslav singers, so far as they do premeditate, seem not to realize at all fully whatever ideas they may have of the perfect state of any song. The variations from recital to recital, by even their most accomplished modern representatives, seem to be substantial; they are anything but perfected. They have about as much literary value as most after-dinner speeches by run-of-the-mill public personalities, or as the average sermon in most churches, where the per-

[57]

former delivers what is on his mind with no fixed text written or memorized, but on the basis of a certain degree of premeditation, aided perhaps by a few notes, or memorization of "heads of discourse." The Serb singer nowadays is a mere amateur *raconteur*, as a rule, though a few are semi-professional insofar as coffeehouse owners may give them retaining fees to entertain clients during the thirty nights of the Mohammedan festival of Ramazan. The Serbo-Croatian trochaic decasyllabic lines, unadorned with rhyme or alliteration, and proceeding in simple speech rhythms with one caesura, strike an outsider as a very rudimentary verse-form compared with the Greek dactylic hexameter. In so far as they are partly improvised, or incompletely premeditated, the result is facilitated by their simplicity of metrical form, and proves nothing regarding the possibility of extemporizing Homeric hexameters. As little would an ability to extemporize a hundred lines in the meter of Longfellow's *Hiawatha* prove a capacity to invent a sequence of fifty rhymed couplets in the manner of Pope, while standing on one foot.

But Murko and Parry agree that the twentieth-century Yugoslav heroic song tradition is decadent; and it may be that in its palmier days, when it was fostered by powerful aristocracies, the singers sought and attained greater perfection and fixity of text. For example, in the 1845 edition of his collection, *Srpske narodne pjesme*, II, 624–27, Vuk. Karadžić printed the song "Jakšići kušaju ljube" ("The Jakšić test their womenfolk") in a version which he claimed to have taken down from the dictation of an 18-year-old youth at Užiće in Serbia. Murko alleges (p.17f) that Karadžić did no such thing, but simply lifted it, line by line, from the volume *Satir,* published in 1779 by the Croat poet A. Reljković, and made a few spelling changes. Murko asserts (p.18) that the identity of a text of the eighteenth century and a text of the nineteenth century would be an impossibility. In view of the example of the Gaelic tale related in 1953 to the International Celtic Congress by Duncan Macdonald, and its substantial identity with the same tale as taken down in 1817, perhaps Murko was too dogmatic, and his attack on the good faith of the respected collector Karadžić may have been erroneous.

Before leaving the Yugoslav material, attention may be drawn to one observation of Lord's that points up a contrast between Homer and the Yugoslav singers of today. Lord

comments (*Singer,* 159) on that passage in *Odyssey* 1 where
Zeus meditates on the return of Agamemnon:

> Such a reference to another tale is highly sophisticated
> and unusual for oral epic. In the Yugoslav tradition
> stories are kept separate and, to the best of my knowl-
> edge, singers never refer in one song to the events of
> another.

Lord's remark ought to shock those who imagine Homer to
have been an illiterate improviser, such as modern Yugoslavs
are supposed to be: for Homer repeatedly refers to other
stories than those of Achilles' wrath or Odysseus' return, for
instance, the voyage of the Argo (*Od.*12.70) and the fall of
Thebes (*Il.*4.406). By these references Homer disqualifies
himself from being ranked among "oral poets."

Lord explains that the Serbo-Croatian singer thinks of his
song "in terms of a flexible plan of themes" (*Singer,* 99).
"Its clearness of outline will depend upon how many times
he sings it . . . a short song will naturally tend to become
more stable the more it is sung" (p.100). Though it never
ceases to be fluid, a Yugoslav song tends to become less fluid
for a particular performer who does it often: yet, Lord finds,
it never acquires a final and perfect scheme of incidents, expressed in a fixed set of words. Be that as it may, it would
be rash to argue by analogy from the Yugoslav phenomena
towards the conclusion that Homer and Hesiod were illiterate
improvisers who did not attempt to perfect their expression
of their ideas in hexameters in the various poems they
created. Perfection, to be sure, is very difficult, given the
frailty of our mortal natures. W.B. Yeats went on rewriting
some of his poems to his dying day. Paul Valéry too was
conscious of the necessary imperfectibility of any poetic attempt. He wrote often of a poem as "un état du poème,"
merely "one state of the poem," considered as an entity
somehow capable of organic evolution. Shakespeare, on the
other hand, "never blotted a line," according to Hemminge
and Condell, editors of his first collected edition. Shakespeare
was perhaps more facile, or less scrupulous, than Yeats, who
wrote:

> Metrical composition is always very difficult for me;

nothing is done upon the first day; not one rhyme is in its place; and when at last the rhymes begin to come, the first rough draft of a six-line stanza takes the whole day [quoted by A.N. Jeffares, *W.B. Yeats: Man and Poet* (1949) 76].

Yeats, among the greater poets, seems to be at the extreme of unspontaneity and infacility in creation. One fancies that Homer was nearer in fecundity and facility to Shakespeare than to Yeats; and yet one could readily conceive that Homer never quite finalized, never got wholly perfect to his mind, either the *Iliad* or the *Odyssey*. Unitarians are not obliged to believe that Homer sat down and wrote the whole *Iliad* from Alpha to Omega just as we have it in, say, the Oxford text. He might have started what became the *Iliad* with a quite short heroic poem on *The Wrath of Achilles*, maybe a four-book affair like the *Argonautica* of Apollonius; then, as audiences liked it, Homer might have added as the fancy took him, and expanded it to the twenty-four books we happily have. That excellent nighttime escapade, the *Doloneia*, could be quite a late addition; so could the funeral games for Patroklos, and even there not every item need have been added to the growing *Iliad* at one effort. James Bridie, the playwright, wrote to his favorite actress Flora Robson: "A play improves by maturing for a bit . . . there are all sorts of delightful accretions that appear with many revisals" (W. Bannister, *James Bridie and His Theatre* [1955] 91). Of the highly effective dream scene in his play *Dr. Angelus* Bridie recorded: "I stuck it in after the play was written" (*op. cit.* 166). Likewise with the *Odyssey*, one can believe that Homer had performed many times various versions of his account of the wanderings and home-coming of Odysseus before he devised, or accepted from another, the good idea of taking the hero to the underworld, and incorporated the *Nekuia*. Even if the *Iliad* as a whole was earlier than the *Odyssey* as a whole, still it is possible that some parts of the *Iliad* as we have it were added after Homer had finished one version of the *Odyssey*: thus formulas and turns of thought that commentators find "Odyssean" may have been put into the *Iliad* by Homer at some revision later than his main spell of work on the *Odyssey*.

Before I come to consider reasons for the frequency of

[60]

formulas in Homer, I wish to draw attention to some aspects of premeditation in more modern literature, having regard to Magoun's proposition 1, about "a lettered poet . . . composing (as he does and must) with the aid of writing materials and with deliberation." And first let us look at some examples of prose authors and their methods of composition.

Edward Gibbon, the historian, in *Memoirs of My Life* (ed. G.A. Bonnard [1966] 159), comments on the composition of his *Decline and Fall*:

> Near two years had elapsed between the publication of my first, and the commencement of my second, Volume. . . . But when I resumed my task I felt my improvement. I was now master of my style and subject: and while the measure of my daily performance was enlarged, I discovered less reason to cancel or correct.

Now here comes the illuminating passage for our purpose:

> It has always been my practise to cast a long paragraph in a single mould, *to try it by my ear, to deposit it in my memory*; but to suspend the action of the pen, till I had given the last polish to my work. Shall I add that I never found my mind more vigorous, or my composition more happy, than in the winter hurry of society and parliament [I italicize]?

Here we have Gibbon, as a member of the United Kingdom legislature, premeditating his history in swatches, a long paragraph at a time, and working it over in his memory till he had each long paragraph, or period, perfected, after which he wrote it down. "Tried by the ear," it was in a sense "oral" prose.

Or again take another eighteenth-century figure, though still alive in 1967, Bertrand Russell, the third Earl Russell. As reported by Ved Mehta, in *The New Yorker* (December 9, 1961) 100, the venerable philosopher explained that "he had two models for his own style—Milton's prose and Baedeker's guidebooks." As a young man he had written with difficulty.

> Sometimes Milton and Baedeker remained buried in his prose until it had been redone ten times. . . . Now, for

many years past, he had learned to *write in his own mind,* turning phrases, constructing sentences, until *in his memory* they grew into paragraphs and *chapters.* Now he seldom changed a word in his dictated manuscript, except to slip in a synonym for a word repeated absent-mindedly [I italicize].

Note that Russell, through long experience of articulate thinking to some purpose, could premeditate and memorize whole chapters of prose. Note also that his early literary training had conditioned him not to repeat words, but to prefer synonyms. This taste for stylistic variation goes back, in prose, to about the fifth century B.C. But not all Greek prose writers thought it reasonable to conform to it. The historian Polybios, for instance, justifies himself (29.12.10) for re-using the same words as on a previous occasion, on the grounds that "in all such matters the large scale of my work is sufficient excuse." F.W. Walbank, *Speeches in Greek Historians* (1966) 13, notes in Polybios a repetition of clichés of metaphor, phrase, and sentiment; and one must accept the conclusion that, for a man who is a philosophical and didactic historian, not merely a verbal confectioner, if a valid point is well stated, it may as well be stated twice in the same good way.

Or again consider the Czech prose writer Jaroslav Hašek, author of *The Good Soldier Schweik,* of whom an editor for whom he worked, Josef Kodíček, testified (as quoted in *The Times Literary Supplement* [September 7, 1962] 665):

> I myself induced him to write two volumes of stories, by the simple device of withholding payment until he had written them in my presence. He would sit down at my desk, and, without a pause, and mostly without a single correction, wrote each story in the neatest of scripts with extreme rapidity.

This shows that Hašek had premeditated and memorized a whole set of stories, perfected in his head without setting pen to paper. Facsimiles of his holographs reveal "a clerkly hand altogether at variance with their rampant subject matter."

Hašek premeditated his stories, and wrote them down

"with extreme rapidity." Shakespeare premeditated his plays, and wrote them down "without blotting a line." What about the glorious hexameters of Homer? Surely there is no difficulty in believing that Homer could premeditate and memorize them, whole books or epics at a stretch, and then write them down without ever blotting his papyrus or leather scroll. About a creator's memory for his creations, one might mention Nikos Skalkottas, the Greek composer (1904–49), of whom John G. Papaioannou writes (in H. Hartog's *European Music in the Twentieth Century* [2 ed., 1961] 345): "He remembered practically all his works, and actually rewrote by heart his entire first orchestral suite six years after it was composed."

Incidentally, Skalkottas was a Euboian from Chalkis, and thus, in some sort, a distant connection of Homer's: for Homer's family, the Homeridai, lived on Chios, and most of the colonists of Chios had come from northern Euboia, along with some from the homeland of Achilles, Thessaly. It is worth noting that the distance from Chios to Euboia is no farther than from one end of Euboia to the other. Our chairborne historians of Greek literature tend to exaggerate the degree of separation between the Greeks of the mainland and their colonists over this or that stretch of water, at a time when water was the easiest highway at seasons when folk wished to travel. Euboia and its vicinity, including the Helikon area, where Hesiod's father settled after coming from Aeolian Kyme where he had been some sort of sailor or merchant, should be regarded as central to the sphere of undisturbed transmission, during the four or five centuries between Achilles and Homer, of the saga material that Homer used for his epics. Probably the least rehandled portion of that material is the Achaean Catalogue in *Iliad* 2, based on an old poem about the mustering of the Greek contingents at Aulis, opposite Euboia.

Homer and Hesiod share a common dialectal mixture, consisting mainly of Ionic, with about a ten percent admixture of Aeolic forms, mostly metrically useful as alternatives, but also perhaps having for Ionian ears a somewhat archaic or poetical flavor, as distinctively Scots words may have for English ears listening to a Border ballad. Supposed Arcado-Cypriote or other dialectal words in Homer are best explained as old words, originally common to wider areas, that happened to survive in classical times only in Arcadia, Cyprus, or elsewhere. Homer and Hesiod, of course, share some formulas, for example, Ὀλύμπια δώματ᾽ ἔχουσαι ("having homes on Olympos"), used of the Muses, which may derive from liturgical hymns in the "paroemiac" meter, used also for proverbs. But Homer and Hesiod also have distinctive formulas preferred by each one of them, just as was found with the writers of the *chansons de geste*. They share a certain linguistic community, and a common tradition of poetic diction for poems of high style about deities and heroes; but they each make an individual use of their inherited materials and expressive means, and each develops his own innovations in phrase-making, just as Marlowe and Shakespeare did among Elizabethan dramatists.

Let us recall now the general cultural background of epic style utterance that, in various measures, influenced Hesiod and Homer, who are likely to have been contemporaries in the eighth century B.C., with Hesiod perhaps the elder of the two. Lord (*Singer*, 156) remarks that in the eighth century Sargon II (722–05) established the library at Nineveh, with tablets inscribed with epic, mythic, magic and historical material in several languages, some of it from 2000 B.C. Lord thinks it would be normal for Greeks to look to the East at that period, for it was in the East that the cultural center was then located. He suggests "that the idea of recording the Homeric poems, and the Cyclic epics, and the works of Hesiod, came from observing or from hearing about similar activity going on further to the East." Dr. Martin A. West, in his admirable edition of Hesiod's *Theogony* (1966), observes (p.31) that "Greek literature is a Near Eastern literature." Certainly some of Hesiod's mythic material is derived from Near Eastern sources; and his father came from Asia Minor. T.B.L. Webster, in *From Mycenae to Homer* (1958) 70, discusses the way in which court formalities affected the language of poetry in Middle Eastern kingdoms of the second millennium B.C. Their written epics show frequent repetitions of word groups. Thus (*op. cit.*, 72), in the Ugaritic poem *Keret*, the god El orders Keret in a dream: "In a bowl of silver pour wine, honey in a bowl of gold. Go up to the top of the tower; bestride the top of the wall." After Keret has woken up, we read: "In a bowl of silver he poured wine, honey in a bowl of gold. He went up to the top of the tower, bestrode the top of the wall." According to the Parry-Lord-Notopoulos theory the repeated word groups, or formulas, in *Keret* exist to safeguard an improvising "oral poet" from metrical breakdown in rapid extemporization.

Comparable to the *Keret* repetition of word groups would be what occurs in *Iliad* I, where 208f repeats 195f, with the change of *gar* to *de m(e)*. 195f means: "For the pale-forearmed goddess Hera sent [Athena] forth, loving and caring for both of the pair alike in her heart." 208f is spoken by Athena, and has a consequential modification: "And the pale-forearmed goddess Hera sent me forth. . . ." Homer's self-repetition may have been motivated by a didactic propensity, to insure that his audience appreciated Hera's equal concern both for the Greeks' commander-in-chief and for their best fighting man. Similarly in *Iliad* 1, lines 372–79 repeat two earlier passages, 13–16 and 22–25, telling how the priest Chryses came to the Greeks' camp to ransom his daughter, and how Agamemnon repulsed him at first. Achilles at 372ff tells his mother Thetis about the proceedings, and uses the exact language of two different sets of four lines. Parryites are compelled to argue that Homer repeats his earlier formulation because he is an illiterate improviser anxious to avoid metrical breakdown. Homer's motivation may have been didactic, to impress on his hearers the exact way in which the quarrel of Achilles with Agamemnon began.

On the Parry theory an "oral poet" does not think in advance just what he is going to say, and does not remember later exactly what he has said. How then can Parryites account for such a passage as *Odyssey* 17.427–41, where Odysseus recounts to the Wooers his arrival in Egypt in the same fifteen verses as he had used in 14.258–72, when telling the tale to Eumaios? Similarly, in *Od*.4.333–50 Menelaos speaks eighteen hexameters about the prospect of Odysseus' homecoming, and in *Od*.17.124–41 Telemakhos quotes Menelaos' statement word for word. On the Parryite principle the whole passage is a formula, and the primary reason for the existence of formulas is that they are metrical devices to facilitate extemporary "oral composition." A. Hoekstra pertinently asks:

> If Homer was always improvising, how could the 36 lines of Agamemnon's offer to Achilles (*Il*.9.122–57) be repeated in exactly the same form (264–99) (with only

a few insignificant variations, made necessary by the change of subject) after an interval of some 100 verses [*Homeric Modifications of Formulaic Prototypes* (1965) 19]?

Hoekstra, by the way, errs in thinking here that Odysseus' repetition of Agamemnon's offer of gifts has "only a few insignificant variations, made necessary by the change of subject." There is a highly significant variation of a different type at *Il*.9.276, as compared with the earlier verse at 134. Agamemnon had seized Briseis, a beautiful war-captive whom Achilles loved as a wife. Agamemnon, in offering to return her, says he will swear that he had never mounted her bed or had intercourse with her "as is the fashion of mankind, of men and women" (9.134). In repeating Agamemnon's offers to Achilles, Odysseus realizes this is a touchy topic, and alters Agamemnon's hexameter to run: "as is the fashion, my lord [*anax*], of men and women" (9.276). Considering that Odysseus had earlier addressed Achilles as *pepon* (252), "my dear fellow" (perhaps more literally "old fruit" in 1967 British English of a certain wide stratum), that "my lord" shows a tactful solicitude for correctness and deference, appropriate to Odysseus' wily character and to the dramatic juncture.

In the same scene, note that Odysseus reminds Achilles how his father Peleus had sent him to help Agamemnon (9.253), and Phoinix re-uses the same line (9.439). Parryites must call this line a formula, and believe that its reason for existence is to avoid metrical breakdown. Critics who understand creative literature may perceive a dramatic and didactic value in the precise repetition. Again, in the Embassy scene, Achilles, still in the same frame of mind about Agamemnon as when they quarreled in *Iliad* 1, re-uses a formula of his own, calling Agamemnon "clad in shamelessness" (9.372, cf. 1.149, with the case inflexion varied to suit); but he also varies the expression of another obsessive idea he has about Agamemnon. Instead of re-using the phrase κυνὸς ὄμματ᾽ ἔχων (1.225, "having the eyes of a dog"), he says something metrically equivalent with substantially the same sense, κύνεός περ ἐών (9.373, "doglike as he is"). Thus we see again how Homer could either re-use good phrases he had made up himself, his own "formulas," or create fresh expressions, just like any other conscious artist. It is a grotesque libel on a supreme man of letters to assert that Homer used repeated word groups to avoid metrical breakdown when uttering, without thinking in advance what he was going to utter.

Again, consider Hesiod, 23 percent of whose extant corpus is reckoned by Notopoulos to consist of repeated lines or phrases. Can anyone seriously contend that Hesiod improvised—that is to say extemporized without previous preparation—that elaborate genealogical system of the gods, or those moral and practical admonitions about plow-making, sowing, chiropody, and so forth? Albin Lesky, in his *A History of Greek Literature* (English translation [1966] 100), wisely observes: "Recent misconceptions make it necessary to say once more that the part played by formulae in Hesiod does not instantly make him an 'oral poet'." On Hesiod's style West remarks (*op. cit.* 75):

> Prolixity and repetitiousness are particularly noticeable in what may be called the hymnic parts of the *Theogony*, the hymn to the Muses which forms the proem, and the passage commending Hecate. Hesiod's enthusiasm for the Muses and for Hecate inspires him to speak of them at some length, but he has not a great variety of things to say about them.

A hymnic background may be assumed for many of Homer's formulas also, of the type "the bright-eyed goddess Athena," "the pale-forearmed goddess Hera," relating to deities; and for heroes who are likely to have been honored with hero cults, or simply mentioned with stock epithets in sagas, whether in prose or verse, for instance, μέγας Τελαμώνιος Αἴας, "big Ajax Telamon's son" (who had to be distinguished from the lesser Ajax, Oileus' son).

But in evaluating Homer's and Hesiod's uses of formulas one must bear in mind that most current speech is highly formulaic, consisting overwhelmingly of recurrent word groups, or clichés; and that prose, too, exhibits recurrent word groups. Naturalistic playwrights today, like Arnold Wesker, Harold Pinter, and Edward Albee, continually represent their characters as talking in conversational clichés. Of Albee a critic in *The Times Literary Supplement* (February 27, 1964, p.166) wrote:

[67]

The attack on America in *The American Dream* has a different kind of actuality, projected through the contemporary dialogue of logical clichés from everyday language. The trivial speech of casual intercourse is recreated as a terrible formula for ritual communication.

In *Newsweek* for March 9, 1964, I noticed President Lyndon B. Johnson described (p.17) as "resorting time and again to the rotund clichés of diplomacy," and about Governor Rockefeller of New York it was stated (p.20) that "his set speeches are humorless and full of bromides." As a synonym for *formula*, the term *bromide* is even more pejorative than *cliché*, which French term Murko uses quite non-pejoratively about the repeated word groups of Yugoslav singers. Now Governor Rockefeller is better able than most statesmen to hire expert *logographoi*, or script-writers; yet they turn out his set speeches "full of bromides." Presumably they mean to. They cannot use formulas for the purpose for which Parryites think formulas were invented, to avoid metrical breakdown in improvising verses: for Governor Rockefeller does not couch his well-measured discourses in meter. Probably their motive is, like Homer's and Hesiod's, stylistic: they think that formulas are an appropriate embellishment of the statesman's style, just as literate Gaelic court poets thought that formulas were an appropriate embellishment of poems for formal occasions. I am told, too, that in Arab lands one may buy tombstones with strings of clichés ready engraved upon them, extolling the deceased for generosity, courage, and all the virtues that a respectable Arab deceased ought to have had, with spaces left for adding the name and date.

Milman Parry himself, in 1928, thought that the formulas of epic poets existed to facilitate a poet's composition of verses with a noble tone, a grand style; that is to say, for two concurrent purposes: (1) to express proper ideas suitably and (2) to diminish the difficulties of making up hexameters. Thus it may be from his sense of what was proper style that Homer said so often "but when early-born rose-fingered Dawn appeared," or rang the changes on two paroemiac clichés for King Nestor, "the Gerenian chevalier Nestor" and "the clear-voiced orator of the Pylians." One is reminded of the ambience of royal households and legislatures, in which people use such formulas as "Her Royal Highness," "His

[68]

Grace the Archbishop," "the right honourable and gallant gentleman, the Member for Great Snoring." The hexametric poems of Homer and Hesiod sprang from a courtly and formal ambience. Dr. West, indeed, believes that the *Theogony* may have been Hesiod's competition piece for the funeral games of Amphidamas at Chalkis, where he won an eared tripod (*op. cit.*, 43). To be sure, ceremonial clichés used by Homer or Hesiod in hexameters would have to scan in hexameters, and sometimes one finds them pressurized into doing so, for instance by lengthening the initial short alpha of the epithet ἀθάνατος ("immortal"). But mere scannability, mere metrical utility, was not the reason for their existence, as Parryites opine, or for their incorporation in the poems.

The Parryite C.H. Whitman, in *Homer and the Heroic Tradition* (1958) 14, admits that "all speech is to an extent formulaic." Parry remarks (*Harvard Studies* . . . [1930] 115) about two post-Homeric poets who were contemporaries and literate, Apollonius and Theocritus:

> If we find almost no Homeric formulas in Apollonius, for example, it does not at all mean that they would not have helped his verse-making, but that he wanted very much to avoid them. If Theocritus, on the other hand, used twelve formulas in his little epic *The Infant Heracles*, it means that he was seeking, in a rather amusing way, for the epic note.

In other words, it is a question of the individual poet's taste. For all we know, Homer and Hesiod may have been earlier poets with the taste of Theocritus in the *Herakliskos*, literate poets using formulas for a special archaizing effect. This is certainly true of Quintus Smyrnaeus in his *Posthomerica*, from about the fourth century A.D., who, as Hoekstra notes (*op. cit.*, 17), in regard to formulaic diction, probably imitated Homer more closely than Homer had followed his own predecessors.

Parry is, of course, correct in emphasizing that Apollonius of Rhodes very much wanted to avoid Homeric formulas; and so did Callimachus. In general the major poets from the fifth to the third centuries B.C. were keen to eschew the more natural ways of expressing ideas. They were keen to coin phrases, and even coin words of their own, and did not at all worry whether a large public could immediately appreciate their concoctions. Callimachus indeed remarked, "I feel a disgust for everything to do with the general public" (σικχαίνω πάντα τὰ δημόσια). This sophisticated avoidance of self-repetition and quest for novelty of utterance is carried to its extreme in Lycophron, so beloved of the Byzantine eggheads, the Hellenistic equivalent in this respect of "Euphues" Lyly or of James Joyce. That Hellenistic fashion was not followed by Quintus Smyrnaeus, who was quite happy to imitate Homer, and even, as Hoekstra notes (p.17, n.2), to work out in a formulaic manner certain expressions which are found in Homer sporadically. Worth considering also is the situation with Nonnos, about 450 A.D. His self-repetition has never been quantified, but there is a great deal of it in the 48 books of the *Dionysiaca*. I have the impression that Nonnos re-used lines and word groups somewhat reluctantly, and usually at intervals of a good many hundreds, or thousands, of lines, so that we should notice the repetition less; and I suspect he was more or less compelled to the repetitions because of the scale of his work, 21,287 hexameters, and the rigorous rules he set himself, far more strict than those of Homer, or even those of Callimachus (see R. Keydell's preface to his edition [1959] I.35ff). Nonnos relaxed these rules somewhat in his hexametric *Metaphrasis* of the Gospel of St. John, where the obligation to keep reasonably close to the sense of the original text was a further restriction. Because Homer's two extant epics extend to a quarter more than Nonnos' epic, namely some 27,803 hexameters, it is not astonishing that Notopoulos could reckon 33 percent of Homer to consist of repeated lines or verses. Once Homer had a good formulation of an idea, in a metrical form accommodated to hexameters, what artistic motive had he for *not* repeating it? He lived in the Geometric age, when artistic motives commonly were repeated, by potters for instance. What would Homer gain artistically by using fifty phrases for Achilles or Odysseus instead of using fifty times the phrases he had selected as most appropriate to emphasize? To reject self-repetition and the re-use of phrases devised by himself would be for Homer as futile as the exercise of Nestor of Laranda in Lycia, who, somewhere around the fourth century A.D., concocted an *Iliad Omitting Letters* (Λειπογράμματος), in which one book omitted alpha, the next omitted beta, and so forth.

Homer is, by common consent, the greatest of all composers of epic, in any language at any time; and one must presume that he understood the art of making epics thoroughly well. If Homer thought fit to repeat lines and phrases to the extent of a third of his now extant corpus, what critic is qualified to say that Homer was wrong?

There are, to be sure, some modern savants who imagine that they can catch Homer out in misuse of formulas. Thus F.M. Combellack writes on "Formulary Illogicalities in Homer," *TAPA* 96 (1965) 41–56, and remarks: "It has become a commonplace of contemporary Homeric criticism that the formulary style and the oral method of composition occasionally produce results which, to us at least, seem illogical and even absurd." For instance, it is thought by some "almost insulting that Penelope . . . is said to have a fat hand," at *Odyssey* 21.6. The version "a fat hand" is a tendentious mistranslation of the phrase χειρὶ παχείηι, which is used also for Athena, Hera, Poseidon, Hector, Menelaos, and other heroes. It means "stout hand, strong hand, massive hand." Such a hand is appropriate to deities and heroic persons, and eminently appropriate in general to the strong-minded Penelope, especially after all that weaving and unweaving she had been doing for so long. More precisely, in the context of *Odyssey* 21 Penelope uses her massive hand to take an instrument called a κληΐς, described as well-bent, handsome, and of bronze, with an ivory handle; she used it to open the massive doors of the palace treasury (47–50), doors so massive that, when being opened, they made a noise like a bull's bellowing. It is not clear just what the fastenings of the doors were, but the use of the κληΐς evidently needed substantial strength as well as dexterity and sureness of aim. Apart from that, Penelope is visualized as δῖα γυναικῶν (1.332), a noble specimen of womanhood; and Homer's ideal of female beauty included supernormal height and massiveness, as we know from *Odyssey* 18.195, where Athena made Penelope "taller and more massive" (πάσσονα, which it would be tendentious to translate as "fatter"). In calling Penelope's hand "massive" Homer knew what he meant, and so did his audiences. It would take scores of pages to disprove all the modern accusations against Homer that he misunderstood the Greek language; but it can be done, granted an adequate knowledge of Greek and common sense.

Supposing those are right who find "almost insulting" the Homeric statement that Penelope had "a fat hand," one wonders how such an "insulting" phrase should have survived the process of dictation assumed by some Parryites. Granted that the putatively illiterate and improvising Homer blurted out the "insulting" words χειρὶ παχείηι, and granted that his literate son or grandson or some non-Homerid scribe duly wrote it down, surely the scribe or some contemporary reader or hearer would have protested, and Homer would have had the opportunity to order a correction in the dictated text. In fact, the phrase came down in the tradition because Homer and the Greeks through the ages felt that a "massive hand" was appropriate to a great lady of the heroic age.

What "illogicalities" there are in Homer do not derive from his alleged misunderstanding of formulas, but are the sort of trivial inconsistencies that can be demonstrated in lengthy modern works that are known to have been written. For example, in *Il*.5.576 Pylaimenes, king of the Paphlagonians, is killed, but in *Il*.13.643f Harpalion, son of Pylaimenes, is killed, and his father accompanies his corpse, shedding tears (658). Dante is just as "illogical" when in *Purgatorio* 22.113 he puts Manto in Purgatory, though in *Inferno* 20.55 he had put her in Hell. Pindar, too, whom no one has yet accused of being a committee of rhapsodes or Peisistratid editors, is capable of grave "illogicalities." Let us search the writings attributed to Pindar for answers to these questions: (A) Where did the dithyramb originate? (1) Proto-Pindar says Corinth, *Ol*.13.13; (2) Deutero-Pindar says Naxos, fr.104 Bowra; (3) Trito-Pindar says Thebes, fr.67 Bowra. (B) Where is Neoptolemos? (1) In Epeiros, *Nem*.4.51; (2) at Delphi, *Nem*.7.46. (C) How did Neoptolemos die? (1) Apollo slew him for killing Priam, *Paean* 6.111; (2) a man slew him in a fracas about meat, *Nem*.7.42. (D) Where is the deceased Achilles? (1) On an island in the Black Sea, *Nem*.4.49; (2) in the Islands of the Blest, far in the West, *Ol*.2.79. One wonders how many co-authors, interpolating rhapsodes, or editorial diasceuasts must be postulated, on the principles of post-Wolfian Homerological theorizing, to account for the body of texts transmitted under the name of Pindar.

Even if Homer could be shown to have committed much graver inconsistencies, they would not suffice to prove him either an illiterate improviser or a syndicate of ghost writers.

Tolstoy's structural inconsistencies in *War and Peace* do not prove Tolstoy an improviser or a syndicate, but are explicable in terms of author's self-revisions extending over many years and many drafts, about which an excellent account in English is given by my colleague Professor R.F. Christian, *Tolstoy's "War and Peace": A Study* (1962). More closely relevant to the Parryite theory is Tolstoy's self-repetition. Christian remarks (p.148):

> A novelist who writes at such length as Tolstoy cannot afford to say a thing once only. Facts are repeated two, three or four times even. Their repetition aids the memory. It facilitates reading.

Christian comments also on Tolstoy's "constant reiteration of some external detail designed to characterize an individual," such as Napoleon's small white hands, Hélène's bare white shoulders, Princess Marya's radiant eyes. Tolstoy has his share of obtrusive verbal idiosyncrasies, frequently recurring expressions constituting linguistic mannerisms, characteristic of one author and not another (p.149). Christian finds an

> insistent use of identical words to express identical content. . . . Tolstoy repeats the same words because he wants to repeat the same idea, which can only be repeated exactly by using again the form in which they originally occurred [150].

For instance, early in the novel, Tolstoy uses five times on end the Russian phrase to be rendered: "There arrived. . . ." His well-known translators, the Maudes, translate it five different ways. Christian stresses (p.154) that "repetition, of one type or another, is the most characteristic single feature of Tolstoy's style," and also (p.162) that "the hallmark of Tolstoy's style is lucidity."

Tolstoy's repeated word groups, or formulas, cannot be motivated by a desire to avoid metrical breakdown in improvisation, for Tolstoy was not writing in meter. Tolstoy simply lacked the *cacoethes variandi* which derives from the Isocratean tradition. The Finnish neighbors of Russia were likewise Tolstoyan or Homeric in their attitude to self-repetition. In *The Kalevala and Its Background* ([1954] 50, n.1) Björn Collinder remarks:

> The old poets did not shun to call a thing by the same name every time they had to mention it, whereas many modern newspaper reporters think they cannot mention Paris twice or thrice without calling it "the French capital" for the sake of variation. Xenophon says, in his *Anabasis*, an infinite number of times, "from there he went to B, *x* parasangs," and why should he not?

Sir Maurice Bowra, in *A Companion to Homer* (p.34), hits, to my mind, on the main reason for Homer's ornamental epithets when he says:

> Because they are so familiar, and do not trouble us, they emphasize the words to which they are attached, and help the clear flow of the narrative, which would be slower and less easy to absorb if the poet adorned his nouns with too many different epithets.

Aristotle observes (in Fyfe's Loeb version, 1460B *init.*): "Too brilliant diction frustrates its own object by diverting attention from the portrayal of character and thought." Homer, I believe, was primarily motivated by artistic considerations, applying skilfully a suitably chosen repertory of phrases proper to a long poem of high style dealing with deities and heroes.

At the same time I am not sure how far one should suppose Homer to have been *fully* conscious of the reasons for his repetitions. Did Homer ever ask himself just why and where and how often he should repeat a word group? Alexander Pope claimed that he himself "lisped in numbers, for the numbers came"; and Ovid said that he automatically spoke in meter: "Quicquid conabar dicere uersus erat." Bernard Shaw, on the other hand, frivolously remarked that he repeated himself "to add spice to his conversation." One must allow something for unconscious mental associations that bring up words together, even as *discrete formulas*, that is to say in the same sentence without being immediately juxtaposed. Consider, for example, some hexameters from Nonnos:

ὃς δὲ μέσας στεφανηδὸν ἐπ᾽ ἄντυγι χεῖρας ἑλίξας·   46.135

χεῖρας ἑὰς στεφανηδὸν ἐπ᾽ ἀλλήλῃσιν ἑλίξας   37.600

καὶ διδύμας στεφανηδὸν ἐπ᾽ ἰξύι χεῖρας ἑλίξας   48.130

στικτὸς ἱμάς, στεφανηδὸν ἐπ᾽ ἰξύι κύκλον ἑλίξας   41.104

κυκλώσας στεφανηδὸν ἐπ᾽ ἰξύι λευκάδα μίτρην   38.294

Here we have various word groups occurring by semi-automatic word-association, with no obvious metrical utility as safeguards against breakdown in unprepared extemporization. Their occurrence does not prove Nonnos to be an illiterate improviser, and similar phenomena in Homer and Hesiod are compatible with their being literate premeditators. Aristotle knew about improvisation (*Poetics* 1428B23), but he classed Homer among poets far evolved beyond primitive improvisation: on which see A.W. Gomme, *More Essays in Greek History and Literature* (1962) 9.

Comparativists have been interested in Serbo-Croatian material in relation to Homer for about two centuries now, since Herder and Goethe. Regarding the repetitions and fixed epithets Grimm remarked: "Alles so wie in Homer" (quoted by D.H. Low, *The Ballads of Marko Kraljević* [1922] xxxvi). In 1912, in that admirable synoptic study *The Heroic Age* (p.313), H. Munro Chadwick concluded:

> It is clear enough that Servian heroic poetry bears little resemblance to the Homeric poems as we have them. But we may strongly suspect that at an earlier stage in the history of Homeric poetry the resemblance would be closer.

The Serbo-Croatian heroic songs, in fact, may correspond to the pre-Homeric and pre-Hesiodic verse and prose material from some of which Homer and Hesiod drew before premeditating and writing their works, much as Tolstoy used orally circulating anecdotes and family traditions as part of his material for *War and Peace*. We must all pay warm tribute to the work of Milman Parry and Albert B. Lord in collecting and investigating Serbo-Croatian data; but so far their main utility for Homerology is to demonstrate once more the fact that formulas are characteristic of individual poets rather than of the group-traditions of a district, a fact borne out by studies of Middle English romances and French *chansons de geste*. Appreciating this fact, George E. Dimock, Jr., wrote (ARION 2 [1963] 54) concerning the *Iliad* and the *Odyssey*:

> That the same poet made both poems is strongly suggested, if not proved, by the remarkably similar way in which stock passages are handled in each, and by the fact that each uses the same formulas in the same situations almost without exception.

Incidentally, in view of the fact that the Greeks retained traditions of epics ascribed to such authors as Eumelos, Arktinos, and Stasinos, whom they dated in the eighth century B.C., it would be odd that they should have had no vestige of a tradition of a different name other than Homer for the author of the *Odyssey*, if in fact that epic was not by the same author as the *Iliad*.

If we are to take account of the Classical Greeks' traditions about Homer, what are we to make of the tradition that he was blind? The *Certamen Homeri et Hesiodi*, which cannot be later than the third century B.C. papyrus in which it appears in part, and may be substantially much older, says that Homer was not blind from birth, but in his *Hymn to Apollo* (172) he calls himself a blind man from rocky Chios. This hymn runs to 546 lines. The *Certamen* (OCT,237) tells how he recited this hymn on the altar of horns during the Ionian πανήγυρις at Delos, and the Delians inscribed the verses on a whitened board and put it in the temple of Artemis. From his similes one may be sure that Homer saw a lot before he went blind. If his blindness was total, and not merely a partial purblindness, presumably he would, at that stage, be unable to write himself, and would dictate, like the ageing Milton. Several years before he began *Paradise Lost* as an epic, Milton had designed a tragedy on the subject. He kept in mind the opening ten verses of his abortive tragedy and put them into the fourth book of the epic. John Aubrey records:

> His Invention was much more free and easie in the Aequinoxes than at the Solstices .... All the time of his writing his *Paradise lost*, his veine began at the Au-

tumnall Aequinoctiall and ceased at the Vernall or there-
abouts (I believe about May) and this was 4 or 5 yeares
of his doeing it.

Jonathan Richardson states that, as the ageing Milton was
"not in Circumstances to maintain an Amanuensis," he had
to be "perpetually asking One Friend or Another who
Visited him to Write a Quantity of Verses he had ready in his
mind, or what should Then occur." Much of his premeditation was done at night, and in the morning the blind poet
would become impatient, comparing himself to a cow waiting to be milked.

One knows, too, of premeditation in the dark by medieval
Irish poets and taletellers (R. Flower, *The Irish Tradition*
Oxford [1947] 96). They were trained over seven winter
sessions, from November to March. In the original composition of poems with elaborate assonantal schemes, each undergraduate aspirant was incarcerated in a dark cubicle till he
had perfected his poem, after which he had to write it down.
The obligation to improvise impromptu pieces was confined,
as a rule, to quatrains. The highest grade of poet, *ollamh*,
was required to know 250 main tales, and 100 subsidiary
tales, which were in a prose approximating to "free verse," in
poetic diction, heightened at points of major excitement into
rhythmic runs, embellished with alliteration. In the aristo-
cratic society of twelfth-century Ireland there were hereditary professional families of learned poets. In Greece we
know of hereditary heralds, seers, physicians, and so forth;
and, besides the Homeridai, we may recall examples of
poetry running in families, as those of Simonides, Aeschylus,
Sophocles, Euripides, and Aristophanes. Homer's sons are
likely to have been at least as apt at taking dictation as Milton's daughters, when their father had gone blind; and they
would be as likely to produce Homer's epics well as Wagner's
grandsons, the Wagneridai, produced Wagner's operas. One
cannot, to be sure, guarantee that they never made an un-
authorized insertion or alteration or deletion in the original
text, as authorized by its "onlie begetter," just as Countess
Tolstoy took a hand in revising *War and Peace*. But, by and
large, we can have fair confidence in believing that the *Iliad*
and the *Odyssey* as we have them are at least 98 percent the
work of a single great literary creator, who was no less of a

conscious artist than Hesiod or Milton or Tolstoy, and ought to be judged by similar standards.

Granted that, in making a hexametric poem, it is easier to repeat a well-made line or phrase than to think up a new substitute every time one wishes to say the same thing, one may still ask two overriding questions. First, do Homer's ornamental stereotyped phrases impair the narrative structure and dramatic impact of his epics and hymns? No. Second, do they make his poems more memorable? Yes. Accordingly it is grossly impertinent to suggest that the primary function of his repeated word groups was to avoid metrical breakdown in improvising. Homer knew what he was doing, and did it about 98 percent perfectly.

Plato's hostility to art (Vol. III, no. 1)

Thomas Gould

WHEN READERS OF PLATO COME TO one of the many passages where he questions the respectability of stories, verse, song, drama, painting or dance, they are usually upset. And well they should be; for Plato's conclusions are absurd —that Homer, for instance, and all of the great Attic tragedians would have to be banned if society were to have a chance at universal happiness. Which of us does not gladly side with Aristotle, who reversed his teacher's decision in this matter and tried to show that the pleasure that we get from poetry and drama is not only harmless, but beneficial? The exhilaration cleanses us, Aristotle argued, and gives us insight more philosophical than the examination of actual facts and events.

Plato's mistakes have a way of haunting us, however. When he criticizes men for preferring imaginative literature to reasoned discourse, we recoil with distaste. The fact is, however, that we instantly dissent from almost all of Plato's most momentous, most original decisions. Indeed, if we were to dismiss as trivial and not worth further thought the discussions in the Dialogues that lead eventually to incorrect conclusions or foolish recommendations, we should have very little left. Consider Plato's most characteristic suggestions. There is the theory of the Form-patterns which exist, Plato thought, independent of sensed phenomena; there are the several demonstrations of the ability of the human psyche to survive separation from the body; the idea that beauty is literally the creator of reality; the recommendation that teachers fall in love with students in order to attain the vision of reality that alone can make them masters of life; the belief that every instance of intellectual understanding is the recovery of ecstatic knowledge once possessed before birth. There is Plato's plan to obliterate the family, his theory of soul as self-generating motion, his vision of intelligent stars, a spinning world soul, post-mortem reward and punishment, the transmigration and reincarnation of human souls in animals and heavenly bodies, and so on and so on. The fact that Plato has triumphed, that he is still the most widely read philosopher in the world today, can surely *not* be traced to the regularity with which he has come out on the right side in his thinking! We reject almost all of his novel conclusions, as most of his immediate students did also. If we admire him it is only because we are nevertheless never quite the same after having gone through the process of demonstrating to ourselves that he must be wrong.

Plato's decision that the older poets would have to be banned

from a well run city, on the other hand, has not been treated as
just another instance of this penchant of his for profound thought
leading relentlessly to perverse conclusions. It has almost always
been treated as a special case. There are several reasons for this.
First, we are, I think, repelled by Plato's hostility to art, more
than we are by his other errors. We even feel a little threatened
by it, somehow. Why, we ask, should anyone want to deprive us
of all our wonderful works of the imagination or submit future
artists to rigid control by a conscious, calculating political rationalism? A civilization that tolerated only those writers, printers and
composers who could pass a test for scientific or political useful-
ness would surely be a nightmare. Second, we are moved by the
memory of countless attempts to censor art down through the
centuries, the best of which have been useless, the worst savagely
destructive. Plato knew of only one society in which the artists
tended to limit themselves to the embodiment of their civilization's ideals and did not often allow their personal imaginings to
carry them where they would; that was Egypt, which he professed
to admire for its rigidity in this respect. (*Laws* II 656, ff. and
VII 799) But surely, we say, the example of Egypt should have
been enough to alert anyone, especially a citizen of Athens in
Plato's time, to the superiority of a society where the artists are
free and genuinely individual, not impersonal instruments of a
state-sponsored morality. And third, it is certainly very difficult
to read Plato's own brilliant, dramatic dialogues and his haunting
myths without being struck by the thought that he is essentially
an ally of the lovers of art and imagination. He gives a thousand
proofs of his sensitivity to the delights of poetry, and he himself
perfected new literary forms to enchant his readers and draw
them toward his visionary's grasp of life and reality. A man who
is moved by literature cannot but be moved by the Dialogues and
lovers of Plato will always also be lovers of literature.

And so, philosophers, scholars, and historians, from the sixteenth century to the present, have regularly tended to ask, not
could Plato's wrongheaded advice have grown, as so often, from
a disturbing germ of truth, but could we not explain Plato's attacks against the arts as not really meant seriously, or at least not
worth our serious attention today. Plato's other ideas have met
with a similar fate from time to time, of course. There is, for instance, quite a respectable group of philosophers today who cannot bring themselves to believe that Plato ever seriously entertained the theory of separate Form-patterns. It is always a temptation, I suppose, whenever we find a great man arguing something contrary to our own feelings, to look for some way to believe that he did not really say what he appears to say. But none
of Plato's doctrines has suffered more from this kind of treatment
than his recommendations concerning the control of artists. Aristotle's *defense* of poetry has always appealed to lovers of the

Dialogues as far more Platonic than Plato's own jibes and sneers. It is significant, perhaps, that interest in Aristotle's defense of poetry was quickened, during the Renaissance, at exactly the same moment that interest began to shift from Aristotle back to Plato. In fact, while Aristotle's system was taken dead earnestly by first rate minds all over the world, his treatise on poetry was ignored; but when his influence declined and the important philosophers were no longer Aristotelians, then and then only did men discover the *Poetics* and begin to apply its ideas to current literature. The year 1536 saw both Ramus' famous doctorate demonstrating the falseness of all of Aristotle's major philosophical positions and also the work of Trincavelli, Pazzi, Daniello and others, which suddenly focused attention on the *Poetics* and made it Aristotle's best loved essay.[1]

The ways in which men have attempted to reduce the harshness of Plato's questioning of art and literature vary from the crude to the subtle and intelligent. First there are those who dismiss as simply false the very possibility that Plato could have been serious. He was ironical, they say, teasing, mischievously exaggerating, or throwing out a wild challenge in hopes of stimulating just such a defense as Aristotle produced. This idea is supported by two arguments, one outrageous and one disturbing. The outrageous argument goes as follows. The only thing one needs in order to see that Plato was having fun here is a sense of humor; anyone who takes the attack against Homer and the tragedians as a serious thrust is showing *ipso facto* his lamentable want of such a sense of humor.[2]

The more challenging argument is the one that points to a passage in the Tenth Book of the *Republic* where Socrates says:

Let it be declared that if the poetic, mimetic art, the aim of which is pleasure, could defend its right to exist in a well-governed state, we should be delighted to admit it, for we are certainly conscious of its charm . . . We should even permit non-poets who are lovers of poetry to give us a defense in prose, showing that, in addition to being pleasant, it is also beneficial to the state and to the life of man; and we shall listen well-disposed toward them, for we can hardly help but be the gainers if poetry should turn out to be not only pleasant but beneficial as well. (607 c-e)

So lovers of Plato must be correct, it is concluded, when they prefer Aristotle's defense of the poets to Plato's attacks against them. Is this not precisely what Plato would have wanted us to feel?[3]

Two additional observations make this suggestion an attractive one. First is the fact that there are indeed several clear instances where Aristole does pick up a challenge in one of the Dialogues and works it out in a perfectly Platonic way—as in the first book of the *Rhetoric*, for instance, where he responds to the call of the *Phaedrus*, or in the *Eudemian Ethics* where he makes explicit the correct Platonic answer to the puzzle of the *Lysis* as to whether love is the attraction of likes or of unlikes.[4] And then, secondly, there is the notorious fact that every single idea and every single major term in the *Poetics* can be traced to one or another of the passages where Plato discusses art and poetry: imitation, for instance, organic unity, pleasure, benefit, seriousness, universality, pity and fear, even catharsis, perhaps. Might we not relax, therefore, and take Aristotle's *Poetics* to be, not a rebuttal, but a loyal working out of his teacher's real views?

Next, there are those who have believed that Plato was not attacking art in general but only certain art. These, too, have ranged from the crude to the challenging. According to the crude form of this argument, Plato was interested only in combating decadent trends in the art and literature in his own generation.[5] This suggestion has been largely discredited now and is seldom heard anymore. Subtler and more serious versions are still current, however, based mostly on the undeniable evidence that Plato had in mind some substitute which, in a well run state, would take the place of Homer and his followers. A number of passages have been scrutinized again and again in this regard. There is the passage in Book Three of the *Republic* implying that only offensive parts would be cut out of the old poems (392); a phrase in Book Ten which seems to suggest that not all poetry is mimetic and therefore to be banned[6]; also the specific statement in that same book, repeated in the *Laws*, that hymns to the gods and praises of good men would have an honored place in the perfect state (*Republic* 607a, *Laws* VII 801e). More important than any of these is the implication, in the Allegory of the Cave and elsewhere, that even the philosopher-rulers, when they are children, can be taught only by stories and songs. Plato clearly believed that these tales could be made to be true and beautiful and should be made so, in order that when the guardians reach the age of reason they will be able to salute reality as an old friend (*Republic* III 402a). People have also pointed to the role that beauty and ecstasy play in the *Symposium* and *Phaedrus*, and to Plato's habit of equating the Good and the Beautiful, as well as his comparisons, in the *Republic*, *Timaeus*, and *Laws*, between the art of the law giver, or even that of the Demiurge himself, and the art of the painter or sculptor[7]: all of which seems to imply that there is indeed a good kind of art as well as a dangerous kind. There is one famous passage in the *Laws* where Plato states outright that the dialogue he is writing is an example of the right kind of art (VII 811c). And the criticism of imaginative literature in the last book of the *Republic* is followed almost immediately by one of Plato's great, haunting myths. This suggests that the myth too, as well as the dialogue, must be an example of reformed literature, based on truth such as only a philosopher can see.[8]

Arguments like these which emphasize the fact that Plato was reforming art, not banishing it altogether, are attractive because they offer an explanation for the apparent inconsistency between his own devotion to art and the caustic tone that he takes toward other artists. It was his high hopes for art, it is argued, not his contempt for it, that led to his sharp criticisms; and it was his unusual sensitivity, his awareness of the power that Homer could have over him, not any imperviousness, that led him to suppose that Homer was dangerous. This line of argument easily degenerates, however, into yet another way of getting around the disturbing quality of Plato's complaints. This is the biographical approach, one of the most popular of all the ways to stop thinking about what Plato says. Plato was neurotic on the matter, it is argued. He was strongly drawn to poetry, but he was tortured also by an obsessive rationalism. This is a personal problem, therefore, and one that need not interest us seriously. There is no profound thought underlying Plato's attacks; he just tried one argument after another, exactly as he did, for instance, when he attempted to rationalize his private and misguided conviction about the immortality of the soul.[9]

It is often pointed out that in the *Republic*, Plato was in any case constructing, not a real or possible state, merely an ideal one. He would have reared in horror, it is suggested, if someone were to recommend that we actually ban Homer for an existing community.[10] It is noted with satisfaction that Plato does not specify clearly what the philosopher-rulers themselves, after they have been indoctrinated with the antidote of philosophy, would read in *their* spare time—as though it were very likely that Plato envisioned a heightened admiration for Homer to be a regular result of his austere program in mathematics and dialectic. Much has been made of the fact, too, that as he grew older, Plato seemed to make more and more concessions to the poetic tradition. In the *Phaedrus*, for instance, the image maker is closer to reality than the manufacturer of artefacts, not the other way around as in the *Republic* (*Phaedrus* 248). And in the *Laws*, Plato's last dialogue, he softens his hostility, even to the point of admitting some mimetic drama—*if* it is carefully censored.[11] In the *Republic*, Plato had condemned poetry as mere play, but in the *Laws* he admits that play has a role both in the education of the young and in the full life of adults.

Akin to the biographical approach, but rather more fruitful, have been the various attempts to put Plato's hostility to poetry into its broadest historical setting. The scholars who have worked at this task have taught us a great deal. There is, for instance, Cornford's attempt to show how Socrates and Plato, like the Sophists before them, inevitably came into conflict with the remnants of an older way of thinking, because they were struggling to displace the bards, sages, and shamans of old who were their true ancestors.[12] And there is Jaeger's monumental study of the older *paideia* of Greece, an education based for centuries, just as Plato says, on the study of Homer and the other poets: Jaeger showed, among other things, that Plato's complaints about the poets' treatment of the gods, was actually in the best manner of an ancient tradition, a tradition which included, not only Heraclitus and Xenophanes, but even Aeschylus and the poet of the *Odyssey*.[13] And most recently Eric Havelock has followed the trail of evidence which shows that oral, memorized verse undoubtedly played a much more important role in the Greek world that it does in our own.[14] Havelock concludes that there was a certain justice in Plato's apparently wild complaint that the poets had a deadly grip on all thought and imagination.

Now there is truth in almost every one of these many ways of explaining Plato's recommendations for the censorship of the arts. The only argument that is just plain false, I think, is the suggestion that Plato really wanted us to draw Aristotle's conclusion, that he never really meant to imply that the quarrel between poetry and philosophy was serious. The differences between the recommendations of the two philosophers on the subject of Homer and the tragedians is surely every bit as dramatic and decisive as their differences, for instance, concerning the substantiality of the visible world, or the origin of knowledge, or the nature of the psyche. But as for the rest of what has been written about Plato's criticism of art, most of it is, as I say, quite valuable. Plato did indeed regret having to condemn the older poets as subversive; he most certainly did harbor hopes of replacing the traditional poetry with something else, something which would play a very important role in his new scheme; he does modify the harshness of his plans a bit when he shifts from an ideal to a more practical and less ambitious dream; and there are conditions, peculiar to Plato's time and absent from our own world, which go some way in explaining the violence of Plato's advice. There is one thing wrong with all of these lines of approach, however; and that is that every last one of them, if taken as the real answer to the puzzle, is really just a way *to stop thinking about what Plato says*. Every one of them tends to put a premature end to any serious consideration of the possibility that Plato's arguments, taken literally, might, to a certain point at least, be *true*—for us as well as for the Greeks.

Aristotle's *conclusions* are right and Plato's wrong. So much is certain. The question is, what do we do with that fact. Is it quite fair just to elucidate and expand upon Aristotle's rightness, and to search for historical or psychological explanations for Plato's error? Surely, in other cases where we have decided that Aristotle was right and Plato wrong, that decision has rarely, if ever, put an end to debate. As I have said, the bigger, the more important, the more original the pronouncement, the more likely it is that Plato was dead wrong. Aristotle, when he softens or reverses his teacher's more shocking conclusions, has the better of it in the judgment of the vast majority of readers, at least in our own generation. (The essence of a species, for instance, does *not* exist apart from instances of individual specimens unless the mind abstracts it; knowledge is built up somehow from sense perception, it is *not* the recovery of a prenatal vision of perfect types; an attempt to obliterate the family would *weaken*, not strengthen, men's loyalties to one another; and so on.) But the important thing to remember is that Aristotle has rarely, if ever, settled a matter for good. In fact, what has usually happened is this: first, Plato has made a suggestion which is moving, hard to forget, based apparently on an heroic attempt to apply intelligence everywhere, but a suggestion which is nevertheless somehow bizarre and unconvincing; next Aristotle has made a move in what seems clearly to be the right direction, he has offered a sensible and necessary correction; but then, in the end, Plato's perversity, rather than Aristotle's sensibleness, has turned out to be the thing that has opened up new horizons for us and prevented us from a complacent acceptance of vulgar myths.

It ought to have been obvious long ago that it would be foolish to examine any individual difference between Plato and Aristotle, as this one on the question of the value of poetry and drama, without relating it to the larger differences between their philosophies as wholes. It is only very recently, however, that we have begun to understand the relation between these two great systems. For centuries it was customary to say that everyone was either a Platonist or an Aristotelian according to the temperament with which he was born. (If one was a visionary, he responded to Plato; if he banked on common sense and the reality of the visible objects around him, he instinctively believed Aristotle.) But then, forty years ago, Werner Jaeger revived the feeling of the ancient Neoplatonists that Aristotle, in many of his writings at least, was still so close to Plato that his treatises could be used to fill out and make explicit the system implied in Plato's Dialogues. "Surely there can be only one positive standard for Aristotle's personal achievements," said Jaeger, "and that is not how he criticizes Plato, but how he himself Platonizes—since that is what philosophizing *means* to him."[15] After all, Aristotle came to Athens to study with Plato when he was only seventeen years old. He then lived in the Academy for many years, until Plato's death, by which time Aristotle was already thirty-seven or thirty-eight. Jaeger argued that it was surely reasonable to assume that as a youth, Aristotle was an orthodox Platonist, and that he only gradually developed his own more characteristic system as he found difficulties in Platonism and tried to correct them. There is no general agreement as to the exact nature of this development, but at least most people would now assume that Aristotle ought not to be described as merely an anti-Platonist; it is fairly clear that he must have been a dedicated Platonist trying to make his master's system perfect wherever he found a defect. Aristotle's system was not set up *de novo* as a rival to Plato's, then, but was worked out slowly in a series of revisions from within—a profound but essentially loyal attempt to "correct" many of Plato's individual arguments in order to make his greater system perfect.

But we all know also how momentous some of these "corrections" by Aristotle have been. In fact, if we took all of the philosophical problems that were first defined by Aristotle's attempts to shore up his teacher's system, we would find that we had most of the puzzles that have engaged philosophers down through the centuries, and most of those that still engage them today. The history of philosophy has been, not so much the adding of footnotes to Plato, as Whitehead once suggested, as a series of attempts, beginning always with Aristotle, to avoid Plato's fiendishly wrong-headed conclusions. Just as a paradoxical statement by Socrates will outrage his interlocutors and so set in motion a Platonic Dialogue, a Platonic Dialogue will point to a solution that outrages its readers and so will set in motion the dialogue that is the history of Western philosophy.

We usually have two tasks, therefore: to understand what drove Plato to his unnerving idea, and then to find the basic changes that Aristotle introduced into Plato's larger vision enabling him, *or forcing him*, to come to a different conclusion. Not only can Aristotle never be understood without a careful study of Plato, but even in our attempts to understand Plato, we can never afford to neglect the study of Aristotle's treatment of his teacher's conclusion. And we should expect the reward to be great. Such an investigation is rarely of interest only to historians. It regularly brings us close to the heart of some extraordinarily interesting and ultimately unsolvable problem. Where Aristotle decided to alter Platonism, it was never out of spite or for trivial reasons of taste or temperament.

This last point is particularly important in the study of Plato and Aristotle on poetry. Many scholars, especially those who have been impressed by the brilliance of Aristotle's *Poetics*, have talked as though Aristotle decided to reverse Plato's conclusions about the harmfulness of poetry and drama simply because he liked poetry more than Plato did. This idea cannot survive a reading of Aristotle's complete works,—the logic, the physics, the biology, and the rest. Aristotle was fairly well read in the poets, he had flashes of taste and insight, and he is justly praised for a few isolated remarks, like the celebrated one about the ability to invent metaphors (*Poetics* 1459a5); but compared to Plato, he was insensitive about literature. Occasionally a line from one of the poets, usually a mediocre one, will pop into Aristotle's head as an appropriate and superior way to say something he is trying to express; usually, however, his infrequent and notoriously inaccurate quotations are made for the driest academic reasons.[16] By contrast, to find the influence of the poets on Plato's language would require a minute examination of the whole of his works. The Dialogues are extraordinarily rich with poetic words and reminiscences. Plato sometimes even preserves gorgeous fragments for us in the very act of belittling the poetic tradition. Over and over again a beautiful line will just well up in him and he will let himself be captured by it. In the Allegory of the Cave, for instance, in trying to describe the revulsion that the philosopher will feel when he must descend again into the murky world of everyday politics, he quotes the words of the embittered ghost of Achilles, that he would rather be the slave of a landless man and be alive than be the king of all the souls in Hades (*Odyssey* XI 489; *Republic* VII 516d). This very passage was cited a few books back in the *Republic* as an example of the sort of thing that a rational society could not possibly allow (III 386c).

This fact, that Plato, the lover of poetry, condemned the greatest poets of Greece, whereas the relatively uninterested Aristotle defended them as rational and health-giving, should be treated, I would suggest, not as two problems, why Plato went wrong and how Aristotle excelled himself, but as one problem: what was the change that Aristotle made in Platonism that allowed him to avoid the necessity to condemn the poets and led him to defend them as rational and as allies of the philosophers? Here then is what we must do: first, sum up Plato's various criticisms of the arts, then determine the extent to which Aristotle accepted the Platonic arguments, next, pin-point the exact nature of Aristotle's differences from Plato on the subject, and then, finally, trace these differences, if we can, to some even more basic difference in the systems of the two philosophers. Everything that we know about the relation between Plato and Aristotle demands that we at least try this approach. And if we are lucky, we should be rewarded by the discovery that Plato's surprising departure from common sense and from his own inclinations stemmed, not from a provincial or trivial consideration, but from a truly interesting problem.

Let us list Plato's specific complaints against the poets. First, in the *Apology* (23c) and *Ion*, he points out that poets are inferior to philosophers because their apparent wisdom comes in the form of inspiration from without, not from true understanding. When they are asked about what they sing, therefore, they are helpless to explain or defend themselves. In the *Protagoras*, the first book of the *Republic*, and elsewhere, he demonstrates the foolishness of the Greek habit of constructing a philosophical argument on a quotation from some poet. In the *Gorgias* (502 b-d) and in the middle books of the *Republic*, he links poets with rhetoricians and includes them among the false demagogues who pander to the foolish desires of the multitude instead of trying to substitute new desires for old. In the second and third books of the *Republic,* he argues that men can never be strong and good so long as their earliest introduction to the ways of the world comes in the form of tales about vicious, quarreling gods or neurotic heroes, and descriptions of the dreadfulness of what awaits us after death. He also rails against the impersonation of trivial and evil types, on the grounds that such imitation forms habits and habits shape character. Music, too, he says, can have a deep and lasting effect on a man and must be carefully censored. Aimless versatility, the search for novelty for its own sake, and irresponsible titillation of the passions must all be avoided. Then in the tenth book of the *Republic,* he charges that poets and painters merely imitate the fleeting and unsubstantial world of external appearances, how men look and act and talk, and do not, like philosophers, dive straight to the heart of a matter and root out the reality, the universal patterns that alone can give us power over events. And in the process of such imitation, he says, the poets feed and water the lowest part of the psyche and demand of their audience that their rational element relax its control—always a profoundly dangerous thing to accustom a man to. Some years later, in the *Phaedrus,* Plato returned to the manic, inspired character of the poet, and, though he admits that this can be a divine gift, he insists that the inspiration of the best part of the psyche does not result in poetry at all but in philosophy. In this dialogue, imitators are said to be one small step closer to reality than the manufacturers of artefacts; still later, however, in the *Sophist* (234), Plato returns to the even more insulting order of the *Republic.* In the *Laws,* his last dialogue, he covers once again the reasons for the necessity to censor the arts and the principles on which this should be done. This time his biggest concern is the molding of the right desires in young children. His discussions include the dance as well as the right rules for drinking parties, also the place of festivals and ceremonies all through life. He concludes that all of these activities are conducted for the pleasure that they bring, but points out that good men and bad men take pleasure in different kinds of art. Good art, the only kind to be allowed in a well-governed state, is the art that is enjoyed by the best men; it is the exhuber- ° ant delight in and exercise of dignity, self respect, responsibility and rationality. As in the *Republic,* the net result of Plato's program would still be to banish most of the great poets of Greece, from Homer on down.

Next, let us list the features of Plato's treatment of the arts that were entirely acceptable to Aristotle. First, he accepted, apparently without a qualm, Plato's odd-sounding assertion, made many times in many dialogues, that poetry is a species of the genus imitation. He even takes over intact Plato's occasional vacillation

°for 'exhuber-'] *read* 'exuber-'

between "imitation" in the sense of mimicry or impersonation and "imitation" in the sense of the making of a likeness.[17] Next, he agrees with Plato that the accomplished philosopher, not the inspired poet, is the real wise man among us (*Metaphysics* A ch. 1, etc.). He agrees also that the arts exist for the pleasure they bring. Good art, exactly as in Plato, is the art that delights good men, bad art the art that delights inferior men. And Aristotle goes along wholeheartedly with Plato's assertion that imitation is inevitable and the natural way in which small children begin to learn, also with his observation that the most usual and effective subject for imitation is the kind of human event that arouses strong emotions—especially the emotions of pity and fear. This arousal of pity and fear, however, just as in Plato, is assumed to be a form of pleasure; it is, Aristotle says, the very essence of the satisfaction that men seek when they become addicted to the theatre. Nor does Aristotle demur from Plato's insistence that such experiences have a significant effect on the character and emotional stability of the listener. He even goes along with Plato when he insists that the best works do not depend for their effect on such things as spectacle, or even verse, but draw their power above all from a profound *mythos* (a word always translated as "myth" in Plato but as "plot" in Aristotle). And, most surprising of all, Aristotle agrees with Plato that a Socratic dialogue in prose would be an example of true poetry at its best (*Poetics* ch. 1). But he shares Plato's special regard for Homer, too, and his assumption that Homer is the true father of Attic tragedy. Georg Finsler has even argued that Aristotle's famous remark about the cathartic effect of tragedy is taken over from a Platonic theory, traces of which can be found in the *Timaeus* and the *Laws*.[18]

This is an impressive area of agreement. It seems almost as though Aristotle never did think about poetry, only about Plato's theory of poetry. But, perhaps, that impression would be changed somewhat if we had Aristotle's other treatises—on comedy, on Homer, and on other poets. In any case, Aristotle did—we must not blur this fact—for all of his dependence on Platonic terms and theories, turn Plato's conclusions upside down.

First, notice how consistently Aristotle pulls the teeth from Plato's favorite terms when he takes them over and makes them into technical terms of his own. Imitation, for instance, seems like a splendid idea as Aristotle talks about it. It is no great disgrace, according to him, that poets must present lively make-believe mimickings of individual men and cannot, like philosophers, articulate the universal laws, draw the appropriate conclusions, demonstrate the necessary truth of their discoveries, and so on. Nor is there anything sinister in the fact that the philosophers have more to teach us than poets. The "ancient quarrel between poetry and philosophy" (*Republic* X 607 b5) did not appeal to Aristotle as either very profound or very dramatic. The poets had their place as well as the philosophers. Men needed the cleansing effect of the exhilaration that accompanies artificial stimulation of pity and fear. As for bad art, that was all that more limited men were capable of enjoying. Why deprive them of it (*Politics* VIII ch. 7)? And at their best, poets are even a little philosophic, in their minor way, because they do, after all, go through a process of selecting and typifying when they compose their imitations. As for Plato's philosophical *mythoi*, is this not just what the ancient legends are—the ones that have proved such effective vehicles for the better tragedians? The older poets do not have to be banned. Nobody will take those ancient, ready-made *mythoi* literally. What we have to do is make a careful analysis of Homer, Sophocles, and the rest of the great ones and see if we cannot teach the younger poets to avoid vulgar tastes and give us more works such as are enjoyed by good men like us—the philosophers.

Not that Aristotle's slim, cramped little essay is merely a piece of emasculated Platonism, of course. It bristles with his own usual jargon. Students of Aristotelian philosophy looking in the *Poetics* for signs that this treatise, too, like all the rest, is part of Aristotle's great, unified vision of reality, are quickly rewarded.[19] We could almost have reconstructed some of the things that Aristotle must say about poetry if the *Poetics* had not survived. We should have known, for instance, especially from the *Protrepticus, Physics I and II,* and *Metaphysics Z,* that the activity of realizing dramatic performances would have to have been shown to be sparked by a formal-final cause. That is, the essence, "what it is to be a tragedy," could not be assumed to be a pointless accident or a local and recent invention by individual men; it would have to be shown to be a Form which has survived forever, passed on from realization to realization somehow and a good that men must inevitably try to actualize. That, presumably, is why Aristotle accepted so gratefully Plato's idea that the *Iliad* and *Odyssey* were primitive attempts to realize tragedy, and his decision to connect this activity with the eternal and universal tendency to learn by imitating. From *Politics* VIII, we might even have been able to predict that he would find the final cause of tragedy, its *telos* or good, in the notion of catharsis, whether that notion ultimately came from Plato too or not (1341b38, ff.). On one level, the *Poetics* is far from a literate, enlightened, common-sense account of the nature of tragedy. It is as peculiar and as idiosyncratic as Plato's hostile analysis. Plato, the prototype of all deep lovers of poetry had felt compelled to banish Homer and the rest as reason's most dangerous rivals; and Aristotle, to whom poetry meant relatively little, was under the same kind of compulsion when he was forced to try to demonstrate the benefit to a man's moral excellence that can be derived only from drama (or at its best only from there), the inevitability, universality and eternality of the activity best realized in Attic tragedies, and the

[91]

essential agreement between poetry and rationality. In other words, *both* Plato *and* Aristotle were driven to their surprising ideas in loyalty to more basic principles.

This brings us to the heart of the problem. Is it possible to detect in Aristotle's more basic revisions of Platonism as a whole some momentous decision that entailed his specific departures from Plato's theories about poetry and drama? Can we find some all-important point where Aristotle refused to go along with Plato and so was not only freed from the necessity to banish the older poets but was forced to defend them as allies of reason?

We might sum up Aristotle's chief innovations in three points.[20] One: the Form-types, though known to the intelligence as unchanging universals, actually exist, Aristotle suggested, only insofar as they are informing matter at any given time, and they are permanent, therefore, only by virtue of a serial succession. This innovation allowed Aristotle to avoid two of Plato's most upsetting conclusions, that Forms are real whereas particulars are not, and that knowledge of Forms cannot be accounted for by our experience of particulars. Two: if the ideal Form-types are causes of perceptible events, as Plato suggested in the *Phaedo* that they were, then the underlying stuff of the perceptible world did not have a random energy of its own, as Plato had thought; it was motivated, Aristotle argued, only by a desire to realize the Forms, nothing else. This suggestion obviated the necessity for a Demiurge who struggled to superimpose the patterns in an unruly receptacle. God could be the perfection that was the final cause of the revolution of the universe, the source of the motion that alone could guarantee the perennial survival of all of the Forms embedded in matter. Three: psyche, which Plato thought must be a third kind of thing, neither Form nor perceptible particular, but perpetual, self-generating energy, is really only another Form after all—the Form that is the final cause of some plant or animal. It animates, not by being itself in motion, but by being a motionless perfection acting as a formal-final cause. This is true on every level of psychic activity, Aristotle thought, from the simplest movement toward growth and nutrition to the realization of the active intellect in man and in God.

Now it will be noticed that all three of these ideas are elegant ways of unravelling problems that worried Plato deeply. They are presumably *not* solutions, however, which Plato would have welcomed. The single most important thing that would have made him balk, I would suggest, is Aristotle's failure in this revised scheme to account for the reality of failure and irrationality. Aristotle did not deny that there was waste and imperfection in the world, of course, but it will be noted that he tried always to explain failures in his version of Platonism *without* resort to his teacher's assumption that there must be powerful random energy in the universe in addition to energy toward excellence. An examination of Aristotle's various treatises reveals that this is so on every level of his universe, from unseasonal rainstorms and monstrous births to ill-considered moves by impassioned men. He proposed a single, monistic explanation for all activity everywhere. We are never to suppose that there is any cause of activity in the universe, he thought, other than forms acting as the goals pursued by matter.[21] Plato, by contrast, had remained an emphatic dualist all through his life. Indeed, as he had grown older, he had become ever more profoundly convinced that, in addition to the pull of the perfect Forms, there was another kind of energy, both in the world at large and in the lower parts of the psyche, that could not possibly be described as intelligent. Though with luck and hard work it could be made subservient to intelligence, he thought, it could never be converted permanently or obliterated entirely.

It is Plato's thinking that is the harder of the two for us to understand, I believe. We must go back to *his* mentor, Socrates. Socrates originally quarrelled with the Sophists and rhetoricans, it will be remembered, because they assumed that there was no higher function for intelligence than rapid, effective calculation in the service of cynical and selfish ambitions. Real intelligence, Socrates maintained, was much more than this, it was the ambition to be happy when that was functioning clearly, the passion for true well-being, the energy generated by a correct understanding of real power and success. Now Plato and Aristotle both inherited this notion; both assumed with Socrates that intelligence was not mere calculation but motion and activity toward good. They also agreed that such activity rules the universe for the most part, and that knowledge of the world, therefore, can be gained only by a comprehension of what excellence means for each thing and for the whole. Rationality, in other words, is the perception of good, both in the pursuit of our own success and in the attempt to understand phenomena.

But where does that leave *ir*rationality? Plato drew what is, in a way, the most logical conclusion: if we define intelligence or rationality in this Socratic manner as motion toward true good, irrationality, Plato decided, can never, under any circumstances be preferred to it. Irrationality is by definition always dangerous, always regrettable. And if all objects of intelligence are perfect Forms, the beautiful patterns that the perceptible world is struggling to realize, then all tendencies that are *not* rational, *not* surges toward the realization of these patterns, must necessarily be unintelligible. The *tertium quid,* whatever it is that frustrates the perceptible world from achieving perfection in each type, can therefore be known, Plato concluded, only by a λογισμὸς νόθος, a "bastard reasoning" (*Timaeus* 52b2). It cannot be an object of knowledge; its existence can only be surmised from the fact that *something* is preventing the perceptible universe from complete success, beauty, and permanence. And in the human psyche as in the world, Plato observed, energy toward true success is constantly being interfered with by another kind of energy. This, too, must be by definition inevitably bad when it goes counter to reason, and it must be in itself essentially unintelligible. Probably the two were really the same, Plato thought, or at least very closely related, the random tendencies in nature and those within our own personalities (*Laws* X). Whatever they are, they are the very essence of what makes it so hard to live a life dominated entirely by intelligence.

But this is precisely where Aristotle parted company with Plato. There is nothing unintelligible in the universe, he asserted. Matter yearned only for Form. Confusion is to be attributed to the criss-cross of the pull of many Forms on matter. Failure, which he called στέρησις, "privation," was always the result of the pull of some other Form-patterns which excluded the one we expected. Even the so-called "irrational" passions in men were not really random drives. They were irrational, according to Aristotle, only in the sense that they were simple (*Metaphysics* θ ch. 1–5) and did not allow for the multiple needs of a human being pursuing his ultimate fulfillment, εὐδαιμονία. Such unambiguous goals inevitably come in mutually exclusive pairs, Aristotle thought, and the best course for a man always lies between the two. If most men fail to be pulled by their true good most of the time, that is merely because unenlightened habit has strengthened unduly one of the pair of simple drives.

Here then, I would suggest, is where we ought to look for the reason why we find Aristotle defending the poets as allies of rationality, whereas Plato had had to condemn most of them as dangerously irrational. Aristotle had dismissed one of his teacher's most important premises, the assumption that there existed energy not caused by any genuine good whatever. Aristotle was not only *able* to defend the rationality of tragedy, therefore, he *had* to defend it. Plato, on the other hand, once he had determined that Homer and the rest appeal, not to the intellect, but to the passions that so frequently frustrate intellect, *had* to condemn them as enemies. The fact that Plato was himself easily and deeply moved by these poets did not save them in his eyes; it made them all the more sinister.

Now let us return to Plato's specific complaints against the poets and see if we do in fact have the key.

In extended discussions of stories, music, rhythm and dance, both in the early books of the *Republic* and again in the *Laws*, Plato argues that these activities have a far more important effect on us than men generally suppose. Education is not a process of putting knowledge into the mind, he points out, it is the turning around of the whole personality, a conversion of the soul from an initial acceptance of shabby appearances to unshakable loyalty toward remoter things (*Republic* VII 518, f). But that process, he argues, must start in childhood, long before reason is developed. Anyone who supposes that we can leave our young alone for many years and start their training only when they are able to think is a fool. The stories he is told, the heroes he is led to admire and mimic, the melodies that arouse him, the movements of the dance that he enjoys, even the very architecture surrounding him affect a child profoundly (*Republic* III 401 b-c). And so a state set up to lead its entire citizenry to happiness by putting reason in control within each psyche could not possibly afford to allow the vulgar tastes of the centuries to determine which of the poets, musicians and artists are to be the ones that will accompany our everyday experiences.

This is the point at which the discussion ends in Book Three of the *Republic*. But it is not Plato's last word on the subject in this, his most important dialogue. In Book Ten he returns once more to the question of the arts.

Now there is a very silly theory that Plato had originally published the *Republic* without this last discussion and had tacked it on in a later version because he had been severely criticized for his plan to censor the poets.[22] Before we have recourse to a conjecture like that, however, we had better see if the structure of the dialogue does not make sense as it stands.

At the end of the discussion in Book Three, Socrates says that he is not yet in a position to explain his plan for censorship more precisely. He then turns in following books to the theory of the tripartite psyche, the theory of Forms, and a description of the ideal training for philosophers. Finally, in Book Nine, he says he is at last able to answer the question raised at the beginning of the dialogue, whether the man ruled entirely by selfish passion is the happiest or the most miserable of men. Socrates shows that such a man is the least enviable of all creatures, because he is essentially insane; he is in the grips, even when awake, of those dark, monstrous desires that in better men take command only when they are asleep. He is driven, compulsive, and inevitably wretched, because that part of him that urges the whole man toward his true well-being has all but shriveled away.

If the *Republic* had ended here, we should probably not have felt any incompleteness. But it does go on. Socrates starts a tenth and last book with the statement that now, and only now, is he able to explain why Homer, Sophocles, and the rest could not be permitted, in a really good city, to enjoy the freedom and the position of influence that they have in ordinary cities. He had been unable to make this clear before, he says, *because he had not yet shown how the psyche was divisible into three parts.*[23] First he translates his earlier remarks about imitation being akin, not to real value, but to shabby appearances, into the terms of his theory of Forms. Then he goes on to make a second point

which he says is the most important of all,[24] namely that the arts
are only effective if they encourage the lower parts of the psyche
at the expense of rationality. They feed and water mad impulses
which better men repress during their waking hours, but which
govern the compulsive criminal twenty-four hours a day. The
madness of inspiration, which can be communicated so swiftly to
an audience, is therefore a dangerous thing. Years later, in the
Laws, Plato had the Athenian Stranger point out that an inspired
poet gets his words un-willed, from hidden places below, like the
water in a spring welling up from under the earth (IV 719b).
Poetry, then, or at least the popular poetry that includes the *Iliad*
and *Oedipus the King,* is the child of the lowest part of the
psyche, the part that is noticeable in dreams, the free play of
infants, compulsions, and the inexplicable excitement of rhythm,
melody, and dance. Socrates *must* be taken at his word, therefore,
when he says at the beginning of Book Ten that only now is he
able to explain the need to curb the poets. We cannot understand
the attack against the poets until we have understood what is
demonstrated in Book Nine, that to put the lowest part of the
psyche in command of the whole person is literally to surrender
to a kind of insanity.

Aristotle does not attack this feature of Plato's theory point-
blank. Like ourselves, Aristotle simply did not see anything very
alarming in the discovery that the arts do not proceed from reason
but from something unwilled and beneath the surface. He was
able to avoid Plato's argument, however, only by asserting something which Plato could never have accepted: the idea that our
non-rational energies are neither alien nor, when it comes down
to it, entirely different from our rational energies. They are not
to be shuddered at and suppressed, he thought, but to be trained
and balanced. They are perfectly natural and easily explained.
A dark passion is, by Aristotle's definition, one of a pair of
natural and useful drives that a clever man must learn to steer
between. That is all. And so when men exercise their passions in
the music and fantasy of the theatre, they must, as in all natural
activity, be fulfilling some rational need. Aristotle settled for the
idea of a catharsis of emotions which might otherwise be trouble-
some.

In Plato's discussion of the activity of the irrational psyche in
dreams, he put first and foremost the terrible incestuous dream of
Oedipus.[25] The dream is horrifying to Plato because he presumed
that it was, not a pointless fantasy, but a genuine wish; it represents, Plato thought, a course of action which the dreamer would
take in actuality if that part of the psyche that is in control in
sleep were ever allowed to take control by day as well.[26] Aristotle
may have seen in this passage a reference to Sophocles' *Oedipus.*
Or at least, the passage may have suggested to him that the
Oedipus was a kind of test case. After all, if Plato is right that the

tragedians sway us primarily because their stories release pent-up desires quite properly suppressed from consciousness in our responsible moments, then what play can be more heinous than *Oedipus Tyrannus?* Aristotle's only answer to the challenge is to show over and over again how the *Oedipus* is a model of excellence in its technique, a deft handling of a serviceable *mythos*. He says nothing at all about any special significance that this among all *mythoi* might have for each of us in our inner struggles. The predicament of Oedipus is merely an unusually useful one for arousing pity and fear. It is interesting, I think, that in modern attempts to revive Plato's question, in psychoanalytic explorations of the relation between fiction and the repressed unconscious, it is still the Oedipus story that appeals to investigators as the most disturbing example of all.[27]

How much credit should Aristotle be given for having avoided Plato's distressing conclusions about the value of Homer and the tragedians? Not as much as he has been accorded in the last few centuries, anyhow. His was the easy conclusion, after all, the one with which we will readily agree and the one, therefore, from which we have the least to learn. Plato raised an extraordinarily interesting problem and a problem which we can hardly pretend to have solved since his time: namely, how are we to understand the relation between fictional stories, rhythmical language, melody and so on and the repressed or partially repressed lives we live in our dreams, daydreams, play, rituals, and compulsions? Aristotle did not settle this question any more than modern writers do when they talk easily about "poetic truth" as opposed to the truth we gain from conceptual thought and discursive reasoning. The real heirs to Plato's endeavor are, of course, the psychoanalysts, especially the Freudians; but when these daring explorers try to find the darker sources of art, literary critics are apt to cry "reductionism," then turn their backs and content themselves with the elucidation of details: structure, character, metaphor, and so on, all the things that Aristotle taught them to admire.

Aristotle's *Poetics* contains, to be sure, a number of passages which show intelligence and perception. As an answer to Plato's discovery, however, the work is not especially profound. Aristotle avoided Plato's most disturbing question simply by denying that there is any such thing as genuine, irreducible irrationality in the activity of nature or in the more brutish desires of man. The same thing, it will be noted, has happened in our own time in psychoanalytic theory. Freud, like Plato, was certain that there were at least two forces at work in us, only one of which was a drive toward happiness; his most famous student, Jung, on the other hand, exactly like Plato's most famous student, settled for one force only. Aristotle and Jung both took exception to their teachers' tendency to treat man's lower drives as fearful and essentially incorrigible enemies. So Jung, like Aristotle, has become the greater favorite with lovers of literature. It seems, indeed, that the dualists' vision of reality has been maintained only rarely by theoretical men, a few great heroes down through the centuries, and that the first innovation introduced by their followers has usually been to reduce the system to a monism again. This is natural enough, however, inasmuch as a dualism of the sort that Plato maintained and Aristotle denied entails the assumption that there is part of the world and a part of ourselves that we can never know completely, a part so essentially inimical to intelligence that it is unintelligible—theoretically unintelligible, not just in practice. This is a position which a theoretical man cannot easily consent to. Touch anything with theory and the irrationality has vanished. Also, most people instinctively side against the Jobs and with Job's would-be comforters: they cannot bear the thought that, somehow, deep down, irrationality cannot ever be explained in such a way that it becomes a friend again.

And so, in their difference concerning the value of poetry, as in their differences on so many points, the quarrel between Plato and Aristotle turns out to be based on a puzzle which is just as interesting and just as difficult today as it was in antiquity. My guess would be that Aristotle's versions of imitation and catharsis might very well be made to work if they were translated into terms of modern studies of our non-rational activities; but such a translation, we should not forget, would involve assumptions about the nature of this irrational life which Plato first brought to light and which Aristotle denied. The quarrel is, in any case, still very much alive.

FOOTNOTES

1. See J. E. Sandys, *A History of Classical Scholarship* (Cambridge, 1908) v. II 133, ff.

2. E.g. "It must be read rather as a dramatic gesture, as a bit of satire on the accredited educators of Hellas. Plato himself adopted the role of the poets, and the very excess of his argument is almost a sufficient indication that he did not mean us to take him altogether seriously." W. C. Greene, "Plato's View of Poetry," *HSCP* 29 (1918) 56. Cf. H. Gauss, *Philosophischer Handkommentar zu den Dialogen Platons,* II Teil, 2. Hälfte (Bern 1958) 223–8 and I. Edman, "Poetry and Truth," *Journal of Philosophy* 33 (1936) 605–9.

3. So Schadewaldt, for instance, concludes, "Furcht und Mitleid? Zur Deutung des Aristotelischen Tragödiensatzes," *Hermes* 83 (1955) 129–171.

4. Cf. Ingemar Düring, *Aristotle's Protrepticus* (Göteborg 1961) 180.

5. E.g. F. Egermann, *Vom Attischen Menschenbild* (Munich 1952) 89, ff. F. M. Cornford suggests that Plato was attacking not art but modern theories about art, "Plato's Philosophy of Art," *Mind* (1925)

154–72. This idea has been severely criticized by H. D. Lewis, "On Poetic Truth," *Philosophy* 21 (1946) 147–166. Cf. S. H. Rosen in *Phronesis* 4 (1959) 135–48.

6. 605 a 2: ὁ δὲ μιμητικὸς ποιητής . . . Cf. 595 a 6: ὅση μιμητική·

7. Cf. J. Tate, *New Scholasticism* 12 (1938) 114, also his review of Koller's *Die Mimesis in der Antike: CR* N.S. 5 (1955) 259.

8. Although it is clear that the myth is *not* intended to be higher than philosophy: see L. Edelstein, "The Function of the Myth in Plato's Philosophy," *Journal of the History of Ideas* 19 (1949) 463–81.

9. E.g. "It is as if he was conscious that the conviction at which he had arrived was the outcome of his temperament and training, and that it was therefore incumbent on him to give rational grounds for the position then adopted. And this is borne out by the method he adopts for convincing his readers of the justice of his position; for throughout his work, he calls attention to whatever supported his instinctive conclusion, while ignoring for the most part facts of an inconvenient kind." J. W. H. Atkins, *Literary Criticism in Antiquity* (Cambridge, 1934) v. I 49–50. Cf. K. Freeman, Greece and Rome 9 (1939/40) 137–49 and K. W. Wild, *Philosophy* 14 (1939) 326–40, esp. 334–8.

10. E.g. Greene, *op. cit.* 55.

11. II 667–672 and VII 817 a–d. On the admission of comic writers: XI 935d, ff. Greene says of the passage in Book VII that it "may be regarded as Plato's answer to *Republic* 607b." (*op. cit.* 65).

12. Especially in ch. V–IX of his *Principium Sapientiae* (Cambridge 1952).

13. *Paideia*, tr. by G. Highet (Oxford 1957) v. II 211, ff.

14. *Preface to Plato* (Cambridge, Mass. 1963).

15. *Aristotle*, tr. R. Robinson (Oxford 1934) 1.

16. In *Rhetoric* II 1388a6, for instance, he quotes Aeschylus to back up a statement that we are most jealous of people near us in age, reputation, etc. At *De generatione animalium* V 785a15 he quotes *Iliad* VIII 83–4 to confirm his description of the structure of a horse's skull. In *Historia Animalium* III 513b27 he quotes *Iliad* XIII 546 on the position of a blood vessel. At VI 574b34 he quotes *Odyssey* XVII 326 and says that Homer did well to represent Odysseus' dog at twenty years old when he died. At 578b1 he quotes a garbled mixture of *Iliad* IX 539 and *Odyssey* IX 190, interpreting χλούνης as "castrated," to prove that castrated boars are the fiercest! At XI 633a19 he quotes a long passage from Aeschylus on the habits of a hoopoe bird. In *Metaphysics* Γ 1009b2 he quotes *Iliad* XXIII 698 (which he thinks refers to Hector) to show that Homer agreed with Anaxagoras and others in their belief that thought alters with a physical alteration. In *De anima* I 404a29 he quotes the same passage, this time remarking that it had been quoted with approval by Democritus and interpreted rightly by him to mean that mind and soul were identical. Similarly, at III 427a25 he quotes *Odyssey* VIII 136 ("for such is a man's mind") taking it to mean that, according to Homer, thinking was identical with perception. In *Nicomachean Ethics* II 1109a31 he quotes *Odyssey* XII 219–20 ("hold the ship beyond that surf and spray") which he says are Calypso's words, though they are Odysseus' to his steersman, in obedience to *Circe's* advice (XII 108): the passage is cited by Aristotle to illustrate that "he who aims at the intermediate must first depart from what is more contrary to it." In III 1118a22 he quotes *Iliad* III 24 and quibbles

that lions do not really delight in seeing a stag or a goat; what they delight in, he says, is the fact that a meal is in the offing! And so on.

17. Contrast *Poetics* ch. iii and ch. xxiv. Cf. H. House, *Aristotle's Poetics*, revised by C. Hardie (London 1956) 122–3. Some writers have tried to vindicate Plato against the charge of having used the word μίμησις in two distinct senses, e.g. G.M.A. Grube, *Plato's Thought* (Boston 1958) 185, ff. and J. Tate, *CQ*·22 (1928) 16–23 and 26 (1932) 161–9. But more comprehensive studies of the occurrences of this word in Greek literature (by Kroll, Else, and others) lend support to the impression that it would have been very easy indeed for Plato to have slipped from one meaning to another with no clear idea as to which one was primary and which derivative.

18. *Platon und die Aristotelische Poetik* (Leipzig 1900) 67, ff. The key passages are *Laws* VII 790d and *Timaeus* 89a. A. Gudeman argues against Finsler on this point, in his edition of the *Poetics* (Berlin/Leipzig 1934) 21–8. See also J. Tate, *Hermathena* 50 (1937) 1–25, W. Trench, *ibid.* 51 (1938) 110–34, and Tate again, *New Scholasticism* 12 (1938) 107–42, especially the last 6 pages. Fensler's suggestion can never be more than a guess, in any case.

19. The most widely read handbooks, those by Ross, Jaeger, Robin, Zeller, Stooks, Allan, Taylor and the rest, make little effort to interpret the *Poetics* as an integral part of the Aristotelian system. Butcher and Else do make an attempt, however, as does Anna Tumarkin, "Die Kunsttheorie von Aristoteles im Rahmen seiner Philosophie," *Museum Helveticum* 2 (1945) 108–122.

20. I have defended this analysis of the relation between Aristotle's system and Plato's at much greater length in ch. VII and VIII of my *Platonic Love* (London and New York 1963), also in "Aristotle and the Irrational" *Arion* (Summer 1963) 55–74, and in my review of Else's *Poetics*, *Gnomon* 34 (1962) 641–9.

21. *Physics* I ch. 9, Cf. *Metaphysics* Λ ch. 10, ϴ ch. 9, Ν ch. 4, *De anima* III 430b22.

22. See Cornford, in his translation of the *Republic* (London and New York 1945) 321. Collingwood, too, *op. cit.* 169, argues that Plato assumed the subject to be exhausted when he finished Book III. But according to Collingwood, Plato later developed a new, "positive" theory, and that is why he added the discussion in Book X. But see Paul Shorey, *The Unity of Plato's Thought* (Chicago 1903) 51, who points out, among other things, that the discussion in Book III closes with the remark, ἴσως δὲ καὶ πλείω ἔτι τούτων, 394 d.

23. What he says is that the necessity to banish the poets νῦν καὶ ἐνεργέστερον · · · φαίνεται, ἐπειδὴ χωρὶς ἕκαστα διῄρηται τὰ τῆς ψυχῆς εἴδη, 595 a 6–7.

24. οὐ μέντοι πω τό γε μέγιστον κατηγορήκαμεν αὐτῆς . . . 605 c 6.

25. μητρί τε γὰρ ἐπιχειρεῖν μείγνυσθαι · · · οὐδὲν ὀκνεῖ, IX 571 c 8–d1. (Cf. Sophocles, O.T. 981: πολλοὶ γὰρ ἤδη κἀν ὀνείρασιν βροτῶν/ μητρὶ ξυνηυνάσθησαν, also Herodotus VI 107.) A whole generation has grown up in America on Jowett's translation of the *Republic*, which softens Plato's words to "not excepting incest," and on Yeats' translation of the *Oedipus*, which leaves out lines 981–2 altogether!

26. ὅταν τὸ μὲν ἄλλο τῆς ψυχῆς εἴδη · · · τὸ δὲ θηριῶδές τε καὶ ἄγριον · · · σκιρτᾷ τε καὶ ἀπωσάμενον τὸν ὕπνον ζητῇ ἰέναι καὶ ἀποπιμπλάναι τὰ αὑτοῦ ἤθη, IX 571 c 3–7. Rohde, Frazer, Dodds, Greene (*op. cit.* 7)

and others have quoted Homer, Aeschylus, Pindar, and at times, even Plato himself (e.g. *Phaedo* 60, *Crito* 44) to show how seriously the Greeks took their dreams as a possible source of divine revelation; but nobody before Plato, even Sophocles, had suggested that the real reason for taking dreams seriously was that they could be used to infer what our own unconscious desires might be. Contrast Aristotle's facile remark, *De divinatione per somnum* 463 b 13: τὰ ἐνύπνια, he says, are not sent by divinity, but δαιμόνια μέντοι· ἡ γάρ φύσις δαιμονία, ἀλλ' οὐ θεία.

27. E.g. Freud's "Dostoevsky and Patricide".

HORACE AS A LOVE POET:
A READING OF *ODES* 1. 5

Kenneth Quinn

For two connected reasons the Pyrrha ode must be regarded as a test case. The first is the paradox of its popularity: the ode has long been well liked, as well as well known; but its admirers are chiefly to be found outside the schoolroom or the lecture theatre, among those who read Latin for pleasure—a class of reader one meets less, of course, today than formerly; from professional scholars the Pyrrha ode wins a curiously grudging recognition. The second reason also involves a paradox: as a craftsman Horace has always been praised, and is still so praised today, even by his most spinsterish interpreters; but as a love poet he has been for a century and a half more often derided, or patronized, than praised.

At the core of each paradox lies the very different appeal that Horace makes to different audiences. But there is another common factor: what has swung opinion most firmly against Horace as a love poet, and against that group of poems of which the Pyrrha ode is the best known representative, is a transfer of authority from one kind of audience to another. As a result of a number of factors, the status of Roman poets has become increasingly a matter to be settled by professional scholars rather than on grounds of general esteem among the lettered public; our understanding of the classics has been improved enormously in the last century and a half by the industry of scholars; when, however, understanding has depended on the possession of taste and imagination by the interpreter (qualities which, when we study poetry, must enlighten constantly the disciplined labour of reason), the result has been more often a corruption of our understanding than a refinement of it; a corruption that has gone almost unchecked as a result of the authority increasingly conceded professional scholarship—conceded not because taste and imagination, unguided by learning, were incompetent to intervene, but because the extraordinary impact of the Romantic movement made it seem for a time that classical poetry, Roman poetry in particular, had been permanently superseded.

The affection lavished on the Pyrrha ode by lovers of Horace— a class that has dwindled steadily during a century and a half of alienation of general esteem from Roman poetry—is extraordinary. Hundreds of them have translated it and taken the trouble to get their translation of it printed. Sir Ronald Storrs claims he has tracked down 451 versions of the poem in 26 languages.[1] Milton's prim, puritanical Pyrrha is the most famous—yet surely, despite stiff competition, among those least like her prototype. But when the student turns to the standard commentators, eager to win more intimate possession of these sixteen sinewy, elusive lines, he discovers a remarkable reticence. Campbell (*Horace* [1924]) contents himself with a dozen words (p. 222): they frame a shrewd initial pronouncement ('thus I. v. is *to* Pyrrha, but *at* her too-credulous latest lover'), but take us no further. The index to Pasquali's great work on Horace (*Orazio lirico* [1920]) is unfortunately full of mistakes; the one reference given is a false one, and all I have been able to discover is a short discussion of Horace's Greek sources (p. 500). Mr. L. P. Wilkinson (*Horace and his Lyric Poetry* [1945]) limits himself, apart from a note on Milton's translation, to citing one phrase from the ode (*miseri quibus intemptata nites*) in support of Tennyson's famous tag 'jewels five words long'; oddly enough, of the five examples Wilkinson quotes, all but one are *four* words long. Professor Eduard Fraenkel (*Horace* [1957]), unless his index is defective too, hasn't even a footnote on Pyrrha. Dr. Walter Wili (*Horaz* [1948]) has a one-sentence summary (p. 182) and a note on word-order in the last stanza (p. 249). Mr. N. E. Collinge (*The Structure of Horace's Odes* [1961]), apart from several terse, cryptic *obiter dicta*, allows himself two short sneers (pp. 85 and 117). Professor Steele Commager (*The Odes of Horace* [1962]), the latest author of a book on Horace, alone attempts to discuss the poem, but confines himself chiefly to a sympathetic appreciation of structure (pp. 51–2 and 65–9); when he comes to consider what the poem is about (p. 144), sympathy vanishes. The best scholarly reading of the poem known to me, the only one that will help the reader to read it as a poem, is contained in a short lesson which J. W. Mackail gave to schoolteachers at Oxford in 1924; though both perceptive and exciting, it seems to have passed into oblivion.[2]

It might be supposed that scholars who write on Horace regard the merits of the Pyrrha ode as self-evident and that they hold themselves in check for poems more worthy of their mettle. One gathers, however, from chance remarks that what they find admirable are the complex patterns into which Horace has woven the 65 words that make up the poem; there is no sign they have given much thought to the poem as a piece of poetic *statement*, capable perhaps of producing, in addition to the aesthetic satisfaction we derive from words adroitly manipulated, some intellectual or emotional impact upon its readers. The ode's merits as a poem about *love* are clearly not something they give serious consideration; somehow it's taken for granted that the poem's status need not be affected by what seems to them the evident fact that Horace has nothing in particular to say.

Now there are love poems by Horace where one can set out from some kind of aesthetic satisfaction with the words and end up regarding the whole as a piece of elegant whimsy, without feeling that something that caught the eye at once has collapsed unexpectedly in our fingers the moment we try to grasp it firmly. Most readers are content with the graceful badinage of 3. 9 (*Donec gratus eram tibi . . .*), and it cannot be said that it ruins that poem to take it that way; though I think it is a pity to miss the ironical psychological acuity with which Horace has thought himself inside the characters he sets sparring with each other in words, so apparently nonchalant, till the moment comes for reconciliation to be plainly talked of. We cannot patronize the Pyrrha ode in this way. To the sensitive reader the very complexity of statement, and the sober, measured tone which that complexity dictates, amount to an assertion on the poet's part that something worth reflecting on lies wrapped in the words. The tone is far from solemn, but Horace is plainly not just jesting either. If therefore careful reading shows his thought sentimental or shallow, then the poem has compelled reflection by false pretences, and we must regard it, for all its elegance, as meretricious, if not downright fraudulent.

The idea that Horace is a serious poet is uncommon among his professional interpreters. Any attempt to claim a status for him as a love poet is apt to meet with particular derision. Mr. E. J. Kenney speaks more bluntly than some, but he expresses the prevailing attitude:

> Horace was undoubtedly a poet, and erotic themes are to be found in his poems; but that he ever wrote anything which in the ordinary acceptance of the term could be called love-poetry I most earnestly deny.[3]

Horace's tendency to portray himself as a lukewarm lover is taken usually as a clear confession of inadequacy, as though the ability to fall helplessly in love were an indisputable demonstration of some kind of strength of character. And what critics suppose about Horace as a lover seems to them confirmed by the way he writes.[4] The Pyrrha ode has in fact been singled out as a telling example of how Horace's shallow insincerity, devoid of emotional commitment, leads to a kind of graceful ineptness.[5] Even Commager, despite the many sensitive things he has to say about the Pyrrha ode, is not concerned to make a case for the ode as a poem intellectually or emotionally worth while.

We may feel this is only the usual state of affairs; that scholars have always tended to be dull dogs; that the splendour of the poetry they expound has always tended to be veiled for them by what that fine scholar Viktor Pöschl calls the schoolroom dust of the centuries (*der Schulstaub der Jahrhunderte*);[6] that, if matters are worse now than formerly, this is just one more instance of a new *trahison des clercs,* of which we read a good deal at present in the serious press—a failure of academics to measure up to their social and cultural responsibilities. Does any of this matter, we may ask, when a reviving popular enthusiasm for classical literature, of which we also read in the serious press, is outstripping scholarly guidance, running on ahead unaided?

Unfortunately it does matter. For it is only the writers who are most easily appreciated (Homer, the tragedians, those people can read in translation with ready, genuine enjoyment, those most independent of changing fashions in literature) that can today survive a lack of scholarly guidance; where Horace or Virgil, indeed Roman poetry in general, is concerned, the lettered public needs assistance. To begin with, you can't get anywhere with Horace through translations; you need to know some Latin as well. Here the trouble starts. Unless you're very perceptive, you won't learn to read Horace in Latin without imbibing, too, your teacher's opinion of the poetry.

So long as the ability to read Horace in Latin was an accomplishment that was almost universal among the lettered public, a scholar's opinion was not the last word; now, it usually is the last word. Small wonder if lovers of Horace are by now reduced to a very small band indeed. Small wonder if the point has been reached, in fact, where it has become really quite rare to read anything sensible about Horace's poetry, to hear it treated as poetry at all. Those who have studied it systematically have been taught to despise it. Those who have not had the warmth of their casual, superficial reaction chilled by the ice of learned opinion, run the risk of incurring the derision of what passes for authority if they open their mouths.

It's interesting to consider a moment this increasing domination of opinion about classical literature by professional scholars. The thing is, on the face of it, surprising. For, though sprightliness of taste and imagination are not—happily—always checked by weight of learning, one would have supposed it common knowledge that men whose authority in scholarly matters must pass unquestioned are often men endowed with a more limited sensibility than is needed to ensure reliable opinions about literature.

From the renaissance until the end of the eighteenth century the major classical writers had been a matter of intimate, enthusiastic concern to a large proportion of those occupied at a creative level with contemporary literature. Throughout this time Roman poetry was read, enjoyed and talked about by people who knew from their intimacy with contemporary literature what poetry was and how it worked. Scholars were listened to with respect, but by a lettered public competent to distinguish exegesis from critical opinion and to allow to each its proper weight. The nineteenth century saw an immense change. To Romantic poets and critics, Roman poetry seemed worn out, debased by association with English classicism and the English Augustan age. Discussion of Roman poetry fell more and more into the hands of professional scholars, who, having now to work unenlightened by contact with an audience that understood poetry, were forced to fall back upon their own taste and their own ideas about poetry. Their taste and their ideas were, to begin with, merely reactionary: the ideas and taste of a previous generation. But quickly the men who became classical scholars were more and more men who found the poetry written and admired by their contemporaries incomprehensible or actually distasteful. Unable any longer to fall back upon the standards of the eighteenth century now that these were generally rejected, unguided by any kind of true participation in the making and discussion of literature, the professional interpreters were soon pronouncing judgment according to their own lights with a confidence that may seem surprising but should not surprise; for, as Housman once remarked, the worst of having no judgment is that one never misses it. Being not generally men of ill will, or stupid, they did not in the main isolate themselves consciously from current ideas about poetry, in so far as they could understand them and were not repelled by them. The standards they applied became those of a kind of superficial Romanticism, diluted and poisoned by common sense.

Remember I am talking about Roman poetry. With other departments of the classics—Homer, Greek tragedy—the tyranny of Greece over Germany (and England) never allowed scholars a free hand to the same extent. But with Roman poetry they were given a free hand. And taking it, scholars reduced Latin poetry too often to a kind of prose that oscillates unhappily between the trivial and the nonsensical.

In Germany the main victim was Virgil, though happily it is no longer fashionable in German scholarly circles to disparage Virgil, thanks to Professor Friedrich Klingner of Munich, who pioneered his rehabilitation in a vigorous campaign of reparation, launched during the last war with his celebrated manifesto, *Wiederentdeckung eines Dichters*, published in 1942.[7] In English-speaking countries Horace has suffered more than Virgil at the hands of a common-sense Romanticism that demands passion of poetry and scorns subtleties that stand in its way. Among the odes of Horace there are only a few that can be reduced without disaster to a series of explicit propositions with an evident appeal to common sense; and there are none that give unrestrained expression to violent passion.

The Pyrrha ode cannot survive scrutiny by such standards. Yet it is a real poem. It manages, by means of techniques that have little to do with those of logical prose, to say something meaningful and discerning. But to show this, I must deal with the ode in a way that will seem confusing and fanciful to those familiar with scholarly discussion of Horace, though normal-sounding enough, I think, to those acquainted with the methods of post-Romantic criticism. The claim I shall make for Horace as a

love poet will startle those accustomed to think of him as a
sensible, easy-going fellow with no particular ideas about the
world around him, who liked dabbling in unusual metres. I do
not see how this can be helped.

We may usefully set out from Mackail's summary (p. 64):

> The picture, the *chose vue*, is a couple in a rose-arbour just
> seen; a slim boy with his arms clasped tight round a girl, who
> sits knotting back her hair.

And yet, while Mackail's thirty words tell us well enough what
Horace's twenty-one say when recast as factual statement, Mackail's words give, of course, no hint of *how* Horace's words say it,
or of the effect Horace's words produce, no inkling of their power
to arouse the reader's continuing interest in this dramatic vignette
which the poet's eye has taken in at a glance, and the poet's
sensibility as instantly comprehended:

> Quis multa gracilis te puer in rosa
> perfusus liquidis urget odoribus
>   grato, Pyrrha, sub antro?
>   cui flauam religas comam,
>
> simplex munditiis?

> What slip of a boy amid a profusion of roses,
> smell-drenched, gleaming, importunes you, Pyrrha,
> in this attractive grotto? For whom do you
> bind back your blond hair,
>
> all chic simplicity?

Here is evocation of scene, not description. Heinze's comment
'Bis in Einzelheiten deutlich malt sich H. die Situation aus'[8] is
misleading, as a moment's reflection shows. What is the scene of
our dramatic fragment? What are the actors doing? Mackail's
summary provides answers with which we need not really quarrel;
but we must remember it is Mackail who is satisfying our
curiosity, not Horace. For clearly, despite the zeal of editors,
unequivocal statement cannot be extracted from *multa in rosa*;
and clearly, *urget* means both more and less than Mackail's 'with
his arms clasped tight round.'

We must remember, too, that Horace's lack of clarity does not
come from failure to achieve clear statement in a recalcitrant
form, nor is it an attempt to evade charges of banality under what
Commager calls 'the shelter of ostentatiously literary language'
(*op. cit.* p. 156); it is an integral, necessary component of his
technique. The problem Horace faces it twofold. He wants, first,
to make words convey what he has seen, in fact or in imagination,
and to convey as well his intuitive sympathy with the participants
in that scene. But the words have a second, and harder, task: to

[108]

compensate for the loss of immediacy that must occur when words set out what the eye can see, and the mind apprehend, in a flash. For it is not the *chose vue,* the thing seen, alone that justifies the poem; indeed, the absence of clear descriptive detail suggests the thing seen is everyday enough for the details to be left to our imagination. It is the immediacy and the depth of Horace's reaction to the thing seen that make the poem worth Horace's trouble to write and ours to understand.

Not everyone can see the eternal in the everyday, the deeper significance of things that seem too trivial to most of us to be significant, or too familiar. Those who are more sensitive than the rest of us, or who reflect more on life's ironies, sometimes feel impelled therefore to explain how their insight into human relationships moves them. But because, *if* they try to explain, explanation inevitably takes time—so much time, if they try to be logical and precise—what they say runs the risk of becoming long-winded, boring, and therefore ineffective.

I imagine this problem faces every social scientist and psychologist, just as it faces every literary critic, and I suspect few of them overcome it. The artist can overcome it because he can evade the need to explain. He does this by creating the illusion in us of a flash of intuition, like the one that came originally to him. In a visual art such as the film it is easily done: the camera lingers for a moment on a boy and a girl together, and suddenly we feel the flash of understanding and are moved. The maker of the film, however, has not brought this about simply by allowing the camera to linger; he has had to create an atmosphere beforehand that makes us more than usually responsive. Otherwise we should not have that flash of intuition; we might laugh instead of feeling a catch in our throats.

The poet has to use *words.* His technique, therefore, is necessarily remote from visual media which can aim at what may look like a reproduction of the scene that moved the original observer. Because clear statement dissipates the effect he is trying to recapture, the poet finds himself led away from the normal prose employment of words. In place of description he is liable to resort to some selective, evocative, oblique technique that will ensure compactness. Then he must find some way of *detaching* us from the everyday scene, so that our commitment to it no longer blinds us to what the poet can see; for we should feel we see for ourselves, not that we have been told. There are many ways of achieving this end. Most of them depend on some form of what critics call distancing, some illusion of alienation,[9] that results somehow in a heightened responsiveness in the reader. This is not of course a device that is confined to verse; obvious forms of distancing are the fable, the funny story, the strip cartoon, many kinds of satire and comedy. The everyday is made to look odd, absurd in externals of appearance; animals instead of men, but dressed and behaving like men; or very ordinary men in very unordinary situations continuing to behave as ordinary men. We laugh first at the obviously funny. Our laughter (the intellectual pleasure of wit is a more refined trick that is common in novels) severs our commitment to the everyday. We begin to see things in everyday occurrences we couldn't have seen before; we begin to wonder whether a situation or a course of conduct that we normally accept without question should go unchallenged; whether situations we judge conventionally shouldn't be thought over afresh.

Horace, it seems to me, put a lot of thought into bringing his readers to think afresh about situations of everyday life so familiar ° people ceased to think about them at all. The normal function of poetry was clearly a debated issue and one much in the foreground of Horace's thoughts. His concern tends, of course, to be detected only in those poems where it is explicit—the *Satires*, the *Epistles*, and the handful of odes that deal manifestly with patriotic and philosophic themes; where the majority of the odes are concerned, it is assumed Horace's slogan is *dulce est desipere in loco*, rather than *omne tulit punctum qui miscuit utile dulci;* it does not seem to cause much surprise that, when the moralist has gone on holiday, the craftsman seems harder at work than ever.

If I am right, Horace worked out, in an attempt to arouse our responsiveness, a technique that depends on a style which is common enough in modern poetry, but hadn't, I think, existed till Horace created it. It depends essentially on a *terse complexity* of statement, enlivened by what I can only call a *subdued flippancy* of tone—an ironical, understating lightness that would not have seemed compatible with poetry at all until Horace proved it was more effective than a vague, rhetorical sublimity, which is apt to dull our responsiveness instead of sharpening it. Horace was already, I think, working in this direction when he stated his ideal formula for satire (*Satires* i, 10, 9–14):

> est breuitate opus, ut currat sententia, neu se
> impediat uerbis lassas onerantibus auris;
> et sermone opus est modo tristi, saepe iocoso,
> defendente uicem modo rhetoris atque poetae,
> interdum urbani, parcentis uiribus atque
> extenuantis eas consulto.

> But briefness is essential: make your statement lively,
> don't clog it with words to burden ears already tired.
> Then language: it must be now austere, now facetious,
> playing at times the part of orator or poet, at times
> the sophisticated citizen holding eloquence in check
> and understating deliberately.

This combination of complexity and flippancy ensures that a situa-

°for 'normal'] *read* 'moral'

tion is presented with no explicit, one-sided judgment of it. Our minds are set working to form our own judgment, and Horace's purpose is achieved more economically and more memorably than by the clumsy techniques of prose.

The Pyrrha ode begins with a double question. But, like the questions with which the Sybaris ode (1. 8) begins, they're hardly questions we can imagine Horace putting in actual conversation. Moreover it's clear Pyrrha isn't expected to answer the questions, or even to hear them—she is otherwise engaged. The questions are a structural convention or trick: the poet's thoughts in a scene are turned into a dramatic soliloquy which we can imagine ourselves overhearing. Opening with a question suggests the directness, the intimacy of conversation. But, while it is important to secure this illusion of the poet's speaking voice, it is equally important in so compact a poem, in which the poetry must work fast, that the poet should win from us a more careful alertness to each word spoken than we are accustomed to find necessary in everyday life. Hence the intricately woven pattern of the words, the metrical pattern,[10] the measured, balanced tone of the questions as they run on through four lightly end-stopped lines, to halt on the striking phrase *simplex munditiis* in the middle of line 5. An effect is built up, confirmed by a distinctly felt tension between ironical lightness of detail and an equally patent seriousness of general intention, that counterbalances the suggestion of conversational tone.

As the questions unwind, they sketch in the scene that prompted them: the artificial grotto (a garden feature the Romans seem to have been fond of), the profusion of roses, the boy, the girl; a few light strokes, and the rest is left to our imagination. The technique is not so much that of the cartoon as that of an impressionist painting, for the scene is dominated by the splash of colour implied by *multa in rosa* (the Romans had only pink and white roses) and a vague, pleasurable radiance conjured up by *grato* that seems equally aimed at suggesting how the actors' surroundings help them to feel they are enjoying themselves and at securing from us an initial mood of tolerant approval.

For the actors are more important than the scene, and it is time our attention shifted to them. The boy, too, is treated impressionistically, but it is an impressionism aimed at suggesting personality as well as appearance. We are told he is *gracilis*; the obvious translations are 'slim' or 'slender'; but perhaps 'slight' or 'slip of a boy' (if one could give them contexts that would make them poetically adequate to the occasion) would suggest better the power of *gracilis* here to evoke the fragility of the boy and the risk he runs of being crushed by an experience beyond the strength of his emotions or understanding. The girl is, by implication, not *gracilis* in appearance, though Mackail's 'more opulent contours' makes disastrously precise what we should no more than sense; nor is she as emotionally fragile: the boy's appearance is the symbol of his fate.

To these connotations of *gracilis* the second line,

> perfusus liquidis urget odoribus,

> smell-drenched, gleaming, he importunes you,

adds an action shot in which only one detail of his appearance is sharply defined. At the same time the words used demand a clearly marked inflexion of disparagement; the very emphatic *perfusus* ('drenched') and the imprecise, depreciatory plural *odoribus* underline the speaker's assessment: the boy, forgetting, in his keenness to look his smartest for the girl, that it is the function of scent and hair-dressing to be no more than discreetly perceptible to nose or eye, has succeeded only in looking a little ridiculous.

Horace stresses the detail because it tells so much. What the boy lacks is above all experience. Without experience, he is emotionally fragile; without experience, his endeavours to look smart are clumsy and ineffective—he overdoes things. Just as he gauchely overdoes his advances to the girl: the verb *urget* gains its terse effectiveness from the same trick of impressionistic imprecision. What it denotes depends on how we relate it to Horace's second question:

> cui flauam religas comam?

> For whom do you bind back your blond hair?

Has the boy kissed Pyrrha and deranged her hair? Or is she warding off his advances by pretending to be busy with her hair?[11] It makes little difference what precise action we individually read into *urget*; what the word connotes matters more: the clumsy ardour of the boy, rendered ineffective by inexperience. Whereas Pyrrha symbolizes experience; all she has to do to control the situation is to 'bind back her blond hair.' It is the one visual detail precisely stated by Horace; the gesture dominates the tiny drama: she is cool where he is ardent; she has learned the effectiveness of restraint while he has yet to learn it; the gesture of combing back her hair is almost an instinctive reflection of her reproval. But it shows, too, that Pyrrha's control of the situation is conscious: she takes it for granted the boy will not dare to interrupt her; at the same time she knows her action will fan desire; her seemingly oblivious nonchalance is directed at an audience, as the dative *cui* discreetly reminds us. For though she reproves she does not repel: the boy is going to get his way—this is the clear prediction of the poem—but on Pyrrha's terms and only for as long as she chooses.

We begin to sense the drift of Horace's moral comment. Here

is a situation where convention talks of the conquest of the girl by the boy. In fact, however, it is often the passive partner, the girl, who is the real conqueror, and the active partner, the boy, who turns out the victim in the end, when the girl decides to assert her power. Horace makes no attempt to say this—his poem would cease to be a poem if he did attempt plain statement. His method is to set out from impressionistic, symbolic detail rather than analysis.

The central section of the ode brings a more thoroughgoing symbolism. But first Horace ends his second question with a telling summing-up of Pyrrha, a two-word paradox that focuses our attention on her at the moment when the opening verbal tableau begins to dissolve, and the poet's thoughts to unwind. Pyrrha is *simplex munditiis.* The order of the words lightly underlines the paradox: *munditiis simplex,* with the instrumental ablative first, would imply, I think, that it was a normal function of *munditiae* to make *simplex*; Horace's order invites us to reflect that it isn't. Moreover *munditiae* is a trivial, jangling word; it means getting the details of appearance just right, paying attention to neatness and cleanliness; but connotation and sound suggest how close to triviality and fussiness too scrupulous a concern with detail can come. The girl who neglects details will never look smart; the girl who pays too much attention to them runs the risk of overdoing things—like the boy. Restraint is the secret of chic—effective understatement in dress and appearance which is the result of a lot of trouble does not show it.

Pyrrha in fact—because of her attention to *munditiae*, not despite it—looks *simplex*; because there's no sign of fussiness one might think there was nothing to it. But *simplex* is another of the telling ambiguities built into this poem. It describes not only how Pyrrha looks, but implies the judgment of her character that the way she dresses is designed to invite. She looks so frank, so innocent, so incapable of dissimulation—all common meanings of *simplex*; another overtone not drawn out till we read the poem a second time and relate the central section to the first is 'unchanging,' 'always the same.'

But though Pyrrha's apparent innocence, like her chic, is studied, the effect of art not ingenuousness, Horace's judgment implies, of course, no condemnation: *simplex munditiis* is a quality he appreciates; the words could provide a serviceable judgment of the poetry he writes. Nor is it his object to make fun of the boy. Horace's attitude is neutral: a complex, unprotesting, understanding compassion.

The next eight lines first carry us away from the scene of the opening five in a flourish of rhetoric; this blends into some seriously poetic imagery; then we return to the opening scene in a double relative clause, whose strongly emphasized rhythm checks the flow of the preceding lines; at the same time dense,

compact statement takes over again from rhetoric and imaginative
fullness. In syntax it is all one lithe, elegant sentence:

> heu! quotiens fidem
> mutatosque deos flebit et aspera
>   nigris aequora uentis
>   emirabitur insolens,
>
> qui nunc te fruitur credulus aurea,
> qui semper uacuam, semper amabilem
>   sperat, nescius aurae
>   fallacis.

> O dear! what wailings about
> promises and gods who let men down, when he gazes
> shocked on a sea rough and storm-black,
> innocently presuming,
>
> because your golden self is now at his disposal,
> he can hope to keep you ever his, ever lovable—
> unaware that calm airs cannot
> be trusted.

The rhetoric is, of course, not Horace's. Horace takes it for granted
that Pyrrha and the boy will not last long; he is convinced that
passionate love never lasts, that the loss of a mistress is too predictable an experience to constitute tragedy; on this issue he is
firmly with Lucretius and firmly against Catullus and the elegists.[12] Many scholars, looking down from the Gothic battlement
of their ivory towers on Pyrrha and the other beautiful creatures
that smile mischievously at them from the pages of their Horace,
find it hard not to see satire of a type singled out for condemnation. Dr. Walter Wili (p. 170) speaks, for example, of *'jene
Frauenart, die wir Vampyr nennen, und die merkwürdig römisch
(und romanisch) zu sein scheint.'* But for Horace, love—passionate,
romantic love—and infidelity simply went together; sooner or later
one followed the other.

The boy, of course, is going to be dreadfully upset when this
happens to him. He will be sure that tragedy has overtaken him.
And thinking himself the victim of tragedy he will feel entitled,
not only to protest, but to protest in tragic terms. To those who
see no tragedy in what has happened, he will naturally look a
little ridiculous. Horace's *heu!* is rather like our 'o dear!.' It expresses his discomfiture at the thought of the fuss the boy is going
to make; how he will complain that he has been betrayed, that
the gods have turned their faces away from him; the condensed
syntax of *quotiens fidem mutatosque deos flebit,* for *quotiens
fidem (Pyrrhae) mutatam mutatosque deos flebit,* neatly suggests
the boy's identification of Pyrrha's infidelity with the cosmos.
When they quarrel, or rather when Pyrrha casts off her inno-

cent young conqueror in a blaze of scornful anger, the boy will stand horror-stricken, amazed like a man encountering his first storm at sea. Notice however Horace does not waste space on a formal simile. The image of the storm-tossed sea acquires its effectiveness from an interesting piece of poetic ju-jitsu. Our readiness to take the four words *aspera nigris aequora uentis* as a fully developed poetic image is due, I think, to the grand manner in which this sentence began. If Horace had continued in the subdued, sinewy style of the opening lines, which he resumes in the double relative clause (lines 9 and 10), the four words could hardly have succeeded in eliciting the vivid image that they do elicit; the change of tone would have come too much as a shock. Yet Horace disowns the rhetoric of lines 5 and 6, as his gently ironical *heu!* makes clear. The sea imagery of lines 6 and 7, however, he wants accepted without reservation, for it introduces a symbol on which the remainder of the poem will depend: like the sea, woman is irresistible, fascinating to man, but unreliable, freely accepting him when it is her whim but turning ultimately on him in angry rejection; the ambiguity in *aspera*—(1) 'rough,' 'turbulent,' (2) 'angry,' 'intractable'—justifies the use of a sea in storm as a symbol of anger. So long as things go well, man may delude himself with the belief that some understanding, some kind of mutual collaboration exists between him and his temporary partner; but woman, like the sea, is ultimately alien, however much a part of our lives. Her anger, like the sea's, is as impersonal as her compliance with our will—more a projection of our feelings than conscious anger.

We must remember that Horace is only talking about passionate love. What he is offering us is not an undiscriminatingly cynical comment on all possible relationships between man and woman. The application of the imaginative comment of the central eight lines is limited by the vignette of the opening five. Even so, the moment we turn the implications of Horace's imagery into a series of prose propositions, its power to arouse moving near-truths is lost. The logic of prose requires a clear equation; before we can accept it, a host of qualifications must be added; and, by the time we have added them, the equation is hardly worth making. But poetry does not assert correspondences, it merely implies them for us to ponder on. It implies them, however, with a force that compels reflection. And when accepting the challenge of Horace's image, we turn its implicit assertions over in our minds we will see, I think, that, however much we should want to hedge them in with qualifications, we are brought none the less to feel something that is movingly, frustratingly close to truth.

It isn't until the sea imagery has been fully explored in the final stanza that the richness of implication latent in it at its first introduction is completely elicited. All Horace expects of us for the moment is a mental picture of the boy's shocked surprise (the forceful compound *emirari* is found only here in classical Latin) when his mistress turns on him. He invites next our admission that the boy's indignation at what seems to him betrayal and disaster is unjustified. The concluding word in the stanza, *insolens*, makes the point more plainly by means of a remarkable triple ambiguity. The meaning of *insolens* that suggests itself first is 'lacking experience'—the meaning of the word closest to its etymology, though it does not seem to have been the commonest meaning in ordinary usage: it is the boy's lack of experience that will make his grief and indignation disproportionate when Pyrrha deserts him. But the context draws out simultaneously the meaning 'presumptuous'—the commonest meaning of the word. The boy is presumptuous in supposing he has any claim on Pyrrha or on the gods, any reason to behave as though the world were his oyster. Will Pyrrha even condescend to promise to love him for ever? If she does, how foolish to believe her, for 'what woman says to eager lover should be written in the wind and running water.'[13] Whether she promises or not, by putting her *fides* alongside that of the gods, Horace implies that the boy is reading his own thoughts and desires into her mind, just as he is reading them into the mind of the universe. But with this second meaning of *insolens* a constructional ambiguity is introduced, in addition to the pun ambiguity,[14] which I have tried to represent by the two words 'innocently presuming': 'innocently' tries to cope with the meaning of *insolens* first discussed; 'presuming,' taken as an adjective, with that discussed second; and 'innocently presuming' ('presuming' taken as a participle) with the connotation of *insolens* when linked with *fruitur* (and *sperat*). For, once the meaning 'presumptuous' is drawn out, we feel we want to attach *insolens* to *fruitur* (and *sperat*) as much as to *emirabitur*, to take it as part of the following double relative clause as well as with the preceding clause.[15] The boy presumes upon Pyrrha's present serene condescension; he takes it for granted she will always be at his disposal—the slightly contemptuous *uacuam* undercuts the boy's ideas of romantic love. More than that, he takes it for granted that he will always be able to love her: *amabilem* means 'that can be loved'—the meaning 'amiable' or 'loving' is not classical. This will be the truly terrible revelation: the Pyrrha he now loves is going to turn into a creature it will be impossible to love.

At this point the symbolism of the sea is reintroduced with the words *nescius aurae fallacis*—again a striking phrase to round off a section of the poem. The words introduce a further ambiguity. The primary function of *aurae* is to re-establish the sea imagery by stressing how the calm breeze that sends the sailor on his journey happy and confident is not to be trusted, for without warning it can turn into an angry gale. But *aura* is an interesting word. The Roman love poets from Catullus onwards use it in an attempt to come to grips with that power of fascination an attractive woman possesses which cannot simply be accounted for by good looks. The word builds upon the old idea of a special emanation, some breath of divinity, associated with goddesses, even when they assumed human shape, that gave them away: the moment you spotted it you knew to be on your guard. Perhaps, influenced by Lucretian materialism, the Roman poets did in fact think of woman's power to fascinate as some subtle breath of fascination, ascribing to it a physical reality where we should more readily think of a psychological phenomenon.[16] This meaning of *aura* is drawn out here by the syntax of the sentence. For though the primary meaning of the words *nescius aurae fallacis*, 'unaware that calm airs cannot be trusted,' attaches the phrase more readily to the sea imagery of the principal clause in lines 7 and 8, their position after the double relative clause in lines 9 to 11 invites taking them as direct statement about Pyrrha and the boy, giving thus to *aurae* its less common meaning; my translation suggests only the presence of an ambiguity, not the proper force of its secondary meaning.

In the final section of the poem, the sea imagery is maintained:

> miseri, quibus
> intemptata nites! me tabula sacer
> uotiua paries indicat uuida
>   suspendisse potenti
>   uestimenta maris deo.

>   What miseries await
> the wretches your splendour unassailed allures! Me? —
> a votive plaque on holy wall declares I've hung my
> sopping garments up to the mighty
> sea-divinity.

Pyrrha, like the sea, has victims yet to claim, waiting ready—note that *nites* is present, not future. But 'victim' is really the wrong word to use, it implies the boy's evaluation of the experience, not Horace's. Horace is not thinking of those who lose their lives at sea, but of those who have had a nasty fright. They could have been expected to know better. Horace does not withhold pity, but *miser* extends a curiously qualified pity: it is the word the elegiac poets use of themselves when they are helplessly in love—not so much 'miserable' or 'downcast' or 'dispirited,' for usually a kind of elation accompanies the lover's anguish, as 'having a lot to put up with.'[17] But there are overtones suggesting an acknowledgement of folly, that the lover should have had more sense; overtones which are apparent in Virgil's use of the word, in a very different context—the exclamation wrung from Aeneas when Anchises shows him the souls of the blessed, eager for reincarnation (*Aeneid* 6. 721):

quae lucis miseris tam dira cupido!

The second personal singular attaches *quibus intemptata nites* to Pyrrha, and both *intemptata* and *nites* might be used only of her, with no reference to sea imagery. But, like *nescius aurae fallacis,* the words become more meaningful once we perceive their double function: *nites,* the shimmering radiance of the sea gently stirred by a light wind (*aura*) on a fine day, provides a metaphor for Pyrrha's less easily described loveliness—an essentially linguistic problem this time, to solve which all words that connote 'shining,' 'glistening,' etc., are pressed into service by the Roman poets; *intemptata* is an uncommon word, but the verb *temptare* from which it comes suggests first a primary meaning 'unhandled' that passes easily into metaphorical meanings which can be represented by the translation 'not come to grips with'; the primary meaning is half drawn out, as we think of Pyrrha, by the *urget* of line 2, but the word is directed mainly at eliciting thoughts of the terror, equally unanticipated by lover and by traveller, that both will have to come to grips with when the storm breaks.

We feel toward the boy something like ironic condescension, when the final sentence brings an unexpected twist: the spotlight that has been turned on Pyrrha and the boy is switched off and Horace walks on to the stage himself. It is a trick Horace is rather fond of: in several odes a sentence beginning with *me* introduces the kind of transition we have here.[18] But, though boy and girl fade from sight, the double-edged sea imagery keeps them in our thoughts.

One purpose of the sentence is clear enough. Without it, Horace's confident prediction of trouble ahead for the credulous young lover must sound over-cynical; even if we accept the intellectual basis for Horace's prediction, his conviction that love is always impermanent and irrational, the rupture, though inevitable, needn't, we feel, turn out as Horace predicts. Couldn't it be the boy that will throw the girl over? Horace must tell us why he makes his prediction with such confidence. The answer is simple: Horace has weathered the storm himself. But he makes no attempt to describe the storm he experienced, for that would involve him in the kind of rhetoric he disowned in lines 5 and 6. Instead we have something much less grand.

It was a common practice in antiquity among those in peril on the sea to offer a gift to the appropriate divinity, to be placed, if the sailor's life was spared, at a conveniently adjacent temple along with a formal statement of the circumstances. We gather from a glance at the custom in *Aeneid* 12. 767–9, that it was also customary for the clothes in which the sailor was nearly drowned to be hung up in the shrine along with the promised gift. This is the image Horace chooses to end his poem with, an image that *uuida* makes gently humorous—Horace lost no time in carrying

out his promise. There is no tragedy here, only the story of someone who ran into trouble he hadn't perhaps bargained for, was
perhaps lucky to get out of it without disaster, but, having escaped, harbours no resentment against the universe.

At each point what is said of the sailor can be felt to hold good
of the lover. But it is an essential feature of the poem that the
equation Pyrrha=the sea is never made explicit: Pyrrha is never
said to be like the sea, or to be the sea; the sea is never *said* to be
like Pyrrha, or to be Pyrrha; the one experience is simply talked
of as though it were the other, using words that are sometimes
ambiguous, sometimes applicable to one of the two experiences
only. An essentially poetic technique circumvents the clumsy apparatus of logical argument.

Many commentators, bewildered by the way Horace talks about
one experience as though it were the other, have found the absence of a cross-reference intolerable. Some have sought to supply
one by turning the last word of the poem, *deo,* into *deae.* Mr. Nisbet is the latest to want to make Horace's meaning clear. 'If Horace did not write [*deae*]', he says (p. 183), 'he must have been
less than usually alert.' If you read *deae* (which is not found in
the manuscripts), then your potent divinity of the sea is Venus
—the Venus Marina of *Odes* 3. 26. And, not surprisingly, there are
many Greek epigrams which make capital out of the dual function
of Aphrodite as protectress of sailors and goddess of love. Heinze
quotes *A.P.* 5. 11, ascribed by some (though not by Heinze) to
Philodemus. Pasquali (pp. 499–501) discusses the *topos* at length
with several more examples. Actually the repair is unnecessary,
even if you assume Horace wants Venus to have the last word,
since *deo* can quite well refer to a female divinity.[19] But surely
it is better that we should no more than infer Venus' presence;
better that nothing in the sentence should point explicitly to the
goddess of love.

The careful reader who noted that, though *quis . . . gracilis
. . . puer?* indicates the boy is unknown to Horace, he knows the
girl since he addresses her by name, will be tempted to find in the
concluding sentence an explanation of her relationship; it doesn't
seem to require much imagination to sense, lined up beside Pyrrha's unhappy lovers yet to come (*miseri, quibus intemptata
nites*) a shadowy line of former lovers, among them Horace himself.

The sea imagery should warn us, however, against over-particu-
larization: the sailor setting out on his first voyage has heard about
storms; no amount of advice will dispel the confidence that the sea
on a calm day inspires in one who hasn't yet learned to know
better; but, having once faced and survived the danger of shipwreck, he learns not merely to beware of a particular stretch of
water, but to beware of all waters said to be dangerous. Pyrrha
is a type, after all: the beautiful, irresistible woman who goes

through life accepting and rejecting admirers, turning before long on those who claim to conquer her with an impersonal violence that it is almost arrogant of us to find cruel. To call such a woman a *Vampyr* is to miss something very like admiration in Horace's attitude to Pyrrha.

For the sailor who has just eluded shipwreck does not give up the sea.[20] He is properly grateful to the powerful divinity who answered his entreaties and spared his life. But from now on he is prepared for danger; he will never again put to sea with the same rash innocence; and he will watch with a mixture of amusement, cynicism and compassion the innocence of those who have yet to learn the lessons of experience.

NOTES

1. *Ad Pyrrham: A polyglot collection of translations of Horace's Ode to Pyrrha. . .*, assembled with an introduction by R. Storrs, edited by Ch. Tennyson (1959); Storrs's anthology comprises 144 versions.

2. J. W. Mackail, 'A lesson on an Ode of Horace' [*A Lecture in a Course for Teachers of the Classics, given at Oxford, 1920*], reprinted in *Studies in Humanism* (1938). Another symptom of scholarly reticence is to be found in Erich Burck's *bibliographische Nachträge* to the eighth edition of Heinze: 1.5 is almost the only well-known ode that failed to win scholarly attention in the period covered by Burck's list.

3. E. J. Kenney, reviewing Erich Burck's *Römische Liebesdichtung* (1961) in *Gnomon* 34 (1962) 313.

4. Commager's remark on *Odes* 3.9 is revealing (pp. 147–8): 'We may feel that the Ode's formal cast betrays its own distance from any real feeling.'

5. *E.g.*, by R. G. M. Nisbet, in *Critical Essays on Roman Literature* (Edited by J. P. Sullivan) vol. I: *Elegy* and *Lyric* (1962) 181–4. Nisbet's conclusion is: 'None of Horace's love-poems (if that is the right name for them) reaches the first rank.'

6. Viktor Pöschl, *Die Dichtkunst Virgils* (1950) 10.

7. F. Klingner, 'Wiederentdeckung eines Dichters' in *Das Neue Bild der Antike*, vol. II (1942) 219 ff.

8. *Horaz*, Kiessling's commentary re-edited by R. Heinze, *Oden und Epoden* (8th edn 1955) 31.

9. This seems, to me at any rate, an important component of Brecht's *Verfremdungseffekt*.

10. This aspect of the Pyrrha ode is well dealt with by Commager, and L. P. Wilkinson, *Golden Latin Artistry* (1963) 219–20.

11. I don't think we can gather much from other passages where Horace mentions women's hair, *Odes* 2. 11. 22–4, 3. 14. 21–2 and 4. 11. 5, except that he found the subject interesting; Ovid, *Ars* 3. 133–58, does his best to exhaust it.

12. I have discussed this question in *Latin Explorations* (1963), Chapter 6.

13. Catullus *Carm.* 70.

14. My terminology, which is intended to beg as few questions as

possible, is taken over from my article 'Syntactical ambiguity in Horace and Virgil,' AUMLA no. 14 (1960) 36–46.

15. Mackail (p. 67) notes this constructional ambiguity.

16. See *Latin Explorations*, p. 176

17. See *Latin Explorations*, p. 152.

18. Discussed by J. P. Elder *HSCP* 60 (1951) 114; he instances, as well as 1. 5. 13, 1. 1. 29, 1. 7. 10, 1. 16. 22 and 3. 5. 13.

19. The form *deus* is used (of Venus!) by Virgil in *Aeneid* 2. 632, and probably 7. 498. Servius on the former passage quotes a fragment of Calvus, *pollentemque deum Venerem; cf. Catulus'* epigram on Roscius, quoted in Kenneth Quinn, *The Catullan Revolution* (1959) 14. ✲

20. It is an error of careless reading to compare the Pyrrha ode with 3. 26 (*Vixi puellis nuper idoneus . . .*).

ADDENDUM

My interpretation of the Pyrrha Ode is discussed by David West in his *Reading Horace* (1967), 99–107. Mr West agrees with me in resisting those who complain that the poem lacks seriousness and involvement; but his interpretation suffers, in my opinion, from a somewhat limited vision of the imaginative and moral implications latent in Horace's sensitively organized poetic structure.

✲for *'Catulus''*] *read* 'Catulus''

LUXURY AND DEATH IN THE SATYRICON

William Arrowsmith

> Every book becomes clean just after one has read
> the New Testament: to give an example, it was
> with utter delight that, right after Paul, I read that
> most graceful, most prankish mocker, Petronius, of
> whom one might say what Domenico Boccaccio
> wrote to the Duke of Parma about Cesare Borgia: *è
> tutto festo*—immortally healthy, immortally cheer-
> ful, and well turned out.
>
> Nietzsche, *The Antichrist*, 46

THE SATYRICON IS A BOOK OBSESSED
with luxury (*luxuria*, that is) and death, and Trimalchio, the
central character of the central episode, is a man with wealth and
death very much on his mind. Throughout the entire banquet at
Trimalchio's house, Petronius plays on these fundamental themes
—mortality and money, surfeit and sickness, impotence and plenty
—intertwining them, with intricate variations, first gently, then
insistently, and finally blending them into the blaring brasses of
the apocalyptic funeral that closes the *Cena*. In technique the
Cena seems to be, and has always been regarded as, brilliant
realism. But that realism is directed and supported by remarkable
thematic concentration and symbolic economy. It is this thematic
concentration—its purpose and implications for the whole of the
Satyricon—that I want to consider here. It is my view that the
Satyricon, even in its mutilated and fragmentary state, possesses
remarkable coherence and unity, and that if we understand this
and the power of thought behind it, we shall be forced to revise
our estimate of Petronius' value. He has traditionally been re-

garded as a minor classical writer; it is my contention that Petronius is one of the greatest Latin writers, certainly the finest *imaginative* writer after Vergil, and easily the greatest master of Roman satire.

These are, I suppose, brave words. Any attempt to revise our estimate of a classic will inevitably seem an impertinence. A reasonable economy, it will be said, supports the notion that sixty or seventy generations cannot have been wholly mistaken about a classic. On the other hand the classics, simply because they are classics, are particularly susceptible to distortion and stultification. They constantly serve, after all, extraliterary purposes, and these other, "cultural" uses of the classic frequently interfere with critical judgment, preventing the reassessment, or even the assessment, of the work. Many classics—I think of Sophocles—are far more subversive of Christian culture than we suppose, and for this reason interpretations that reveal subversiveness are particularly resisted. This is oddly enough also the case with the *Satyricon*, which is traditionally classified—alongside Boccaccio and Rabelais, and even alongside Burroughs and Nabokov—as a "bawdy" or "surreptitious" classic. Hence the critic who wants to argue, as I do, that the *Satyricon* is a fundamentally serious and even moral work, a sophisticated Epicurean satire, is apt to sound as implausible as the critic who maintains that *Oedipus Rex* is really a comedy. And to some extent my difficulties are insensibly compounded by the picture of Petronius which Tacitus has left us (and Hollywood embellished)—that image of a refined, sybaritic, and corrupt courtier who ministered to Nero's pleasures and committed suicide like an Epicurean fop, languorously and courageously. A second objection is the fragmentary state of Petronius' work; we simply do not know whether the *Satyricon* was a big book or a small one, and this is unsettling. Doubtless the knowledge that the *Satyricon* is fragmentary has deterred critics from looking at it with analytical eyes, since no unity could be conclusively claimed. Certainly all I claim for my own interpretation is that it fits the fragments of the work as we have it, and fits them far too well to be dismissed as accidental. Finally, there is the superbly controlled realism of Petronius' narrative, a realism so convincing and colloquial, combined with so fine a satirical eye for detail, that one is tempted to look no further, to suppose that surface is everything. I myself translated the entire *Satyricon* without ever suspecting the presence of the

[123]

pattern which now seems to me so incontrovertibly *there*. The *Satyricon* I tried to translate was in fact the familiar *Satyricon* of literary history: a splendid bawdy novel, told with fine realism and a typically Roman relish for high sound, whose purpose was literary parody and broad comic satire of Neronian Italy. In all this there is, fortunately, nothing radically wrong. It was the underlying pattern that was missing.

To observe that pattern, we should look first at the *Cena*, the only complete episode of the book and the one in which the pattern is most clearly elaborated in its two central themes.

The setting is the house of Trimalchio, in a Greek settlement somewhere in the bay of Naples. Invited to dinner are a group of Trimalchio's freedmen friends and that trio of picaresque perverts—the narrator Encolpius, his friend Ascyltos, and his minion Giton—with whose adventures the story is mostly concerned.

Trimalchio, as I said earlier, is a man obsessed with death. And for that reason, I should like to plant here, large as life, the apocalyptic funeral in which the whole episode culminates, and then to show from the beginning how the pattern is developed and sustained. Toward the close of the *Cena*, Trimalchio, thoroughly drunk, reads his will aloud in the presence of those people who are to inherit from him, and then, with the entrance of Habinnas, a monumental mason, a maker of tombs, proceeds to order, in detail, his own tomb. Even this gruesome episode, however, is not enough to placate Trimalchio's obsession with mortality, and he concludes as follows, with full diapason, his whole being concentrated on death:

> "Take my word for it: money makes the man. No money and you're nobody. Big money, big man. That's how it was with yours truly: from mouse to millionaire.
>
> "In the meantime, Stichus," he called to a slave, "go and fetch out the clothes I'm going to be buried in. And while you're at it, bring along some perfume and a sample of that wine I'm having poured on my bones."
>
> Stichus hurried off and promptly returned with a white grave-garment and a very splendid robe with a broad purple

[124]

stripe. Trimalchio told us to inspect them and see if we approved of the material. Then he added with a smile, "See to it, Stichus, that no mice or moths get into them, or I'll have you burned alive. Yessir, I'm going to be buried in such splendor that everybody in town will go out and pray for me." He then unstoppered a jar of fabulously expensive spikenard and had us all anointed with it. "I hope," he chuckled, "I like this perfume as much after I'm dead as I do now." Finally he ordered the slaves to pour the wine into the bowl and said, "Imagine that you're all present at my funeral feast."

The whole business had by now become absolutely revolting. Trimalchio was obviously completely drunk, but suddenly he had a hankering for funeral music too and ordered a brass band sent into the dining room. Then he propped himself on piles of cushions and stretched out full length along the couch. "Pretend I'm dead," he said, "say something nice about me." The band blared a dead march, but one of the slaves . . . blew so loudly that he woke up the entire neighborhood. Immediately the firemen assigned to that quarter of town, thinking that Trimalchio's house was on fire, smashed down the door . . . Utter confusion followed . . . and we rushed out of there as though the place were really in flames.

(77.6–78.8)

If this is the note on which the *Cena* closes, it is also the note on which it begins. When we first hear of Trimalchio, we are told that he has "a great big clock in his dining room and a uniformed bugler (*bucinatorem . . . subornatum*) who blows a horn every hour so the old man won't forget how fast his time is slipping away." Death at the beginning and death at the end: death by bugles. The patterning will be obvious. But as the theme is developed, it begins to attach other themes to it, and then gradually to subsume them into a larger, more comprehensive theme—that satiety of body and spirit which is *luxuria*. Thus there is almost a cyclical rhythm here of associations between thematic ideas. The thought of death invariably arouses the thought of wealth; wealth brings thoughts of defecation (for wealth is symbolically a satiety that cannot evacuate itself). Defecation in turn brings thoughts of death and money. And so the tropes pursue each other in an end-

[125]

less chain, but also relentlessly forward to the finale—the vision of satiety and *luxuria* as a description of an entire culture, or that version of a culture which one might call, to borrow from Tertullian, *Romanitas*, and its living death.

The note is at first struck gently. Trimalchio orders a silver skeleton brought into the dining room and the servants flex it into "suggestive" postures, a scene which provides Trimalchio with the opportunity to recite a little poem on the theme of *carpe diem*—a drunken doggerel meditation on death:

> Nothing but bones, that's what we are,
> Death hustles us humans away.
> Today we're here and tomorrow we're not,
> So live and drink while you may.
> (34.10)

Now there is nothing in all this which is, for a Roman banquet, particularly unusual. Trimalchio's skeleton is merely a heightened version of the ancient custom of reminding people, even in the midst of their pleasures, of their mortality, a *memento mori*. Thus dining-room mosaics from Pompeii and elsewhere show us reclining skeletons or skeletons with an accompanying Greek inscription ΓΝΩΘΙ ΣΑΥΤΟΝ. Trimalchio's only refinement is to confound things further by using a silver skeleton and having it flexed, perhaps into sexual postures. But the innovations themselves serve insensibly to widen the theme—to extend *luxuria* beyond money to sex and death. The one thing Trimalchio does not know is what might be called the mortal modalities, and his whole concept of a feast, based upon satiety to the point of nausea or constipation, bears out his immense lack of knowledge. So terrifying is his own habit of *memento mori*, the skeleton which reminds him of death, that he drives himself toward death by satiety. By eating he proposes to forget death, to "seize the day" and to live; he passionately desires life, but with every mouthful he takes, he tastes death. And this (thoroughly Epicurean) point is made, I think, with extraordinary comic neatness and firm realism as well, in Trimalchio's famous constipation-speech at table:

> Well, anyone at table who wants to go has my permission, and the doctors tell us not to hold it in. . . . Take my word for it, friends, the vapors go straight to your brain [*anathy-*

miasis in cerebrum it]. Derange your whole system. I know
some who've died from being too polite and holding it in.
(47.4–6)

This seems on the surface like simple realism, an exquisite parody
of monumental vulgarity, but Petronius' point is also this: food
consumed to the point of satiety is an instance, a symbol, of
luxuria; the end of satiety is constipation; and flatulent vapors "go
straight to your brain and derange your whole system," and especially the reason which should, at least in Epicurean ethics,
control the appetites. "I know some who've died . . . from holding
it in." That is, *luxuria* is death, extinction of the rational will.

That this is everywhere Petronius' essential symbolism can be
seen by a brief glance at the obsessive *sexual* themes of the book.
Now it is odd, to say the least, that in the *Satyricon,* so commonly
regarded as a naughty or orgiastic book, successful sex of any
kind is rare, and that the impotence of the hero seems to provide
the mainspring of the plot. There is also the fact of perversion
which, it will be remembered, is the subject of explicit condemnation as *unnatural* in Eumolpus' epic effusion on the decay of
Romanitas (cf. 119.19–27). Though it is doubtless true that
classical attitudes towards homosexuality were more lenient than
our own, they were not entirely permissive, especially in the stern
context of Republican morality, and I am inclined to believe that
perversion is a theme in this book precisely because Petronius
believes that perversion and also impotence are typical symptoms
of a luxurious and unnatural society. And in the field of sexual
appetite, satiety, indulgence to the point of debility, appears as
impotence. As constipation stands to food, so impotence stands to
sexuality; both are the products of *luxuria* in a society which has
forgotten its cultural modalities and which cannot recover life,
except by Epicurean *askesis*—by rediscovering the sense of true
need, of necessary economy, in pleasure. The *pain* of loss is the
pain which is suffered by the constipated Trimalchio and the impotent Encolpius, and although their pain is comic to the reader,
to them it is total since it affects the appetites to which their whole
lives are in fact devoted. If your name happens to be Encolpius
—which means, literally, something like "The Crotch"—and you
are stricken with impotence, you are in some clear sense a dead
man. Circe makes the point abundantly clear in the mocking letter
she sends to Encolpius:

[127]

I have heard doctors say that impotent men are incapable of even standing up straight. So, my dear, you must take good care of yourself, or your paralysis will be total. Never before have I seen a young man in such *infirm* health, or *so close* to *death*. One might almost say you were *dead* already.
(129.5–6)

That this is Petronius' theme—the death which *luxuria* brings in sex, food, and language, that is, in the areas of energetic desire and social community—is made abundantly clear in the *Cena*. The evidence is, in fact, so overwhelming that I can deal with it only in the most schematic way. But those who will reread the episode with the connection between satiety and *luxuria* and death firmly in mind will quickly recognize the deliberate symbolic intent beneath the comic realism.

A few examples. After Trimalchio leaves the room, the freedmen's conversation is begun by Seleucus who, strange to say, has just come from the funeral of a man called Chrysanthus (which means, strange to say, Goldflower). Goldflower's funeral reminds Seleucus of what might be called a drunkard's modalities: "Just goes to show you. What are men anyway but balloons on legs, a lot of blown-up bladders? Flies, that's what we are. No, not even flies. Flies have something inside. But a man's a bubble. . . ." And on he goes, establishing the modal verities which will eventually appear inverted in the final scene, when the whole feast turns into a funeral.

Even small things assume the size of symbols when the context becomes so death-centered. Thus Trimalchio's famous remarks on the Sibyl—"For with my own eyes I saw the Sibyl at Cumae, hanging in a bottle, and when little boys asked her, 'Sibyl, what do you want?', she said, 'I want to die' "—begins to loom large, to look, in fact, remarkably like what Joyce called an "epiphany," one of those little revelations designed to set before the reader, like an explosion, the "whatness" of a particular event. And in this event it is clearly the death of *Romanitas*—*Romanitas* turned inside out and upside down in a slavish Saturnalia—which we witness at Trimalchio's dinner.

There, the linking of death and wealth and food is persistent, overwhelming. One of the freedmen is described by another as follows:

What a life he had! But I don't envy him. And, you know, he had a nice respectable business. *Undertaking. Ate* [my

[128]

italics] like a king: boars roasted whole, pastry as tall as buildings, pheasants, chefs, the whole works.

(38.14–15)

In short, what might be called the *luxuria* syndrome. When Trimalchio brags about his silver, he confuses not only the minor conventions of taste, jumbling together scenes from mythology with contemporary gladiatorial games, but the major modalities. "I've got a hundred bowls," he says, "all engraved with the story of Cassandra: how she killed her sons, you know, and the kids are lying there dead so naturally that you'd think they were still alive." Comic confusion, true; but also indicative of Trimalchio's governing inability to distinguish between the modalities.

In answer to Niceros' werewolf story, Trimalchio tells the tale of the slave who tried to fight off the witches, and the theme of death-in-life makes its appearance, introduced by the *luxuria* motif:

When I was just a little slave with fancy curls—I've lived in the lap of luxury from my boyhood on, as coddled as they come—my master's pet slave happened to die one day. He was a jewel all right, a little pearl of perfection, clever as hell and good as good. Well, while his mother was tearing out her hair and the rest of us were helping out with the funeral, suddenly the witches started to howl. They sounded like a whole pack of hounds on the scent of a hare. Now at that time we had a slave from Cappadocia, a giant of a man, scared of nothing and strong as iron. That boy could have picked up a mad bull with one hand. Well, this fellow whips out his sword and rushes outside with his left arm wrapped in his cloak for a shield. The next thing we knew he had stabbed one of those wild women right through the guts —just about here, heaven preserve the spot! Then we heard groans and when we looked out, so help me, there wasn't a witch to be seen. Well, our big bruiser came stumbling in and collapsed on a bed. He was covered from head to toe with black and blue spots as though he'd been flogged, though we knew it was that evil hand that had touched him. We shut the door and went back to work. But when his mother went to give him a hug, she found there was nothing there but a bundle of straw. No heart, no guts, no anything. As I see it, the witches had made off with the body and left

[129]

a straw dummy in its place. But it just goes to show you: there *are* witches and the ghouls go walking at night, turning the whole world upside down. As for our big meathead, after the witches brought him back, he was never the same again, and died raving mad a few days later.

(63.3–10)

No heart, no guts, no anything. Diagnosis: *luxuria*.

At the close of Trimalchio's dinner, the crescendos gather with the kind of obsessive power that makes analysis unnecessary. The decisive turning point is the entrance of Habinnas, a man who has grown rich by making grave monuments; he too, like Seleucus, has just come from a funeral. He gives a few meager comments on the funeral, and Trimalchio interrupts him: "But what did they give you to *eat*?" There follows a detailed description of dinner by Habinnas, the real point of whose speech is one more instance of the modalities in confusion. If Trimalchio turns a feast into a funeral, Habinnas turns a funeral into a feast, completely confounding life and death. It is this confusion, and the related theme of the living dead, that fill out the rest of the episode. Thus Habinnas' appearance—and his profession—not only announce the theme but permit Trimalchio to discuss his tomb and then to read his will aloud in public. That will is Trimalchio's only power over the living: nothing else sustains either him or those who depend upon him but that knowledge. "Nobody in this house," he says, alluding to his dog Scylax, "loves me as much as that mutt." And he is right. It is for this reason that he turns the feast into a funeral, in the hope of stimulating by the *pretence* of his own death the love and gratitude, the immortality of memory, which he covets but does not know he covets. It is a terrible picture, but one done in full realism and charity. No heart, no guts, no anything. This is what has happened to this society. "Never has there been greater lust for life (*maior cupido vitae*) or less care taken of it," says Pliny. The *numen,* the radiance in ordinary things, in simple necessities, the divine economy of Epicurean simplicity, has been destroyed by the compulsive, insatiable satiety of *luxuria,* by the *devouring* terror of death.

Consider the parallel theme of brutalization. Like the life-in-death theme, it is introduced naturalistically first and then widened in its implications until it reaches its climax at Croton. The distaste with which Petronius' contemporary Seneca viewed

[130]

the animal games of the Empire is well known. Spectators, gladiators, and animals all exist on a single common level; if anything, the spectators are lower than the animals. The emphasis in Petronius is extremely similar, as the quite Senecan passage in Eumolpus' effusion on the Civil War makes clear:

> Rome rampant
> on a victim world.
> New shapes of slaughter everywhere,
> Peace a pool of blood.
> With gold the hunters' snares are set:
> driving through Africa, on and on; the hunters at Hammon,
> and the beaters thrashing the thickets where the flailing
> tiger screams.
> Hunters, hawkers of death. And the market for murder at
> Rome:
> fangs in demand. At sea sheer hunger prowls the ships;
> on silken feet the sullen tiger pads his gilded cage,
> crouches at Rome, and leaps! And the man, gored and dying,
> while the crowd goes wild.
>
> (119.13ff)

That the sentiment here is Petronian, however, and not merely a parody of Lucan or Seneca, becomes clear in the remarkably apposite speech of one of Trimalchio's freedmen guests. During Trimalchio's brief absence from the table, the freedmen speak their minds openly. First Ganymedes makes a splendidly serio-comic speech on the decay of the times, rounding it off with the standard explanation of Rome's decay, that men have neglected the gods. To this the freedman Echion replies, somewhat irritably, that things are no worse than anywhere else—as though *that* argument disposed of Ganymedes' complaint. As evidence of his contention, he enthusiastically describes some forthcoming gladiatorial games and a public handout. First the gladiatorial games:

> And don't forget, there's a big gladiator show coming up the day after tomorrow. Not the same old fighters either; they've got a fresh shipment in and there's not a slave in the batch. You know how old Titus works. Nothing's too good for him when he lets himself go. Whatever it is, it'll be something special. I know the old boy well, and he'll go whole hog.

[131]

Just wait. There'll be cold steel for the crowd, no quarter, and the amphitheater will end up looking like a slaughterhouse. He's got what it takes too. When the old man died —and a nasty way to die, I'm telling you—he left Titus a cool million. Even if he spent ten thousand, he'd never feel it, and people won't forget him in a hurry either.

(45.4–6)

The phrase "like a slaughterhouse" catches us up and once again suggests the close link between food and death. And the coarse relish of Echion's enthusiasm is ironically concentrated in the remarks about the death of "old Titus'" father; Echion seems utterly unaware that the gladiators' death in the arena might also be a "nasty way of dying." Petronius thereby allows us to see both Echion's callousness to the gladiators and his attitude to Titus' father as governed by a common obsessive hunger for death in all its forms. Death, food, and money: these are Echion's world. And the obsessive theme is thereupon repeated for emphasis, this time in even sharper terms—food and death, interminably:

Well, they say Mammaea's going to put on a spread. Mmmm, I can sniff it already. There'll be a nice little handout all around. And if he does, he'll knock old Norbanus out of the running for good. Beat him hands down. And what's Norbanus ever done anyway, I'd like to know. A lot of two-bit gladiators and half-dead at that: puff at them and they'd fall down dead. Why, I've seen better men tossed to the wild animals. A lot of little clay statues, barnyard strutters, that's what they were. One was an old jade, another was a clubfoot, and the replacement they sent in for him was half-dead and hamstrung to boot. There was one Thracian with some guts but he fought by the book. And after the fight they had to flog the whole lot of them the way the mob was screaming, "Let 'em have it!" Just a pack of runaway slaves.

(45.10–12)

Now as stated, Echion's garrulous enthusiasms here are little more than a dramatically vivid and concentrated statement of the moralist's commonplace of "bread and circuses" (*panem et circenses*). The mode is seemingly realism, but the irony of Petronius' structure and symbolism again cuts deeper. It reveals, first,

[132]

what the satirist's denunciation does not, that the man Echion is literally brutalized by *what he sees* and *what he eats,* and this brutality is confirmed in the animal vigor of his language. In the second place, it shows starkly that "bread and circuses "are merely diverse expressions of the same fact—the satiety which is death. Satiety of food kills; satiety of death kills; satiety in the *Satyricon* is to become animal, to become all belly, pig or hog, wolf or cannibal.

That this is so the sheer volume of animal metaphors clearly indicates. "Women," says a freedman, "they're a race of kites." The Zodiac dish, as explained by Trimalchio, systematically equates men's fates with their animal equivalents. Trimalchio places nothing on his sign, which is Cancer, because he fears "queering" it, inviting disaster. The meaning he gives his sign is that he, like the crab, is at home on land or sea, because his possessions lie in both elements. The bad omen he tries to avert is death, death by Cancer, the inward crab. His fate is, of course, both: the cancer wealth which kills. "We're big lions at home, and scared foxes in public," comments a freedman on his own political hypocrisy. The centerpiece of the brutalization theme in the *Cena,* however, is Niceros' story of the werewolf, the soldier who turns wolf and slaughters the sheep. "The place looked like a butcher shop, blood all over," says Melissa, and we remember the arena, and how it is that men are turned into animals: by literal metamorphosis, by being eaten alive. And Habinnas promptly makes the echo explicit. Describing the funeral feast he has attended, Habinnas says that the *pièce de résistance* was bear meat, which is to say, strong meat. It was so strong that his wife lost her supper, but Habinnas put down about a pound of it, because, as he says, "it reminds me of wild boar, and besides . . . if bears eat men, why shouldn't men eat bears?" The transitions are revealing, as is the whole speech. Between wild boar and bear, there is no difference; satiety and savagery both equal death. Habinnas means by bears here precisely the bears of the arena, to whom criminals were fed. That is, Habinnas will be the thing he eats, just as Echion will be the thing he watches. But if bears eat men, what is the word for men who eat man-eating bears? Cannibals, surely.

If it were not for the scene at Croton, all this might perhaps seem merely so much tiresome ingenuity. But at Croton all the themes of brutalization are gathered up with supreme horror in a cannibal apocalypse. That cannibalism is the master metaphor is obvious. Croton itself is described as "a place which is like a countryside ravaged by the plague, a place in which you will see only two things: the bodies of those who are eaten and the carrion crows who eat them" ("oppidum tamquam in pestilentia campos, in quibus nihil aliud est nisi cadavera quae lacerantur aut corvi qui lacerant," 116.9). And the episode as a whole concludes with the reading of Eumolpus' will, which requires the people of Croton to become in fact what they symbolically are: cannibals. Here realism and symbolism combine to produce an effect of grotesque horror which is, I think, unique in literature prior to Swift. Here are Eumolpus' words:

> With the exception of my freedmen, . . . all those who come into money by the terms of my will shall inherit only upon satisfaction of the following condition: they must slice up my body into little pieces and swallow them down in the presence of the entire city. . . .
>
> *   *   *
>
> We know that in certain countries there exist laws which compel a dead man's relatives to eat his body. So rigorously, in fact, are these laws enforced that men who die of sickness or disease frequently find themselves reproached by their relatives for having made their meat inedible. So I warn my friends not to disregard my last wishes, but to eat my body as heartily as they damned my soul.
>
> *   *   *
>
> I am not in the least disturbed by any fear that your stomachs may turn. They will obey you quite without qualms so long as you promise them years of blessings in exchange for one brief hour of nausea. Just close your eyes and imagine that, instead of human flesh, you're munching a million. If that isn't enough, we'll concoct some gravy that will take the taste away. As you know, no meat is really very tasty anyway; it all has to be sauced and seasoned with great care before the reluctant stomach will keep it down. And if it's precedents you want, there are hundreds of them. The people of Saguntum, for instance, when Hannibal besieged them, took to eating human flesh, and did so, moreover, without the slightest hope of getting an inheritance out of it. And when a terrible famine struck Petelia, the people all became cannibals, and the only thing they gained from their diet

was that they weren't hungry any more. And when Scipio captured Numantia, the Romans found a number of mothers cuddling the half-eaten bodies of their children in their laps. . . .

(141.2 ff)

Like *hybris, luxuria* affects a man so that he eventually loses his sense of his specific function, his *virtus* or *aretē*. He surpasses himself, luxuriating into other things and forms. It is for this reason that the *Satyricon* is so full of luxuriant falsenesses, pretenses, fakes, metamorphoses. Forms of life are jumbled incongruously, transformed, degenerated. If men are bestialized both literally and metaphorically, Trimalchio's chef Daedalus is a wizard of changes, making "pigeons out of bacon, doves from ham, and chicken from pigs' knuckles." Out of a roast boar comes a flock of thrushes; out of another tumble sausages in imitation of intestines. Transvestism is everywhere: Encolpius walks with mincing steps, whorelike; Ascyltos' lips are painted scarlet; Eumolpus complains poetically of:

the mincing gait, effeminate, the girl-men, their hair curried to silk, and the clothes, so many and so strange, to mew our manhood up. . . .

(119.24–26)

If it is not perversion, it is posing, or play-acting, or simulation. Thus Giton feigns suicide and castration; Trimalchio apes the equestrian; a painted dog terrifies a man; Eumolpus plays slave owner. And everywhere the language of mime and rhetorical tragedy take over in situations of love or terror or passion, subverting them, emptying them of meaning. Hypocrisy, by etymology the actor's nature, touches everything. And behind hypocrisy stands *luxuria,* that abundance and satiety which make men lose their sense of human function and turn unnatural, or even bestial.

Associated with *luxuria* in food and sexuality is *luxuria* in language. In contrast to rhetoric or the *bella figura* of language grown luxuriant, Petronius sets his own ideal of "pure speech" (*sermo purus*) and "verbal candor" (*lingua candida*). The theme opens with Encolpius' splendid tirade against the Fury-haunted language of the schools, is continued in the parody of epic poetry put in Eumolpus' mouth, and concludes at Croton. Encolpius' tirade is directed particularly against excess in style, the so-called

"Asianic" or "opulent" manner represented by those "twin Atreidae" of fustian, the rhetoricians Agamemnon and Menelaus:

Action or language, it's all the same: great sticky honeyballs of phrases, every sentence looking as though it had been plopped and rolled in poppyseed and sesame. A boy gorged on a diet like this can no more acquire real taste than a cook can stop stinking. What's more, if you'll pardon my bluntness, it was you rhetoricians who more than anyone else strangled true eloquence. By reducing everything to sound, you concocted this ridiculous drivel, with the result that eloquence lost its sinew and died.

But in those great days when Sophocles and Euripides invariably found the exact word, talent had not yet been cramped into the mold of these set-speeches of yours. Long before you academic pedants smothered genius with your arrogance, Pindar and the nine lyric poets were still so modest that they declined even to attempt the grand Homeric manner. Nor are my objections based on poetry alone. What about Plato or Demosthenes? I never heard it said of them that they ever submitted to your sort of formal training. No, great language is chaste [*pudica*] language—if you'll let me use a word like "chaste" in this connection—not turgidity and worked-up purple patches. It soars to life through a natural, simple loveliness. But then, in our own time, that huge flatulent rhetoric [*ventosa istaec et enormis loquacitas*] of yours moved from Asia to Athens. Like a baleful star, it blighted the minds of the young; their talents shriveled at the very moment when they might have taken wing and gone on to greatness. And once the standards of good speech were corrupted, eloquence stopped dead or stuttered into silence. Who, I ask you, have achieved real greatness of style since Thucydides and Hyperides? Poetry herself is sick, her natural glow of color leached away. All the literary arts, in fact, cloyed with this diet of bombast [*omnia quasi eodem cibo pasta*], have stunted or died, incapable of whitening naturally into an honest old age. And in painting you see the same decay: on the very day when Egyptian arrogance dared to reduce it to a set of sterile formulas, that great art died.

(1.3–2.9)

What we should notice here is the way in which the terms used to describe *luxuria* in language are skilfully transferred from the related *luxuriae* of food and sex. Language in rhetorical use is like "great sticky honeyballs of phrases, every sentence looking as though it had been plopped and rolled in poppyseed and sesame." When Encolpius says that "eloquence lost its sinew," he means sexual sinew. Rhetorical language is impotent. For the same reason he tells us that "great language is chaste language" and then, as though to stress the point, adds: "if I may be permitted to use a word like 'chaste' in the connection." As for poetry, it is "sick," while all the other literary arts, "cloyed with this diet of bombast," have stunted or died. In sum, *luxuria* of language is on the same level as *luxuria* in food and sex; all three are symptoms of satiety and excess, and all three culminate in death unless controlled.

It is clearly part of Petronius' design that the section dealing with rhetoric, mostly lost, should be set against the *Cena*, with its pointed display of freedmen speech in all its vulgarity and energy. What is Petronius' attitude toward freedmen speech? It is not easy to say, but there are, I think, reliable hints. That it was genial snobbery, as many scholars seem to think, strikes me as quite untenable, a view borrowed from Tacitus' portrait of the fastidious Neronian courtier. Two factors militate against it. First is the fact that Petronius' effort here is unparalleled in Roman literature, and this tells us something about the bent of his mind, that he was not willing simply to indulge in contempt for vulgarity, but described it in minute and loving detail. And in a Mandarin literature like Latin, the fact is doubly unusual. Petronius' narrative, that is, deals precisely with those people who have traditionally been regarded, both in Latin and Italian, as "unworthy" of art, lives too sordid to be redeemed by rhetoric. The second hint is to be found in Encolpius' remarks to Agamemnon, when he inveighs against sophistic education as artificial, and complains that it keeps children "utterly ignorant of real life. The common experience is something they never see or hear [*nihil ex his, quae in usu habemus, aut audiunt aut vident*]." Where one speaks in this way, it is clear that one has something like "common culture" in mind, and also a common language—which is the sign of an integrated culture. It is my belief that Petronius views the speech of freedmen with amusement and delight in its energy—is there anything more self-evident in the whole *Satyricon* than the sheer electrical joy of language?—and that he saw in it something like the possibility of renewal, a source of freedom, invigoration, and reform for a language grown artificial, rhetorical, and stale. I cannot, of course, prove such a point, and I realize that such a view is at odds with the older view of Latin literature. But then so is the *Satyricon*. And in no point is it more unusual than in this relish for life in language, however vulgar, and the sympathy which is, despite satire and parody, diffused over all the freedmen alike.

What is Petronius' point then in the vulgar Latin of the *Cena*? Is he making merely the point that freedmen's culture is a hit-or-miss affair, compounded of bad mythology, garbled Vergil, vulgar astrology—in short, high-culture-in-caricature? That is, to be sure, one of his points. But he is also telling us, I think, of the failure of a Mandarin culture to diffuse itself, to make itself available. And his point is as much the snobbery and parasitism of the educated as the vulgarity of the freedman. If Trimalchio is capable of applauding an atrocious recitation of Vergil, Encolpius applies, with shocking effect, Vergil's splendid description of Dido's reception of Aeneas in the underworld, how she:

> *turned her head away* and gazed upon the ground . . .
> (132.11)

to his own impotence. If the freedmen vulgarize, Encolpius, Eumolpus, and Agamemnon *desecrate* the culture they profess. The point is important, I think, since it emphasizes the equality of educated and uneducated in a world whose sole standard is wealth. If the freedmen show that they secretly hate culture, Encolpius and Eumolpus are hypocrites and snobs whose culture is no more than a veneer. In practice, they betray it on every possible occasion.

With this in mind, consider Eumolpus' preface to that appalling parody of Lucan which Petronius assigns to him:

> Serious poets, of course, despise this dilettante approach to their art; from hard experience they know that the imagination is utterly incapable of conceiving, let alone producing, a real poem unless the poet's mind has been literally saturated in the poetry of the past. Cliché and cheap language, for instance, must be ruthlessly resisted. No great poetry has ever been founded on colloquial language, language that has

[138]

been, so to speak, debased and corrupted by popular usage. Its motto is that of Horace: *I loathe the vulgar crowd, and shun it.*

(118.3–4)

These words are, I think, an accurate description of traditional upper-class Roman attitudes toward literary culture, and their parody in the poem which Eumolpus claims is based upon such principles makes Petronius' lack of sympathy evident. Needless to say, the poem does not necessarily impugn the principles, but Petronius here suggests, I think, that the luxurious and self-indulgent language which Eumolpus regards as traditional and elegant is in fact more corrupt than the language against which he protests. And its corruption is clear in the luxuriousness which it exhibits even while excoriating the death of a culture by general *luxuria*. Typically Petronius makes any part of his work do double duty, and this epic on the Civil War is no exception. It is not only that Eumolpus' rank and tortured language proves his poetic point—that *luxuria* did destroy Rome—but that Eumolpus elsewhere is a flagrant practicer of the very moral vices he so roundly lashes here, particularly pederasty. He is, in short, the hypocrite of a traditional culture, whose values have become words without substance—that is, rhetoric.

This theme of *luxuria* in language is finally rounded off at Croton. Our evidence is fragmentary, a single unfinished sentence, but it makes the point with great effectiveness. Eumolpus makes his announcement that the people of Croton must turn cannibals in order to inherit from him, and then the text says merely: "Gorgias stood ready to manage the funeral. . . ." Petronius' names are almost always used to carry meaning, either ironic or descriptive. In this case the meaning is descriptive: Gorgias as the actual founder of sophistic rhetoric, the man who first systematically developed the artificial style, and whose language later became a model of the Asian manner. Gorgias, as Petronius observes, is always professionally willing to assist at a funeral. That is his profession: undertaker of language.

One incident in particular—the speech of the freedman Echion —reveals Petronius' attitude to culture and class, as well as the extraordinary economy of his narrative. Childlessness is, among the Roman moralists, the typical trait of an unnatural society organized on the principle of *luxuria*. It is also an overt theme in the *Satyricon*, culminating in the cannibalism at Croton, and the final sentence of the book: "When Scipio captured Numantia, the Romans found a number of mothers cuddling the half-eaten bodies of their children in their laps." The Numantine mothers could at least have pleaded necessity, whereas the Roman mother can only plead profit. And, as a general rule, children appear in the *Satyricon* only to be prostituted by their parents or tutors, either literally as in the story of Philomela, or figuratively in the words of the rhetorician Agamemnon: "As with everything else, even the children are sacrificed on the altar of [their parents'] ambition" (4.2). And typically these prostituted children are less innocent and more corrupt than their corruptors: one thinks of Giton, or the children of Philomela, or the boy in the Pergamene episode. These are, of course—like Nabokov's Lolita—the children of satire: they exist as exaggerations, meant to make a special, shocking point about the toxicity and pervasiveness of *luxuria*. There is, however, one instance—and only one—in the book, which deals with something like normal, everyday paternity, and this is the case of the freedman Echion. For this very reason, its uniqueness and realism, the account has a particular significance.

Echion's speech begins as a rambling answer to Ganymede's attack on the times, and its relish for gladiators and death is part of the over-all theme. Before long Echion's vulgar relish for the games evidently brings a pointed yawn from the "refined" Agamemnon, and Echion replies in some irritation:

> Well, Agamemnon, I can see you're thinking, "What's that bore blabbing about now?" You're the professor here, but I don't catch you opening your mouth. No, you think you're a cut above us, so you just sit there and smirk at the way we poor men talk. Your learning's made you a snob.
>
> (46.1)

One notes parenthetically here that Petronius' genius for dialogue lies partly in his managing to give, simply by warping the speech of the speaker, the sense of the response to the speech. Echion thereupon proceeds to ask Agamemnon to his house, an invitation which must have met with doubtful response from Agamemnon since Echion promptly reassures him, "Don't you worry, you'll find food." Theme and realism merge here; it is only the promise of a good meal that can move Agamemnon, just as Agamemnon

[140]

adapts his rhetoric to the hunger of his audience. Echion knows his man. He then proceeds as follows:

> You remember that little shaver of mine? Well, he'll be your pupil one of these days. He's already doing division up to four, and if he comes through all right, he'll sit at your feet someday. Every spare minute he has, he buries himself in his books. He's smart all right, and there's good stuff in him. His real trouble is his passion for birds. I killed three of his pet goldfinches the other day and told him the cat had got them. He found some other hobby soon enough. And, you know, he's mad about painting. And he's already started wading into Greek and he's keen on his Latin. . . . The older boy now, he's a bit slow. . . . Every holiday he spends at home, and whatever you give him, he's content. So I bought him some of those big red law books. A smattering of law, you know, is a useful thing around the house. There's money in it too. He's had enough literature, I think. But if he doesn't stick it out in school, I'm going to have him taught a trade. Barbering or auctioneering, or at least a little law. The only thing that can take a man's trade away is death. But every day I keep pounding the same thing into his head: "Son, get all the learning you can. Anything you can learn is money in the bank. . . . Take my word for it, son, there's a mint of money in books, and learning a trade never killed a man yet."
>
> (46.3–7)

One notices immediately the delicate double viewpoint that Petronius brings to bear upon the monologue. Echion's younger boy is simply a reader, one of those wonderful childlike readers, who read because they are rapt away, quite without motive, for the sheer joy of it, in a state of what one might call free innocence, the condition of all true education. To Echion, however, the innocence is regrettable, because impractical. It is on a level with the three goldfinches, and he reveals his gratuitous practical brutality in killing them. And so he rambles on, everywhere advancing his own motives, and finally culminating with the practicality that education is good because it makes money. Indeed, the whole section is a superb example of Petronius' wonderful skill in mingling and reporting double realities. Echion the gladi-

[141]

ator-enthusiast has a son who reads, who keeps pet goldfinches (which his father kills); it is a familiar, but subtly observed, pattern. The picture of Echion himself is remarkably vivid: an affectionate father, proud of his children, coarse-natured, with a strong streak of practical brutality. He has an awareness of money which is downright Roman, hard-headed and shrewd; he feels ambiguous toward culture—he thinks he admires it, but actually despises it unless it produces money. But it is important to note the *rounded* quality of the portrait—we are not being offered a stock portrait of freedman vulgarity, but a portrait based upon clear, realistic contempt, with some sympathy. There is nothing exaggerated: such, we are meant to think, must have been a middle-class freedman. If Echion does not understand the fineness of his son's nature, the point is that these things go together, that where there is death, there is life; too much brutality creates the reaction of gentleness; coarse fathers often have fine children. It is an important point.

Can we leave the *Satyricon* at that? The moralist Petronius, preoccupied to the point of nausea and despair by the hopelessness of a culture corrupted by *luxuria*, a culture which turns men into the living dead, which degrades, desecrates and finally annuls, a culture without joy, without hope, without animal faith? This is where a recent critic, Miss Helen H. Bacon, for instance, leaves him. Side by side, in fact, with T. S. Eliot. In Miss Bacon's own words:

> Sweeney, Doris, Mr. Eugenides, Encolpius, Trimalchio, Circe, Giton,
>
> > De Bailhache, Fresca, Mrs. Cammel, whirled
> > Beyond the circuit of the shuddering Bear
> > in fractured atoms. . . ,
>
> a polyglot society with no realities but money, and frustration. The over-educated Greek and the Syrian freedman are atoms adrift in the heterogeneous world which Rome ruled without uniting. The safe, parochial standards of their individual cultures have been invalidated, by science, by comparison with other cultures, by the sheer brutality of experience in a world of famine, where luxury tries to tease the satiated senses into the appearance of life. The Sibyl is the

symbol for this waste land as well as Eliot's. With this difference, perhaps, that to Petronius she does not seem to suggest the possibility of rebirth when the longed-for death has been achieved. . . . The heart is dead. Love is an attitude.

. . . The "Satyricon," like the "Waste Land" contains a series of rapes, seductions, intrigues, and esoteric sexual adventures in high and low life. And here too is sensuality without joy, satiety without fulfillment, degradation without grief or horror.

The traditional comparison to Aristophanes, Rabelais, and Sterne is as inappropriate for Trimalchio and Encolpius as it is for Sweeney and Doris. Real laughter is rare in Petronius. There is little joy. The characters lack just what Eliot's characters lack—the feeling of being alive, the sense of good and evil.*

It is all a little depressing. Right up to a point, Miss Bacon sees for the first time that the *Satyricon* is not a symptom of a corrupt society, but a penetrating *description* of it, remarkably like Fellini's *La Dolce Vita*. And she also sees what almost no other scholar has seen—that Petronius' narrative, though realistic on the surface, is controlled with extraordinary symbolic and structural skill. But when she forces the whole book to yield that Christian, almost Manichaean, desolation of Eliot's *Waste Land*, she goes, I think, deeply wrong. And when, in order to support this view, she denies that the *Satyricon* is basically comedy, and that the characters are not alive, I think she is violating her text, its plain comic ambitions and its extraordinary liveliness in both life and language. Whatever else readers have made of Petronius, nobody has ever denied him a fundamental gaiety; the gaiety may seem wicked or innocent, but *gaiety* is the word for the book. Indeed it is this very gaiety which has prevented scholars from seeing what is, I maintain, so obviously there—the deep, searching analysis of the death throes of classical *Romanitas*. Like many

* "The Sibyl in the Bottle," *Virginia Quarterly Review* 34 (1958) 276, 267.

scholars and good Christians, Miss Bacon tends to assume either that comedy and moral seriousness are incompatible, or that deep gaiety and the description of cultural decay are incompatible. She is, I believe, wrong.

Is it really true that there is little laughter in the *Satyricon*? But what response are we intended to make to Trimalchio's table conversation on the topic of constipation? That it is vulgar? And nothing more? When Encolpius says, "I don't know whether to be angrier with my mistress for seducing my boy, or with my boy for seducing my mistress," are we to note, with appropriate solemnity, that Petronius is describing the quandary of sexual ambiguity? Is the story of Philomela and her children only satirical description? What Miss Bacon fails to notice is that Petronius' charity is the source of his comic attitude—a charity which is based upon realism, a resolute cheerfulness in the face of the facts of human nature, and it is this good cheer that represents him best: the good cheer derives from relation to the realities, the modalities, and not from a sick indulgence of degeneration like Seneca's, or narrow-minded and heavy-handed denunciation in the manner of Juvenal.

What about the characters? Do they "lack the sense of being alive, of good and evil"? The very words are revealing in themselves, with their suggested equation of "life" and "the sense of good and evil." A sense of "good and evil" is precisely what these characters don't have; life they *do* have. Like children, precisely, and what this means is nothing less than an improbable kind of innocence, a *comic* innocence in which immoral actions are incongruously set against a fundamental and rather charming naiveté. Encolpius' deepest trait is innocence; he is either beyond or below good and evil. His love for Giton is, true, pederasty, but it is also love—and what is more, it is unrequited love, as Petronius takes pains to show us. If we recognize Encolpius' deformity and pathos, we are also meant to recognize that he is not a monster, but pathetic. For all his defects, Encolpius has the basic gifts of life: love, generosity—poverty and bad luck. He is a marginal man, an Augie March, or even a dissolute Huck Finn, one of those who refuse to turn cannibal, to ape the ape, to brutalize themselves. With the gift of life, he has other traits which belong to death. Eumolpus may be an atrocious poet, a lower-class Lucan, a hypocrite, a pederast, and a thief, but he also has *style*; he is like Khruschev in Frost's description, "a grand old ruffian."

[144]

And however we may finally condemn those characters, we must bear in mind that they are all fictive devices for bringing society to account. Just as Nabokov in *Lolita* shows us that poor old Humbert is an amateur of vice compared to Lolita, that sub-teen-age professional, so Petronius sets his charming rascals and rogues in sharp contrast to society's greater immoralism, hypocrisy and vulgarity. Compared to the people of Croton, Eumolpus and En-colpius are likeable and innocent con-men, the bearers of poetic justice.

Another example is the treatment of Lichas, not what anybody would call a sympathetic character. Merchant, captain, and per-vert *par excellence,* he is cruel, jealous, proud, and unforgiving —even his very name is an obscenity, though he too has famous forebears. But when he dies in the wreck of his own ship, and his body drifts slowly shoreward, the tone of the narrative suddenly changes. Encolpius feels the tears tugging at his eyes, and reflects:

> But drowned! To think our every human hope must some-day come to this, this corpse of great ambitions, this poor drowned body our dreams! O gods, and was this once a man, this thing that floats now merely?
>
> (115.10)

And then he recognizes that the body is that of Lichas, and bursts into tears, weeping openly, unashamedly at the death of his enemy:

> O god, how far he lies from his destination! Why, doom is everywhere, at any time. . . . Why, if you calculate our chances in this life, what do they cry but death? Shipwreck is everywhere. . . .
>
> (115.15–16)

Encolpius is given to melodramatic outbursts, but the language here is not that of melodrama; it is that of mourning. Petronius crowns the death of the despicable Lichas with a funeral oration, and what gives this oration force and power is precisely the sense that Lichas, for all his crippled life, carries, in his death, the whole tragedy of human existence, helplessness, and futility. We feel what we feel at the funerals of strangers; that our lives and deaths are involved in theirs, that we mourn all men in every

[145]

funeral. If life refuses us solidarity, death does not. Encolpius' compassion is total, not sentimental. And behind it stands, I think, Petronius' extraordinary charity. Total clarity and total charity, with nothing missing.

Finally there is the story—I almost want to say "parable"—of the Widow of Ephesus (111 ff). In context an urbanely cynical Milesian fable on the inconstancy of women, it also immediately and forcibly suggests a wider symbolic meaning. When Christopher Fry based his charming *A Phoenix Too Frequent* upon the Widow of Ephesus, he did no more, I think, than dramatize the obvious symbolic intent of Petronius' tale. The symbolism itself is still another of Petronius' vivid oxymorons, but one this time weighted on the side of life rather than death: the symbolism of love-in-the-tomb, of life rising phoenix-like from its own ashes. Against Trimalchio, who turns a feast of living men into a funeral, is set the story of the soldier who celebrates his marriage in the tomb. The design could hardly be more schematic, and it is confirmed by the convergence of all the familiar themes of the *Cena*, but this time inverted. Thus whereas the *Cena* insists that satiety is death, the story of the Widow insists upon the stimulus conferred on desire by denial, frugality, *askēsis*. The widow's vigil for her dead husband, we learn, takes her to the point of starvation before she is tempted by the soldier's food. As for the soldier's supper, it was, we are told, a "little one," "a frugal repast" (*cenula*), but evidently it satisfied. At least Petronius immediately proceeds:

> Well, you know what temptations are normally aroused on a full stomach. So the soldier, mustering all those blandishments by means of which he had persuaded the lady to live, now laid determined siege to her virtue.
>
> (112.1)

And the result of his siege is, as we know, the consummation of love in the tomb, love doing its work beside the corpse of the dead husband. *Consummation*: the very word itself, set against the pervasive theme of sexual impotence, is revealing. And when to the fact of consummation we add the only instance in the book of satisfied heterosexual love, the force is doubled. Here Petronius seems to be saying, I give you an image of the rebirth of human life; here are the hope and energy, which everywhere else are

baffled by satiety and thereby transformed into death. In place
of perversion, natural marriage; in place of impotence, consummation; in place of unappeasable appetite, satisfied desire; in place
of death, life. It is the same miracle that occurs elsewhere in the
books, but always oppressed by circumstances, or overwhelmed
by its context—the flock of thrushes which bursts from the stomach
of the roast boar served at Trimalchio's; the gentle goldfinch-
and-book-loving son of the coarse freedman Echion. And finally
it is thematically bound up with those splendid bursts of poetry
which throughout the book seem to hover over the action like
blessings of fertility or shapes of irrecoverable felicity, our lost
power and innocence. Thus when Encolpius and Circe make their
first ill-fated attempt at love, the scene is haunted not only by the
memory of Odysseus and another Circe, but of the even greater
scene that all human love-making tries to imitate, in fertility and
naturalness:

> Such flowers as once on Ida's peak the fruitful earth
> in gladness spilled, when Jupiter with Juno lay
> in lawful love, and all his heart was touched to flame:
> bursting roses blew, and violets, and such,
> and from the fields, like snow, the sudden lilies laughed.
> Such earth, it seemed, as summons Venus to the grass:
> the light spilled brighter, bursting on our hidden love. . . .
> (127.9)

Like everything in Petronius, the effect of these miraculous de-
scents of the poetic dove is multiple. They are emblems of lost
power, great memories against which the corruption of the present is measured, but with which the future is also blessed. Eating
and sex, sex and food, it is all rehearsal, repetitions which are
designed to recover the old rapture and rediscover the divine
presence, the *numen,* with which the world once was filled, the
world of our beginnings, *illud tempus.* Every whore, every woman
in love, recalls Circe; every Encolpius has the hope of being
Odysseus; this is a countryside where, as Quartilla says, "one
might more easily meet a god than a man." That is the *hope,* not
the *fact*; but it is a hope of which Petronius, even in the midst of
so much degradation and death, never loses sight. If society has
organized itself around the satiety that brings death, man's hope
is to rediscover the old pagan landscape, the radiance here and

[147]

now, in which everything had *numen,* and nobody needed eternal life because life itself was good and had god in it. As a description of cultural crisis, the *Satyricon* is as extraordinary an achievement as Joyce's *Ulysses,* and is as fundamentally bright, cheerful, and gay. But Petronius is also the last great witness to the pagan sense of life, and the last classical author in whom we can feel the firmness of moral control that underlies the Greek tragedians.

To see the *Satyricon* this way is, I know, to see it as it has not been seen before, but this does not deter me. For clearly, if I am right, Petronius is squarely in the Latin moralist and satirical tradition—and the greatest moralist of them all. The *Satyricon* is a book about the loss of the modalities, but a book whose effortless good cheer, whose *comic* control, require a writer who made his peace with necessity. Comedy, great comedy, requires nothing less; of all the genres of literature, it is the one which most requires balance, wholeness, sanity, and the comprehensive sense of human life. Juvenal can only *denounce* vice because his humanity is not large enough to confront what is disorderly and anarchic and dangerous in human life. But Petronius *describes* with realism, and that realism allows him to keep faith with man by keeping faith with the possibilities and realities of men. What matters is not pleasure but being rapt away by need, rediscovering joy and eternal life by the discovery of the necessary and the possible, the economies of body and spirit. There is none of the Christian hatred of life and the body here—like bread or wine, the body is good, provided that its function and powers are not abused. In both satiety and asceticism lies death. And what matters is not the dingy virtue of self-control or spiritual calisthenics, but being carried along rapturously by one's necessities. In short, by love of fate, *amor fati.* To rediscover the reality of need, the joy of acceptance of one's fate, the submission to the world as it is—this is the classical sense of life *par excellence.* What it requires, of course, is not less than everything, including pain. Submission is not easy, as those who suffer the pain of submission know, but the only pain which can be borne with something like joy and gaiety is that pain. Nietzsche, better than any other modern writer, reveals the pain and the rebirth which *amor fati,* love of fate, creates:

> Only great pain is the ultimate liberator of the spirit. . . .
> Only great pain, that long, slow pain in which we are burned

[148]

with green wood, as it were—pain which takes its time—only this forces us . . . to descend into our ultimate depths and to put away all trust, all mere good-naturedness, all that would veil, all mildness, all that is average, things in which formerly we may have found our humanity. I doubt that such a pain makes us "better," but I know that it makes us more *profound*. . . . What is strangest is this: afterwards one has had a different taste—a *second* taste. Out of such abysses . . . one returns newborn, having shed one's skin, more ticklish and sarcastic, with a more delicate taste for joy, with a more tender tongue for all good things, with gayer senses, with a second dangerous innocence in joy, more childlike and yet a hundred times more subtle than one has ever been before.

That is the pagan spirit, the spirit of Petronius.

PETRONIUS: ARTIST OR MORALIST?

J. P. Sullivan

AN EVALUATION OF PETRONIUS that will convince everyone is perhaps impossible: the *Satyricon*, as we have it, even after the most searching attempts at reconstruction, is too fragmentary, the movement and the denouement of the plot too obscure. But there is enough of it left to allow some sort of judgment on its merits as a cultural and literary document, and a more or less informed assessment of its probable intentions and success. Were enough not extant, it would be hard to explain, pragmatically or plausibly, the interest aroused by it and the labors expended on it. Several obstacles have stood in the way of any attempt to see what its virtues are, or to relate it to the development of Latin literature in general: besides the mutilated text, the persistent doubts about its date and authorship, although, to my mind, largely unnecessary, made critical comment hazardous, just as the scabrous nature of some of the episodes made a scholarly interest in the work eccentric or suspect. (Arguably, the whole question of the sexual strain that runs through Latin literature—and Greek, for that matter—is overdue for serious scrutiny, with the hope of separating what is, and what is not, of true literary and human interest to the twentieth century. But perhaps, as a recent bowdlerization of Catullus suggests, classical scholarship is not quite ready for this.) It was, no doubt, this lack of moral earnestness, real or apparent, and its *recherché*, and therefore incomprehensible, literariness that militated against its survival intact through those early centuries whose growing Christianity went hand in hand with increasing intellectual barbarism. The rather specialized nature of its sexual interests—homosexuality, voyeurism, and castration—and its learnedly allusive and blatantly topical qualities might appeal as a combination to a *jeunesse dorée* of low habits and refined tastes, but hardly to those whose hopes of heaven denied them a number of more earthly interests. A modern reaction to this standard view has been to read into the work the sort of seriousness we associate with the classics of moral satire or the philosophical novel.

In an earlier issue of ARION, Kenneth Rose[1] tried to dispel, as far as possible, the factual uncertainties about the *Satyricon* and its historical setting; in his essay on Juvenal, H. A. Mason[2] tried to counter certain critical, perhaps even unconsciously moral, assumptions about the necessary nature and spirit of all satiric writing in Latin literature. Similarly, I will argue that however we finally evaluate his achievement, Petronius was, in certain clear senses, a literary opportunist. Menippean satire presumably suggested itself as a very suitable form for such opportunism because of the comparative freedom it offered in terms of structure and theme. The *Satyricon*, as Rose has pointed out, was almost certainly written for the amusement—or, I would add, for the *literary* instruction at most—of Nero's court circle. There seems evidence that it was used, incidentally and without too great a fuss, not only to present a classical critique and an Epicurean theory of literature, but also to snipe at various literary and philosophical targets: Lucan and Seneca, rhetorical moralizing, and Stoic doctrine in general.[3] What prompted the dislike behind this sniping, whether personal antipathy, literary or philosophical disagreement, the wish to please or influence the emperor, we naturally have no means of deciding. Luckily the personal motives of an artist are irrelevant to an assessment of his esthetic principles. Such principles underlie an author's responsible choice of sexual, local, biographical, political, or literary themes, and dictate his handling of them; as such they are a proper subject of our concern. They may be invoked to explain local inadequacies or limitations, just as the unifying vision behind the work determines our total impression of its larger intentions and its classic status.

The main critical question is: Was Petronius a true satirist? There have been many attempts to make him one, and, as with any classical author, the defense counsels have been learned and ingenious. He has been credited with personal satire against his own ex-slave, against various court ladies such as Agrippina, and even against Nero himself; he has been depicted as dwelling on the turbulence and unhappiness of passion and vice simply to inculcate the lessons of Epicurean *ataraxia* and contented imperturbability; he has been ascribed more traditional castigation of the luxury, materialism, and sensuality of his Roman contemporaries; and, more subtly, he has been praised as seeing the skull beneath the skin of his world, of seeing around him a Waste Land, with fear in a handful of dust. This Waste Land is supposedly represented in the *Satyricon* by such things as Trimalchio's obsession with death and by the sterile childlessness and materialistic preoccupations of his company. The only sane answer amid all this is that given by the Sibyl to the teasing children: "I want to die" (48.8). Doubtless T.S. Eliot's use of this story as an epigraph for *The Waste Land* helped, if it did not suggest, such a critical interpretation. The world that Petronius presents, then, would be

> A heap of broken images, where the sun beats,
> And the dead tree gives no shelter. . . .

I find it difficult, however, to substantiate any of these interpretations. There seems to be an occasional hit at some contemporary fashion at court or at large, but the theory of a consistent satire, directed against a person or persons, will not stand up to an examination of the literary and historical evidence. The positive advocacy of a morality which is associated more with Epicurus himself than with his later, less orthodox, Roman followers, such as Lucullus and Petronius, an advocacy posited by the more strenuously moral apologists for the work, seems flatly contradicted, not so much by what we know of the author's own life—that is critically irrelevant—but by the views expressed at 133.15, where Epicurean principles about literature and sex are invoked to quite different effect.

This has been recognized as a key passage for our interpretation of the work. It is eight lines of verse in which the author, in a sort of aside to his audience and in a grotesquely humorous context, Encolpius' address to his genitals, explains part of his intentions and principles in a defense of the sexual subjects of the *Satyricon* and his literary treatment of them. It runs:

> quid me constricta spectatis fronte Catones,
>   damnatisque novae simplicitatis opus?
> sermonis puri non tristis gratia ridet,
>   quodque facit populus, candida lingua refert.

> nam quis concubitus, Veneris quis gaudia nescit?
> quis vetat in tepido membra calere toro?
> ipse pater veri doctos Epicurus amare
> iussit, et hoc vitam dixit habere τέλος.

A translation of this would not be very helpful, but the following paraphrase perhaps brings out Petronius' meaning:

> The work you are now hearing no doubt provokes the usual strictures from the more censorious who believe that, in accordance with Stoic principles and literary theories, a work of art should be instructive and moral, not least in the narrowest sense of that term. Such critics will condemn this work, which is a reaction against our present modes of writing and old-fashioned puritanism, and has its own literary and stylistic intentions. Its pure Latinity has one end: to charm you, not to instruct you. My subject is human behavior and the narrative is realistic, although *honest* might be a better way of describing it. No one is unaware of the important place sex has in ordinary life. Does anyone take a moral stand against harmless and natural sexual enjoyment and comfort? As an Epicurean, I could even invoke philosophical principles in their defense and point to Epicurus' doctrines about its supreme importance.[4]

Similarly the passages in the prose and the verse that present some straight moralizing, and which are used to buttress the theory that Petronius, in a conventional but sincere manner, is satirizing the vices of his times, become suspect through the irony of their context, because of the disreputability of the *personae* that utter them, and in the light of their parodic intentions. Even the subtler, though (to me) anachronistic, interpretation that claims a consciously felt and expressed *Angst* or *Weltschmerz* simply does not survive an inspection of the humorous irony that pervades the work, and the interested vitality that comes through all the elaborate literariness. Such evidence for this interpretation as may be collected from the repetitive themes and images of death in the *Cena* may be more plausibly seen as examples of philosophical parody or satiric characterization: the middle and lower classes of many societies *are* preoccupied with money, and many Romans, including Pacuvius and Seneca, were, like Trimalchio, obsessed with the thought of death, whether their attitude was one of didactic resignation or fearful preparation. But these aspects of the *Cena* seem to me to derive from the satirical and amused observation, not the disgusted and symbolic condemnation, of a society.

The words "satire" and "satirical" turn up constantly, when one is clarifying Petronius' aims, techniques, and achievements. And it may seem paradoxical to deny him his status as a major satirist in spite of this. But Petronius' use of the satiric mode, however original and inventive in some ways, is not, as it were, *classical*: he employs themes and techniques, he follows certain models, of the genre, but he is not interested in morality in the larger sense, but only in art. And this means that the centrality of the great satirists, Horace at his best, Persius, Donne, Pope, and Johnson, for instance, is beyond him—or is not his main concern, depending on the criteria we choose to apply.

When I speak of "great satire," I do not mean "negative" satire, although this may be forceful and brilliant. Satire has always presented critical problems, and there is (or used to be) a tendency to dismiss all satirists as somehow impure or inferior artists, or think of them in terms recalling Louis Macneice's lines:

> He is not creative at all, his mind is dry
> And bears no blossoms even in the season,
> He is an onlooker, a heartless type,
> Whose hobby is giving everyone else the lie.

The best satire, to my mind, has to be conceived as an art form that is self-avowedly concerned in some sense with morality (including under this head esthetic and intellectual principles) and it expresses, implicitly or explicitly, an ethical or para-ethical standpoint. This constitutes, as it were, the center from which the description and the treatment of the objects of the satire emerge. The best satire embodies, in proper artistic form, a coherent and positive sensibility. One need hardly point out that just to have a moral or semimoral position and good intentions is not enough: it is the intimate fusion of art and morality that makes satire *literature*. This also generates the critical problems, particularly as the reader does not have to, and often does not, share the ethical assumptions of the satirist.[5] But the triumphs, the paradigms, of the genre, *The Dunciad*, *The Vanity of Human Wishes*, effectively dispel any a priori doubts we might feel.

A satirist of this type Petronius is not. He is, so to speak, Alexandrian—in the modern rather than the ancient sense. His unswerving devotion to literature and his more or less coherent esthetic theory go hand in hand with a deliberately limited "realism"; it looks like the selective and seamy "realism" of the genuine satirist, who naturally focuses on the darker side of life, but the impulse behind his restricted choice of low characters, cynical motivation, and the high preponderance of sexual situations (insofar as this is not to be analyzed in social or psychological terms), is a *literary* impulse, and devoid of any obvious moral commitment. The satiric subjects are chosen on *literary* grounds, for their traditional connotations or humorous possibilities, not the other way around, as might be the case with the true satirist. Like all Roman writers Petronius has a strong sense of literary decorum and tradition. His choice is not prompted by any *saeva indignatio*.

The result is a curious distancing, a wry irony, and although at times this makes the author seem almost ambivalent toward his characters and topics, and distracts from their consistent and integrated presentation, it does, for one thing, drain the more shocking episodes of any pornographic effect. For instance, the rich Latin vocabulary of obscenity is hardly ever called upon, except for an inoffensive joke or a sexual pun. Petronius' self-conscious sophistication may be seen in the careful dissociation of the author and the ostensible narrator, who is constantly made the unconscious butt of the author's ridicule and satire to achieve this very purpose. This in turn blunts the edge of the conventional satire against other targets in the work, by removing any acceptable moral criteria, except for the uninteresting possibilities in the reader's stock responses. The satire seems then the product of a literary, rather than a moral, impulsion, a view that is confirmed by the very traditional satiric themes selected. Even when Encolpius steps out of his dramatic role to deliver the well-known defense of the work, and to claim that it is prompted by candor and describes life as it is, the partial revelation he offers of the author's principles is still given an ironic and mocking context of literary allusion.

All this surely must throw doubt on any claim that Petronius is a genuine classic, however minor, of satire in the proper sense. If there is a "quasi-moral" principle at work, it is the principle, invoked sometimes by Horace also, of taste, be it taste in literature or behavior, but taste itself dictates that even this be not taken too seriously—*surtout pas de zèle*. Petronius tries to strike a balance—and he is sometimes successful—between the traditional demands of his chosen genre, which he cannot altogether resist, and the spirit that animates his work. And perhaps this indicates that he had in mind something different from the true satirist.

An English critic, W. W. Robson, long ago pointed out to me that there are two kinds of judgment that one makes about literature. In one case, and this covers light reading and the literature of escape, one judges the thing as a specimen of a class: the mere subsumption in a category predetermines the *range* of critical predicates. And this allocation to genre is not necessarily trivial or futile; it can be a way of indicating what things are relevant to our critical examination. If one condemns a thriller as lacking in suspense, everyone would agree that the comment, whether true or not, was to the point. One may say that thrillers are a shocking waste of time, but no one can question the relevance of the criterion. The judgment operates in terms of a *class* of literature, and thus whether the work in question has or has not certain expected properties. But with the other sort of literary judgment, which is perhaps best exemplified in such verdicts as "that's a good poem," or "that's a significant novel," one is not assigning to a category, and the audience has virtually no idea of the range of appropriate predicates.

Of course the criteria for good poems, indeed for any works in which creative originality is an important element, seem far more varied than the criteria for good thrillers. It looks as though whenever we judge a poem good, we are not thereby considering it to have satisfied some pre-existing criteria for a particular class or category of poems. We seem to be valuing the thing as it is in itself, as something unique.

Naturally our usual literary discussions are full of over-lappings of these two types of judgment. (In classics, there is the further complication of making a preliminary decision, often on the basis of an incomplete set of facts, about what the work was intended to be in its entirety, or even what it said or meant locally. Both of these problems are important and relevant to such fragmentary works as the *Satyricon*.) When we compare two works with a view to establishing a preference between them, we may only do this in virtue of some hypothetical end or aim which they are presumed to share; but in so doing, we must give up the claim for either of them of an ideal purity and singularity of intention. On the other hand, when we analyse a work with a view to showing how it attains its characteristic effect, we may, if we wish, retain the implication that its particular realization of its individual aim is unique. (Of course in practice the critical and descriptive vocabulary we employ, if it is to be intelligible, has to relate to the audience's experience of other works: comparison is implicit generalization.) It is important, however, to be aware when we are doing the one or the other; to know what criteria are relevant and when; and to see where and why we can convincingly invoke, with reasonable safeguards, the privilege of singularity for a given work.

In the light of this, denying Petronius any claim to be a serious satirist doesn't mean denying him all claim to an integrating vision or to artistic seriousness in other ways. And the principle of uniqueness is a tempting one to invoke for a work that is so manifestly different from the rest of Latin literature; certainly the adjective "unique" occurs frequently in critical comment on the *Satyricon*. Petronius' decision to use humorous narrative as the vehicle for his artistic ends—and *ad hoc* purposes—was a natural one: the form was flexible, and so adaptable to his particular aims and even to his Epicurean views on the non-utilitarian value of literature. Behind the basic conception of the *Satyricon* there was genuine critical thinking. Certainly some of the literary discussions interspersed in the narrative echo certain important critical debates, common to the Neronian and earlier periods, that affected, to some degree at least, Petronius' esthetic principles. The controversies that obviously influenced the genesis of the *Satyricon* were, first, that carried on between the Atticists and the Asianists over style in general, and, second, the more defensive fight waged by the writers of *satura*, epigram, and the earthier, more "realistic" genres of Latin literature against both moralistic censors, waving the banner of Cato, and the exponents of the loftier, more prestigious and ambitious types of poetry and prose—historical and mythological epic, drama, and philosophy. If my view of the *Satyricon* is correct, namely that the framework was the parodic Wrath of Priapus, that the style was *tenuis* with frequent parody of other styles, notably Seneca's, that the subject matter was mainly humorous sexual adventures with literary divisions, and that the narrative method was the han- * dling of low and trivial personages and adventures in a highly sophisticated way through irony and literary allusion, then Petronius was on the side of the Atticists and, despite his admiration for Vergil and other standard classics, the "realists." The other factors governing his choice of sides are not difficult to guess at. As far as we can see, there was a sterile imitativeness about much of Neronian literature, both in poetry and rhetoric. The evidence is there in the harsh criticism of Persius' first satire, in Lucan's radical attempt to get away from traditional mythological structure of epic, and in the minor literature that has survived from the period. Almost in the spirit of Callimachus, who turned away from the grander forms of poetic composition, not because of their intrinsic inferiority, but because epic and tragedy had reached their peak with the Cyclic poets such as Homer and with the Attic dramatists and were now unsuited to the demands and talents of a very different, sophisticated and academic age, Petronius chose the Latin tradition that offered him, as it did Persius, Martial and Juvenal, the greatest freedom for experiment and originality, and the desired tolerance of such things as criticism, parody, literary versatility and the sophisticated treatment of subjects that were alien to more classical forms. This tradition, whose vitality did at least insure that the evolution of Latin poetry, a sicklier, if more precocious, child of the Roman and Italian genius than Latin prose, did not come to a halt with the Augustan or Neronian eras, but continued to produce classics, in the standard sense, well into the second century A.D. Petronius' exploration and expansion of the comparatively minor sub-

[159]

*for 'divisions'] *read* 'diversions'

genre, Menippean satire, was prompted by the many oppor-
tunities it offered, although, like the novel or *vers libre* in
more recent times, it also presented certain temptations to
self-indulgence.

Of course the "freedom" that modern authors like to think
they possess was psychologically impossible for any, even
the most revolutionary, Roman writer. The power of tradition, of formal conventions and requirements, of literary decorum, even of the audience's expectations, was greater than
our romantic and modernist imaginations can readily grasp
—yet it was gladly acknowledged. Revolutions in literature
took place within established, or at least acceptable, frame-
works: they were not violent or anarchical attempts to tram-
ple underfoot the achievements of predecessors, or the heritage of Greek and Latin literary theory. The call for *novae
tabulae* in Rome was always political, never literary, whatever the faults of contemporary practitioners in the eyes of
the reformers. For all his originality, Petronius is no exception to this rule.

The *Satyricon* had still to conform, minimally at any
rate, to the rules of *satura*, which was still a more encom-
passing form than our "satire," even though by this time it
was, one suspects, being gradually pressed into the Juve-
nalian mold. It remained of course an appropriate form still
for literary, as well as moral, criticism and for humorous
parody as well as philosophical censure; it invited also the
coarseness and sexuality, not always strictly relevant or
necessary, that presumably appealed to the Roman readers
of Catullus, Horace, Martial and Juvenal, and which dis-
tresses many of their modern admirers.

The *nostalgie de la boue* which went along with such
tastes, and which must be postulated in the simultaneously
refined and gross upper-class circles of Petronius' age (and
later), the impulse that sent Nero the *artifex* wandering and
brawling through the lower quarters of Rome like any
Tityre-tu in seventeenth-century London, is hard to over-
look in the *Satyricon*: it is visible in the lack of admirable
characters; in the sympathetically detailed, if ironic, description of Trimalchio and his milieu; and, above all, in the recurrent, bizarre sexual scenes. This had to be a determinant
of the choice of form and subject matter, just as the motive
behind the criticism of Lucan's *Pharsalia* and the parody of

Seneca's tragedies and of the later philosophical work produced by that presumably uncongenial Stoic was another determinant. The form once fixed upon exercised its prerogatives in stricter ways: *some satire*, in our standard sense, had to be introduced to satisfy its demands. Petronius was *obliged*, as it were, by his literary principles to gratify some of the expectations of his hearers. Fundamentally his engagement, apart from minor excursions into topical, or even personal matters, was with *literature* (as much a part of life of course as any other), but he had now to set up, with misleading consequences for us, some at least of the standard *moral* targets of his predecessors in satire, whether this went against his artistic grain or no. Into the accommodating framework of his comic *Reiseroman*, therefore, with its affectionate parody of the Homeric Wrath of Poseidon, he inserts such obviously "satiric" episodes as the Crotonian imposture (against legacy hunters); the *Cena Trimalchionis* (against wealthy and pretentious freedmen); and, most congenially for his sexual "realism," the various scenes portraying that favorite subject of satirists through the ages, female lust—in the persons of Tryphaena, Quartilla, the Ephesian matron, Circe, Proselenos and Oenothea. The number and variety of these characterizations of what is, at bottom, a simple enough literary and satirical type provide a clue to Petronius' real achievement: how he transcended the limitation and exigencies (for him) of his chosen, but in certain ways uncongenial, form and, to an admittedly limited extent, unified the disparate intentions of the different parts of the work. As a result, a piece of coterie writing, a loosely knit assortment of occasional criticism, parody, humorous adventure and perverse sexual themes, impresses us, in certain areas, as artistic writing of a high order.

The Flaubertian objectivity of his style; the complete absence of the author's personality from the main narrative, achieved through the use of a dissociated and carefully "placed" narrator; even the ironic and detached expression of his principles through the medium of different (and differentiated) *personae*: while these cannot, or at any rate do not, produce great satire in the classical sense, they are Petronius' means to a different sort of end: a creative and humorous presentation of an imaginatively realized world. (Despite her satiric potentialities, Emma Bovary is not satir-

ized either.) It is not a world that corresponds with our
world, nor one that stretches as far as the horizons of the
greatest and more humane writers of other ages. But it is the
sort of creation that one is hard put to parallel in comparable
Latin writers: the microcosm of Plautus and Terence is
schematic and insubstantial by comparison, and the universe
of Apuleius is as dreamlike and unlocalized as Cupid's palace
in the story of Psyche.

In the most obvious and impressive case, the episodes in-
volving Trimalchio, we see how an initial conception, which
might have developed along traditional satiric lines, as did
Horace's *Cena Nasidieni*, is transformed into something
different in kind rather than degree; so vigorous is the artistic
power, and so vivid the delineation, that the subordinate
motives of Senecan parody, and the topical criticism of current fashion and earlier folly, are fused into, rather than
stand in the way of, the total effect. A sardonic caricature of
a volatile, ignorant, superstitious, and boastful freedman,
who seems initially arraigned for condemnation on grounds
of taste, would be no difficult feat for a writer as good as
Petronius, given also the wealth of earlier literary models
and the material for observation offered by first-century
Rome. But by an impressive variety of structural devices,
changes of tone and point of view, ironic reversals of the
expected signals and responses, carefully planned rhythm
and dynamic symbolism, and plausible detail and dialogue,
the episode ends up a convincing and sympathetically *felt*
creation of a memorable fictional character, or rather of a
whole society. The rounding out of what might have been
an essentially flat figure in a static situation is accomplished
by the gradual revelation of Trimalchio's personality, and
by a corresponding and increasingly complex development
of our attitude toward him: he is presented through his physical surroundings, then through Encolpius' own personal impressions of him, then through the conversation of his guests;
we are given, concomitantly, a prejudiced account of his
behavior and hospitality by Encolpius, the effect of which
is offset by an unwittingly naive account of his own poor
behavior; finally the last strokes are added with Trimalchio's
great outburst at Fortunata, followed by his autobiographical
reminiscences and his mock funeral. He is dramatically presented from successive points of view, much as Socrates is

presented in Plato's *Symposium*, and this is a true novelist's technique. (One remembers that D. H. Lawrence, in "Surgery for the Novel—or a Bomb," described Plato's dialogues as "queer little novels.")

So if satire in the full sense was alien to Petronius' genius and outlook, the more disinterested and tolerant observation of the novelist was not. The satiric realism he limited himself to, in following the tradition, does indeed concentrate on the blacker, meaner, and seamier aspects of life, but this limitation, although serious enough by the highest standards, which are anyway not in question here, is partially surmounted by Petronius' refusal to associate himself (as the omniscient author, say) with Encolpius' narrative, criticism, or self-pity. His humorous and ironic detachment insures that we do not see the low-life adventures and cynical immorality of the characters through pessimistic eyes, but with amusement, and even, in the cases of Trimalchio and Eumolpus (whose devotion to poetry is touching, if a little absurd), with sympathy. Trimalchio is admittedly larger than life, but this in no way excludes the careful and controlled observation that is characteristic of the detached sympathy of the artist, as opposed to the directed and highly selective purview of the satirist. It has been said that the future of realism in literature may lie in the ease with which it can sustain, as it does in certain recent English and American novels in the picaresque vein, the properly timed commentary of humor. When all reservations are made, the *Cena* stands out as an early anticipation of this, a successful and self-contained example of such comic realism. The *Cena* accordingly offers us a standard for the rest of the work, and it is not without reason that this part has received most scholarly attention, although the comparatively intact text and the relatively inoffensive nature of the realism have also helped. There is no more successful character in the rest of the work than Trimalchio. And Petronius' claims as an imaginative writer must begin from this. Admittedly none of the other characters in the work can compete with this creation. Encolpius, although sometimes a vehicle for the author's critical views, is too drastically distanced by Petronius' self-conscious irony for us to have more than an idea of his character. He has to step out of his dramatic role at least twice, and his reaction to situations seems partly dic-

tated by an effort on Petronius' part to milk the humor of
each episode rather than to present Encolpius as all of a
piece. As a consequence, his behavior is not just melodramatic but psychologically inconsistent also, without any discernible artistic reason. The rest of the characters, unfortunately, with the exception perhaps of Eumolpus, are known
to us from very fragmentary episodes. The women in the
work, although clearly differentiated one from another, are,
as we see them, too lightly sketched, or too stock as characters, for us to linger over them as major creations, although
we may appreciate some of the nice personalizing touches
put into the creation of Quartilla and Circe. Eumolpus is,
in a way, an important exception, but the consistency of his
amusing hypocrisy and his satirized *furor poeticus* is slightly
marred by his selection as an alternative vehicle for some
of the author's literary views. His poetic effusions, which
have to be taken seriously by him and Encolpius in the context of the narrative, have, after all, parodic or exemplary
purposes from the point of view of Petronius and his audience: their rationale and Eumolpus' eminently reasonable
critical remarks do not properly jibe with the dramatic presentation. Here Petronius's local opportunism has meant artistic sacrifices. This ironic knowingness, of course, protects
the author from too much responsibility for his literary exercises and opinions. But this in turn strikes the reader as an
ambivalent attitude to a literary creation, and produces in
him a sense of unease.

Indeed, one might say, in general, that this sort of opportunism *is* a crucial weakness in the work as it stands; it is
one of the temptations inherent in any sort of *satura*, and
perhaps Menippean satire particularly is subject to it. The
form, as we can see, leads to other and similar self-indul-
gences, partly because it is expanded by Petronius beyond
its original circumscribed limits. Petronius works hard to im-
pose, and keep obvious to the reader, the mock-epic structure that to some extent unifies the *louche*, unpredictable
adventures of Encolpius; true, the *Cena* may be defended
as a digression that is a self-contained and successful work of
art, but even so Petronius, perhaps in response to the cir-
cumstantial incitements which his arguably serial method of
composition and publication may have encouraged, is sometimes too ready to display his artistic versatility, and this leads

to a blurring of the dramatic focus and an inconsistency of treatment. Almost any opportunity may serve for the introduction of a rhetorical parody or an amusing, or clever, and *ad hoc* poem, which cannot, in the nature of things, rise to any great heights. And this willingness to be irrelevant shows itself in larger ways.

The humorous realism of the *Cena* is almost thrown aside in the Croton episodes; the realism here is confined to the sexual scenes, and the rest of the story has an air of unreality, which is alien to the tone so far developed in the work. The themes of legacy hunting and cannibalism, although not in themselves incapable of humorous treatment, lack the ironic gravity that a Swift might bring to them. The humor is usually farcical, and is liable to strike the reader as rather heavy-handed even when he allows for the fragmentary state of the text at this point. And this crystallizes the main dissatisfactions that one feels with Petronius, the want of a unified viewpoint throughout the successive episodes—Encolpius is not enough for this—and the lack of a properly controlled tone, or at least recognizable justification for its inconsistency. And the suggested circumstances of its production, with perhaps the haphazard, and *ad hoc* or *ad hominem*, selection of themes and models, once the basic plot and general scale were established, serve only to *explain* these faults.

These criticisms suggest some further reflections. If one had to characterize the vision that dominates the work, as distinguishable from the narrator's pessimistic outlook, it might be described as an amused and snobbish, but interested and tolerant *acceptance*, in literary terms, of things as they are. In Petronius' world they are not altogether well or admirable, unless the neo-Epicurean defenses, ironic humor and the refined, humane pleasures of literature, social life and taste, are kept intact. Much like Lucretius, looking squarely at what is for ordinary people a cold, blind and depressing universe and accepting it in a philosophical spirit, so Petronius looks at a world of men, which he deliberately, and unnecessarily, depicts as uniformly mean, immoral and ridiculous. And he is saved from pessimism, if my reading is correct, by two things: an interest in the sheer vitality and variety of even this sort of life, particularly when it is the material of art, and by his sophisticated irony and humor.

For many, it may be that the deliberately limited subject matter that the *Satyricon* presents is scarcely saved by the author's subtle and disengaged style, and by his unemotional observation of his world. Nevertheless, the horrors *are* distanced, even become funny, when observed with his ironic, and yet sympathetic, detachment.

In fine, it must be confessed that Petronius' literary theories and artistic practice finally impress the reader, despite their successes, as not quite fully thought out. His complaints about the unreality of contemporary rhetoric are not consonant with his traditionalist's admiration of Vergilian epic; his defense of the realism of the *Satyricon*, so decisively limited in its scope anyway, conflicts with the differently conceived fantasy of much of the Crotonian episode, as well as many of the irrelevant insertions, prose and verse, which serve merely to display his stylistic invention and skills. His choice of a satiric genre, his rehandling of various conventional satiric topics, although partly dictated by this very choice of a loose and adaptable form, are admittedly suspicious in the absence of any consistent and positive standards. Here his detached irony and meticulous style may, or may not, have interesting results: it may produce a Trimalchio or the bizarre, if scarcely pornographic, scene with Philomela's children. His conception that the artist, in epic or satire, must be highly literate and well-read is of course almost a commonplace of Roman criticism and literary practice, and it is obvious how seriously he himself took it. Still, there are temptations in a form as loose as Menippean satire to display gratuitously one's familiarity with earlier models, and the range of one's reading. And Petronius is sometimes guilty of this. Yet this might also be seen as breaking in a different way the rule he lays down for epic: that *sententiae* should be subordinated to the narrative. Perhaps some of Petronius' literary set pieces might be similarly criticized in terms of the whole work.

Against these deeper faults, which are not entirely to be laid at his door, but may be partly attributed to the straitjacket of Latin literary theories and the tastes of his milieu, we have to set the clarity and vigor of his style, the pace, humor and invention of his narrative, the independent treatment of his models and his chosen form, and his correct decision as to the strength of the Latin literary tradition. Despite his admiration for Vergil he eschewed the dessicated banalities of mythological or historical epic to which Valerius Flaccus and Silius Italicus were to succumb; he avoided, in general, some of the stylistic Sirens to which Seneca listened in both his prose and his verse. And if his achievement, apart from the *Cena*, seems more art than matter, Silver Latin writers have left us works that are notable for neither. If Petronius has profited too much from the mystery of the *Satyricon's* genesis, other writers, without even the excuse of that mystery, have profited from our inertia.

NOTES

[1] See Kenneth Rose, "The Petronian Inquisition: An Auto-da-Fé," ARION 5 (1966) 275ff.

[2] See H. A. Mason, "Is Juvenal a Classic?" ARION 1 (1962) 8ff.

[3] Cf. the critique of Lucan in *Sat*.118 and compare, e.g., *Sat*.100.1 with Sen.*Ep*.73.6–8; *Sat*.115.8–19 with *Ep*.101.4.6; 99.31; *Cons. Marc*.11.3–5; *Ep*.99.8–9; *Ep*.92.34–35; *Rem.Fort*.5.2,4,5; *Cons.Marc*. 10.6: *Sat*.88 with *Ep*.115.10–12; *QN*7.31.1ff: *Sat*.125.4 with *Ep*.105. 7–8. *The Letters to Lucilius* are of course very close in date to the *Satyricon*; see K. Münscher, *Senecas Werke, Untersuchungen zur Abfassungszeit und Echtheit, Philologus Supplbd*. 16 (1922) 76ff, and Rose, *art. cit.* That the sniping was not one-sided is suggested by a comparison of *Ep*.122.15 (on the *turba lucifugarum*) with Tacitus' portrait of Petronius in *Ann*.16.18.

[4] For similar programs, see Mart.3.85, 4.49, 8.3, 11.15, and for general discussion, H. Stubbe, *Die Verseinlagen im Petron, Philologus Supplbd*. 25 (1933) 150ff. On the more significant points of the interpretation: for *Catones* and Cato's symbolic function in Latin literature, see Cic. *Ad Att*.16.1.16; Sen.*Ep*.97.8,10; Mart.1.*Epist. ad lectorem*, 1.1, 5.51.5, 9.28.3, 11.39.15, 12.6.8, 2.89.2, 11.2.1–2, 11.15.1, 11.16.6, 10.19.21; Juv.2.40, 11.90; Val.Max.2.10.8; on *simplicitas*, cf. Mart.1. *Epist. ad lectorem* (*Absit nostrorum iocorum malignus interpres*) and 11.20.10 (the *Romana simplicitas* of Augustus' obscene epigrams); for the stylistic implications of *simplicitas*, see E. T. Sage, "Atticism in Petronius," *TAPA* 46 (1915) 47ff, and G. M. A. Grube, *The Greek and Roman Critics* (London 1965) 202; for *nova* as opposed to *prisca simplicitas*, which was associated with the Stoic admiration for the good old days of Republican hardihood and frugal living (cf., e.g., Sen.*Ep*.86 on Scipio Africanus), see K. Borszak, "Die *Simplicitas* und römische Puritanismus," *EPhK* 70 (1947) 1ff. That it could have literary connotations is clear from Juvenal's *illa priorum scribendi . . . simplicitas* (1.151–53); for Epicurean teaching on the subject of sex,

cf. H. Usener, *Epicurea* (Leipzig 1887) Fgt. 68: οὐ γὰρ ἔγωγε τί νοήσω τἀγαθόν, ἀφαιρῶν μὲν τὰς διὰ χυλῶν ἡδονάς, ἀφαιρῶν δὲ τὰς δι᾽ἀφροδισίων, κτλ.(the quotation is in fact from the περὶ τέλους); and cf. Fgt. 68 and Varro, *Sat.Men.*Fgt. 402 (Buecheler); further details in C. Bailey, *Epicurus* (Oxford 1926) 390, and N. de Witt, *Epicurus and his Philosophy* (Minneapolis 1964) 292–93.

[5] Critical discussion of Latin satire is further bedeviled by problems of its own. It is worth perhaps restating briefly the obvious: whatever the literary origins and influences, there became early established in Roman literature a broad multifarious genre called *satura*, one important strain of which usurped even in classical times, as we know from Juvenal (*Sat.*1.8), the name as its particular prerogative. This strain becomes the paradigm for our own notion of satire, the other types of Roman *satura* being "satire" only in a historical sense (literary histories still find it convenient to talk of *satura* as Roman satire). The particular and easily isolatable aims, qualities, and techniques of the predominant strain, which made its way in an identifiable form into later literatures, were easily transferable to other literary genres, although they could be independently hit upon, granted the moralizing tendencies—or *Schadenfreude*—of men. Such satiric qualities and aims were not of course original to this strain of Roman *satura*; they were to be found in previous literature (Attic Old Comedy being an obvious example, as Horace saw, *Serm.*1.4.1ff). Consequently the title "satire" or "satiric" could be applied retroactively to earlier literary forms which exhibited the main characteristics of our modern conception of satire: one can obviously talk of Greek satire.

Senecan tragedy (Vol. V, no. 4)

SENECAN TRAGEDY

C. J. Herington

1581 AND 1927 SHOULD COUNT AS THE two most important dates in the long and, for the most part, shadowy afterlife of Senecan tragedy among the English-speaking peoples. In the earlier year, still during the first light of English drama, Thomas Newton's collection of translations of the tragedies was issued in London; and almost from that moment, whether by chance or not, "it was dawn, and the sacred day was growing." But it is characteristic of the malevolent fate presiding over the

    ◦ Senecan plays that nearly two and a half centuries were to pass before any great poet of the English language should again feel their impact, or before they should again become a reputable subject of conversation among serious lovers of literature. That second epoch is marked by the reissue, in London and New York, of Newton's translations, introduced this time by one of T. S. Eliot's most masterly essays. And few who are familiar with both Eliot and Seneca will believe that Eliot's response stopped dead at a single critical delineation. In Eliot's art the agonized sense and gorgeous sound of the Latin verses met, and befriended, something like their equal, as once they had with the Elizabethans.

Now, in 1966, appears a reprint of the 1927 edition.[1] To hail this event as the prelude to yet a third poetic renaissance would be unwise, no doubt. Yet I for one welcome the book; and also feel that, after a generation's lapse, it brings with it a suitable occasion to reflect afresh on the old translations, on Eliot's essay and, above all, on the ultimate source of both—the half-forgotten Roman master, Lucius Annaeus Seneca.

Apart from those who will be required to possess the book merely for professional reasons, I see two classes of reader, both in search of a new poetic experience, who may be interested in

[170]

◦for 'two and a half'] *read* 'three and a half'

the translations themselves. There are those who have no Latin, and hope for a fresh approach through these versions to the mysterious Seneca himself, the remotest, even though not the most closely guarded, of classical fastnesses. And there are those who will be looking at the book primarily as English poetry in its own right.

The Latin-less can be assured that as a whole, even if we take into account the considerable differences in quality between the various hands,[2] Thomas Newton's collection comes nearer than any later English translations to capturing those qualities of Senecan poetry which most grip a reader of the Latin original. The violence of the imagery; the intense (though, as we shall see, severely restricted) moral feeling; the unerring choice of the thunderous epithet; the steady rhythmic punch; above all, and probably most neglected of all in modern times, the superb *speakability* of Senecan verse; all these things the Elizabethan translator clearly felt down to his bones, and all these he conscientiously tried to reproduce with the means available to him. On the other hand, later translators, whether scholarly or amateur, probably have not felt in the first place or, if they have, certainly have not tried. Let the reader test this judgment for himself by declaiming aloud three versions of the opening of Hippolytus' speech in *Phaedra* 671ff—the moment of detonation in that most powerful scene of all ancient drama, the meeting, face to face, of Phaedra and Hippolytus. (He should declaim with shame, disgust and rage, for, in the very word before, Phaedra has finally unveiled her obscene desire.)

> Magne regnator deum,
> tam lentus audis scelera? Tam lentus vides?
> Et quando saeva fulmen emittes manu,
> si nunc serenum est? Omnis impulsus ruat
> aether et atris nubibus condat diem,
> ac versa retro sidera obliquos agant
> retorta cursus; tuque, sidereum caput,
> radiate Titan, tu nefas stirpis tuae
> speculare?

> O soveraygne Sire of Gods, dost thou abide so long to heare
> This vile abhomination? So long dost thou forbeare
> To see this haynous villany? if now the Skies be cleare,

[171]

Wilt thou henceforth at any time with furious raging hand
Dart out thy cracking thunder dint, and dreadfull lightnings
    brand?
Now battred downe with bouncing bolts the rumbling Skies
    let fall
That foggy Cloudes with dusky drouping day may cover all,
And force the backward starting starres to slide a slope
    wythall.
Thou starry crested crowne, and Titan prankt with beamy
    blase
Come out, with staring bush upon thy kindreds guilt to gase.
                                          (John Studley, 1581)

                    O King of gods,
Dost thou so mildly hear, so mildly see
Such baseness? When will fly the thunderbolt
Sent from thy hand, if thou art now unmoved?
Oh! Let the firmament be rent apart,
The daylight be by sable clouds concealed,
The backward driven stars be turned aside
To run inverted courses. Thou bright sun,
Chief of the stars, canst thou behold the crimes
Of this thy offspring?
                                   (E. Isabel Harris, 1904)

Great ruler of the gods, dost thou so calmly hear crimes, so
calmly look upon them? And when wilt thou send forth thy
thunderbolt with angry hand, if now 'tis cloudless? Let all the
sky fall in shattered ruin, and in murky clouds hide the day;
let the stars be turned backward and, wrenched aside, go
athwart their courses. And thou, star of stars, O radiant Sun,
dost thou behold this shame of thy race?
                    (F. J. Miller in his Loeb translation, 1917)

Of these three translators only the Elizabethan Studley (by no
means the most gifted of Thomas Newton's contributors) seems
to me to have had much understanding of Hippolytus' contorted
horror, or to have heard the riot of Latin sound in which that horror is expressed, or—above all—to have *seen* the storm clouds
gathering and the stars racing backwards in the boy's moral
heaven. Miller's version is merely what it was intended to be, a

useful and workmanlike crib, but (literally) unspeakable. Behind Harris'—which is still made to represent Seneca in such a widely read handbook as P. W. Harsh's *Anthology of Roman Drama*—I hear, perhaps uncharitably, little more than the rhythmic tinkling of teacups.

Newton's collection remains, then, the furthest point on the road to the real Seneca that the Latin-less reader, as yet, can hope to reach. But the truth must now be admitted, both to that reader and to that other reader whom I have in mind, the reader who comes to this book for love of *English* poetry. Though I said earlier that the Elizabethan of 1581 did his best to express Seneca with the means available to him, in 1581 these means were not impressive. (Another twenty years, perhaps—the maturing was so fast—and who can tell how a translation of Seneca would have read, supposing it had still been needed?) Eliot, though establishing this point with his customary learning and clarity, especially in the last section of his introduction (xlv ff), still seems to me somewhat overgenerous in his final judgment on their verse (liii–liv). The reader who wishes to know exactly what he is in for should reflect on Alexander Nevile's preface to his translation of the *Oedipus* (1.191): "In fine, I beseech all together (if so it might be) to bear with my rudenes, and consider the grosenes of our owne Countrey language, which can by no meanes aspire to the high lofty Latinists stile." We shall be hearing more of Nevile's opinions, all thought-provoking in spite of his tender years (he was sixteen when his translation was first published—another of those omnicompetent Tudor adolescents); but this one in particular seems completely accurate. Our language was indeed still gross, with a rustic tendency to redundance and verbosity. And the tendency, in these translations, is made into an obligatory rule by the fatal choice, for all the plays except *Octavia*, of fourteeners as the standard verse of the dramatic dialogue. Just as our iambic pentameter is usually a little too short to carry the full load of meaning packed into the Greek and Roman six-foot iambic line, so the fourteener is a little too long; and padding becomes inevitable. Add the restraint of rhyme, as these translators did, and you have a medium which, from the start, cuts you off from all hope of achieving the concision of a Senecan phrase or the sustained forward thrust of a Senecan period. It is no wonder that Eliot's two examples of the poetic excellence occasionally to be felt in the translations are both taken not from the dialogue but

[173]

from choruses, which are regularly rendered more freely, and in rhymed quatrains of pentameters. Even so, I doubt whether it would be easy to find many more than those two.

To read through these translations is in fact no great aesthetic experience. Pleasure one feels, but it is akin to the pleasure of ruins—of early Elizabethan ruins, rambling, whimsical, repetitive in their effects, wavering still in provincial uncertainty between Gothic and Renaissance. From this touristic point of view almost any page offers agreeable surprises: the "Great Guns in Carts" brought against the city wall in a chorus of *Thyestes* (1.67), the "prety dapper cutted Beard" on the chin of the youthful Theseus (1.159), and the unmistakably sixteenth-century tackle of the ship Argo (2.69). Above all, the immense wealth of obsolete but expressive adjectives, amply illustrated in the passage from Studley's *Hippolytus*, quoted above; add the dankish dabby face of the South Wind, and the Danube's waumbling streame (2.81). Without doubt Polonius, a generation out of date, slept with these translations under his pillow ("That's good, 'waumbling streame' is good"). For us, however, the luxuriance of such oddities, the lack of proportion or selection at any point, the relentless alliteration,[3] the numbing ding-dong rhythm of the fourteeners, page after page—all these things make it difficult to treat the translations seriously as works of art.

To summarize: these translators, partly through the accident of having lived just when they did and partly through their own natural gifts, possessed a still unrivaled feeling for what Seneca was about. But, again partly through an accident of time, their poetic technique is too unsure to communicate their feeling to a modern reader directly, without great labor on his part. One last example. There is a compact, devilish sentence towards the end of *Thyestes* (1067–68), where the insatiate Atreus is wishing that he could give the banquet all over again, because neither father nor sons had been conscious of the horror at the moment of eating. A modern who seeks to know Seneca will need much patiently acquired understanding of the Elizabethan translators' ways before he can sense that behind such vividly felt yet grotesque verses as:

> He rent his sonnes with wicked gumme, himselfe yet wotting
>   naught,
> Nor they thereof,

[174]

there lies anything like this:

> Scidit ore natos impio—sed nesciens,
> Sed nescientes!

Yet the vivid feeling is there, as it is in no other versions.

I do not mean to discuss Eliot's "Introduction" at any length, because it is certainly familiar to most readers (a reprint of it, of course, is available also in his *Selected Essays*), and because, within the areas which he chose to cover, there can be little serious disagreement with him even at this date. I draw attention only to one factual error, which may prove to be more important than at first sight it seems, if we seek a just understanding of Senecan drama: "The most unpleasantly sanguinary [of Senecan tragedies] is the *Thyestes,* a subject which, so far as we know, was not attempted by a Greek dramatist" (xxiii–iv). That is simply untrue. Eight Greek dramatists, including Sophocles, Euripides and Agathon, wrote tragedies entitled *Thyestes*; although all are now lost and the fragments of them, as so often, are scanty, at least the Sophoclean *Second Thyestes* (and possibly, also, his *Atreus*) almost certainly dealt with the cannibalistic dinner. (And incidentally, as if for good measure of horrors, Sophocles seems to have treated Thyestes' subsequent outrage, the rape of his own daughter Pelopia, in the *Thyestes in Sicyon*.)[4] This mistake of Eliot's may, in fact, be classified as a Freudian slip: even in a passage when he is, quite rightly, protesting against the widespread belief that Senecan drama is simply crammed with horrors, he still cannot shake off the even more widely spread ancestral opinion that at any rate it ought to be gorier than *Greek* drama. Even the extant Euripidean versions of the deaths of the Princess and Kreon in the *Medea,* and of Hippolytus, and of Pentheus, or Sophocles' version of the agonies of Lichas and Herakles, or Aeschylus' extremely precise account of the Thyestean banquet itself (*Agamemnon,* 1587–1602) should long ago have put an end to such an idea—if only people had been content to read the poems for themselves, and with the help of all five senses. Seneca is indeed horrific, but not, as I hope to show later in this essay, in the same sensuous, physical way as the Greek dramatists can be when they choose.

Otherwise, I still see little that I should wish to change in Eliot's essay, and only find myself admiring once again his mastery of, and immediate transcendence of, what scholars call (often with quite straight faces) the "Literature"; his perfectly tuned ear for the original dramas both in Latin and English; and the felicity and precision with which he expressed his findings. Little that I should wish to change; but very much that I wish to add. The essay, it will be remembered, falls into three sections: the first treating "the character, virtues and vices of the Latin tragedies themselves"; the second, their influence on Elizabethan drama; the last, the Elizabethan translations as such. The first of these sections, which primarily interests me here, remains to this day the most intelligent sketch of Senecan tragedy available in English, outranging by far the current academic handbooks.[5] Yet I will confess that even it seems to me a collection of piecemeal observations—nearly always just, and often excellent—on the superficies of Seneca, on his style, his characterization, his Stoic slant, his metric. What I miss is any final synthesis, any sustained attempt to reach the heart of these tragedies, to appraise their status as works of art in themselves. One still comes away with the feeling that had they not, by the accident of their preservation, exercised a vast influence on Renaissance drama, they would be remarkable only for a few casual felicities. In that sense Eliot's approach to Seneca, for all its superior intelligence, remains squarely in the nineteenth- and twentieth-century Anglo-Saxon tradition. Senecan drama *as a whole* we refuse to take seriously; even the most benevolently disposed, after admiring a phrase here, a scene there, will go on to speak of matters that are strictly irrelevant, of Greek derivations, or European influences, or Silver Latin rhetoric, or, in extreme cases, the fact that Seneca prophesied the discovery of the American continent.[6] In the following part of this article, turning away from such things, I shall first concentrate on the man himself. For I believe that there and there only we shall find our clues to the criticism of these tragedies—in that terrible moral sensitivity which imperiously compelled their creation, and in that concrete, pictorial imagination which brought them into shape. Whether this examination will show that they are great works of art I do not know. But it may suggest, at least, that neither their contents nor their technique are anything like so remote from modern experi-

[176]

ence (or indeed from the human experience of all ages) as is usually supposed; that they are perfectly serious, honest works of art, not frivolous exercises in gruesome wit; finally, that they represent an art form almost without parallel in antique literature, a truly religious drama.

It has always been known that there are two distinct lives of Seneca: the life—very largely an *inner* life[7]—which can be reconstructed from his own writings, and the primarily political biography which has to be pieced together from allusions in other ancient authors. The inner life, as perhaps with most of us after reaching maturity, is an almost timeless thing, showing little essential change as the years pass. Against it, in vivid contrast, stand the mountainous fluctuations of Seneca's secular, political life, with its abrupt tragicomic peripeties and its ultimate catastrophe. This outward life is, I believe, of little moment to the critic of Seneca's extant writings, with two important qualifications, which will appear shortly; so I will spend only a few sentences in recalling its main features.[8] He was born in Spain, within a year or two of the birth of Christ;[9] early brought to Rome; in adolescence, obsessed with philosophy, especially in its more ascetic manifestations, from which he was rescued by the common sense of his father, M. Annaeus Seneca (*Ep.*108.17–22). During the same period, and indeed throughout his life, he suffered from ill health. There was a significant moment, late in the reign of Tiberius, when this actually impelled him towards suicide (*Ep.*78.1–2); but he was diverted from it, partly (like his own Hercules in the *Hercules Furens*, 1302–1317!) by his aged father, and partly by the consolation of philosophy. Meanwhile, however, so far as the world at large could see, he was succeeding in life during his thirties and early forties: quaestor, perhaps shortly after 32 A.D., and thereafter an advocate so famous in the courts as to arouse the maniacal hatred of Caligula. Here is our first evidence of his contact with princes, of his presence at the edge of that tiny group of men on which there bore down, night and day, the concentric pressure of a monstrous weight, the post-Augustan Empire. That pressure is almost unimaginable to the ordinary citizen of the present day, perhaps even to the statesman. We can only stare, helpless, at its psychological effects on the individuals. Some of

them found release in madness or cruelty; some (among whom I
see Petronius) cushioned themselves in detached pleasure; others
(Seneca and Marcus Aurelius are obvious examples) armed themselves in the ponderous carapace of Stoicism and lumbered for-
wards as best they could. But all these reactions have one point in
common: they are extravagant; not only vice (as in the mirrored
room of Hostius Quadra),[10] but virtue itself is magnified into monstrous images.

And nothing, no one, is secure. . . . After a narrow escape from
the murderous Caligula, Seneca survived into the reign of Claudius only to be exiled before its first year was out (41 A.D.) to
Corsica, where he lingered hopelessly for eight years. In 49, however, his fortune again reversed itself, totally and with staggering
abruptness: he was recalled by Agrippina, now Claudius' wife in
succession to Messalina, and made tutor to Nero. From then on he
stood in the center of the world, at Nero's side through his ac-
cession in 54, the murder of Britannicus, the murder of Agrippina, and the death of Burrus in 62. At this last point his luck (if
it was luck) broke again; his final three years, from 62 to 65, were
lived in semi-retirement, under the constant threat of trial and
death, until his suicide in the aftermath of the Pisonian conspiracy.

So much for the turbulent outward career, our main concern
with which is its relationship to the more static inner life and
convictions revealed in the writings. I do not intend here to spend
time on the eternally discussed question of Seneca's hypocrisy or
otherwise during his years as adviser to Nero. This, surely, can be
judged by such scholars or philosophers, if there are any, as have
found themselves in anything like Seneca's situation; at any rate,
it is not relevant to the present inquiry. What does seem relevant
is the clear fact that Seneca himself lived through and witnessed,
in his own person or in the persons of those near him, almost every
evil and horror that is the theme of his writings, prose or verse.
Exile, murder, incest, the threat of poverty and a hideous death,
and all the savagery of fortune were of the very texture of his
career. Such themes, at least where Seneca is concerned, are traditionally dismissed as rhetorical commonplaces, an emotive
phrase which really contributes nothing to our understanding of
the problem. Rhetorical commonplaces, like early epic formulae
(which in fact they closely resemble), can be adopted by a writer
with or without feeling, disposed with or without art. Everything
in Seneca's career, as well as a dispassionate study of his writings,

would suggest that these themes, for him, were or became urgent realities.

The second point about the outward life which seems worth making here is that, at any rate in the last three years of semi-retirement from the court, it merged in an almost perfect harmony with the inner life. "Was man in der Jugend wünscht, hat man im Alter die Fülle." Where we can still trace Seneca in action, he is fearless. And the *Naturales Quaestiones* and *Letters to Lucilius*, known to have been composed in those same years, have the ring of an almost religious fervor; there are places, indeed, where neither the contents nor the very sound of the language seem to belong any more to the pagan classical world, but to late antiquity or the so-called Dark Ages. "Intellego, mi Lucili, non emendari me tantum sed transfigurari"[11]. . . . "Cresco et exulto et discussa senectute recalesco. . . ."[12] Finally, there is an extraordinary passage where he in effect defends the integrity of his inner life, whatever men's opinions of his words or actions may be.[13] It is written in old age, evidently in ill health, and evidently in daily expectation of death from these (or other?) causes:

> So I have no fear as I ready myself for that day on which, without any of the turns or colors of rhetoric, I am to pass judgment on myself: is my courage in my words, or in my true feelings? Were they pretense, were they a masquerade, all those proud words which I uttered in the face of Fortune? Away with the opinion of mandkind, always uncertain,   *
> always a split vote; and away with the studies that I have pursued all my life: Death (I tell myself) is about to cast his verdict on you. . . . I accept the terms, I do not shrink from the judgment. *Non reformido iudicium!*

Neither here nor elsewhere in this essay do I propose to discuss the validity or practicability of the eclectic Roman version of Stoicism which finds startling expression in such passages as these. My purpose will be served if I have indicated how it molded and dominated Seneca's inner life from the time of his earliest extant writings (about 40 A.D.) until his suicide; how his whole career from that date was such as inevitably to reinforce its vitality and meaning for him; how during his last years, if not earlier, it certainly invaded his external actions in return. It is a datum which we must imaginatively accept for the moment, as Seneca him-

[179]

*for 'mandkind'] *read* 'mankind'

self accepted it, if we are fairly to judge either his prose or his verse.

In seeking the springs of Senecan tragedy we must begin with his prose, for here both the convictions of the man, and his pre-occupations, and—I would dare to add—his unique artistic talents, are most easily seen. This is not to suggest for one moment that any of the Senecan prose treatises, *as wholes*, can be considered works of art. Indeed, it is hard to classify them in any artistic, lit-erary or philosophic category; which is, I believe, one powerful reason why they have fallen into neglect since the early nine-teenth century, precisely when books began to become the pro-vince of the systematizing professor. Their philosophical approach is too casual for the philosopher, or even the historian of philoso-phy. Their lack of formal structure frustrates those who look to ancient literature for aesthetic reasons. Historians of Roman Im-perial politics, approaching a source which should be so prom-ising, are met by discreet silence or bland generality;[14] and the inquirer after scientific information is understandably maddened by a page or two of the *Naturales Quaestiones*. As for Seneca's three *Consolationes*: Consolation is simply no longer part of our academic curriculum, and the same holds for Benefaction (*de Beneficiis Libri Septem!*), Anger (*Libri Tres*), Leisure, Clemency and The Happy Life. In short, there's only one phrase to describe Seneca's prose works: *frozen conversations*. Almost all of them deliberately adopt the tone of conversation, and bear the traces of having been set down almost at conversational speed (the near-est thing to an exception, in an entire work, is the *Consolatio ad Helviam*). Indeed, I have sometimes suspected that they were in large part actually dictated to a stenographer.[15] Works of art, naturally, do not emerge, nor do systematic bodies of informa-tion. In compensation we have something hardly less interesting, the speaking voice of an extraordinary man. The speaker ranges over a vast number of topics, though always referring them in the end to his most urgent preoccupation, Stoic ethics. As a rule, the level of conversation, over any five-minute section, is high, and the verbal and notional wit is sustained with great virtuosity for sentence after sentence. There are certainly dull periods, as in any conversation, and there are a few entirely dull conversations, notably the *de Beneficiis*.[16] But equally there are passages—again, hardly ever lasting for more than five minutes at a time—when the entire eye, soul, imagination of the speaker seem to leap into the

words. Such passages are not few, and, as will be seen, I believe
they are of considerable interest to a student of the tragedies.

Bitterly opposed as I am to anthologizing in general—it is not
only the history of the declining Roman Empire that teaches us
how the epitomizers and anthologists move in not more than a
century before the barbarian hordes—I would make an exception
of Seneca's prose works, for the reasons stated. Very few can reasonably be expected to find time to listen to the entire extant conversation of any man, however brilliant, that extends over nearly
1100 pages of close print,[17] in a highly idiomatic and sophisticated
Latin. Seneca's reputation would certainly gain by a sympathetic
anthology of his inspired moments. In a way, the following pages
will contain an approach, in miniature, to such an anthology; they
concentrate primarily on Seneca's sensitive reaction to the phenomena of his world, and on the means by which he expressed
that reaction.

It was *one* world. An essential preliminary to the understanding
of Seneca is the realization that, however eclectic he is, he is still
Stoic enough by habit to draw little or no distinction between
spiritual, moral and material realities. Though he protests in theory against some excesses of the earlier Stoics in this matter,[18] in
practice he treats *all* phenomena as belonging to the same order
of being. His discourse slips, without warning or break, from the
vastness of the soul to the vastness of the starry sky.[19] The stormy
wanderings of Ulysses are equated with the daily experience of
the soul.[20]

There is no difference for Seneca—and this is a point which
should interest readers of his tragedy *Thyestes*—between physical
and moral light or darkness: the soul of the good man, if we could
look into it, would prove to be ablaze with soft light, and in fact
we can actually *see* some of that fire in his eyes;[21] on the other
hand, the external darkness in which the debauchee spends his
existence is matched by the darkness in his soul.[22] "You are wrong,
Lucretius," Seneca says, "we aren't afraid in the light; we have
made everything into darkness for ourselves: *omnia nobis fecimus
tenebras.*"[23] Again, I will not pause to pass judgment on this view
of reality, nor to inquire whether we should describe it as total
materialism or total idealism, totally objective or totally subjective.
The important word is *total*: in Seneca the passions, the tides and
the orbits are phenomena of the same kind, are causally interrelated, and can be discussed in interchangeable terms. Nor shall

I here do more than tentatively suggest that our own world view, in the latter part of the twentieth century, may again be trending in a similar direction. All I ask is that the reader should do his best, for the moment, to see the world through Seneca's eyes.

At any level below the fixed stars, it is in great part a world of fear. Beside what we should call the terrors of nature, the earthquake,[24] the thunderbolt,[25] the city-destroying fire,[26] are ranged (as usual with no consciousness that they could be different in kind) the fury of tyrants,[27] envy, pain, poverty, bereavement; and beside them again, the no less solid terrors within the individual soul, the annihilating passions, above all anger, lust, and fear. It is this last group which naturally concerns Seneca most, and bulks largest in his writing. Not only is it the nearest and the ultimate danger, the fifth column within every man's citadel, but its effects are contagious: they extend from the individual across the body politic (nature created Caligula *ut ostenderet quid summa vitia in summa fortuna possent*),[28] and in time can reach out and destroy not only the earth, but the fabric of the universe, stars and all.[29] You want the true image of our human existence (*vitae nostrae vera imago*)? Seneca can tell you: it is the sacking of a city.[30]

All human beings, even if they should miraculously escape the onset of the passions or the tyrant, are in any case headed for nothing but death. In passage after passage, august ancestors of lines in Dante and Eliot ("I had not thought Death had undone so many"), are seen vivid pictures of the crowds hurrying to Hades, and the pompous funerals of the Caesars jostling the quiet, taper-lit obsequies of infants.[31]

With all such terrors Seneca's imagination was obsessed; and I think it is true to say that he spends quite as much time in picturing them as on the more positive function of instructing his hearer in the remedies against them. The receptive artist, in fact (as we shall see in more detail shortly), time and again takes over from the dogmatic moralist. But those remedies are simply described, if one strips away, as Seneca, Epictetus and Marcus Aurelius did, all the elaborate foundation of dialectic, and most of the foundation of physics, on which the Hellenistic Stoics had based them. A single crucial battle has to be fought within the soul itself, the battle between reason and the passions. A victory by either side is total. If the passions win, the result is at once visible and concrete (such is the instant causal connection between moral and physical realities): the regular lineaments of the human face col-

[182]

lapse into the contorted mask of mania, *furor*; and another terror
has been added to the world.[32] Reason, on the other hand, anni-
hilates every vice at a blow by its conquest,[33] and the soul is
henceforth impenetrably armored for its lifelong duel with externals—in other words, with Fortune. This is still a hard-fought
battle, but a glorious one: in the strange second chapter of the *de
Providentia*, the universe dissolves into a mighty amphitheater,
in which an immortal audience, breathless, looks down on the only
gladiatorial pair worthy of the sight of God—Fortune and Cato,
fighting it out. And this, says Seneca (with one of those mild
lapses from his sense of humor which rather endear him to me)
—this is definitely a more adult sport than our human practice of
goggling at wild-beast fights.

Death itself, to such a man, is of no consequence. Though knowing as well as the rest of us that ". . . every mother's son/Travails
with a skeleton,"[34] he accepts this fact as in accordance with nature, and indeed, under certain circumstances, positively wel-
comes it. The theme of Death the Liberator—liberator not only
from the stress of the wise man's battle against Fortune, but from
humiliation or dishonor—appears constantly in Seneca's prose and
verse;[35] and to this moment one is impressed by its ultimate appearance, not in his prose nor in his verse, but in physical action
taken one day in 65 A.D. (If that was a "rhetorical commonplace,"
as the type of Senecan commentator with which I have no pa-
tience would call it, we must at least admit that Seneca took his
commonplaces very seriously indeed—and, with that admission
alone, a vital contention of this essay is established.)

I have now surveyed, briefly and impressionistically, the most
prominent features of Seneca's world. It is not, of course, a world
of his own creation, for it differs in no important respect, so far as
we can tell, from that of many earlier Stoics. Yet, I think, enough
has already been said to suggest, first, that Seneca had completely
assimilated it for his own purposes, and second, that his personal
experience at the feverish center of the Julio-Claudian empire
enormously intensified his understanding of it. He operates within
its framework no less surely than Dante within the framework of
the Thomist universe. And, I would now add, with something
of the same creative and pictorial imagination: to turn from the
fragments of the earlier Stoics, or even from the pages of Marcus
Aurelius, to Seneca, is to turn from the philosophical technician to
the born artist. Once again, we must bear in mind the patchy, con-

versational character of Seneca's prose works. But they provide abundant evidence, scattered here and there, of a facet of Seneca's genius which I believe has been almost completely neglected: his painter's eye, his almost Leonardesque visual imagination and fantasy.

When gifts such as these operate on the physical and moral realities of the Stoic universe—or simply on the Roman world as observed by Seneca—the result is startling. They can bring out, in color and perspective, minute details: the muddy alleys and eroded, cracked, uneven walls of the Roman slums (*de Ira* 3.35.5); the delicate miniature rainbow made by the fuller as he sprays water from his mouth over the stretched cloth (*Q.N.* 1.3.2); the gourmet whetting his appetite by observing a costly fish as it expires in its prison of glass, white stealing under pink (*ibid.* 3.17.2–18.1). In such mastery of visual detail, it is true, Seneca is not quite alone among Neronian writers, for something very like it is found in—of all people—Petronius (perhaps their only point in common). But when he moves out to wider perspectives, Seneca seems to me to leave behind him most of the writers in the Latin language. Here is a landscape from the eighteenth chapter of the *Consolatio ad Marciam* (or from the background of some canvas by Bruegel, "The Fall of Icarus," "The Return of the Cattle"?):

> hinc camporum in infinitum patentium fusa planities, hinc montium magnis et nivalibus surgentium iugis erecti in sublime vertices; deiectus fluminum et ex uno fonte in occidentem orientemque defusi amnes et summis cacuminibus nemora nutantia et tantum silvarum cum suis animalibus aviumque concentu dissono; varii urbium situs et seclusae nationes locorum difficultate, quarum aliae se in erectos subtrahunt montes, aliae ripis lacu vallibus pavidae circumfunduntur; adiuta cultu seges, et arbusta sine cultore feritatis; et rivorum lenis inter prata discursus et amoeni sinus et litora in portum recedentia; sparsae tot per vastum insulae, quae interventu suo maria distinguunt.

On that side, the level spread of plains that stretch off into infinity. On this, great snowy mountain ridges rise into skyward-soaring spires. Tumbling rivers; streams falling off eastward and westward from a single spring; woods waving on hilltops; and all that forest with its animals, with its harmony fused of different birdsongs. Towns variously sited; people cut off by the wildness of the land, some of them withdrawn into soaring hills, others moated by lakes, valleys, marshes.[36] Cornfields thriving through agriculture, wild copses with none to tend them. Streams wander softly through meadows; then there are fair bays, and shores that here and there retreat into harbors; beyond, all those islands scattered through the deep, punctuating beween sea and sea.

The traditional response to such passages is what, by now, amounts to a dirty word: they are ecphrastic, part of the rhetor's stock in trade. But I would ask the reader, before he dismisses them on such a ground, to consider a possible objection to it. Every age has its own forms and conventions, which cannot be judged as good or bad in the abstract, but only by the way in which the individual writer employs them. No one would think it any sort of criticism of the third section of Bach's Suite No. 2 for Flute and Strings to remark merely that it is a *sarabande*. Why the rhetorical forms such as *commonplace* and *ecphrasis* should be otherwise treated, as if their use in itself put an end to all criticism, is beyond me.

Now there is in fact considerable difference between the *ecphrasis* of a Seneca and that of a Longus, say, or a Philostratus. Not only does a Senecan landscape (or starscape, of the type which we shall shortly mention) seem to arise far more directly from the writer's own inward or outward eye—that is my, admittedly subjective, impression—but it is informed by a deeper meaning and urgency. For example, the passage just quoted from the *Consolatio ad Marciam*, if read in context, will be found to be no casually inserted purple patch. It is part of a vision that lies open before the infant just born into the world. To find its like we must look far afield, perhaps to the late seventeenth-century Christian mystic, Thomas Traherne.[37]

Seneca's vision carried him far beyond a single landscape, however: again and again, in the tragedies as well as in the prose, we meet passages which suggest that he carried in his mind's eye, almost continually, an astronaut's view of the entire Roman world, and of the shadowy regions on its borders. The Scythians tramping across their frozen lakes (*Prov.*1.4.14); the Ethiopian pygmy imposing his will on the elephant (*Ep.*85.41); or the pomp surrounding Parthian kings (*Ep.*17.11)—such pictures flash across his conversation hardly less often than images drawn from the areas where he actually spent most of his mature life, Latium and Campania. Perhaps slightly more often in the tragedies than in the prose, the vision pierces far beyond the Roman boundaries. The pearl from the Indian Ocean is found only in *Phaedra* (391–92); the silk of China, startlingly enough, in *Phaedra* (389) and *Thyestes* (379); and it is to *Hercules Furens* (533–41) that we owe our most imaginative picture of the frozen seas in the far north, with their silent, spiky waves. More than any other extant Latin writer, Seneca is preoccupied with ocean discovery. "Videbis hic navigia quas non novere terras quaerentia."[38] In the *Naturales Quaestiones* (4.2.24) we see a glimpse of the navigation of the African coast; and, in the same work (1.*Praef.*13), occurs the astonishing statement that the voyage from the western shore of Spain to the Indies takes a very few days, given a following wind.[39] For a moment, the vision unites the two far ends of the earth.

Such Senecan passages, taken together, convey perhaps as vividly as anything in Latin writing the sheer immensity of the Imperial Roman world, as seen through the eyes of a sensitive observer stationed at its administrative and diplomatic center. But even from a more restricted, literary point of view the phenomenon is interesting: Seneca's Stoic habit of mind here combines with his practical experience as a Roman administrator to produce a truly ecumenical poetry, a poetry in which location and race are almost non-significant. Since Aeschylus (who, from very different causes, seems to share something of the same internationalism, the same sense of the coherence of the known and half-known worlds) such a thing is not easy to parallel. But there are more surprises to come: Seneca, unlike Aeschylus, is aware not only of the immensity of the earth in the eyes of man, but of its minuteness in relation to the universe. A characteristic passage in the *Naturales Quaestiones* (1.*Praef.*8–11) is worth quoting; it comes near to a familiar modern simile for our earth, the ants on the billiard ball. The human soul, says Seneca, cannot quite discipline itself to despise material luxury,

> until it has made the circuit of the entire universe; until it
> has looked down from the heights on to our earth—narrow,
> largely covered by sea and, even where it emerges from the

waters, wild over wide spaces, and either scorched or frozen; until it has told itself, "So that's the dot which so many nations compete to carve up with fire and steel! How absurd are mortal frontiers! (*o quam ridiculi sunt mortalium termini!*)" . . . If human intelligence were granted to ants, wouldn't they, like us, carve up their single threshing floor into many a Province? Once you have lifted yourself into that region which is truly great, you will be content, whenever you see our armies marching with their standards aloft, their cavalry squadrons (as if something important was going on) scouting in advance or clouding the flanks, merely to quote: *it nigrum campis agmen.*[40] All that rushing to and fro is ant labor, labor in a tiny space. . . . The scene of your voyages, your wars, your allocation of empires, is a dot! The mighty spaces are above our heads; and into their freehold the human soul is admitted.

From the period of his exile,[41] through the height of his power,[42] and into the years of his retirement,[43] we can follow Seneca's preoccupation with the starry heavens in a series of passages which for splendor and vivid realization are scarcely to be paralleled between Plato and Boethius. For him the stars have a triple fascination: their majesty and the regularity of their movement are reminders—wherever you stand on the earth's surface, whether in Corsica or on the Palatine Hill—of the divine order; the fire of which they consist is identical with the fire of the human soul, they are *cognatae res;*[44] finally (a grim fascination, this), being one with us, they may ultimately, for all their remoteness, perish with us and through us. Seneca's universe, I would repeat, is one, and all its parts are interrelated.

Here I reach a side of Seneca's mind and art, his visual fantasy, which is hard to parallel at all in extant ancient writings—the great myth at the end of Plato's *Phaedo* is the nearest thing that occurs to me. That he possessed the power of projecting himself imaginatively into regions which he could never see is shown by many casual passages—his description of the measureless caverns in the bowels of the earth, with their sightless fauna,[45] his visions of the deep seas of future time,[46] and of scientific discoveries opened up by remote posterity.[47] But of all such visions, the greatest and the most terrible are those which concern the destruction of the universe. For neither earth nor stars are immune

to human sin, and the time will come when we shall destroy
them all. This idea is never far from Seneca's consciousness:
again we can trace it throughout his career,[48] but perhaps the
most fantastic of all such passages is to be found near the end,
in the *Naturales Quaestiones* (3.27–30), where he envisages the
destruction of the world by water, the *fatalis dies diluvii:*

> First, there are immense showers of rain. The suns are seen
> no more, but heaven's face is grim with clouds and uninter-
> rupted mist. There is thick, humid darkness with never a
> wind to dry it out. Corruption seizes the crops, and the
> growing cornfields rot, grainless; and when the sown plants
> have perished, marsh grasses grow up to take their place
> all over the plain. Soon even the stronger vegetation feels
> the hurt, as the trees heel over with their roots loosened,
> and the vines and every other shrub can no longer keep
> their grip in the earth, which has turned soft and liquid.
> . . . The houses, soaked through, begin to slip, for their
> foundations are sinking; the water has filtered deep, the en-
> tire soil is a swamp. No use, their efforts to shore up the
> tottering structures. Every solid building is set in a slippery,
> muddy earth: nothing is firm. And now the storm clouds
> gather and gather, and layers of snow, which have taken
> centuries to accumulate, melt; a torrent rolls down from the
> utmost mountain heights, catches up the loosely clinging
> forests, bowls down rocks set free of their twisted settings,
> scours away farms, transporting herdsmen in confusion with
> their flocks, plucks up the little buildings in passing, and
> storms away against the greater—whole cities it pulls away,
> whole peoples entangled in their towers!

But this is only a stream; what of the earth's truly great rivers,
the Rhône, the Rhine, the Danube? Can we imagine the Danube's
flow,

> when it is no longer scouring the spurs or the middle of the
> mountains but is harassing their very crests, carrying in its
> course the sodden flanks of hills, and shattered cliffs, and
> headlands of vast extent which have torn away from their
> parent body as their foundations collapsed? At last, finding
> no outlet (for it has dammed itself up by its own action),

[188]

it turns in on itself, a global mass, and swallows an immense region of lands and cities in a single maelstrom. And all this while the rains persist, and the sky grows heavier and piles evil on evil with the passing of time: it was cloud before, now it is night, night dreadful with the terror of a flickering, ghastly light. Again and again the lightning flashes, the storm winds make the ocean shudder . . . .

A very similar word picture of the Deluge (which, I believe, may ultimately be derived from Seneca) will be found in a Windsor manuscript of Leonardo da Vinci;[49] but I do not know that anyone ever dismissed *that* as an *ecphrasis*.

Seneca had also, in his mind, seen the stars collapse on themselves. Leaving aside, for the moment, a surrealist chorus in the *Thyestes* (827–84), I would draw the reader's attention to a strange passage in the *de Beneficiis* (6.22), where he pictures the consequences of a lapse of benevolence in the sun and moon.

All those heavenly bodies, separated by immense intervals, and posted for the protection of the universe, would desert their stations. There would be instant confusion in nature. Star would ram star. Natural harmony dissolved, the divine world would collapse into ruin. In mid-course, the lattice-work moving at immeasurable speed would abandon its alternations, guaranteed for so many ages; the bodies that now pass and repass in turn, and so maintain a proper balance in the firmament, would be burned up in a sudden blaze; that great variety would be fused, all would end in one. Fire would be master of the whole, fire succeeded by a motionless night. So many divine beings sucked into an endless whirlpool!

And once, for a brief moment, there is a fantasy worthy of a Michelangelo or a Blake: the lonely God after such a cosmic collapse, a God totally at rest, sunk in his own thoughts.[50] Here the wheel comes full circle, however; for in this passage Seneca is making the point that those thoughts will be no different from the thoughts of the Stoic sage in prison, exile or shipwreck. I cannot too often stress the unity of the world which Seneca had inherited and made his own; a moral and physical unity from the depths of the universe to the individual human soul.

[189]

Enough, perhaps, has now been said to demonstrate the range of Seneca's visual imagination, and the manner in which it can illuminate and realize his Stoic cosmos. But one special aspect of it remains to be considered—an aspect predictable enough, no doubt, to an ancient Stoic, but not so immediately obvious to the modern reader. Moral realities, in this mind, assume shapes no less pictorial, and indeed dramatic, than physical realities:

> *Thus let us picture Anger!* Her eyes are on fire; she is clamorous, hissing, bellowing, groaning, screaming, making any fouler noise you care to think of. In both her hands—since she never thinks about protecting herself—she is waving weapons. Wild, bloody, scarred, bruised dark with her own lashings, with the walk of a maniac, clouded deep with darkness, charging here and there, ravaging, routing, agonized by the hatred of all, and of herself more than any if she can find no other way of doing harm. She is as dangerous as she is hateful: she longs to overturn earth, oceans, heaven.

Such is the "hideous face of a hideous emotion."[51] It will be observed, with interest, that the destructive force of this emotion is no less powerful than that of the Deluge in the *Naturales Quaestiones*; equally, it extends to the whole cosmos. Briefer, but hardly less vivid, moral personifications of a similar type occur several times elsewhere in Seneca: Virtue and Pleasure (*Vit.Beat.*7.3); Fortune (*Cons.Polyb.*2.2); and Clemency, bringing sudden peace at her entry into the house (*Clem.*1.5.4). Seneca visualized these —to him—fundamentally important powers with the same clarity as he could visualize, say, the collapse of the stellar system. But no passage makes this mental habit of his clearer than a quite casual remark in the *Letters* (113.26), where he is reducing to absurdity the earlier Stoic view that the Virtues are *animalia*. It is a remark which, I suppose, briefly allows us a glimpse into the innermost part of his workshop. If virtues are animals, his argument runs, then it will follow that all sorts of improbable entities are animals also. "I just split with laughter when I try envisaging a Solecism as an animal, and a Barbarism, and a Syllogism; and when, like a painter, I try assigning them their appropriate outward shapes—*et aptas illis facies tamquam pictor adsigno.*"

Tamquam pictor: like a painter. There, I believe, is one important clue to the creation of the Senecan tragedies. Another clue is Seneca's total imaginative assimilation of a basically Stoic cosmos and Stoic ethics. A third is the terrible immediacy which these ideas came to acquire for him, probably in his middle years as exile and dynast, certainly by the time of his retirement from court in 62 A.D. And not only for his own sake: I have already given instances, earlier in these pages, of his preoccupation with the destruction of the world through human passions, and of the missionary urgency that appears in his last works.

Longum iter est per praecepta, breve et efficax per exempla: instruction is the long road around, the short and effective road is through example. This truly Roman principle, laid down in *Ep.*6.5, operates from end to end of the rambling, conversational prose works of Seneca. Again and again the modern reader, bored (as he well may be) by a page or so of exhortation to Virtue, is on the point of dropping the book, when he is shocked back into attention by a brilliantly realized, nervous paragraph; the inevitable *exemplum* has succeeded the *praecepta*. Seneca, as he himself several times admits, is but an amateur moralist.[52] As a creative word-painter, he is a superb professional, as we see both in the prose *exempla* and, above all, in those extended, fantastic *exempla* in verse, the tragedies.

Having said that, one has said, in a sense, all that matters. In the dramas those Senecan qualities which I have tried to delineate through the survey of the prose works, but which appear in those works only by brilliant flashes, operate continuously and on the grand scale. The acute moral sensitivity, the painter's eye and fantasy, the indifference to the modern (and, I would add, high classical) distinction between the moral and physical worlds—all these are combined and sustained. Further, unlike any other surviving works from Seneca's hand, the dramas aim at being works of art. For they are molded by a triple discipline. The Senecan moral-physical universe, strewn in confused pieces through the conversational prose writings, is here shaped and defined by the limitations of verse, of dramatic form, and of mythic subject.

Before exploring the consequences of this view in more detail, I think it right to pause over certain external aspects of the tragedies. I shall put forward my opinion about them rather dogmatically, not because I do not know that they present complex and important problems to any serious student of Seneca (or of

European drama), but because they belong only to the background of the present essay.

Were the tragedies intended for acting on a stage? We cannot, in method, be certain. Not a scrap of unambiguous evidence concerning the production or non-production of *Senecan* drama has come down to us; we have simply the bare Latin scripts, without commentary, without any of the enormous apparatus with which the Greeks of antiquity surrounded *their* classical tragedies. Nor is much light shed by a consideration of the Neronian theater in general: the results point all ways. Though I do not know of any evidence which indicates beyond doubt that any first-century play was written for recitation by a single voice, there are certainly indications that some plays were composed for recital rather than full theatrical production.[53] Leaving aside the intervening quasi-theatrical phenomena which also delighted Neronian audiences, the mime, the pantomime, the operatic rehashes of scenes or parts from Greek drama, we come, at the other end of the scale, to straight theater. For this last there is, in fact, a fair amount of evidence in Seneca himself.[54] Where the Senecan tragedies are concerned, therefore, our only resource is the texts themselves. In these I find nothing unactable, if allowance is made for a few stage conventions that would be moderate by Jacobean, let alone Aeschylean or Restoration, standards. But that decision is, admittedly, subjective; far less subjective, if subjective at all, is the question of the speakability of Senecan drama. Practical experiment in the tape recording of scenes from the *Phaedra*[55] convinced me, and I believe would convince anyone else who tried it, that Senecan dramatic verse is designed, no less than the verse of Marlowe or Racine, for its effect on the ear, not on the eye; and that that effect is shattering. Retranslated, even by amateurs, into the sound-medium, the long speeches almost of themselves generated passion, the verbal epigrams (dull on paper) acquired a cutting edge, the texture and forward movement of the scenes were restored. That the verse was intended for speaking, then, I have no doubt; and if that can be admitted, the conclusion inevitably follows that it was intended for speaking by *different voices for the different parts*. Those, and there are many, who blandly assume that the Senecan dramas were recited in an auditorium by a single voice, like an epic or a history, are hereby recommended to try, say, *Medea* 168–171:

[192]

Nurse: Rex est timendus. *Medea*: Rex meus fuerat pater.
N.: Non metuis arma? *M*.: Sint licet terra edita!
N.: Moriere. *M*.: Cupio. *N*.: Profuge. *M*.: Paenituit fugae.
N.: Medea, *M*.: Fiam! *N*.: Mater es. *M*.: Cui sim vides![56]

What can a *single* reciter make of that? Does he speak alternately out of opposite sides of his mouth, or what? And indeed, what does a reader make of it when he eyes it on the printed page? I believe that there is only one answer to this, and to the innumerable similar passages in Seneca: they are meant to be spoken; and they are meant to be spoken by a separate voice for each part.

If that point is conceded, the Senecan tragedies are, for all essential purposes, true drama, and to be treated as such by the critic. Whether they were accompanied by action (in fact, anyone who has tried to *speak* a Senecan scene will probably find that some action and gesture follow irresistibly), whether there was a raised stage, scenery, masks—these are marginal and antiquarian questions, insoluble on our available evidence. On the external aspects of Senecan drama I shall speak more briefly. *The Choruses*: by the standards of fifth-century Greek tragedy their behavior is flatly incomprehensible. But why judge Seneca, in this or other matters, by the standards of fifth-century Greek tragedy, as if nothing had happened since to the world or to the theater? (I suppose it is some time since people abandoned the practice of measuring Horace by Alcaeus, or Lucan by Homer.) The often-made suggestion that Seneca's choruses operate somewhat in the sporadic manner of Hellenistic comic choruses[57] seems to me very plausible, and to dispose of almost all the difficulties; though certainty cannot be attained. Of the contents of the songs in Seneca we shall see more later; but a word should be said here about their technique. Once again, as with the dialogue, the *sound* matters immensely. Seneca's generation, like ours (and like Euripides'), was suffering from a failure of nerve, and the tragedies are compelling evidence of this; but, unlike ours, it was certainly not suffering from a failure of ear. In their purely rhythmic aspect, the Senecan choruses are to me the most interesting poems that survive from the first century A.D. And for the rhythmic virtuosity—to put the matter at its lowest—of the so-called "polymetric" choruses with which he experimented in his *Oedipus* and *Agamemnon*, there is just no parallel in ancient Latin. We have to range more widely, backward to classical

Greek lyric, forward to . . . Milton? I do not try to fool the reader into supposing that Seneca's poetry, or his technique, is up to those standards. I do ask him, if he has any Latin, to reserve his judgment and to listen:

> Heu quam dulce malum mortalibus additum
> vitae dirus amor, cum pateat malis
> effugium et miseros libera mors vocet
> portus aeterna placidus quiete.
> Nullus hunc terror nec impotentis
> procella Fortunae movet aut iniqui
> flamma Tonantis.
> Perrumpet omne servitium
> contemptor levium deorum
> qui Styga tristem non tristis videt
> audetque vitae ponere finem.[58]

A prose paraphrase might run:

> Ah, it is sweet yet cruel, the evil love for life imposed on man, when he has an open refuge from his troubles—Death's freedom beckoning to the sufferer, a waveless harbor of everlasting calm. He who hears her will feel no terror, not the gale of raging Fortune, not the flames shot by the cruel Thunderer. He will break his way out through any slavery if only he can despise those ever-changing Gods; if he can look on Hell's sad river without sadness; if he dare end his life.

The relation of the Senecan tragedies to the Greek tragedies on the same themes is a subject which long mesmerized the learned. Term papers and dissertations pullulated, comparing (with a small, mad smile) the *Agamemnons* of Aeschylus and Seneca. Perhaps the most accessible summary of such labors is to be found in F. J. Miller's appendices to his Loeb edition of Seneca, where "Comparative Analyses" of the respective Greek and Senecan dramas are laid out on facing pages. They form an entertaining study. The spoken scenes rarely correspond—and then only with the aid of yawning blank spaces on one side or the other—while the choruses just don't correspond at all. With equal sense, and with equally disconcerting results, one might draw up Comparative Analyses of Homer and the *Aeneid* on facing pages, or of the *Antigones* of Sophocles and Anouilh. But even a Comparative Analysis, in fact, does not suffice to reveal the profundity of the differences between Seneca and the Greeks: it is hard even to think of any single line in the Greek so-called originals which Seneca has, in any sense, translated. He has, indeed, borrowed his general plots from the Greeks, and he has borrowed (or presumed his hearer's knowledge of) many scenes and several speeches. And it is true that in such cases a circumspect comparison of Seneca with his models can throw light on the art of both—in very much the same way as, for instance, a comparison between the *Eclogues* of Virgil and Pope would throw light on *their* artistic methods. But on the whole the relation is not particularly close, and for most critical purposes is probably best ignored. In my experience, one comes closer to a just understanding and enjoyment of, say, the Senecan *Oedipus* if one thinks of it neither as a "translation," nor as an "adaptation," but as a "Neronian Fantasia on a Theme by Sophocles." A fantasia in a musical idiom all its own.

This brings me back from an admittedly condensed review of externals to the main topic of this essay: the Senecan tragedies in themselves, as expressions—perhaps the finest, certainly the most artistically shaped—of the unique Senecan sensibilities and talents which I have traced in the prose works.

Let us review four propositions about Evil, which I suppose are of vital importance to Senecan thought generally, but above all to the creation of the tragedies:

1) Evil is something material, with effects no less material than those of, say, fire. "Is a napalm bomb a sin? Is sin a napalm bomb?" Seneca would have had difficulty in distinguishing be- •
tween the two questions; witness his Ghost of Tantalus in the Prologue of the *Thyestes*, whose advent sears the orchards, dries up the streams and melts the mountain snow; or his Oedipus, who carries with him an evil that has infected the Boeotian skies with pestilence.[59]

2) Evil takes its rise within a tiny but measureless space,[60] the individual human soul. If it is not checked within that space by the opposing force of reason, no check remains between it and the stars. There, in the soul, is the crucial and the final battlefield.

3) The most terrible and most immediate disasters result from

[195]

•for 'Seneca would'] *read* 'Seneca might'

the victory of evil in the soul of a prince. It is at once amplified. A nation, or a world, will feel its consequences.

4) Although there is no check to evil once let loose on the world, there is one thing which it cannot vanquish—a soul within which *reason* has won the battle. To such a soul even physical death is no injury, but a sort of triumph. Its integrity remains.

Though the phraseology of these propositions is out of fashion, they are in themselves perhaps not so farfetched as might appear to a modern at first sight. On some not altogether superficial views, 3) has been exemplified in our own time, in the histories of Germany and Russia, and was certainly not meaningless to Roman contemporaries of Caligula and Nero. And I do not think that we customarily sneer at 1), 3) and 4) when we find them operating, as we do, throughout the dramas of one of the greatest of ancient poets, Aeschylus. Only 2), the most characteristically Stoic of them all, implies a psychology that has never been fash-ionable, at least in such rigorous terms. But be that as it may, let us temporarily accept all four for the purposes of Senecan criticism.

For it was undoubtedly with these propositions in mind that Seneca selected his Greek mythic themes, and transformed them. Thereafter, the unrestrained pictorial imagination came into play, giving color, form and depth to Evil itself; creating, as it were, violent impressionist canvases which bear little relationship to the Greek Old Masters. People speak much of what they call Seneca's rhetorical exaggeration, when phenomena occur such as the Ghost of Tantalus or the Senecan Oedipus, just cited. They might equally well use the same language of Van Gogh's "The Starry Night" in the New York Museum of Modern Art. Stars aren't like that, like great catherine-wheels; but that is what stars feel like. A Senecan tragedy, by similar means, tells what evil feels like to an acutely sensitive mind under abnormally evil conditions. The perpetual criticism that Seneca's characters and situations are unrealistic seems to me to miss the point. He is not trying, even in the sense that Aeschylus did (let alone Sophocles and Euripides), to present the actions of human beings. His emphasis is on the action of Evil, and of the emotions which generate it; the human actors, the palaces, the landscapes, the starry heavens themselves, are subordinate to this action; they are its external manifestations. If to us they seem pictorially exaggerated, the Stoic moralist will probably have his answer ready:

[196]

"You *cannot* exaggerate the shape of Evil, if you have ever confronted it in your own soul; it fills your heaven."

Although I am primarily concerned, through most of this essay, to rescue Seneca from what seem to me misapprehensions about his art, I do not wish to glide over its limitations. One of the most serious of these appears in the very fact that it is possible, in some degree, to draw up the scheme of a typical Senecan tragedy—something which no one in his senses would try to do for the tragedies of the Greeks. The minds of the Greek dramatists were wide open (which is perhaps one reason for the fascination they have exerted on many subsequent revolutionary periods, including our own). The mind of Seneca, on the other hand, is not open, but operates within a well-defined, quasi-religious system. Hence a greater intensity, and a surer sense of direction, in the Senecan dramas, but at the same time a loss of flexibility in composition. Personally, I am grateful to Time for preserving our seven complete Senecan tragedies;[61] they provide an experience for which I look in vain elsewhere in European literature. I doubt, however, whether Seneca could profitably have composed many more than seven in so limited a genre.

The scheme of a Senecan tragedy is easily defined. Although the tragedy is formally divided into five acts by the choral songs,[62] the course of the plot, viewed as a whole, falls into three movements only, of gradually increasing length. For short, I will give them titles: The Cloud of Evil (this coincides with a formal division, the Prologue); The Defeat of Reason by Passion; finally, The Explosion of Evil, consequence of that defeat.

A Senecan Prologue has none of the dynamics of a Sophoclean, nor even the detailed, lively narrative of a Euripidean. We see a solitary,[63] over-life-size figure brooding on the stage. Neither its physical nor its intellectual lineaments become clear to the audience in the course of its opening speech. Instead, that speech creates an aura of evil around it; either the soul (and, of course, the landscape) is clouded with the terror of past wickedness, or passion is gathering, threatening wickedness in the future. In *Agamemnon* the figure is the ghost of Thyestes, carrying a load of guilt that checks the stars in the sky (53–56). Likewise under a night sky, spangled with the constellations that commemorate the illicit loves of Jupiter, appears the figure of Juno in the Prologue to *Hercules Furens*, lashing herself into rage. The guilt of Oedipus, of Tantalus (in the Prologue to

Thyestes), even of Hecuba (Prologue to *Troades* 40), is reflected, or externalized, in the entire surrounding landscape, and
beyond; and the raging sorceress Medea will shake the light from
heaven as easily as she will shake the marriage torches from the
hands of her enemies (*Med*.27–28). Only once is this pattern
varied, in *Phaedra*—a play which, together with *Thyestes*, is complicated by the presence of a noble character who confronts, and
ultimately is overwhelmed by, the central stream of evil. *Phaedra*, by a brilliant stroke, opens with a solitary figure whose state
of soul is symbolized in the landscape, but it is the figure of the
noble Hippolytus—noble by Senecan standards, for he is an out-
rider of the Age of Gold. The dark figure of Phaedra, in the
throes of the battle between passion and reason, is postponed
until the next scene.

This Prologue to *Phaedra* deserves further consideration, for it
embodies, in a short space, much that is typical of Senecan art.
It is composed in light, running anapaests, a rhythm which Seneca
handled with great *brio* and tunefulness; we have to wait four centuries, until Boethius, for anything near a similar mastery of it.
As with all Senecan verse, only reading aloud will do it justice,
but I invite the reader to weigh the Latin sounds of, for instance,

Ite, umbrosas cingite silvas,

or of

si quem tangit gloria silvae.[64]

The content of the song, a solo by Hippolytus, will enrage the
literal-minded. It is a lighthearted summons to a hunt, a hunt that
rampages all over Attica from the wooded glens of Phyle[65] to
the headland of Sunium, from Marathon to Thria. This is no picture of any single hunter's glade: it is a wide aerial view (reminiscent of the landscape in the *Consolatio ad Marciam*, quoted
earlier), which occasionally dives to ground level and picks out
a detail, the alder copse in the plain, the victim's spoor sharp in
the morning dew. Then the song moves to the Huntress, Diana,
and her far-flung worshipers across the known world, from Hyrcania by the Caspian Sea to the ridges of the Pyrenees. It ends with
the clear baying of hounds calling Hippolytus from the stage—

to join a monstrous hunt that never was and never could be, *except in a young man's imagination*. In short, just as in the normal Senecan prologue, so here: whether horrific or beautiful, the visible scene described by the speaker is not described for itself—indeed, in itself it is impossible—but is the amplifying medium which conveys the state of the subject's soul. For it is on this last that all issues depend in Senecan tragedy, no less than in Senecan prose. How else (Seneca might ask) should one convey the fresh, cool integrity of Hippolytus—that integrity which belonged to the earliest age of man, described by Hippolytus himself later in *Phaedra* (525ff)?[66] Another typically Senecan element in this opening song is its outward movement from the Attica of the Heroic Age to lands which the Mycenaeans never knew. I mentioned Hyrcania and the Pyrenees; add the Sarmatians of northeastern Europe, the tribes around the Danube, the Armenians, the nomads of Arabia and of the Libyan deserts. Seneca's characters are tied only loosely to any specific place or time, and that by way of a courteous gesture to the Greeks. In practice, they are supranational. They speak with the voice of the Roman Empire, which in turn, for Seneca and some other Stoics, was ideally the Human Empire, the *Cosmopolis*.

To me the same principles which I have here illustrated from the Senecan prologues seem to operate throughout the tragedies. In general, they are obviously not difficult to apply; but it is worth drawing attention to one special application of the principle that moral and psychological states are regularly reflected in, and represented by, what we should call physical phenomena. The descriptive speeches in Seneca have often been criticized; even Eliot, in his introduction to the *Tenne Tragedies* (p. x), makes merry at Seneca's expense over the long description of Hell by Theseus in the middle of *Hercules Furens* (650–827). Why indeed should Hercules' family be entertained in so ghoulish a fashion immediately after the hero's unhoped-for return, and while he is "engaged in a duel on the result of which everybody's life depends"? Eliot might have asked more: why does the first part of the choric ode continue the same ghastly theme? Why did Seneca, in this matter, deliberately and blatantly depart from Euripides, who in his version gave as little emphasis as he could to Hercules' legendary descent into Hell? Sheer artistic irresponsibility, is Eliot's implied answer; poor, weak Seneca has fallen once more for the blowzy charms of Rhetoric, he has committed another *ecphrasis* for the transient delight of some Roman drawing room or other. But experience of Seneca teaches me to beware of such answers, and to suggest another. "So you think, in your pride, that you have now escaped the Styx and the ghosts?" cries Juno in the Prologue to the tragedy (90–91); "*Here* I will show you Hell!" She then conjures the creatures of Hell to take possession of the hero's mind. I suggest that when Theseus, in this great central interlude between the return of Hercules and his apparent triumph over his enemies, describes the dark caverns, the tortures, the waste lands[67] of Hell, he is not only describing what Hercules has been through; he is indicating what Hercules, for the moment, *is*. Many other long descriptive passages in the Senecan tragedies, which either are without precedent in the Greek so-called originals, or fantastically expand hints found there, can be interpreted in a similar way—and, to my mind, gain greatly thereby in relevance and power. Such are the great storm scene of *Agamemnon* (421–578—preceded by the scene in which Clytemnestra collapses before the onset of passion, followed immediately by the chorus on Death as the *harbor* from the storm of life, which I quoted earlier); the incantations of *Medea* (670–842); the necromancy of *Oedipus* (530–658); and the frightful description, not only of the murder of Thyestes' children, but also of *the place where Atreus murdered them*, in *Thyestes* 641–788 (where 641–682 are given entirely to the visual background of the crime). Like the landscape in the *Consolatio ad Marciam*, such passages can be, and usually are, dismissed as mere rhetorical word paintings. But it may be seen on sympathetic inspection that, again like that landscape, they are word paintings with a distinct moral and artistic purpose.

After the prologue, with its solitary figure casting gigantic, distorted moral shadows across a vast background, the second of the three major movements in a Senecan tragedy may appear livelier and less complicated; this is the movement which I have entitled, for short, the Defeat of Reason by Passion. At first sight it is certainly closer to the Greek dramatic norm than the prologue. The shadows fall away, the human figures multiply, move into the foreground, converse in sharp, direct dialogue. For a moment, the perplexed Hellenist may feel that he has come home.

He will soon find out his mistake. Our cool modern assumption that Greek tragedy must be the ultimate criterion for Senecan tragedy leads, almost every time, to a dead end. Similarly, one of the factors in Western Europe's very belated recognition of Greek tragedy was the cool Renaissance assumption that *Senecan* tragedy was the ultimate criterion. Better, perhaps, to avoid either extreme, and to take each type of tragedy, in the first instance, on its own terms.

The second acts of five out of the seven genuine and complete Senecan tragedies[68] present a character meditating a passion or a crime, and arguing with another character (usually an inferior) as to whether or not he should give in to the temptation. It is important to notice that the corresponding Greek dramas, Seneca's alleged models, either do not contain such a situation at all, or handle it in an entirely different way. We are dealing here, in fact, with an element that is peculiarly and demonstrably Senecan. That it was felt as such by near-contemporaries is proved by the two plays in the corpus which are probably by followers of Seneca. *Hercules Oetaeus*—composed by a talented writer who had inherited several of Seneca's gifts, but not, alas, his sense of proportion—devotes more than 300 lines (233–568) to Deianira's discussion with the Nurse as to whether she is to give way to passionate jealousy and poison the robe. And I do not believe it has been sufficiently recognized that the historical tragedy *Octavia*—the work of an inexperienced but not insensitive amateur—is composed of such situations almost from end to end. Octavia dissuaded from passion by her Nurse, Nero dissuaded by Seneca, Poppaea by *her* Nurse, Nero by the Prefect—these are the scenes which form the body of the *Octavia*.[69]

Lest there be any misunderstanding, I here offer a list of such situations in the genuinely Senecan tragedies:

Phaedra 129–273: The Nurse, who already knows Phaedra's rising passion for her stepson, tries to reason her out of it; but finally, when Phaedra announces that no *ratio* (265) will prevent her suicide, the Nurse succumbs to Phaedra's *furor* (268), and instantly offers her services for the seduction of Hippolytus. (The resemblances to the scene between Phaedra and the Nurse in Euripides' *Hippolytus* are few and superficial.)[70]

Medea 150–175: Medea is dissuaded from her *dolor* (151), *furor* (157), and *dementia* (174) by the Nurse, but without effect; the situation is repeated, but more vividly, at the beginning of the third act (380–430), where the Nurse laments Medea's total subjection to *insania, furor, ira* and (389) "every passion." (There is no corresponding situation in Euripides' *Medea*.)

Thyestes 176–335: Atreus, swollen with *ira* (180), *furor* (253), *rabies* (254), *dolor* (299), discusses with an attendant his proposed crime against his brother. The latter at first offers reasons against it, but after line 219 his resistance weakens; during the later part of the scene, while the hideous plan is evolved, he becomes a loyal accessory, as his parting words show. (None of the eight Greek tragedies entitled *Thyestes* is extant.)

Agamemnon 108–225: Clytaemnestra, in a turmoil of passion—*dolor, timor, invidia, cupido, ira, spes* (131–142)—is dissuaded from it by a Nurse, who urges her (129–130) to try the effect of delay, even if she will not accept the claims of *ratio.* In this play, by exception, the inferior's arguments temporarily convince the superior; the intervention of Aegisthus, and a second long argument (226–309) on the relative advantages of passion and reason, are necessary before Clytaemnestra finally and totally capitulates to passion. (There is, of course, no corresponding situation whatever in Aeschylus' *Agamemnon.*)

Troades, 203–352: Pyrrhus, cruelly urging the sacrifice of Polyxena, is dissuaded from his plan by a strangely subdued and gentle Agamemnon, who has learned humility and mercy from the fall of Troy (250–270), and has seen enough of *ira, dolor* and *furor* (280–283). But Calchas' announcement of a new omen ratifies Pyrrhus' plan. (There is no corresponding situation in Euripides' *Hecuba* or *Troades*; though Seneca's moving characterization of Agamemnon here may owe something to the former of the two plays.)

There is great variety in the detailed handling of these scenes; a variety imposed partly by an external factor, the traditional myth, partly by the art of Seneca. But the general similarity is plain, and so is its crucial significance for the plot of a Senecan tragedy. A duel is fought out in each case between the passions of one character and the reasons offered by the other; the passions conquer; and from that conquest catastrophe follows directly. Now it is surely impossible to dissociate this phenomenon of the Senecan tragedies from the Stoic doctrine on the passions which is assumed, with more or less modification, throughout Seneca's prose writings.[71] In particular, one of the details of that doctrine should be recalled here: once passion has completed its victory in the soul, the effects are immediately visible and tangible. There is a ghastly change in the victim's face, coloring, voice and gait; R. L. Stevenson's account of the dissolution of Dr. Jekyll into

Mr. Hyde would be no excessive caricature of the psychosomatic process envisaged by Seneca (who would probably have applauded Stevenson's story from end to end). Nor should we be in too much haste to criticize the Senecan doctrine as unrealistic: Seneca had himself looked into the face of the madman Caligula.[72] The same transformation is described again and again in the tragedies, most notably at the beginning of the third acts of *Phaedra* (363–383) and *Medea* (380–396), when the moral surrender of the respective heroines is complete.[73]

This cannot be coincidence. The Passion-Reason scenes in the *tragedies* must have been created with conscious and deliberate reference to the doctrine so familiar to us from the prose works. Hence perhaps the colorlessness (so often criticized) of the inferior of the two characters in such scenes, and the fact that on two occasions[74] the inferior finally capitulates in the most abrupt and improbable manner, and thereafter serves as accessory to the projected sin; the *idea,* as so often in Seneca, overrides the demands of the factual realism and even of individual characterization. One is almost tempted to speak of allegory, and to interpret some of the scenes as symbols of the crucial battle within the single soul of Phaedra, Medea or the rest. Or even to go further, interpreting those heroines themselves as mere allegories of the passions from which they suffer: "I see the face of Passion (*vultum furoris cerno*)!" cries the nurse at the terrible reentry of Medea (*Med.*396); and indeed, Seneca's whole representation of Medea, yearning for an evil that will shake earth and heaven (line 45), bears a remarkable likeness to his portrait of Anger in the *de Ira* 2.35, quoted earlier. But to allegorize the tragedies entirely is to be too crude. It is to deny Senecan tragic art one of its greatest charms, a charm which it shares with much of our own recent literature—the free, ambiguous interplay between objective and subjective.[75]

Five of the seven tragedies show the defeat of Reason by Passion taking place before our eyes, in a sharply defined Second Movement. *Oedipus* and *Hercules Furens* are only exceptional in that the genesis of evil is placed, respectively, before and outside the body of the action. In Seneca's *Oedipus,* as in Sophocles', the initial errors are already committed before the drama opens. Yet there the resemblance to Sophocles practically ends. The Greek tragedian represented the gradual discovery of the truth through the very brilliance of Oedipus, and his concurrent passage from confident majesty, through nervous tyranny, to psychological and political annihilation. Seneca neglects the latter aspect of the Oedipus story and treats the former perfunctorily (compare his recognition scene with that of Sophocles!). His emphasis, already in the Prologue, is on the evil *per se*; even there its presence is felt by an oppressed and frightened Oedipus, who, without knowing precisely why, at once assumes the guilt for the pestilent skies and the dying citizens. From then on, far from being discovered by him, the evil closes in on him, manifesting itself in ever more elaborate and grotesque shapes—the divine oracle, the obscene details of Teiresias' sacrifice, and finally the ghastly train of royal phantoms. *Hercules Furens* likewise, if I understand Seneca's conception of the story, offered no occasion for a Passion-Reason scene. Hercules, one of the nearest approaches to an ideal Stoic sage that the world has yet beheld,[76] could not be brought on stage dickering with his passions like a Medea or a Phaedra. Seneca, therefore, like Euripides, has the passion violently injected from the outside; unlike Euripides, however, he actually shows the generation of that passion, during the Prologue, in the heart of Juno.[77]

The last, and the longest, of the major movements in a Senecan tragedy was entitled, above, "The Explosion of Evil." (From some points of view "The Implosion of Evil" might be equally appropriate; let the reader choose.) The factual details of disaster in the several plays are to a great extent predetermined by the Greek fable concerned. Oedipus, as you might expect, is blinded; Medea murders her children; and Thyestes duly dines on his. We see the profound difference between Seneca and the Greeks not in such narrative data, but in emphasis and attitude.

Enough has already been said in the course of this essay to indicate what these differences are. In sum: the vivid and sensuous narratives of Greek tragedy can be read (and, I would say, *should* be read in the first instance) as *representations of people in action*, whatever ulterior symbolisms and abstract truths may be discerned through that action. Senecan narratives, on the other hand, cannot be so read, for they are *representations of passion in people and things*. The symbolic and the abstract have entered into the fabric of the drama.

In the Third Movement of a Senecan tragedy the shock wave of evil races outwards, prostrating both the wicked and the noble, and rarely stopping short of the stars—though it is often left uncertain whether those stars really belong to the visible firmament. The modern theater electrician, faced with a Senecan production,[78] would have to ponder the text very carefully before he actually turned down the lights, or set them flickering across the background, at such passages as *Agam*.727 (the light goes out of the sky for Cassandra) or *Med*.787ff (Medea sees the moon racing through heaven); at *Herc.Fur*.939ff (the sky blackens, and Hercules sees the monstrous constellations, Lion and Bull, preparing for a fight) he had better keep his hand from the switchboard;[79] in *Thyestes*, on the other hand, he would certainly be kept busy.[80] But in all these instances, even the last, the moral and physical phenomena are really inextricable. The reader of Senecan drama should never forget that devastating interchange between the Nurse and Medea (*Med*.164–167): "The Colchians, your people, have left you; you can put no trust in your husband; of all your great resources nothing remains."—"*Medea* remains! *In me* you see the ocean and the land, and steel and fire, and Gods and lightning bolts!"

> —Abiere Colchi, coniugis nulla est fides;
>   nihilque superest opibus e tantis tibi.
> —Medea superest. Hic mare et terras vides,
>   ferrumque et ignes et deos et fulmina!

Naive, perhaps, this interplay between the psychological and the celestial? But you will find it in some of the greatest of English tragedies: in the night of Duncan's murder, and throughout *Lear*.

Once seen in this light, Seneca can be left to interpret himself. It is needless to pursue the course of the evil in detail through the several tragedies. But before we take leave of the third movement, I should like to recall the fourth of the propositions which seem to underlie Senecan drama: Evil may overwhelm, but cannot truly vanquish, the soul in which Reason has won the battle. To Seneca, as we saw earlier, the greatest of all dramas was the drama of the Stoic Cato battling with Fortune (a battle which, as we know and Seneca knew, ended with Cato's death at Utica). *Ecce par deo dignum*: here is a gladiatorial duel worthy of the sight of God![81]

A number of the Senecan tragedies contain minor figures who, in the midst of the explosion, give way neither to passion in themselves, nor to the evil which advances on them from the external

[205]

world. Such are Cassandra and Electra in *Agamemnon,* perhaps Jason in *Medea,* certainly the Trojan characters in *Troades.* When these have to die, as all too often they do, they face death itself fearlessly, or even with a kind of exultation. Consider the appearance of Polyxena in the last moment before she dies, victim of the stupid passions of Achaean princes:

> Ipsa deiectos gerit
> vultus pudore, sed tamen fulgent genae,
> magisque solito splendet extremus decor;
> ut esse Phoebi dulcius lumen solet
> iamiam cadentis, astra cum repetunt vices,
> premiturque dubius nocte vicina dies.[82]

Such transfigurations at the moment of suffering we associate more with Christian martyrologies than with tragic princesses. But here we should recall that the Stoics, as well as the Christians, had their martyrology (in which Seneca himself claims an honorable place). It is not, I think, fanciful to see in Polyxena, and in most of the other minor characters mentioned above, *exempla* of Stoic living and Stoic dying, sketched in more or less detail.[83] In two Senecan tragedies, however, such a noble figure is not merely sketched, but brought out in full color: *Phaedra* and *Thyestes.* This is certainly one of the chief reasons why, for me, those plays rank as the finest in the Senecan corpus. There is not merely the obvious consequence of an increase in sheer theatrical power (so considered, the confrontation of Phaedra with Hippolytus, and the scene where Atreus offers Thyestes the regalia before the gates of the Pelopid palace,[84] rival almost any scene from Greek tragedy), but a greater richness and depth in all respects.

Without doubt Hippolytus and Thyestes, as Seneca conceives them, are noble characters; and they are Stoics. Not, of course, perfect Stoic sages, for not one of those is found in many centuries; but Stoics of the large class to which Seneca himself belonged, who have seen the ideal and are struggling after it as best they may.[85] The relationship between the attitudes of Hippolytus, Thyestes and Seneca in his prose works is so close that it cannot be due to coincidence. When Hippolytus is tempted by Phaedra's nurse,[86] he replies with a long speech (483–564) in which he defends the virtuous innocence of the woods, equating

[206]

°for 'martyrologies'] *read* 'martyrs'

it with the innocence of the Age of Gold; the speech is paralleled, even in some verbal details, by Seneca's *Letter* 90 on the same subject.[87] After he has said his say, the Nurse laments (580–582) that her words make no more impact on him than sea waves beating against a rock—an image which elsewhere in Seneca is applied exclusively to the assault of evil on the philosopher.[88]

Thyestes' speeches in *Thyestes* 404–420 and 446–470 parallel the speech of Hippolytus very closely in tone and in detail. But Thyestes' case is more complex. Unlike Hippolytus, he has known luxury, power and guilt; it has taken exile and poverty to bring him to his present understanding. Now, recalled by Atreus in pretended reconciliation, and faced again by the glittering palace, he is filled with sorrow: "Back to the woods [412]! . . . Before, in that state which all men think hard, I was brave and happy [417–18] . . . . But at the height of my power I never ceased from terror, from fear of the very sword hanging at my side [447–49] . . . . Out of experience I speak: one may choose ill fortune in preference to good [453–4]!" It is, to me, almost inconceivable that Seneca could have written such lines without conscious reference to *his own* exile and recall; the language is actually reminiscent of his own words in the *Consolatio ad Helviam.*[89] Certainly *Octavia*, composed a few years after Seneca's death, attributes to its stage-Seneca a speech which combines elements from that *Consolation* with the speeches of Thyestes and of Hippolytus. Seneca is there shown bitterly regretting his recall to the height of power from that happy exile among the remote rocks of Corsica,[90] where he had had leisure to improve his mind by studying the majestic courses of the stars;[91] he ends with a nostalgic picture of the Golden Age, and the decline of the human race thereafter.[92] The *Octavia's* unknown author, who was undoubtedly someone close to Seneca, therefore saw nothing odd in identifying the views of Thyestes and Hippolytus with those of the Master.

Thus seen, the two plays acquire an added poignancy. Into them, and especially into *Thyestes*, there enters something that transcends the mechanics of a plot, or the cold abstractions of a philosophical system. Seneca's own experience is present here. His whole career is a record of that terrible incompatibility between the inward and the outward life, and his struggle to choose between the demands of the two. Abide by the inward life like Hippolytus, and you will be wiped out; weaken, and compromise

[207]

(however innocently) with the outward life, like Thyestes, and you will be worse than wiped out. That is the dilemma of the practicing Stoic, and, some might think, of the practicing human being. Nowhere that I know is it posed with crueller force than in *Thyestes*. Those who have merely read a synopsis of its plot, and some who have read further (including even Eliot), regularly single out this tragedy as the supreme example of Senecan bloodiness. But perhaps we have seen enough in the course of this discussion to realize how these horrors should be understood. The mad, meticulous murder-ritual in the Palace yard, the diabolical cookery, the garlanded reveler quaffing wine and blood with unaccountable tears—for Seneca these are only pictorial by-products of the more terrible realities with which he was concerned in the tragedies, the prose and the Julio-Claudian court. *Thyestes* is in fact the most clearly Stoic, and in some ways the most compassionate and human, of the dramas. Anger, insatiate ambition, the intolerable choice between political kingship and the kingship of the mind, are not exactly dead issues yet, though we may be shy of formulating them this way. Nor, or course, are we accustomed to transcribe psychological and moral collapse into terms of a pre-Copernican night sky; as Seneca does in the last chorus of *Thyestes*, where the Zodiac slides madly into the abyss, its gleaming signs entangled and running wild, the Bull goring Gemini, Sagittarius at long last loosing his arrow from the snapped string. . . .

What kind of drama is this? I have suggested above that Senecan tragedy, on unprejudiced inspection, proves to possess many of the qualities that we still associate with the greatest drama: speakability; actability; powerful theatrical situations; conflict both between minds and within minds; and what we may describe (shortly and, by Senecan standards, not quite accurately) as an unrestricted symbolic use of the concrete universe for the abstract, which gives his text, rightly read, the immediate impact of nightmare—just so do our dreams operate in conveying the psychic state. Yet in one most important respect these tragedies differ from almost all the other great tragedies of the Western world: they do not doubt to the very end, they leave no ultimate questions open. To the Stoic, as (it is said) to Isaac Newton, the Universe is a cipher that only waits to be cracked. If we could see it all, we should see the adamantine chains, cause linked to cause, in which all reality is bound, in which God himself, though by his own will, is prisoner.[93] *Agunt opus suum fata:* the fates go on with their own work.[94] Even as things are, with vast discoveries still to make,[95] the Stoic has seen enough into his moral-physical reality to understand and formulate the practical rules of Fate's game with the individual. And in these tragedies the rules are every time obeyed, the game is played out.

With such a rigid system implied in it, with such unquestioning faith in the ultimate workings of the world, with such a desperately urgent sense of the absolute reality of sin and virtue—this drama can only properly be classed as religious drama. Our earliest ancient tragedies, the first plays of Aeschylus, composed when the Western world was just emerging into an era of free inquiry, show many of the same qualities (some instances have been noted here and there in this essay). Our latest ancient tragedies, those of Seneca, seem in this and some other respects to mark the beginning of the reverse process, the transition from free inquiry to an era of religion.

Yet to suppose on these grounds that the tragedies have now lost their meaning, that they could only make sense to a limited (and long dead) circle of Stoics and Neronians, would be mistaken. Though their formulation is strange to us, they seem, once understood, to touch on permanent realities in the human condition. True, as Regenbogen pointed out in a fine study,[96] the Western world has tended only to come back to them at the periods of its greatest emotional, religious and intellectual strain, when the universe seemed to be falling about its ears: it was during the crisis of the sixteenth century that in England Thomas Newton produced his *Tenne Tragedies*; on the Continent some of the most perceptive criticism—and, incidentally, the last complete commented edition of the *Tragedies* yet [97]—came from the generation that had witnessed the bestialities of the Thirty Years' War. Regenbogen could, perhaps, have offered further examples: his own study of the tragedies, and the distinguished series of German studies on the same lines which succeeded it, coincided with a period when continental Europe was entering and passing through a nightmare. (The sense of immediate reality in those studies contrasts strangely with Eliot's leisurely, detached, purely *literary*

[209]

essay, published in England during the same year that Regenbogen's lecture was delivered.) The pessimistic, in some moods,
may wonder whether the nightmare has not since spread, whether
human passions have not now begun to threaten, literally, the
existence of the earth and the innocence of the sky. "Marke thou,"
says the sixteen-year-old Elizabethan in his preface to the translation of *Oedipus*, "what is ment by the whole course of the History: and frame thy lyfe free from such mischiefs, wherewith the
world at this present is universally overwhelmed, the wrathful
vengeaunce of God provoked, the Body plagued, the mynde and
Conscience in midst of deepe devouring daungers most terribly
assaulted." Nevile was living through the religious crisis of the
Renaissance, but with only a few changes his words would apply
to the crisis of our own time.

NOTES

[1] *Seneca his Tenne Tragedies translated into English*, edited by
Thomas Newton, anno 1581; with an introduction by T. S. Eliot.
(Bloomington and London 1966).

[2] No less than five translators are concerned, all of whom actually
worked in the sixties of the century, with the exception of Newton
himself. See Eliot's Introduction, xlv.

[3] My quotation from Studley's *Hippolytus* provides many examples.
Of all Newton's contributors only Jasper Heywood, the translator of
Hercules Furens, Troades and *Thyestes*, puts up any resistance whatever
to this temptation.

[4] For evidence on the Greek tragedies entitled *Thyestes*, I refer to
A. Nauck, *Tragicorum Graecorum Fragmenta*[2] (Leipzig 1889) 965
(*Index Fabularum*); and, for the Sophoclean versions, to A. C. Pearson,
The Fragments of Sophocles (Cambridge 1917) II.91ff, 185ff.

[5] A fair example of these is probably the third edition of W. Beare's
The Roman Stage (London 1964). It devotes some half-dozen pages
in all to the Senecan tragedies (234–36, 351–54), and even those pages
are mostly concerned to show, not without indignation, that they are
impossible to stage—a conclusion which would have startled the Eliza-
bethans. Beare's general opinion of the tragedies is summed up in a
sentence on 235: "The Senecan tragedies are simply artificial imitations
of Greek tragedy, worked up in the style of the Silver Age, and they
are meant to be declaimed, not acted."

6 Sen.*Med.* 375–79, and, e.g., Beare (*op. cit.* in note 5) 354.

7 The chief exceptions are the two *Consolationes* written in the earlier part of his exile (41–49 A.D.) to his mother Helvia and to Claudius' freedman Polybius, both evidently oblique pleas for pardon; and the *de Clementia* addressed to Nero early in his reign, and apparently designed as a general program for the new regime. But even these contain relatively very few direct references to Seneca's own activities.

8 There is no satisfactory account of Seneca's life (outward or inward) in our language. A convenient assemblage of the hard facts will be found in Schanz-Hosius, *Geschichte der römischen Literatur* II⁴ (Munich 1935) 680–82. As an elegant first introduction to the subject I would recommend a little book by Pierre Grimal, *Sénèque: sa vie, son oeuvre; avec un exposé de sa philosophie* (Paris 1948). Unfortunately, the latter is hardly documented in detail at all, and also paints Seneca in unbelievably rosy colors. I wish those colors were justified; but one does not normally suffer from an acute sense of guilt, as Seneca did from end to end of his life, without reason.

9 M. Préchac, "La date de naissance de Sénèque, *REL* 11 (1934) 360ff.

10 *Q.N.*1.16: one of those surrealist passages in Seneca, of which more will be said later.

11 *Ep.*6.1: "I feel myself, Lucilius, not just being improved, but being transformed."

12 *Ep.*34.1: "I increase, I exult, I shake off my age and grow warm again!" The assonances, as well as the feeling, of this sentence might well belong even to the late Middle Ages. Seneca is here rejoicing over his protégé Lucilius' progress in philosophy; for this missionary zeal, the reader may compare *Ep.*8.1–6, and *Q.N.*3 *praef.*

13 *Ep.*26.1–6: quoted here only in part.

14 Perfectly intelligible, if one recalls mid-first-century political conditions. It is probably no coincidence that the only historian known to me who has made much headway in the political interpretation of Seneca's prose writings spent her formative years in East Germany.

15 There are in fact some indications that Seneca took a practical interest in shorthand. Isidore of Seville (*Etymol.*1.22.2) says that he made great improvements in it; and this is not necessarily contradicted by Seneca's derogatory remarks about its inventor in *Ep.*90.25.

16 This seven-book work is usually thought to have been composed fairly early in the reign of Nero; after rereading it for the purpose of

this article, I cannot resist the conjecture that Nero's professor was subjected to some early version of the publish-or-perish rule. Imposed, perhaps, by Agrippina? One would readily attribute so fiendish an innovation to the later Julio-Claudian epoch.

¹⁷ In Haase's edition (Leipzig 1851) of the complete works—which is also the last edition of any major portion of Seneca's prose works whatever that attempts to help the reader to follow Seneca's thought, both by typographic means and by the inclusion of a full index of subject matter. It is a sign of the general drift of Western classicism since that time that later editions, far more "scientific" though they are, offer no such aids. A solid stream of thoughtfully constituted text, an index of proper names, and an index of *testimonia*, are the most the reader can now expect. This is unfortunately true even of the otherwise excellent text of the *Letters* recently published by L. D. Reynolds (Oxford 1965).

¹⁸ See *Ep.*113, largely on the extreme Stoic view that the virtues are *animalia*. Seneca has a good deal of quiet fun in deducing from this that "circumspect walking" is not only an *animal*, but spherical.

¹⁹ *De Ira* 3.6.1; *Cons.Helv.*6.7; 8.4; *Ot.Sap.*5.6; *Q.N.*7.25.1–2; *Ep.* 104.23.

²⁰ *Ep.*88.7.

²¹ *Ep.*115.3–4.

²² *Ep.*112.4.

²³ *Ep.*110.6–7, answering Lucretius' famous equation of the superstitious man's fear in the light, with the child's fear in darkness (2.55–56).

²⁴ *Q.N.*6.1.

²⁵ *Q.N.*2.59.

²⁶ *Ep.*91.1–2.

²⁷ E.g., *de Ira* 3.16–21.

²⁸ "To show the might of supreme vices in the supreme estate," *Cons. Helv.*10.4.

²⁹ *Q.N.*3.27–30, especially 30.7–8.

³⁰ *Ben.*7.27.

³¹ E.g., *Cons.Marc.*9 and 14–15 (the *funera Caesarum*); *Cons. Polyb.*11; *Tranq.*11.7. But the most vivid picture of all, as so often,

is found not in the prose works but in the tragedies: *Herc.Fur.*838ff, where those crowds are likened to the *populus* streaming towards the theaters of Rome on a festival day—the ultimate ancestor, perhaps, of Dante's more elaborate (but not, to me, more compelling) image of the crowds on the bridge during the Jubilee (*Inferno* 18.28ff).

[32] The Senecan doctrine on the collapse of *ratio* in the clash with the passions is to be found in some brilliant chapters of the *de Ira*, which every reader of the *Tragedies* (especially of *Medea* and *Phaedra*) should consult: 1.1, 1.7–10, 2.35.2, 3.4.1–3. *Ep.*114.22–25 is also worth looking at.

[33] E.g., *Cons.Helv.*13.3.

[34] For which one of the many Senecan equivalents is *mors . . . denuntiata nascenti est,* "death was (our) sentence at birth," *Cons. Marc.*10.5.

[35] E.g., *Prov.*2.10; *Ep.*70.14, 91.21; *Phaedra* 139; *Troad.*144–164.

[36] The Latin text is slightly confused here in the manuscripts. I have translated what seems to me the least unlikely restoration of it, dropping *ripis* and adopting P. Thomas' *palude* for *pavidae*.

[37] E.g., *Centuries of Meditations* 3.3 ("The corn was orient and immortal wheat . . .").

[38] *Cons.Marc.*18.7, from the newborn infant's vision of the world, which I have already quoted in part: "Here you will see vessels making for lands they do not know."

[39] Duly noted by Christopher Columbus, and probably of far more importance in the pursuit of his dream than Seneca's oftener quoted, but vaguer, prophecy of Atlantic discovery in *Medea* (375–79).

[40] A half-line from Virgil's famous ant simile, *Aen.*4.404: "A black column marches in the plain."

[41] *Cons.Helv.*8.6.

[42] *Ben.*4.23.

[43] *Ep.*90.42: compare 102.28, for the brilliance of the light among the stars.

[44] *Cons.Helv.*8.6; cf. 6.7–8.

45 *Q.N.*3.16.4ff.

46 *Ep.*21.5 (*profunda supra nos altitudo temporis veniet*).

47 *Q.N.*7.25.3–5.

48 Apart from the passage immediately to be quoted, see *Cons.Marc.* 26.6; *Cons.Polyb.*1.2; *Epigram* 7.5–6 (if this is really by Seneca); *Ep.*71.12–13; *Q.N.*6.2.9. A speech put into Seneca's mouth in the pseudo-Senecan historical drama *Octavia* (377–437), if taken as a true record of Seneca's opinions, would imply that towards the end of his life Seneca, like the early Christians, expected the catastrophe to happen very shortly. The speech is followed immediately by the entry of Nero, almost as if he embodied the ultimate climax of sin.

49 MS 12665; an easily accessible translation is in Irma A. Richter, *Selections from the Notebooks of Leonardo da Vinci* (Oxford 1952) 187–93.

50 *Ep.*9.16. The bare notion, indeed, does not originate with Seneca, but with the early Stoa; see Chrysippus, *frag.phys.*1064 (von Arnim). But Seneca's treatment of it (actually included by von Arnim as *frag. phys.*1065) is infinitely more imaginative.

51 *De Ira* 2.35.5; cf. 2.35.3.

52 See, e.g., *Ep.*27.1, 57.3, 87.5 (*parum adhuc profeci*).

53 Tac.*Dial.*2–11, passim.

54 The most important passage is *Ep.*80.7–8, where Seneca is speaking of true and false happiness. An example of the latter (*personata felicitas*, happiness residing only in the mask) is the hired actor who acts a royal part on the stage, draws his day wage, and goes home to sleep on a rag quilt. Seneca quotes some of the lines he speaks (*dicit*); they are quite clearly tragic (probably from plays about the Pelopid house), and were so classified by Ribbeck. Other passages which imply that Seneca had seen, and presumed his reader to have seen, straight theatrical performances are: *de Ira* 2.17.1; *Ep.*76.31; *Cons.Marc.*10.1 (on theatrical props); *Q.N.*7.32.3, where three kinds of very popular spectacle are quite casually referred to, the pantomime, the private theater with stage and masks (*pulpitum; sub persona trita frons*), the gladiatorial games.

55 I am grateful to H. A. Mason for the first impulse to make such experiments, and to Miss Rosemary Barton and Mrs. G. Amis for their admirable work in carrying them out.

56 One of the insuperable difficulties for an English translator of Seneca is the slowness of our language in comparison to the Latin con-

cision and speed; but here is a plain rendering of the sense of these lines: "Beware the King!"—"My father also was a king."—"Aren't you afraid of arms?"—"No, not even arms sprung from Earth!"—"You'll die for it."—"That's what I long for."—"Flee!"—"I've long been sick of flight."—"Medea, . . ."—"*Medea* is what I shall become!"—". . . You're a mother!"—"Yes, and look at the father!" Only speech, and Latin speech at that, can fairly reproduce the helter-skelter duel between reason and emotion which is created here.

[57] That is, the Chorus is not always on stage, and need not even consist of the same individual(s) throughout the piece. We do not, of course, know enough about Hellenistic *tragedy* to say whether it followed the same pattern. Yet there is one suggestive piece of evidence. In Seneca's *Hercules Furens* (827–29), and again in his *Agamemnon* (586–88)—in both cases, long after the first choral song of the play—an actor announces the approach of a band of people, who then proceed to sing. This way of introducing a new company of singers is exactly paralleled in numerous passages from Hellenistic comedy, which are collected and discussed by E. W. Handley in his commentary on Menander's *Dyskolos* (London 1965) 230–32. The Senecan examples might be worth adding to his illustrative material there.

[58] *Agam.*589–609, following Richter's text in *Senecae Tragoediae*, ed. R. Peiper and G. Richter (Leipzig 1902). No two of these verses are metrically the same, but I try, by indentation, to show the main rhythmic movements.

[59] *Oedip.*36 (*fecimus caelum nocens*), 79, 631ff, 652, 1052–61.

[60] "So there's nothing you can't measure?" says Seneca to the Roman astronomer (*Ep.*88.13). "If you are a real scientist, measure the soul of a man, tell us how great it is, tell us how minute it is."

[61]This is not the place to discuss in detail the authenticity of the remaining three plays preserved in the medieval tradition of Seneca under his name. Briefly: I would be fairly confident that the historical play, *Octavia*, is not by Seneca, but by a close friend or pupil; my reasons are given in *CQ* 12 (1961) 18–30. The same probably holds good of the elephantine *Hercules Oetaeus*; for some good arguments, see W. H. Friedrich in *H* 82 (1954) 51–84. As for *Phoenissae*, I follow the majority in assuming that its 664 extant lines, though from Seneca's hand, are only an unfinished sketch of a drama—or possibly of two dramas. The discussion of Senecan drama in the following pages does not, generally, embrace these three plays.

[62] Possible, though to me not quite certain, exceptions are *Phaedra* and *Oedipus*, which some rate as six-act plays; see K. Anliker's *Prologe und Akteinteilungen in Senecas Tragödien* (Bern 1960) 93–97.

But Seneca's *general* observance of the five-act rule is interesting, in view of the fact that the rule now seems to have been emerging early in the Hellenistic age (see E. W. Handley, *op. cit.* p. 4 [n.57 above], for temperate comments on this question). This observance, like the behavior of Senecan choruses (see n.57 above), may perhaps count as another indication that Senecan dramaturgy was influenced by Hellenistic Greek practice, and may provide another warning against the direct comparison of his technique with that of the fifth-century tragedians.

⁶³ The appearances of a *second* figure in the Prologues of *Oedipus* (Jocasta) and *Thyestes* (the Fury) hardly alter the dramatic effect of solitude. The extant opening scene of the fragmentary *Phoenissae* (cf. n.61 above) is almost certainly not a Prologue: it has some of the marks of a Senecan Second Act.

⁶⁴ *Phaedra* 1 and 28: "Away, surround the shadowy woods!" and "He who is moved by woodland splendor."

⁶⁵ Giomini's correction, followed by W. Strzelecki, *Rivista di Cultura Classica e Medievale* 2 (1960) 369–70, of the corrupt place name at line 29; it seems to me as certain as such things can be.

⁶⁶ Also in *Ep.*90 and *Q.N.*1.17.5–10; similar views are put into Seneca's mouth by the author of *Octavia* (394ff).

⁶⁷ *Herc.Fur.*698–707, a remarkable passage.

⁶⁸ It will be remembered (see n.61 above) that I am not counting the *Hercules Oetaeus* or the *Octavia* as genuine, nor the *Phoenissae* as complete. By the "Second Act" of a Senecan tragedy, I mean what students of Greek tragedy, following Aristotle, call the First Episode; in other words, I count the Senecan Prologue as the first act of the five.

⁶⁹ The most moving of them, incidentally, and the most interesting to a student of Seneca, is the scene between Seneca and Nero, 377–592. It is by far the earliest extant evidence, apart from such dark allusions as can be gathered from Seneca's own writings, about Seneca's attempted political and moral influence on Nero during the final period of his political ascendency. Though clearly committed to Seneca's cause, the unknown author of *Octavia* should not be ignored on this point. His melancholy and noble Seneca, in daily expectation of the end of the world, confronts the stupid, animal passions of Nero as the very embodiment of Stoic *ratio;* and holds up, as a political model, the mature Augustus (*Octavia* 477ff). The versifier has, of course, recalled Seneca's frequent use of Augustus as a political *exemplum* in the prose writings, especially *Clem.*1.9, addressed to Nero almost at the beginning of

[216]

his reign; but there are signs, here and elsewhere in *Octavia*, that he speaks also from direct personal experience of the events he describes.

[70] It is, of course, almost certain that Seneca followed, in part, the plot of Euripides' *lost* earlier version of the Hippolytus (for a recent reconstruction, which uses Seneca's play as a source rather more freely than I would, see B. Snell, *Scenes from Greek Drama* [Berkeley and Los Angeles 1964], c. 2). But there is no evidence at all as to whether that lost version contained a precedent for the Senecan scene now under discussion.

[71] The more significant of Seneca's references to the doctrine are collected in n.32 above; on the psychosomatic effects of passion, see also *Ep*.52.12, 106.5, 114.3.

[72] Suet.*Calig*.50: "Though his countenance was naturally wild and hideous, he deliberately tried to enhance its savagery by grimacing in front of a mirror, so as to produce every possible effect of panic and dread."

[73] Other such passages in the tragedies are: *Med*.849–69; *Troad*. 615–18, 623–26; *Oedip*.921–25; *Agam*.128 (*totus in vultu est dolor,* "all her agony is in her face"); *Herc.Fur*.329–30. Add the non-Senecan *Herc.Oet*.240–53.

[74] In *Phaedra* and *Thyestes*. A third instance will be found in *Hercules Oetaeus*, 233–568, where, as always, the author of this play has a sharp eye for the typically and essentially Senecan.

[75] These terms and concepts are of course alien to Seneca himself, but the effect is there—imposed, as has been suggested in the survey of the prose works, by the Stoic world view which he had made his own.

[76] In his prose works, the patriotic Seneca usually rates Cato the Younger a little nearer to the ideal; but he follows the Greek Stoics in his deep respect for Hercules. See *Const.Sap*.2.1–2; *Ben*.1.13.1–3 and 4.8.1. Any who doubt that he so conceived Hercules in the *Hercules Furens* also should turn again to the majestic prayer for world peace and world innocence uttered by the hero just before his madness *strikes*, 926–39 (there is no parallel, naturally, in Euripides' version).

[77] *Herc.Fur*.76–86, 108ff. It will be recalled that Euripides' prologue is different (it consists of a dialogue between Amphitryo and Megara); that nowhere in his play is Hera brought on the stage; and that the onset of madness in the center of the play is represented by Lyssa, Frenzy, in person.

[217]

78 An exciting event, if imaginatively handled; but we shall not see it, alas, until someone composes an actable, speakable translation of the tragedies into twentieth-century English—a very difficult, but not impossible, task. The Elizabethan translations, though actable in their day, are actable no longer.

79 See Amphitryo's words at 952–54.

80 *Thyest.*637–38, 776–78, 784ff, 789ff, 891–93, etc.

81 *Prov.*2.9.

82 *Troad.*1137–42: "Through shame her eyes are downcast—yet her cheeks are alight, her beauty, at the last, shines with a strange splendor; so is the Sun's light sweeter at his very setting, when the stars are claiming their turn again, and night presses close on glimmering day."

83 For the radiance of Polyxena in the face of death, see also *Troad.* 945–48. This subtle and powerful play (among the most admired of all Senecan tragedies until c. 1800 A.D.) seems to me primarily a fantasy on the Senecan view of Death as Liberator; a strange fantasy, where the conquerors are in terror, the dead are happy, the conquered and doomed arrive at a sort of happiness. Leopardi comes to mind.

84 *Phaedr.*583–718, *Thyest.*508–45. Both scenes imperatively require acting, or, at the very least, envisaging. If that is done, it will be found that the regalia scene from *Thyestes* is not altogether unworthy of comparison even with the tapestry scene of Aeschylus' *Agamemnon.* A man who has found true kingship, in the Stoic sense of kingship over the passions, is offered false, political kingship; and before our eyes, reluctantly and out of mistaken *pietas*, grasps the scepter and puts on the diadem.

85 For the rarity of the true Stoic *sapiens, quem tot saeculis quaerimus*, see *Tranqu.*7.4–5; also *de Ira* 2.10.6; *Const.Sap.*7.1; *Ep.*42.1 (the truly good man occurs about as often as the phoenix). Throughout his extant works Seneca emphatically denies that he himself is a *sapiens*; rather he is a *proficiens*, an "advancer" (*Ep.*71.29–37; *Cons.Helv.*5.2–3), though as late as *Ep.*87.5 he is still ruefully confessing that he has advanced too little—*parum adhuc profeci.*

86 Reason now perverted to the slavery of Passion? It will be remembered that in the previous act (85–273) the Nurse had at first tried by all means to dissuade Phaedra from her love, but had finally capitulated.

87 Compare in particular *Phaedr.*483 (the woodland life is *libera et vitio carens*) and *Ep.*90.44 (the Golden Age was *egregia . . . et carens*

fraude); 495 (urban man's terror of strange noises) and 90.43; 502–03 (primitive man's aggression is turned only against wild animals) and 90.41; 519–20 (primitive man drinking from cupped hands) and 90.14; 524–25 (sleeping under the stars) and 90.42.

[88] The image is of course common in Greek and Latin, occurring in many different contexts (e.g., *Aen*.6.470–71). But in Seneca I have only found it in the following passages: *Const.Sap*.3.5 (the *sapiens* resisting all external injuries), *de Ira* 3.25.3–4 (the *sapiens* resisting the infection of anger), *Vit.Beat*.27.3 (Socrates impervious to slander). Marcus Aurelius applies the image similarly; see *Meditations* 4.49, where he urges himself to be "like the headland, against which the waves break unceasingly; but it stays upright, and around it the boiling foam is laid to sleep."

[89] With 417–18 compare *Cons.Helv*.6.1 ("let us dismiss the vulgar view of exile") and 20.1 ("I am happy and high-spirited, *laetus et alacer*").

[90] *Octav*.377–82; cf. the passages from *Thyestes* (412–54, *passim*) just quoted.

[91] *Octav*.383–90; practically a condensed versification of a noble passage in *Cons.Helv*.8.

[92] *Octav*.395–435; cf. *Phaedr*.526–62.

[93] *Prov*.5.7–8; cf. *Ben*.6.23.1–3; *Q.N*.2.35.2; *Oedip*.980–97; *Herc. Fur*.178–91.

[94] *Cons.Marc*.21.6–7.

[95] *Q.N*.7.30–32.

[96] Otto Regenbogen, *Schmerz und Tod in den Tragödien Senecas* (Darmstadt 1963) esp. 11–25. The work was originally published in *Vorträge der Bibliothek Warburg* 7 (1927–28) 167–218.

[97] J. F. Gronovius, *L. Annaei Senecae Tragoediae passim restitutae cum Gronovii et variorum notis* (Leiden 1661). This was the basis of Gronovius' son's re-edition (Amsterdam 1682) and of Schroeder's (Delft 1728).

THE GAIETY OF LANGUAGE[1]

D. S. Carne-Ross

'WE NEED AN EYE WHICH CAN SEE THE PAST IN ITS PLACE WITH ITS definite differences from the present,' Eliot wrote, 'and yet so lively that it shall be as present to us as the present.' An eye for the present moment of the past, for those aspects of an old author that most call for attention today, is by and large the critic's eye. It is even more the translator's eye. It is not the scholar's eye. Many contemporary classical scholars, indeed, alarmed by the impurity of method they detect in a Murray or a Verrall, are above all concerned to avoid importing modern interests into their reading of an ancient text. Their business is with those many and complex questions which only an exact scholarship can handle; what remains may be left to the dilettante or perhaps to the scholar himself in his private hours. Such 'purity of method' is no doubt admirable in itself, but when it involves ignoring whatever it is in an author that made him worth reading in the first place, it is time to start asking questions. Professor Page, in his edition of Sappho and Alcaeus, is serious and intent when he is trying to establish the true reading, to sort out some linguistic difficulty, or castigating the blunders of his predecessors; when he comes to the experience offered by Sappho's poetry, the body of realised life, this seriousness gives way to an easy, dismissive irony that is often not far from contempt. 'Here, at the height of her suffering, she devotes a quarter of her poem to such a flight of fancy, with much detail irrelevant to her present theme.' So Page concludes his analysis of the great poem which the Alexandrian editors placed first in their collection of her work. His task, as he himself allows, is 'the difficult and doubtful task of *interpreting* at least the longer . . . pieces.' My italics point to something that the bland, hard surface of Page's prose rather consistently refuses to do. He makes little attempt to engage with Sappho's *poetry* (as distinct from her dialect, meters, historical references and so forth) and whenever she fails to conform to his notion of what a poem should be, it is always Sappho who is at fault.

In reading Sappho one does not have to look for 'the present moment of the past.' Everything is present. More completely than any Greek poet except Homer, she cancels the intervening centuries. But much Greek poetry is far more specialised—in its formal procedures and in the qualities of its sensibility—and it is here that the critic, and the translator, show what they are made of. Attic tragedy, despite its present vogue, is in many ways a

[1] *Bacchylides: Complete Poems* translated by Robert Fagles, with a foreword by Sir Maurice Bowra. Introduction and Notes by Adam M. Parry. Yale University Press, 1961. Pp. xxiv + 123. $3.75.

strange, remote form. We are perhaps rather too easily assuming that it has been domesticated. Choral lyric is stranger still, the most distant province of Greek literature. Of the two choral poets whose work has survived in some bulk, Pindar, superficially the more remote, might I think prove the more accessible—given a critic, or translator, who could wake him into life. Perhaps our approach to Pindar starts at the wrong end; we try (as finally of course we must) to make sense of a Pindaric whole, of a complete ode, even of his entire remaining work, chattering nervously the while about formulae of break-off and transition, gnomic bridge passages, ring composition and the like, in the effort to make ourselves feel at home in his curious world. It might be better if we started with the immediate *donnée,* his diction. The furious pressure to which Pindar subjects language, the incessant dislocations of normal usage, the extraordinary play of metaphor, the systematic exploitation of the sensuous confusions of speech, the way abstract nouns are wrenched into the sphere of sensation (to *taste* toil, to *flame with* excellence, to be *clasped*—or blended, mingled, wedded, almost *bedded*—with praise)—all this induces a state of heightened response in which the facts of everyday experience are dissolved, 'destroyed,' and then recreated in a new sensuous fulness. His poems 'live or die as physical objects radiating the freshness and pleasure of a transformed reality.'[2]

But if Pindar offers something that could excite the student of modern poetry (in a sense, of course, all poetry is modern poetry), it is not at all clear that Bacchylides, who shares with him many of the procedures of choral lyric, could be approached in this way. There is nothing in his language, I suppose, that is particularly close to us today, no single aspect of his poetry as a whole that strongly engages our creative or critical interests. The critic should no doubt be supple and imaginative enough to deal with texts that do not bear on his immediate preoccupations—though in fact little of literary interest seems to have been said about Bacchylides since the sands of Egypt yielded up some 1500 lines of his poetry over sixty years ago.[3] But what is the translator to do? What sort of modern English equivalent can he devise for this poet, a good

[2] I take the expression from Frank Kermode's excellent short study of Stevens (*Wallace Stevens*, Edinburgh and London, 1960, p. 25), a poet who could, I think, help to open an approach to Pindar. For an example of Pindaric 'destruction,' see N. 10.35–6.

[3] It is sad that the excitement caused by this discovery has been allowed to die down so completely. There is a quite 'unscholarly' enthusiasm in the way his second editor, Friederich Blass, refers to the event: 'Resurgunt litterae vetustae, ζῶσιν οἱ γᾶς ὑπαὶ κείμενοι, atque utinam etiam alii, qui nunc nondum videntur!' There is striking evidence of the (lost) unity of European culture, a unity centered in Greece and Rome, in the fact that a couple of Bacchylides' odes should have been *translated into Croatian* within two years of the discovery of the papyrus.

one but not, like Pindar, a great one, working in a difficult remote genre?

The attempt to approach Bacchylides critically has promptly led me into the standard critical cliché, the comparison with Pindar, a cliché as old as 'Longinus' and probably much older. Bacchylides is a delightful, interesting author—so the critical writ runs; his work is full of bright, vivid imagery, he has his moments of suggestive pathos, but—*he cannot be compared to Pindar*. Mr. Parry, in his introduction to the present volume, offers his own (negative) version:

> To blame Bacchylides for not being Pindar is as childish a judgment as to condemn Vermeer for falling short of Rembrandt, or Marvell for missing the grandeur of Milton.

And the comparison duly follows. Now I don't at all want to quarrel with Mr. Parry; he has a number of good things to say in his commentaries on individual poems and I suspect that his insight contributed substantially to the success of this volume. Of course he means no more here than that it is foolish to blame chalk for not being cheese. He is just clearing his throat. Nonetheless the relaxed critical tone is all too representative of the patronising way in which classical scholars like to address the general public. For if it is foolish to blame Bacchylides for not being Pindar, that is just what is always being done, whereas who has ever blamed Marvell for not being Milton? Why bother to make so trivial a point?

But if the critic is to deny himself this Pindar/Bacchylides comparison, what is there left for him to do? What other point can he make? We are always being told now that translation is a form of criticism, so let us take this question to Mr. Fagles' versions and see what sort of answer emerges.

Bacchylides presents the translator with a number of problems. I will single out two: the fragmentary state of the text, and the *embarras* of compound epithets. These are not the most obviously significant problems, but they will serve my present purpose. For the first has a general interest extending beyond Bacchylides, and the second can I think lead us to the heart of his poetry. Or at least to its surface, which may prove to be what he principally offers.

The poem which stands first in most editions, the epinician ode to Argeius of Ceos, has not reached us intact. We have lost (according to Blass) the first 110 lines, of which 46 can be partly reconstructed from separate fragments. It was a clever stroke of the *Zeitgeist* to let Egypt start revealing its tattered treasures just at the moment when a taste for the fragmentary was developing in the arts. An earlier translator would not have made much of the odds and ends assembled by Blass and would probably have started, where Jebb's text starts, at line 111. But to someone

familiar with modern verse there is often a genuine pleasure to
be found in these ruined syllables. The lack of connection we
can altogether take in our stride—we are used to establishing
connections for ourselves. Pound's little poem 'Papyrus', which
aroused the scholarly indignation of Graves and Laura Riding,
shows, playfully, how readily the fragments of Oxyrhynchus can
be assimilated:[4]

> Spring . . . . .
> Too long . . . .
> Gongula . . . .

One's eye, coasting down Blass' column (how much of her
technique did H.D. learn in this way, one wonders), is first
caught by a couple of lines which are not in the papyrus at all—

> oh godbuilt gates / of Pelops' shining island—

but were retrieved from the scholiast's comment on Pindar *O.*
13.4. At line 48 we find two words which can be reconstructed
as ἱστουργοὶ κόραι, 'girls at the loom', and at 50, μελίφρονος ὕπνου,
'of sweet sleep'. The whole section 49–55 is in fact quite promising. I quote Jebb's synopsis:

> One of the maidens, on awaking from sleep, speaks to an-
> other about quitting their ἀρχαίαν πόλιν, and seeking a new
> abode 'on the verge of the sea' (ἀνδήροις ἁλός), in the full
> 'rays of the sun'.

From these bits and pieces, Mr. Fagles produces the following
lines:

> O gates flung up by the gods
> On Pelops' shining island . . .
> Girls at the looms . . .
> Delicious sleep . . .
> A fine old city . . .
> And dunes where the combers
> Crash under searing sun . . .

It was clever of Mr. Fagles to have made this *prosōpon tēlauges*
for himself out of such shaky material. But of course, you say,
this is not what Bacchylides wrote. It proves, does it not, what

[4] 'Who or what is Gongula?' they enquire. 'Is it a name of a person?
of a town? of a musical instrument . . . ? Or is it perhaps a mistake for
Gongora . . . ?' (*A Survey of Modernist Poetry*, London 1929, p. 218.)
No doubt Professor Graves has since discovered his blunder, but as he
has not (so far as I know) apologised for it, it is worth pointing out
that 'Papyrus' is exactly what it claims to be, a poem suggested by an
actual Sapphic fragment, first published in *Berliner Klassikertexte*,
v.2, 1907, pp. 14–15 (95 in the Lobel–Page *Fragmenta*). Pound's
Lustra, in which 'Papyrus' appears, was published in 1916.

you had always supposed, that translation is hardly a serious
business. What a contrast between this light-fingered fellow
Fagles raiding the apparatus, magpie fashion, for whatever gauds
may take his fancy, and Lobel (to invoke the most terrifying
name in the business) austerely dipping into his baskets!

This is not, I agree, the facade that Bacchylides designed.
That facade is ruined. What then is the translator to do? He may
reconstruct radically (and produce something like those restored
'medieval' palazzi the Italians used to build); he may skip and
start half way; or he may do what Fagles has done and create,
out of the old stones lying here and there in the grass, an attractive little archway of his own. It pretends—the notes make clear—
to be no more. But it achieves its purpose. It catches our attention
for Bacchylides; it makes us want to read on and discover what
happens next on this sunlit island. It was simply chance that
allowed Fagles to introduce Bacchylides to us speaking our own
fragmentary poetic speech; but it was creative intelligence that
turned this chance to good ends.

Before I show him dealing with something that Bacchylides
really did write, let me point to one more passage in which he
takes advantage of a break in the papyrus. Near the middle of
the ninth ode, in his translation, this passage occurs:

> Harpinna foamed in a sheen of robes
> To mix with sturdy Mars?
> Corcyra curved in wreaths?

To these attractive lines, the papyrus contributes no more than:

$$\upsilon\pi.\pi\lambda o\nu [$$
$$\alpha\nu\epsilon\lambda\iota\kappa o\varsigma\tau\epsilon\phi\alpha[$$

But this is more promising than it looks, for it yields two likely
adjectives, *eupeplos* and the beautiful *helikostephanos*. And the
context helps to establish the owners of these charming costumes.
The poem was written for one Automedes from Phlius, a small
Dorian state in the northeast of the Peloponnese; and in the passage in question, the poet is celebrating the matrimonial successes
of the daughters of the local river god, Asopus. It was Bacchylides' third editor, Jurenka, who drew attention to a passage in
Pausanias (5.22.6) describing how the Phliasians dedicated
statues to these river nymphs and to the gods they lay with:

> Their images have been ordered thus: Nemea is the first of
> the sisters, and after her comes Zeus seizing Aegina; by
> Aegina stands *Harpina*, who, according to the tradition of
> the Eleans and Phliasians, *mated with Ares* . . . ; after her
> is *Corcyra* . . .

Which of these four ladies is to be brought into the poem is a matter of choice, governed by meter and space. Edmonds, whose text is the most fully—and, in his usual manner, the most hazardously—restored of the five which I have been able to consult, plumps for Harpin(n)a and Corcyra, but the second name seems unlikely on metrical grounds.

The larval purist in me regrets, dimly, that Fagles' translation here cannot, perhaps, quite be squared with the meter. It is nonetheless a genuine recovery, not a clever substitute like the opening of the first poem. For even if the names were different, Bacchylides must have written something very like this. 'It is the charm of his ode,' Jebb writes (p.206), 'that it takes us into the heart of these Peloponnesian uplands,' delicately evoking the pious fancy of this remote Greek people who turned the springs and streams of their land into nymphs whose beauty drew down the shining presences from Olympus. Fagles'

> Corcyra *curved in wreaths*

(an admirable translation of *helikostephanos*), with its suggestions of at once rustic piety and archaic *haute couture,* has created for us, out of a few battered syllables and a scholar's footnote, an image of the garlanded statue of the eponymous river nymph, or the nymph herself as local folk-lore conceived her. His success in releasing the picture enclosed in the compound epithet leads me to my second point.

The imperfect state of Bacchylides' text puts the translator on his mettle; faced with this challenge, Mr. Fagles reveals himself an agile, ingenious man, ready (as all good translators must be) to take his *bien* where he finds it and now and then, maybe, when he thinks no one is looking, to add a little *bien* of his own. (This is, nonetheless, to use the sacramental word, an *accurate* translation; its freedoms are dictated by insight into the original.)

The state of the text is an accidental difficulty; the compound epithets are an essential one. The wealth of such epithets seems to have been a characteristic of earlier choral lyric; they are sown thickly in much of what we have of Ibycus and an ancient critic comments on their 'abundant use' in Stesichorus. Pindar's epithets are of course very numerous and often of breath-taking power, but he does not use them as Bacchylides does, heaping up three and even four around a single noun, as at 5.98–9, for example, or 10.37–9. We find over ninety epithets in Bacchylides which do not occur elsewhere in extant Greek; they are probably the most striking single feature of his style, and they face the translator with a serious problem. (By 'the translator,' I mean the man who wants a picture and a meaning and does not suppose that a literal English equivalence is automatically going to bring over the picture and the meaning in the Greek.)[5]

The English language forms simple vernacular compounds easily enough—long-legged, mealy-mouthed and so on—but the elaborate, 'poetic' compound is another matter. If we turn to the 858 lines of the General Prologue to *The Canterbury Tales*, as clean and strong a draught of our native speech as exists, we find that it yields no more than three compounds, 'gat-tothed' (468), 'short-sholdred' (549) and 'fyr-reed' (624), all of the straightforward vernacular kind. But if we look next at the prelude to *Troilus*, Book V, where Chaucer, with an eye on classical poetry, wants to be rather fine, we discover him talking about '*goldytressed* Phebus' (after *auricomus*, I suppose). One might just imagine a critic of the school of Dr. Leavis, much concerned with the vital relation between poetry and everyday speech and determined to preserve the purity of our native tradition from alien presences, finding here the first sign of those classicising tendencies which were to reach their dark florescence in *Paradise Lost*. Maybe we should not have tried to enlarge the mold of English by raiding the classics, but that is what our poets have in fact done, and the attempt to anglicise Greek compound epithets—and their far less numerous Latin progeny—is simply one small aspect of this long endeavor.

The natural way in English to deal with the more elaborate type of Greek compound is to expand it into an adjectival phrase or clause. Thus the translator who had to render *Zephuros hēdupnoos* would not go far wrong in adopting Chaucer's 'Zephirus *with his sweete breeth*'. Thus Robert Fitzgerald avoids 'rosy-fingered' (an unattractive word, in English, bequeathed us by Spenser, *F.Q.*I.2.7) and writes instead

When Dawn spreads out her finger tips of rose—

This avoids any wrenching of English usage, but as a method it is open to one or two at least theoretical objections. An elaborate adjectival phrase or clause ('Zeus who delights in thunder') tends to obstruct the run of your sentence; and, arguably, it lacks the poetic force that a good compound can have. (How greatly would 'the *to-and-fro-conflicting* wind and rain' be weakened if the compound were replaced by a clause.) Moreover, in a sense it side-steps the problem instead of facing it and thus fails to perform one of translation's most valuable functions, which is to

---

[5] E.g. 'deep-girdled' for *bathuzōnos*. So Mr. Lattimore when he meets the word at Il.9.594, *kai alloi allothi*. I cannot understand this sort of translation. What *is* a deep-girdled woman? What does she look like? Where has Mr. Lattimore seen one?

enlarge the formal and expressive possibilities of the new language.[6]

The compound epithet is a regular feature of the poetic, or elevated, style in Elizabethan poetry and such it has remained. It was not so long ago that Dylan Thomas wrote of 'the *heron /Priested* shore.' Yet between its use in Shakespeare, who developed it as magnificently as he developed every other aspect of our language, and Gerard Hopkins, the poet who exploited its resources most completely, there is relatively little systematic development. The subject is so central to the translation of Greek poetry that I think it is worth glancing at its place in the English poetic tradition.

W. H. Gardner, in the course of some valuable pages on this particular feature of Hopkins' style, suggests that the compound epithet in English may be divided into two main types, the 'poetical-descriptive' and the 'dramatic or rhetorical.'[7] The first type, deriving through Spenser and Milton from the Greeks, 'reaches its fine flower in the *"soft-conchèd* ear" and *"far-foamèd* sands"* of Keats.' As examples of the second type, Mr. Gardner offers Shakespeare's '*steep-down* gulfs' and '*to-and-fro-conflicting* wind and rain.'

This distinction fits the facts, but in its place I would propose, as neater and no less accurate, 'Greek' and 'English'. In the first category I would place Shakespeare's '*fiery-footed* steeds' (from *Romeo*), in the second the two examples from his mature style cited by Gardner, or Chapman's perhaps less powerful but very interesting '*care-and-lineament-resolving* Sleepe'.[8] In the first category, again, I would place Milton's '*flowry-kirtl'd* Naiades', a compound which very exactly recreates the pleasure of the more decorative and ceremonious Greek formations; Shelley's '*eagle-baffling* mountain' and '*isle-surrounding* streams' (from *Prometheus Unbound*); and Tennyson's '*many-fountain'd* Ida'. The latter, although a direct translation from the Greek, is warmed into life by the moving rhythm of the lines in which it occurs;

---

[6] See Roger Shattuck in 'Artificial Horizon: Translator as Navigator': 'In its truest role translation does not consist solely in reducing all foreign works to the limitations of, say, English, but equally in reshaping and enlarging English to reach meanings which it has not yet had to grapple with.' (*The Craft and Context of Translation*, ed. W. Arrowsmith and R. Shattuck, University of Texas Press, Austin 1961, p. 152.)

[7] *Gerard Manley Hopkins* (London 1948)i.126ff.

[8] *Odyssey*, 20.56–7. Chapman here fuses a phrase—*luōn meledēmata thumou*—and a compound epithet—*lusimelēs*. For some comments on this feature of his style, see George D. Lord: *Homeric Renaissance: The Odyssey of George Chapman* (London 1956) pp. 139–41. Yeats may have had this remarkable formation in mind when he produced his magnificent '*haystack- and roof-levelling* wind' in 'A Prayer for My Daughter.'

Shelley's compounds, apparently more enterprising, are too anxious to demonstrate their Hellenic stock; they have not been sufficiently felt into English.

We reach a point of greater interest when my two categories (and also, I think, Mr. Gardner's) begin to break down. Tennyson's 'goldenrinded,' for example, from an early poem, *Eleänore*, feels Greekish, but what about this a line or so further on, the description of the bower

> *Grapethickened* from the light . . . ?

The formation has a genuine sensuous life, and though Tennyson may still be partly thinking in Greek, he is emphatically writing English.[9] What again of the very charming compound from Browning's *A Pretty Woman*:

> That *fawn-skin-dappled* hair of hers . . . ?

In a sense, this falls into Gardner's 'poetical-descriptive' and hence into my 'Greek' category, but it feels wholly English and anticipates some of Hopkins' compounds.

It is no part of my purpose to analyse the enormous wealth and variety of compound epithets in Hopkins. I refer the interested reader to Gardner, who discovers no less than fifteen distinct types of formation (*op.cit*.i.286). What I am concerned with here is the way in which Hopkins was able to extend the formal possibilities of English poetry by his creative insight into the procedures of Greek poetry. The attempt to bring the English and the Greek poetic traditions into the closest possible relation was of course common to many nineteenth century poets, but whereas in works like *Merope* and *Erechtheus* we see the writer depriving himself of most of the native resources of English poetry without being able to call on the resources of Greek poetry in their place, in Hopkins the Greek influence has the effect of making him even more exuberantly English.[10] Hopkins was of course interested in many aspects of Greek poetry, most of all perhaps in the 'beautiful variety' and 'infinite flexibility' of the Greek lyric forms, but also, as Mr. Gardner shows in an interest-

---

[9] I fancy he may have had somewhere in his mind the line about the grove of Colonus, *phullada muriokarpon analion*, at Soph. *O.C.* 676, supplemented by the description of the 'sacred place,' *bruōn/ daphnēs, elaias, ampelou*, at 16–17.

[10] For example, 'Away in the loveable west, / On a pastoral *fore-head* of Wales —' (*The Wreck*, II. 24.1–2) strikes one as a strong piece of English metaphor. It is in fact extremely Greek. Compare the 'shining *breast*' (i.e. hill) on which Battus is told to build a city at Pindar, *P.* 4.8; or the (strictly pleonastic) description of the Isthmus as the 'festal *neck*—or perhaps, *throat*—of Corinth' at Pindar *O.* 8.52 (similarly Bacchylides, 2.7). Alcman, in a vivid fragment(59D.), writes of 'Mount Rhipe, aflower with forest, *breast*—or *chest*—of dark night.'

ing chapter (ii.98ff), in the syntax. His strange adjectival phrases ('the *rolling level underneath him steady* air') seem to be attempts to recreate in English something equivalent to the way in which fifth century Greek poets weld a sequence of words into a single rhythmic and sense unit.[11] But nowhere is Hopkins more Greek than in the loaded vehemence with which he piles up epithets.

> Wiry and white-fiery and whirlwind-swivellèd snow
> Spins to the widow-making unchilding unfathering deeps.

Does this not read like an inspired translation of some unknown fragment of Aeschylus?

The daring, the sensuous fulness, of so many of Hopkins' coinages provides a way—strangely little exploited—of dealing with the feature of Greek poetry that has most consistently defeated translators. Surely the *'evil leisuring hungering dangerous-harboring* winds' at *Agam.* 192–3 would play straight into the hands of the translator who had gone to school to Hopkins? Hardly less so the sequence of six epithets at *Supp.* 794–6 with which Aeschylus builds up the image of a mountain. Or the *'untimely-at-midnight* clamor' (ἀωρόνυκτον ἀμβόαμα) at *Choeph.* 34. Or Sophocles' *'oxsummering* meadow' (βουθερὴς λειμών) at *Trach.* 188. The field is wide open.

But the interest of Hopkins' use of Greek poetry extends beyond the business of translation. What he did was to show, as Arnold and Swinburne were unable to show, that Greek and English poetry could be brought into a close critical relation. This relation is still there—if we want to use it. One is supposed, nowadays, to leave one's modern preoccupations at the door before one approaches a Greek author, but there is surely a difference between bringing an anxiety about the historicity of miracles or votes for women to an ancient author, and bringing a decent interest in the problems of poetic expression. For different in so many ways as the Greek and English poetic traditions are, there is a *lingua franca* of poetry which unites them. (It is this that allows a person with good literary sense to be excited by poetry in a language he hardly understands.) The English-speaking reader, more than any other, with his immediate access to the

---

[11] Gardner (ii.123) cites Aesch. *Agam.*201–4, which he translates: 'The seer proclaimed, urging Artemis (as cause), so that the *earth-with-their-staves-smiting-sons-of-Atreus* [χθόνα βάκτροις / ἐπικρούσαντας Ἀτρείδας] ε.ifled not their tears.' This sort of compression, or fusion, is common in Greek poetry. See Dodds on Eur. *Ba.*866–70: the expression 'χλοεραῖς λείμακος ἡδοναῖς has perhaps the effect of a compound, "green-meadow-joy."' For further examples, see Wilamowitz on Eur. *Her.*468('we must think of the substantives as coalescing into a single compound'), Jebb on Soph.*Ant.* 794, and Fraenkel on *Agam.* 504.

only body of poetry in the West that can compare with Greek, should not hesitate to use his native literary experience to help him get at Greek poetry. Surely the man who has ever really *read* Shakespeare could not say, as Professor Page says in his comment on *Agam.*1180–3, that 'image and reality are confused, as often in Aeschylus.' Surely he is going, unlike Professor Page, to understand how in the second stasimon of the same play Helen can be the gentle lion cub *and* the 'priest of ruin,' the 'spirit of windless calm' that first came to Troy, *and* the 'fiend whose bridal was fraught with tears', the νυμφόκλαυτος Ἐρινύς which later destroyed it. (See Page's comment at 744ff.) To the grammarian, such procedures are puzzling and annoying, but, unfortunately for the grammarian, that is how some great poets write. As a matter of politeness (since Professor Page is a distinguished man in his field) and as a matter of prudence (since Page is a formidable man in any field), this may be the tactical moment to call Coleridge to my aid. He is describing his literary training at Christ's Hospital under the Reverend James Bowyer:

> At the same time that we were studying the Greek tragic poets, he made us read Shakespeare and Milton as lessons .... I learned from him, that poetry, even that of the loftiest and, seemingly, that of the wildest odes, had a logic of its own, as severe as that of science; and more difficult, because more subtle, more complex, and dependent on more, and more fugitive causes.
>
> (*Biographia Literaria,*Cap.I.)

This kind of interrogation of whatever is relevant in our own poetic tradition is something that the translator should surely undertake before he attempts the peculiarly difficult task of turning Greek poetry into English poetry. A study of the particular feature I have been looking at will not, certainly, tell anyone how to form English compounds. *D'abord il faut être un poète.* But it could provide a few rules of thumb—be concrete, be specific, create an image and so on—and, negatively, it might suggest the kinds of compound that will not do. Hardy's '*brown-shawled* dame', for example, will not do; it is too dull. Shelley's '*eagle-baffling* mountain' will not do; it is too Greek. Anybody's '*deep-girdled* woman' will not do; it offers no picture and next to no meaning. Positively, one can I think say that a compound should 'give pleasure', as Hopkins' '*dappled-with-damson* west' gives pleasure; and there should, usually, be some energy in its formation (Shakespeare's '*steep-down* gulfs'), some intensity of perception or variety of sense data that demands the tightest possible juxtaposition. A minor point is that the simpler compounds, at least, are stronger when they are not hyphenated. Tennyson's 'grapethickened', the original spelling of the 1832 edition of his poems, has surely more sensuous life than 'grapethickened', the form to which he reduced it in the 1842 volume, perhaps a result of adverse criticism.[12] The hyphen points to the construction and as it were apologises for it, thus weakening its poetic force. Hopkins tends in fact to hyphenate his adjectival compounds but not, usually, his noun compounds (wolfsnow, Amansstrength etc.). Who would want to parcel out Joyce's grand formation into a run of little words?

Beside the rivering waters of, *hitherandthithering* waters of. Night!

At this point I return to Mr. Fagles and his dealings with the adjectival Bacchylides. One may not invariably like what he does, but he has got seriously to grips with his text. Take a single example, the passage at 5.172 where Meleager describes his sister as χλωραύχην. This is one of Bacchylides' most charming strokes, but it is hard to translate. χλωρός is partly an adjective of color and means something like 'pale green' (the green of young plants); it can also mean 'yellow' and (of the complexion) 'pale'. But along another line of meaning it is used, with no sense of color, of living, growing, glowing things: of fresh sappy wood as against dry, of dew, of a field full of flowers, even of a glistening tear. The sense in Bacchylides, as Jebb says, is 'with the freshness (the fresh bloom) of youth upon her neck.' It may be worth comparing Mr. Fagles' version with the one offered by Mr. Lattimore in his translation of this ode:

Deïaneíra, *her throat still green*
with youth—

I don't understand this. I have seen a girl with green eyebrows but never with a green throat. Once again I ask: where has Mr. Lattimore seen one? Admittedly Berni, in an anti-Petrarchan sonnet, writes of a woman with a *blue* mouth ('bocca ampia *celeste*'), but the reference there is plainly to some gap-toothed hag, whereas Bacchylides wants to paint a picture of a young and beautiful girl. Mr. Fagles' translation is:

Her neck glows
With the gloss of youth.

Unfortunately this won't do at all. 'Gloss' is too hard, too metallic, for *chlōros*, and it hasn't anything like the right sensuous suggestion. What was needed was something as new and imaginative as Browning's 'fawn-skin-dappled hair' or Hopkins' 'brown-as-dawning-skinned' sailor. But earlier on in the same ode he man-

[12] See Joyce Green, 'Tennyson's Development During the "Ten Years' Silence,"' *PMLA* 66(1951)691.

ages one of Bacchylides' most notable adjectival clusters with some success (98–9):

> Constrain the goddess,
> Whose arms are white
> Under wreaths of buds—

Fagles quite often unfolds his epithets in this way, working them into the run of the sentence. But he also coins a number of compounds, and here I think he has been skilful. Almost always he employs the type of formation adopted by Hopkins in his '*silk-sash* clouds,' '*dare-gale* skylark,' *flint-flake* sea,' '*baldbright* cloud'—a pair of monosyllabic verbs, nouns or adjectives (unhyphenated in Fagles). Thus he writes '*stormpace* stallion' (πῶλον ἀελλοδρόμαν, 5.39), '*cragtooth* hound' (καρχαρόδοντα κύνα, 5.60), '*riptide tusks*' (of the Calydonian boar, an energetically compressed treatment of πλημύρων σθένει . . . ἐπέκειρεν ὀδόντι, 5.107–8) and '*bluebraid* Nereids' (17.37–8, which sensibly takes advantage of our uncertainty about the Greek color sense to avoid the hackneyed rendering of ἰόπλοκος as 'violet-crowned' or something of that sort).

These are all accurate translations, in the conventional sense; they are also good, forceful English and if there is nothing specially 'modern' about them, they are at least words that a contemporary poet, given a similar context, might use without loss of face. Let me take one further example, from 9.47–52, this time setting it in its context:

> Roads fan out to the world
> That carry word of your clan,
> Those *sleeksash girls* the gods
> Made flourish as founders
> Of streets that block invasion.

(The last line gives the sense of the Greek very well, but stylistically it 'specifies' too vigorously for Bacchylides, whose poetry does not engage so closely with our everyday world.) 'Sleeksash girls,' for λιπαρόζωνοι θύγατρες, is distinctly a trouvaille. It certainly observes, as a compound epithet should, the third law of Wallace Stevens' universe, 'It Must Give Pleasure.' In a paper on 'The Criticism of Greek Tragedy' (*Tulane Drama Review*, III.3 [March 1959] 34), William Arrowsmith complained that there has been a 'failure to realize turbulence.' There has. There has also been a failure—in our approach to Greek poetry as a whole—to realize *gaiety*. Major Greek poetry is, heavens knows,

> Vested in the serious folds of majesty.

It is also 'crested / With every prodigal, familiar fire.' We have forgotten, somehow, in our dreary translations, in our dreary chatter about the culturally uplifting value of Greek civilisation, the enormous brightness, the αἴγλα διόσδοτος, with which Greek poetry recreates and celebrates the entire phenomenal world. Do we tell our students, as they plough their way through their paperbacks, that a huge period of Aeschylus or Pindar can be as light on its toes as a dancer?

Bacchylides is, certainly, a long way from the great masters who give Greek poetry its claim to be our 'proper study.' Yet in the formal procedures of his verse, he touches their high manner. His λιπαρόζωνοι θύγατρες are, the syllables as they glitter by tell us, very charming. And this charm Fagles has caught with his 'sleeksash girls.' Any sensible man would obviously be delighted to take a sleeksash girl out to dinner. But if his adjective meets the Greek on the ground of gaiety, it is distinctly jaunty, whereas λιπαρόζωνος is stately and ceremonious too, recalling as it does similar formations in earlier Greek poetry—λιπαροκρήδεμνος, for example, in the beautiful passage near the beginning of the Hymn to Demeter, to which Pater drew attention, where the goddess Hecate sits, withdrawn, in her cave, 'veiled in a shining veil,' listening to the cries of Persephone.

We get none of this in 'sleeksash.' How should we? If we want these pleasures of association, we must read Bacchylides in Greek. Fagles was quite right to concentrate on one element in his original and go all out for that. Had he tried for everything, he would probably have missed everything. He has, nonetheless, here and often elsewhere, been faithful to an important element in Greek poetry. And he has approached it with the proper sensual relish.

> Natives of poverty, children of malheur,
> The gaiety of language is our seigneur.

Mr. Fagles has taken Bacchylides' gaiety seriously. There is a suggestion, in his versions, of festal glitter. He has got *aigla* into his lines. He has also taken the meters seriously. Translators of Greek lyric poetry nowadays, profiting by what they feel to be the liberties of modern verse, have mostly abandoned meter altogether and offer a series of irregular, vaguely cadenced lines which sometimes *look* a little like a page of Greek lyric. Mr. Fagles has gone about his job more seriously.

What characterises Bacchylides' metrical composition, it has been noted, is the tendency 'to divide his periods rhythmically into short kola, usually of two or three *metra* each.' (Jebb p. 94). Translated into the common speech, this gives the effect of 'quick and nervous . . . rhythm' to which Parry alludes in his introduction. Fagles has tried to create an *English equivalent* by using a short line; I suppose his average line is of about six syllables, and if he now and then stretches to ten, he often contracts to three. There is a good deal to be said for the use of short lines in translating Greek lyric. The unit of English poetry, lyric as much as narrative, is the line—even where, as in developed blank verse, there is regular enjambment. The metrical unit of Greek lyric is the kolon. H.D.'s brief, incised lines are intended, I have suggested elsewhere, to recreate 'the fiercely edged musical phrases out of which the Greek lyric is built.' The difficulty is that English does not take readily to a series of very short lines—witness the extreme rhythmical monotony of the sequence of tiny phrases with which she tries to handle stichomythia in her *Ion*. The short line requires great rhythmical variety if it is to be effective, the kind of variety which (to take an example) the Scots poet W. S. Graham achieves in his fine poem, *The Nightfishing*. Graham uses a line with strong, almost hammered, irregularly placed stresses, clever variation of rising and falling rhythms and of masculine and feminine endings. I don't at all know if Fagles consulted this poem, but should the occasion of a second edition give him a chance to revise—or if, as we must hope, this is merely his pioneer venture in the field of Greek lyric—I think he might find Graham helpful.

He is often, in fact, successful. Take the opening of Ode 17:

> *B*lack at the *b*eak that craft
> With Theseus *b*raced for *war*
> And fine Ionian sons and *dau*ghters,
> Seven of each a*board* her
> Cutting the Sea of *Crete*,
> As Athena *a*rmed with the *ae*gis
> Bellied her shining *sheets*
> With a wind from *north*.

Isolated, this is not remarkable; in its context, it works. Here and elsewhere Fagles uses alliteration and assonance to pull his lines together; they have thrust and shape, and the movement seems to me right for Bacchylides. But take the opening of the fifth ode:

> Splendid in destiny,
> Marshal of men
> Where chariots
> Whirl through Syracuse—

I don't know how *eumoire* should be translated, but the vapid 'splendid in destiny' is the kind of thing that would have put an epinician poet out of business. And the third line, getting off to a limp start and then stopping before it has established any sort of rhythmic *raison d'être* for itself, is a feeble affair. The short line, to be interesting, needs a tight play of stresses; and whereas Bacchylides could draw his diction from a great and still vital tradition, his twentieth century translator has got to put a spin on his words if he wants them to reach our side of the net.

In looking at these translations, one or two general points about Bacchylides have come up. Can we now—thanks to Fagles—go on and say anything more interesting about this poet than that, though good, he is not so good as Pindar?

It is extremely unfortunate for Bacchylides' reputation, and for our critical sense of his poetry, that in the absence of any other choral lyricist whose work has survived in bulk, we are forced to compare him with Pindar—even while insisting, like Parry, that the comparison is foolish. The best things in Bacchylides are fine, Edmonds writes, but—they do not, 'like Pindar's three-word apocalypses, stir thoughts too deep for tears' (*Lyr. Gr*.iii.647). Well, no. But still, there are things that a poet may do besides stirring thoughts too deep for tears with three-word apocalypses, so it would surely be worth enquiring if Bacchylides does anything else that, in its slighter way, may be interesting.

The vice of this Pindaric comparison, apart from its obvious injustice, is I suggest that it draws attention to what in Bacchylides is, in some respects, questionable, and away from what he has more valuably to offer. It is, for instance, generally agreed that the fifth ode, in which he tells how Heracles meets Meleager among the shades, is his best poem. 'Carmen egregia arte compositum rebusque et verbis splendens facile principem locum inter epinicia tenet,' Blass declares. 'A favourable instance' of his talents, Rose allows. 'This is Bacchylides' most impressive work,' Parry agrees. Let us take a look at it.

After the opening address to Hiero, Bacchylides points to himself preparing to send his song of praise to Syracuse (9–16). My expression 'points to himself' is I think a fair comment on the very deliberately raised tone of this passage. It feels rather 'Pindaric.' Given the frequent difficulty, or impossibility, of dating these poems, it is of course very hard to say when Bacchylides is imitating Pindar or vice versa. At line 9, for example, we find him using an expression which Pindar was to employ two years later. Equally, in a passage where we think we detect a debt, the poet may simply be drawing on a fund of expressions common to the epinician style as a whole. Nonetheless, there is a very marked style, exalted often, sometimes homely, but almost always characterised by an intense poetic concentration, which we recognise as Pindaric. It was quite different, so far as we can judge, from the more playful manner which Simonides adopted in his epinicia;[13] and different, too, from the lighter, more relaxed style we recognise as Bacchylidean. The present passage seems to me one in which Bacchylides is not so much imitating Pindar, as allowing himself to be influenced, to be perhaps a little bullied, by the new elevation and intensity which Pindar had brought into the victory ode.

[13] See Bowra, *Greek Lyric Poetry*, (Oxford 1961)314.

The celebrated comparison of the poet to an eagle follows (16–30): the eagle soars high in the limitless inane while lesser birds cower below. It is a fine anthology piece and duly found its niche in the *Oxford Book of Greek Verse*. To the obvious criticism that it is absurd of Bacchylides to describe his poetry in terms that belong rather to Pindar, we may reply that he is not thinking of himself but of the poet, any poet, writing in the high epinician way. Or we may say, with Blass, that what is being compared is the 'ampla materies carminis cum immenso aeris spatio in quo volat aquila'—for he goes on to say that 'a boundless course' is open to him on every side. The fact remains that the pomp of this extended simile leaves us uneasy; if it were being used functionally, it should prepare the way for a story told with a certain majesty, *modo Pindarico*, whereas the scene which follows is marked rather by a vivid pathos. But before he comes to his myth, Bacchylides adds another short passage in which, with what seems a remarkable emphasis, he calls the earth to witness that no horse has ever reached the winning post ahead of Phere-nikos. The manner may again be strained and Lavagnini's comment sounds reasonable: 'tanta solennità sembra fuor di proposito per elogiare le virtù di un cavallo.' (Bacchylides uses a very similar expression at 8.19–20, but there he is at least speaking of a *human* victor.) Of course, to attempt to be at all inward with a genre as remote as this is very hazardous—who has the faintest conception of what the performance of an epinician ode was really like? It is often hard enough to be sure of the tone of the older poetry in one's own language. All the same, unless one is to accept passively whatever the poet offers—and in that case why bother to read him?—one must at least try to catch his tone of voice. And I think one can say here that while a similar elevation of manner in Pindar is felt to be acceptable, given his exalted conception of the significance of a victory in the games, it is not equally acceptable in Bacchylides; and that, moreover, he has other ways of writing which do not raise these misgivings.

The myth itself is beautiful and has been justly praised. I want to look only at one point, the lines in which Heracles replies to Meleager's long story (160–9). The shade has described his early death and Heracles is for once affected. Ah well, he says, in his gruff Dorian way, best for a man never to be born, I expect. Still —no use talking about that. By the way, you don't happen to have a surviving sister, do you? If she looks anything like you, why, I'd marry the girl! This question, coming at the end of Meleager's touching narrative, is surely very odd indeed and seems as badly out of place as Montano's question at *Othello* II.i—'But, good lieutenant, is your general wived?'—which aroused Thomas Rhymer's indignation. The immediate purpose of both queries is the same: to introduce a description of the lady in question, and certainly Bacchylides' picture of Deianeira, with the fresh grace

[237]

of youth still about her, is very charming and balances the previous account of her brother's young death. More important, no
doubt, it serves as a further indirect illustration of the gnome
which introduced the myth: 'no mortal man is blessed in everything' (53–5). Heracles will return to earth and marry Deianeira,
and suffer in his turn.[14]

My point is not so much the clumsiness of the plotting—though
I think it is clumsy—as Bacchylides' failure to use myth, as Pindar
and the major Greek poets use it, as a means of enquiring into
the structure of man's fate. This is what he attempts to do here:
the story of Meleager is meant to open out, through the concluding hint of what is to happen to Heracles, and bear generally on
the human condition. In fact, we are left with a touching story
to which a not particularly interesting moral is loosely attached.

My purpose in pointing to what I think is Bacchylides' relative
failure here is to get at what I take to be his success elsewhere—
success in a kind of writing we do not find in Pindar. The thir-
teenth epinician has not reached us intact. The opening is missing
and a few lines and part lines have been lost in the course of the
poem. But there is quite enough to be getting on with. The ode
begins, as we have it, with a description of Heracles' victory
over the lion at Nemea, where the young Pytheas has just been
victorious. A general statement on the unquenchable brightness
of victory is made and then transposed into the actual brightness
of the *kōmos*, the festive glitter of the welcome which awaits the
young man as he comes home to Aegina. This is in the usual
epinician manner, but a more interesting transposition, or modulation, follows. Aegina (the eponymous nymph, not the island) is
gracefully invoked—

> Girl of the rapid river,
> O gentle Aegina—

and then—to quote from Parry's excellent commentary—'the joy
and brightness are condensed in the figure of the dancer', the
ὑψαυχής κόρα, a distinctly Yeatsian young woman with a proper
sense of the ancestral glories of her race who goes off with her
friends to sing and dance on the hills. Fagles' translation has just
the right suggestions:

[14] There may be an explanation of the way Bacchylides handles the
scene in a piece of information preserved by the scholiast at *Iliad*
21.194: Pindar also wrote a poem about Heracles' encounter with
Meleager in the underworld, in which *it was Meleager who asked
Heracles to marry Deianeira*. This makes much better sense: Meleager
knows that his sister is being pestered by the local river god and does
what he can to help her by sending Heracles to the rescue. One
guesses that Pindar's poem came first, and that Bacchylides had to be
odd in order to be original. (See Jebb, p. 472.)

When she goes gay
With her famous friends
Who live nearby,
Crowned in reds and reeds
For their island rite
They sing your strength,
O Queen—

They sing of Aegina herself and of the legendary heroine who
bore Peleus (father of Achilles) and Telamon (father of Ajax)—
and there follows a passage of heroic narrative drawn from the
Iliad. It is tiresome that the text is doubtful at this point. According to Jebb's conjecture, accepted in their editions by Kenyon,
Blass, Jurenka and Edmonds, the ensuing narrative is sung by the
girls. According to the supplement proposed by Wilamowitz and
Housman, which Snell adopts in his Teubner edition and Fagles
follows, there is a transition here: the girls' song ends and the
poet takes over and tells the story in propria persona. From the
literary point of view, Jebb's text is greatly preferable. There
is a most suggestive contrast between the voices of the girls and
the grim Homeric scene which they present—a contrast which I
find present in the actual mode of the narration. And even if there
is a transition here to the poet, the point is not altogether lost.
The young women have done their job, for the lyrical prelude to
the narrative conditions the way we take it.

I called it a 'grim Homeric scene,' but that only does for one
aspect of it. Bacchylides presents, with genuine power, the violence of Hector's assault against the ships, the terror of Achilles
raging over the plains of Troy; a number of epithets and phrases
remind us of the *Iliad* and there is even a full-blown simile in the
epic manner. But beside—or rather, below—all this is something
that is not at all Homeric. There is of course the basic modulation
from the powerful Homeric hexameters to Bacchylides' light,
glancing dactylo-epitritic meter. But there is more than this. The
sentence which describes Achilles raging over the plain ends by
presenting him as 'the fearless son of the Nereid wreathed in
violets' (122–3):

$$\text{ἰοστεφάνου}$$
$$\text{Νηρῆδος ἀτρόμητος υἱός.}$$

This is of course the kind of elaboration, so common in choral
lyric, of a Homeric phrase, in this case 'child of fair-haired Thetis'
(Il. 4.512, 16.860). But in fact this way of describing Achilles is
very rare indeed in the *Iliad*. Of the 190 or so times in which his
name, or one of his patronymics, is qualified by an adjective,
phrase or clause, only on the two occasions mentioned above
(or four, counting 'whom an immortal mother bore' at 10.404 and
17.78) is an expression employed which relates him to the gentle

world of Thetis. Elsewhere, except for neutral terms such as *dios, agauos, amumōn* and the like, his name is always qualified by words or expressions belonging to the masculine world of war and leadership. I am not concerned here with the metrical reasons which may have made these forms more convenient, but simply with the impression made on the reader or listener by their constant use.

The question is whether this rather unusual way of presenting Achilles is just a pleasant variation, or whether it is being used more purposefully to modify (in some way) the heroic context in which it occurs. A point perhaps worth noticing is that the epithet ἰοστέφανος—and the variant ἐυστέφανος—is regularly used not of Thetis but of Aphrodite.[15] But in calling this a point, one immediately wonders if in fact it *is* a point. How closely should one read Bacchylides? Are we justified in questioning one of his numerous epithets in this way? I think we are, for although he may sometimes throw in an epithet simply to glitter an otherwise dull line, he often uses them far more functionally. (Mr. Parry provides a few examples, pp. xxii–iii.) We should in fact expect nothing less, for he was a careful artist and well before his time Greek poets had turned the 'ornamental' epithet, which Homer employed with such tireless profusion, into a very precise poetic tool. 'By the end of the sixth century . . . and probably a great deal earlier,' A. E. Harvey writes in an interesting paper, 'the lyric poets were fully conscious of the conventional associations of Homeric diction. Consequently it seems unlikely that they will have used purely ornamental epithets indiscriminately . . .'[16] If this is true—and Harvey offers some convincing stylistic analysis —it is quite reasonable to suppose that Bacchylides is conscious of the fairly well-established associations of *iostephanos* and that he is using the word for a definite reason. The function of this 'ornamental,' very unmilitary epithet, occurring in a passage of heroic narrative studded with warlike Homeric epithets, is surely to lower and gentle the tone. It would come very well off the lips of the girls of Aegina; they would naturally welcome any opportunity of celebrating the softer side of their hero.

It would be silly to make so much of a single word but for a rather similar effect a few lines later on in which the associations I have claimed for *iostephanos* are very much to the point. After the epic simile (124–32), the poem describes how the Trojans took heart 'when they heard that the warrior Achilles was keeping to his quarters because of the soft limbs of blonde Briseis'—

εἵνεκεν ξανθᾶς γυναικός,
Βρισηΐδος ἱμερογυίου—

[15] E.g. at Od.8.267 and 18.193, *h. Hom.* 5.6,175,287 and 6.18, Solon *fr.*7.4. See Allen-Halliday-Sikes on *h. Hom.* 5.175.
[16] 'Homeric Epithets in Greek Lyric Poetry,' *CQ* n.s.7(1957)214.

Once again, Bacchylides has Homer in mind. In the course of the Catalogue, there is a comment on the absence of the Myrmidons; the reason they were absent was that their leader, Achilles, 'was lying among the ships, angry because of Briseis, the girl with the lovely hair' (2.688–9):

κούρης χωόμενος Βρισηίδος ἠυκόμοιο.

Once again, then, we have the customary choral *réchauffement* of an epic phrase; and once again, and more strongly, there is a perceptible change of tone. In Homer, it is of course a slighted sense of heroic honor that keeps Achilles away from the fighting. So it is in Bacchylides—ostensibly. But the epithet ἱμερόγυιος is not only not Homeric (the nearest thing in the *Iliad* is χροὸς ἱμερόεντος which occurs, appropriately, in the sensual context of the *Dios Apatē*, 14.170); it takes us right out of the sphere of Homeric sentiment and into that of 7th and 6th century lyric.[17] If we did not know Bacchylides' Homeric original here, we would surely suppose that he was presenting Achilles as a romantic lover pining for his mistress.

Mr. Harvey, in the article I have already mentioned, points to the existence in archaic lyric of a convention whereby the poet, in certain contexts, notably in dealing with matter belonging to the heroic world, borrowed elements of Homeric diction which he would not normally have used. By the time of Anacreon, we find something much more sophisticated, namely the deliberately 'witty' use of Homeric diction in light-hearted poems about everyday life. Harvey shows with how delicate a stylistic control Anacreon introduces Homeric echoes to produce an effect of mock solemnity. Bacchylides, I suggest, is working the other way round. Where Anacreon had brought a solemn Homeric word into a gay love poem, Bacchylides, with an equal stylistic finesse, introduces a word more proper to love poetry into what claims to be a rather solemn piece of epic narrative. He is not, like Anacreon, witty, yet I think we may find some of the qualities which constitute wit in the way he can hold two levels of style in his mind and move so easily between them. The particular pleasure which his poetry, at its best, can offer is present here in the way, without ever quite denaturing it, he turns the Homeric original into something subtly different. His poetry sets up a contrast—the sort of stylistic contrast which the Greeks, we know, enjoyed: witness their exorbitant taste for parody—between two kinds of poetry, and so between two ways of life. The matter of Greek poetry, one might very roughly say, is sometimes fairly simple, but the manner is usually highly sophisticated. (I have

---

[17] *Himerophōnos*, for example, in Sappho, if no longer in Alcman; or such sensuous compounds as *erasiplokamos* or *aganoblepharos* in Ibycus.

in mind not mere sophistication of *technique,* which can be found in quite primitive poetry, but a sophistication of emotional attitude.) And that is what we have here, the perfection of manner.

Mr. Parry, in his commentary, approaches the ode quite differently. He shows how the initial 'brightness', present in the victory itself and in the festivities that celebrate it, is taken up in the myth and revealed on a deeper level of meaning. 'The Greek heroes who overcame the Trojans have died but "excellence flaming to all" . . . is bright even in that darkness. It is the same excellence that "honors Aeacus' island, harbor of frame."' Everything he points to can be found in the text, but I wonder if this is what should take the critical stress. Isn't Bacchylides here doing simply what was expected of an epinician poet, relating today's bright achievement in the games to some legendary achievement in the past? Moreover, as Parry analyses it, the poem sounds remarkably like a poem by Pindar. To me, it is, in the best sense, much more light-weight, and it seems to me that the critic should try to point to what is original in the poem—the very skilfully handled stylistic level—rather than to the normal features of the epinician which Bacchylides was paid for. As Parry reads it, the poem is rather solemn; I think it is pretending to be solemn while contriving to be distinctly gay.

Even if my point is not critically valid as applied to this particular ode, it may still be worth making insofar as it bears on the way we read Greek poetry. Our critical approach is still markedly influenced by the nineteenth century thirst for high seriousness. What Eliot said of traditional taste in English poetry —that it had been 'largely founded upon a partial perception of the value of Shakespeare and Milton, a perception which dwells upon sublimity of theme and action'—is true of our taste in Greek, substituting Homer and Attic tragedy for Shakespeare and Milton. Thanks to the critical revolution which has taken place in the last forty years or so, we are equipped, in our general reading, to appreciate a great deal in poetry apart from sublimity. But, as *Arion* has argued elsewhere, this revolution has had next to no effect on classical studies. The classical scholar continues to operate with the old critical tools.

The techniques of modern criticism have largely been worked out in new areas of literature or on old authors, like Shakespeare and the Metaphysicals, read in new ways. The pity is that the area of Greek poetry which might (to a lesser extent) have ministered to a fresh critical approach—the work of the 7th and 6th centuries, most of all, perhaps, the great Archilochus—has reached us in so fragmentary a state that the literary critic is shouldered aside by the papyrologist and the philologist. Yet here is a body of writing with which the modern critic might have felt thoroughly at home: poetry that takes much of its material from the everyday circumstance of life, and poets—like Archilochus and the Lesbians—who generally write in the language they speak.

But too little of this wonderful period of Greek literature has survived to change the old critical habits, with the result that we tend to deal very inadequately with the bits and pieces doled out to us by Oxyrhynchus and Mr. Lobel. The 'additions to the text of Sappho have shown that much of her poetry was below the standard by which we were accustomed to judge her,' Professor Page writes (p.110), not without satisfaction. What he means is that none of the new fragments are, as he puts it, 'aglow in the reflection of intensely ardent emotions,' like *Poikilothron*' and *Phainetai moi*. But of course she did not always write like that—nobody ever has done, nobody could. Nonetheless, in the best of the new material we still find the same consummate control of tone, the same power to give significance to the most trivial event or mood. But that is not enough for Professor Page, who knows that the best poetry is about exalted matters, whereas Sappho's verses, reflecting 'a life of *idleness* and comfort at home' (p.226—my italics), are full of stuff about girls coming and going and a brother who misbehaves in foreign parts. Surely *that* can't be great poetry?

Something of the same prejudice, the same high-minded insistence on elevation, has blocked a proper understanding of Bacchylides. A Pindaric ode can at least partly be approached in terms of sublimity. An ode of Bacchylides cannot. But the critical observation is, surely, not that Bacchylides failed to rise to Pindar's heights, but rather that Pindar, in giving the victory ode a great burden of religious emotion, was doing something new and very strange. With Simonides, so far as we can judge, the tone was gay and light-hearted. And properly so. However seriously the Greeks took their athletics, it would probably not have occurred to anyone except Pindar that a victory in the games was quite the occasion for a kind of divine epiphany. Bacchylides was influenced, at the formal level, by Pindar, sometimes to his cost, I think, but at his best he retains the lighter manner of much earlier choral lyric. As such, he is the last accomplished voice of the beautiful tradition which flourished between the grandeur of Homer and the grandeur of Attic tragedy. We should think of him not as a lesser Pindar, but as the successor of Simonides, Ibycus, Stesichorus and, more distantly, of the enchanting Alcman. He retains the element of epic narrative which Quintilian's phrase may point to in Stesichorus, while not usually attempting to rival the Stesichorean gravity; and, at his best, he writes with a grace and a formal intelligence greatly in advance of anything that Ibycus could achieve in the ode—if the unfortunate Polycrates poem, so inferior to the rest of his fragments, is really by Ibycus.

For Bacchylides' qualities at their best we should look to a poem like the 17th, the dithyramb about Theseus' quarrel with Minos on the ship bound for Crete. The 'epic' tone of the angry speeches which the two men level at each other is admirably done (compare, for example, 29–36 with Il.20.206–9); there is just the right stylistic elevation—note, for instance, at 24–8, the grand Hellenic way in which Theseus accepts the dispensations of fate. But, as Parry says, 'the moral and tragic elements alike are subordinate to a mood of patterned gaiety and intricate delight . . . . In no other of (his) poems do we feel so strongly the stylized grace of his lyric narrative.' That seems to me the right way to talk about Bacchylides.

ARNOLD AND THE
CLASSICAL TRADITION[1]

H. A. Mason

THE FIRST IMPULSE ON RE-READING THE *Lectures on Translating Homer* is to comment on the rare exemplification of the qualities that make a good literary critic and on the perfection of manner, its charm, vivacity, and ease. The felicitous formulations come with added force from their successful application, as in this:

'To handle these matters properly there is needed a poise so perfect, that the least overweight in any direction tends to destroy the balance. Temper destroys it, a crotchet destroys it, even erudition may destroy it. To press to the sense of the thing itself with which one is dealing, not to go off on some collateral issue about the thing, is the hardest matter in the world. The "thing itself" with which one is here dealing—the critical perception of poetic truth—is of all things the most volatile, elusive and evanescent, by even pressing too impetuously after it, one runs the risk of losing it. The critic of poetry should have the finest tact, the nicest moderation, the most free, flexible, and elastic spirit imaginable; he should be indeed the "ondoyant et divers," the *undulating and diverse* being of Montaigne.'

This word is still in season, and the *Lectures* remain the first and only book to put into the hands of the beginner who would make something of Homer as a poet. Where else do we find a Homeric critic pressing so directly to the sense of the thing itself?

Nevertheless, without lapsing too excessively from Arnold's canon, the critical re-reader may feel that Arnold is radically inadequate both in his conception of translation and in his formulation of the claims that may be made on Homer's behalf. If so, after saluting Arnold's adequacy and the happiness of his approach, the task devolving on the critic is to explore the grounds for this negative conviction. It may then appear that Arnold suffered from having lost contact with the wisdom of the eighteenth century as we see it embodied in Samuel Johnson and that he failed in his characterisation of Homer because he stood in a wrong relation to all the Greek classics.

To establish so radical a criticism would require the re-examination of the whole of Arnold's work, but a glance at a few texts will give initial support to the main heads of the charge. It may at first sight appear a paradox to maintain that Arnold's wrong relation to the Greek classics was a consequence

[1] *The Complete Prose Works of Matthew Arnold,* edited by R. H. Super. Vol. I. *On The Classical Tradition.* The University of Michigan Press, 1960. Pp. 320. $6.50.

of his failure to appreciate Shakespeare. For the paradox to become a truism one must be convinced that we are for good or ill unable as Englishmen to put the Greek classics above Shakespeare. When we aspire to be European and to find the point of true critical poise, we have no alternative but to look at other literature through Shakespeare. Our greatest poet gets at us in such an intimate way that we can never afterwards cut him out of our organs of perception. And if he does not, there is always a risk that our standards of comparison will betray a weakness.

Because Shakespeare meant too little to Arnold, he likens him illegitimately to the Greek classics and he raises the Greeks above Shakespeare by appealing to a limited standard of simplicity. What is simplicity at its highest, when, in Mr. Eliot's words, it costs not less than everything? The charge against Arnold would depend on the belief that the highest simplicity is not found in the Greek classics, that the greatest moments in English involve in their simplicity an immense complexity and that this duality gives us reasons for being glad that we *must* come to the greatest things in literature through Shakespeare. The gravamen of the charge against Arnold is that, faced with *Lear* and the 'main scenes' of *Lear,* he left the emphasis on the claim that you have to read passages more than once to get their full meaning, and omitted to say that at the crises of those scenes Shakespeare rises to a simplicity that enables us through it to judge all other claims to be sublimely simple.

A second head would be that the Greek classics meant too much to Arnold and that he needed them too exclusively for one purpose. The familiar sonnet must serve to remind the reader of a general position:

> Who prop, thou ask'st, in these bad days, my mind?
> He much, the old man, who, clearest-soul'd of men,
> Saw The Wide Prospect, and the Asian Fen,
> And Tmolus' hill, and Smyrna's bay, though blind.
> Much he, whose friendship I not long since won,
> That halting slave, who in Nicopolis
> Taught Arrian, when Vespasian's brutal son
> Clear'd Rome of what most sham'd him. But be his
> My special thanks, whose even-balanc'd soul,
> From first youth tested up to extreme old age,
> Business could not make dull, nor Passion wild:
> Who saw life steadily, and saw it whole:
> The mellow glory of the Attic stage;
> Singer of sweet Colonus, and its child.

Arnold needed the classics for his very existence or continuing existence in an alien (as he felt it) world. Therefore he saw them predominantly in one light, the light he had to obtain from them if he was not to live in darkness. To prop Arnold's mind, Homer,

Epictetus and Sophocles had to be seen in contrast to Victorian England and remote from its worries and distractions. When we consider how many wise things Arnold said of the classics (though his remarks on Horace in his inaugural lecture *On the modern element in literature* surely point in the direction of my argument) it is hard to realise how subtle was the metamorphosis the classics underwent in Arnold's hands. But he by adverting his *gaze from some things and failing to take an interest in others enabled himself to see the Greek classics fixed in god-like calm, like the statues under glass cases of which the Victorians were so fond. They were made antithetical to much of life somewhat in the spirit of Yeats' 'golden smithies of the Emperor' which 'break the flood':

> Marbles of the dancing floor
> Break bitter furies of complexity,
> Those images that yet
> Fresh images beget,
> That dolphin-torn, that gong-tormented sea.

A hint of the way in which Arnold turns the raw and bleeding heroes of Greek legend into wax figures may be seen in his remark on the story of Merope:

'Maffei did right, I think, in altering the ancient tradition where it represents Merope as actually the wife of Polyphontes. It revolts our feeling to consider her as married to her husband's murderer; and it is no great departure from the tradition to represent her as sought in marriage by him, but not yet obtained.'

No great departure! What if Jocasta had failed to marry her husband's murderer—a far greater cause for revulsion, since the murderer was her own son. But in describing the heroes as 'raw and bleeding' I was thinking of their appearance in the refined literature of the classical period rather than of the findings of modern anthropology. We can now conjecture what those murders followed by marriages with the widow mean. But the significant fact for my argument is that the Greek tragedians were not of the same mind as Arnold, and that they preserved so much in their plays of the primitive and revolting.

That Arnold was not the disinterested critic anxious to see his object as it really was when that object was a Greek classic is revealed in the *Lectures on Translating Homer* by a tell-tale trick of lecturing style, of over-emphatic and too general assertion. No doubt Arnold gave his audience credit for more intelligence than his lecturing method would allow us to suppose. When he reiterated that Homer is rapid, simple and noble, he doubtless expected his audience to go away saying, 'rapid, yes, but Homer is not always rapid; simple, but not always plain; his style is natural but there are passages of great artifice; noble, but not always in

[247]

the sense in which our Alfred is always noble.' Yet Arnold himself betrays that he forgot the saving qualifications that distinguish the true critic from the publicist, the man with a thesis.
When we find him asserting, for instance, that 'Homer *always*
deals with *every* subject in the plainest and most straightforward
style,' or that 'Homer is *never* quaint and antiquated,' we may
wonder whether Arnold was keeping in mind every word of the
Iliad and the *Odyssey* or whether he was stretching the truth for
the sake of making a strong immediate impression on his
audience.

Grant this, and we yet cannot get rid of the suspicion that it
was not only for the sake of his audience that Arnold insisted in
the face of the facts that Homer's concern was to be plain and
natural at all costs. He seems to have had his own reasons for
altering the image that strikes the schoolboy on the very first day
he opens his *Iliad* and begins to construe. In looking for the
cause of the distortion we may note that an element of wilfulness
and flippant insouciance creeps in when Arnold goes to his own
defence. A striking instance occurs when he offers his own translation of a well-known passage, which he renders:

So shone forth, in front of Troy, by the bed of Xanthus . . .

The betraying note comes in his comment on the last line:

While their masters sat by the fire, and waited for Morning.

'I omit the epithet of Morning, and whereas Homer says that
the steeds "waited for Morning," I prefer to attribute this expectation of Morning to the master and not to the horse. Very
likely in this particular, as in any other particular, I may be
wrong; what I wish you to remark is my endeavour after absolute
plainness of speech, my care to avoid anything which may the
least check or surprise the reader, whom Homer does not check or
surprise.'

This will never do. Arnold is imposing on Homer a conception of
plainness derived, as he here admits, from a partial response, a
deliberate selection from the text.

The effect I likened to that of putting a statue in a glass case
is noticeable when Arnold attempts to set Homer on a pedestal
as if the Greek poet were alone exempt from the laws and conditions of poetic composition. A few scattered quotations will
focus the objection:

'Homer presents his thought to you just as it wells from the
source of his mind . . . . In Homer's poetry it is all natural thoughts
in natural words . . . between Pope and Homer there is interposed
the mist of Pope's literary artificial manner, *entirely* alien to the
plain naturalness of Homer's manner.'

I have italicised the over-emphatic 'entirely,' which gives criticism a legitimate foothold. For while nobody thinks that Homer's manner is *identical* with Tennyson's or Pope's, nobody can believe that Homer presents his 'thought' to us 'just as it wells from the source of his mind.' As everybody knows, Homer's heroes do not talk, they make speeches. The *Iliad* is a treasure-house of literary devices. If Homer looked back on more composition in his style, that is, stood in a far longer tradition of epic than Dante, Pope or Shakespeare could look back on for their compositions, so we may argue that Homer's art contains more *artifice* than Dante, Shakespeare or Pope used in their greatest passages. At any rate, it is clear that Homer's natural manner resembles that of all other great poets who have it—it is a triumph of *art*.

It is when Arnold uses the word 'noble' that we become most clearly aware that he is attempting to remove Homer to a distance from life. That in so doing he was avoiding one order of facts he was sharply reminded by Newman. Newman presents with all the honesty of a decent man a Victorian dilemma to which Arnold blandly shut his eyes. He is content to accuse Newman of being grotesque when he translated Il.6.344

O, brother thou of me, who am a mischief-working vixen,
A numbing horror,

and he claims that the original would not excite any such feelings in the breast of a competent scholar. To which Newman replied:

'Mr. Arnold says that I am not quaint, but grotesque, in my rendering of κυνὸς κακομηχάνου. I do not hold the phrase to be quaint: to me it is excessively coarse. When Jupiter calls Juno 'a bitch,' of course he means a snarling cur; hence my rendering, 'vixen' (or she-fox), is there perfect, since we say *vixen* of an irascible woman. But Helen had no such evil tempers, and beyond a doubt she meant to ascribe impurity to herself. I have twice committed a pious fraud by making her call herself 'a vixen,' where 'bitch' is the only faithful rendering; and Mr. Arnold instead of thanking me for throwing a veil over Homer's deformity, assails me for my phrase as intolerably grotesque.'

Now although this does not meet Arnold's point in the strict sense that, pious fraud or not, Newman's translation *is* grotesque, yet a thoroughly disinterested critic might well have confessed that this is only one instance out of a thousand where he as a Victorian could not have both translated the Greek and maintained that Homer is always noble.

But what most convinces the critical re-reader that Arnold was not disinterested in his attempt to see Homer as always noble is his further attempt to fix on Homer his conception of the 'grand style.' A glance at the four snippets Arnold gives to suggest his meaning will bring out the disparity. The Virgil and Milton snippets correspond to the kind of self-conscious nobility, dignity and self-restraint Arnold wished to bring home to us. The Dante piece might with a squeeze be thought similar, but the quotation from the *Iliad* could only be thought to belong here by ignoring the Greek, forgetting its context and substituting Arnold's wishy-washy crib:

> Be content, good friend, die also thou! why lamentest thou thyself on this wise? Patroclus, too, died, who was a far better than thou.

Homer's episode (Il. 21.34–135) is a fine study of the point where the hero turns into the brute. Achilles is not being noble here, he is behaving like a brute and a cad. Homer has as much sympathy for him as a neutral observer might have had if he watched an English soldier, whose wife had been shot, 'taking it out of' a defenceless Cypriot girl or boy. The parallel can be pressed home since the episode comes after the death of Patroclus and Achilles is addressing before butchering an unarmed suppliant. There is no overt comment: Homer's point is made by the dramatic speech which accompanies the brutal act, the unashamed nakedness of the language of Achilles' blood-lust. Homer is humanity gazing on and seeking to comprehend inhumanity.

Homer's dignity is quite another thing than Victorian dignity. Like Shakespeare's and Dante's it is compatible with a great deal of low-level coarseness. For failure to see that it is not a blemish in the highest poetry to use expressions which are in everyday life vulgar or coarse Arnold's Homer resembles Bowdler's Shakespeare. Yet Arnold, had he wished, could easily have found a passage in Dante to match this episode from the *Iliad,* for one of his famous 'touch-stones' is taken from the episode in the *Inferno* where the hero visits the frozen region of lowest hell reserved for traitors. Here Dante uses the same method of making the unspeakable reveal itself by dramatic speech:

> After them I saw a thousand livid faces,
> wizened by the cold. Never again shall I
> look on ice-bound water without a shudder.
> As we moved towards the centre of gravity,
> I shivered in the everlasting chill. Whether
> it was will or chance or fate I cannot tell,
> but as we made our way between the frozen
> heads, my foot struck one of them in the face, and
> tears came, and it said, 'What are you treading on
> me for? Is this a fresh instalment of the
> punishment I am suffering for my treachery?'
> I turned to Virgil. 'Wait for me here awhile,
> master, till I find out who this is. Then you
> may hurry me on as fast as you wish to.'
> Virgil halted, and I said to the mouth that
> was still cursing hard, 'What do you think you

are doing, swearing like that? Who are you?'
'Who are *you*?' it replied, 'and what are you doing
in the region of Antenor, kicking people
in the face? It felt like a blow from a human.'
'That's what it was,' I said, 'and you might be glad
of a little publicity. Shall I include your name in
my travel notes?' 'That's just what I don't want,' it
said. 'Take yourself off and leave me alone. We
don't care to be interviewed in this part of hell.'
So I took him by the hair at the scruff of
his neck. 'You had better give me your name,' I
said, 'or you've seen the last of this lot of hair.'
'You can have every hair on my head,' it replied, 'but you still won't hear my name or
see my face if you give it a thousand kicks.'
I got a good grip on his hair and pulled out
several chunks, but he only screamed and kept
his eyes turned down to the ground. Then another
traitor began to shout, 'What's up? What the devil's the
matter with you, Bocca? Curse with your foul mouth
if you must, but do you have to scream as well?'
'So that's your name—Bocca!' I said, 'You needn't
bother to talk now, you traitor. I'll make
a full report and tell the world what has happened.'
'Tell them what you like,' it said, 'but get out of
here. And if you do manage to return from
hell, don't forget to mention what this fellow,
who couldn't keep his mouth shut, is in for. Put
down this in your report: "among the traitors
kept in cold storage," you can say, "I saw one
Buso of Dovera, known to all readers
as the man who took bribes from the French." And if they
ask you who else was there, I can give you a
few more names.'

The excuse for this otherwise impertinent version is that it may
bring out what is really there in the original, the naked way of
speaking. The speakers are not thinking about the impression they
are making as they speak. They are not keeping up appearances:
they express themselves with crude vigour. This is the impression
I obtain from the episode in the *Iliad*. Achilles seems to be speaking frankly, without airs.

We are not, however, driven back on third-rate translations if
we seek through English to come closer to Homer's nobility. What
I wish to get rid of is all that is Victorian in the word 'noble.' The
note of nobility does not, I contend, involve removing action or
speech from the center of life. Certainly, we must feel above the
brutality presented. We must be allowed to see it through the

eyes of humanity. The modern sickened fascination with brutality
is not noble. Here, then, is a passage that should help us to define
the nobility of great literature when the theme is the hero becoming a brute.

Macd. Turne Hell-hound, turne.
Macb. Of all men else I haue auoyded thee:
  But get thee backe, my soule is too much charg'd
  With blood of thine already.
Macd. I haue no words,
  My voice is in my Sword, thou bloodier Villaine
  Then termes can giue thee out. *Fight. Alarum*
Macb. Thou loosest labour,
  As easie may'st thou the intrenchant Ayre
  With thy keene Sword impresse, as make me bleed:
  Let fall thy blade on vulnerable Crests,
  I beare a charmed Life, which must not yeeld
  To one of woman borne.
Macd. Dispaire thy Charme,
  And let the Angell whom thou still hast seru'd
  Tell thee, *Macduffe* was from his Mothers womb
  Vntimely ript.
Macb. Accursed be that tongue that tels mee so;
  For it hath Cow'd my better part of man:
  And be these Iugling Fiends no more beleeu'd,
  That palter with vs in a double sence,
  That keepe the word of promise to our eare,
  And breake it to our hope. Ile not fight with thee.
Macd. Then yeeld thee Coward,
  And liue to be the shew, and gaze o'th'time.
  Wee'l haue thee, as our rarer Monsters are
  Painted vpon a pole, and vnder-writ,
  Heere may you see the Tyrant.
Macb. I will not yeeld
  To kisse the ground before young *Malcomes* feet,
  And to be baited with the Rabbles curse.
  Though Byrnane wood be come to Dunsinane,
  And thou oppos'd, being of no woman borne,
  Yet I will try the last. Before my body,
  I throw my warlike Shield: Lay on *Macduffe*,
  And damn'd be him, that first cries hold, enough.
         Exeunt fighting.

Clearly, if we consider how much else beside naked dramatic
speech there is in the line

  And to be baited with the Rabbles curse

the humanity of Shakespeare is present in more complex ways
here than in the Greek or the Italian.

If there is anything in these criticisms, does it not begin to look as though Arnold's insouciance, persiflage and 'vivacity' are all symptoms of the wrong sort of ease? May not these, too, be symptoms or rather the mask hiding Arnold's embarrassment over failure to expose himself to Homer and discover himself? And if so, is not his air of superiority, his assumption that he is standing at the center and commanding to the horizon a little . . . maddening?

And I have not dealt with his failure to understand the nature of translation!

ARNOLD, H. A. MASON, & THE CLASSICAL TRADITION

Matthew Arnold's relation to Græco-Roman antiquity has re-
ceived persistent attention in recent years. In 1952 Kenneth Allott
° established the fact that Arnold's successive dealings with classical culture heavily influenced the paralleling of Victorian England
with the Empire of Marcus Aurelius in *Marius the Epicurean*.[1]
The publication of Arnold's earliest prose writings under the title
On the Classical Tradition focussed attention on this thread in the
complex fabric of Arnold's discursive themes, and provided the
occasion for an astute essay by H. A. Mason.[2] More recently I have
myself tried to suggest the peculiar centrality in Arnold's development of his essay on Marcus Aurelius.[3]

It is to Mason's essay that I would like, now, to return. Precisely
because it is astute and balanced it is also worth arguing with.

Mason concerns himself almost entirely with the *Lectures on
Translating Homer*. Limiting himself thus, he begins by paying
them very high praise: not only are they a "rare exemplification
of the qualities that make a good literary critic," but they em-
body a "perfection of manner" characterized by "charm, vivacity,
and ease," and "remain the first and only book to put into the
hands of the beginner who would make something of Homer as
a poet." But an implied emphasis is here already thrown on their
suitability for a *beginner*; and the rest of Mason's remarks are
directed toward showing precisely how Arnold does not satisfy
the requirements of a full and mature evaluation of Homer: an
evaluation which, for an Englishman, is intrinsically and inescap-
ably bound up with his response to the supreme classic of English
literature. Arnold, insofar as his own response to Shakespeare was
constricted and inadequate, did not—could not—bring to Homer
a fully sensitive range of response. And from this derives the
ultimately constricting quality of Arnold's categories of Homeric
"dignity" and "nobility" as we see them in the *Lectures*.

In the development of Mason's argument there are, it seems to
me, two cruxes which deserve close attention. In his second paragraph Mason offers the suggestion that if Arnold's claims for
Homer and his conception of the translator's function are indeed
"radically inadequate," then it may appear

> that Arnold suffered from having lost contact with the wis-
> dom of the eighteenth century as we see it embodied in
> Samuel Johnson and that he failed in his characterization of
> Homer because he stood in a wrong relation to all the Greek
> classics.

A few paragraphs later he writes:

> Arnold needed the classics for his very existence or continu-

[254]

ing existence in an alien (as he felt it) world. Therefore he saw them predominantly in one light, the light he had to obtain from them if he was not to live in darkness. To prop Arnold's mind, Homer, Epictetus and Sophocles had to be seen in contrast to Victorian England and remote from its worries and distractions . . . . By adverting his gaze from ✻ some things and failing to take an interest in others [Arnold] enabled himself to see the Greek classics fixed in god-like calm, like the statues under glass cases of which the Victorians were so fond.

I think it is by now common knowledge that Arnold was not in the ordinary sense a systematic or even a coherent thinker; if we differ at all from his harsher nineteenth-century critics then it is because we find his inconsistencies more interesting, and above all more relevant, than their tidy packages of thought. It *should* be common knowledge (though I am afraid it isn't) that much argument concerning Arnold has taken the form of an endless series of nonsequiturs; that his critics have too often tried to reduce the complexities and ambiguities of his thought—qualities inseparable, I think, from his "charm" and "vivacity"—to a pat sentence or two of paraphrase; the result being, as we might expect, that no one's paraphrase quite agrees with anybody else's. My argument with Mason stems from the fact that he does precisely this in summarizing Arnold's relation to the classical tradition, and that in the process that relation, even as Mason praises the vivacity of the *Lectures,* comes to look in its larger aspects like the operation not of a living and flexible mind but of a Victorian intellectual embalmer.

To take, first, Mason's charge that Arnold "enabled himself to see the Greek classics fixed in god-like calm," and his subsequent characterization of Arnold as one who "turns the raw and bleeding heroes of Greek legend into wax figures" by his inability to see that the Greek tragedians "preserved so much in their plays of the primitive and revolting": It would be perverse to deny that Arnold sometimes spoke of the Greeks in the "god-like calm" vein, and that he was capable of delivering very unfortunate judgments on the nastier aspects of Greek legend; an especially painful example of the latter is quoted by Mason from Arnold's Preface to *Merope.* But that Preface also contains Arnold's most wide-ranging and coherent discussion of Greek tragedy, which, since it is central to any discussion of his relation to classical culture, and is clearly delivered with more forethought than his offhand remarks on Maffei's alteration of the Merope story, surely deserves corresponding weight and attention:

> But it cannot be denied that the Greek tragic forms, although not the only possible tragic forms, satisfy, in the most perfect manner, some of the most urgent demands of the human spirit. If, on the one hand, the human spirit demands

[255]

✻for 'adverting'] *read* 'averting'

variety and the widest possible range, it equally demands, on the other hand, depth and concentration in its impressions. Powerful thought and emotion, flowing in strongly marked channels, make a stronger impression: this is the main reason why a metrical form is a more effective vehicle for them than prose: in prose there is more freedom, but, in the metrical form, the very limit gives a sense [of] precision and emphasis. This sense of emphatic distinctness in our impressions rises, as the thought and emotion swell higher and higher without overflowing their boundaries, to a lofty sense of the mastery of the human spirit over its own stormiest agitations; and this, again, conducts us to a state of feeling which it is the highest aim of tragedy to produce, to a *sentiment of sublime acquiescence in the course of fate, and in the dispensations of human life.*

What has been said explains, I think, the reason of the effectiveness of the severe forms of Greek tragedy, with its strongly marked boundaries, with its recurrence, even in the most agitating situations, of mutually replying masses of metrical arrangement. Sometimes the agitation becomes overwhelming, and the correspondence is for a time lost, the torrent of feeling flows for a space without check; but the balance is restored before the tragedy closes: the final sentiment in the mind must be one not of trouble, but of acquiescence.[4]

This is seriously dated, and woolly in much of its language; but it is surely not incompatible with the fact that the Greek tragedians preserved primitive and revolting elements in their plays, any more than an insistence of the ultimate unifying order of a Shakespearean tragedy nullifies the power of its subsumed representations of the demonic and the anarchical. (The word "agitation" has lost much of its force since Arnold wrote and has, today, slightly comical and old-maidish overtones; but compare it for effectiveness to Pater's harping on that abominable phrase "the pagan sadness.")

My second point of disagreement centers itself on Mason's statement that Arnold saw the classics *in toto* "predominantly in one light"; that "Homer, Epictetus and Sophocles had to be seen in contrast to Victorian England and remote from its worries and distractions"; and that the result was to fix (or, in my own paraphrase, to embalm) the Greek classics "in god-like calm." Arnold's identification of himself with Sophocles, as two who had heard at vastly different times "the eternal note of sadness" in the ebb-tide, should be enough to cast doubt on the sweep of this generalization; but *Dover Beach* is only one example of a persistent element of personal and social identification in Arnold's dealings with classical antiquity. This sense of affinity shows itself as early as the Preface to the first edition of Arnold's *Poems* (1853), when Arnold describes Empedocles as

> the last of the Greek religious philosophers . . . having survived his fellows, living on into a time when the habits of Greek thought and feeling had begun fast to change, character to dwindle, the influence of the Sophists to prevail. Into the feelings of a man so situated there entered much that we are accustomed to consider exclusively modern; how much, the fragments of Empedocles himself which remain to us are sufficient at least to indicate. What those who are familiar only with the great monuments of early Greek genius suppose to be its exclusive characteristics, have disappeared: the calm, the cheerfulness, the disinterested objectivity have disappeared; the dialogue of the mind with itself has commenced; modern problems have presented themselves; we hear already the doubts, we witness the discouragement, of Hamlet and of Faust.[5]

—doubts and discouragements of a kind to which Arnold was singularly prone. Here, already, a characteristic note has been struck: for Arnold finds its easiest to identify himself (the reference to Sophocles in *Dover Beach* notwithstanding) with the post-Hellenic figures and monuments of classical culture. In the 1857 lecture "On the Modern Element in Literature" the age of Pericles emerges as "a highly-developed, a modern, a deeply-interesting epoch," but the period of Roman ascendancy, despite its literary inferiority to fifth-century Athens, excels it in being "a period more significant and more interesting, because fuller, than the great period of Greece."[6] In a letter Arnold wrote to his sister "K" from Nimes on 22 May 1859 the Roman and English spirits are compared.[7] And Arnold's essay on Marcus Aurelius (1863) shows him not only identifying himself with the Stoic Emperor —an identification which accounts, as I have tried to demonstrate elsewhere, for some of the peculiar qualities of the essay as a whole—but making an extended point of the fact that

> Marcus Aurelius has, for us moderns, this great superiority in interest over Saint Louis or Alfred, that he lived and acted in a state of society modern by its essential characteristics, in an epoch akin to our own, in a brilliant centre of civilization. Trajan talks of "our enlightened age" just as glibly as the *Times* talks of it. Marcus Aurelius thus becomes for us a man like ourselves, a man in all things tempted as we are . . . . Neither Alfred nor Saint Louis can be morally and intellectually as near to us as Marcus Aurelius.[8]

In other words, Pater's act of synthesis in drawing up a whole ∗ series of Arnold's writing in the 1850's and '60's in order to establish a parallel between Antonine Rome and Victorian England was (whatever one may otherwise think of Pater) a critical response

[257]

∗for 'drawing up'] *read* 'drawing upon'

to something which is genuinely present in Arnold's prefaces, essays and lectures. Taken in this context, Mason's strictures are applicable not to Arnold and "the classics" and not (without qualification) to Arnold and "the Greek classics," but to Arnold and Homer. It is simply not true that "Homer, Epictetus and Sophocles had to be seen in contrast to Victorian England and remote from its worries and distractions." On the contrary: the movement from Homer to Epictetus becomes, for Arnold, a movement toward a kind of modernity that has strongly contemporary overtones.

Against the background of Arnold's persistent sense of affinity with varying aspects of Græco-Roman antiquity, the *Lectures* themselves take on a peculiar interest which has not, I think, been previously noted: for they represent an act of resistance to precisely this tendency in himself, an attempt to mark off a phase of Greek culture which would be most resolutely resistant to "modernization." In a passage which recalls and anticipates many of his dealings with classical culture, he writes:

> Modern sentiment tries to make the ancient not less than the modern world its own; but against modern sentiment in its applications to Homer the translator, if he would feel Homer truly—and unless he feels him truly, how can he render him truly?—cannot be too much on his guard.[9]

And a remark of Ruskin's on Homer, Arnold continues, represents "a just specimen of that sort of application of modern sentiment to the ancients, against which a student, who wishes to feel the ancients truly, cannot too resolutely defend himself."[10] I think it would be just to say that by the time Arnold, two years later, published his essay on Marcus Aurelius, he had forgotten his own good advice; or at least that part of it in which he tried to fence off from the modernizing impulse not only Homer but the ancients in general.

A final point remains to be made concerning Mason's comparison of Arnold and Samuel Johnson, much to the detriment of the former. Surely the relevant fact here is that the "wisdom" of the eighteenth century as embodied in Dr. Johnson was unobtainable (and, in a basic way, insufficiently applicable) in a world already feeling the characteristic pressures of modernity, a world like our own, in which an immense critical and exclusive effort had to be made before wisdom could even begin to heave into sight; pressures too that made it necessary (as they make it necessary today) for all valuable social and critical thought to incorporate at least a measure of utopian feeling, with the back-reference that usually accompanies it. The process can be clearly seen in Dr. Leavis's dealing wi th Bunyan: it would be absurd to try to dissociate them from Dr. Leavis's concerned analysis of the world in which we live (I need not add that it would be equally absurd to see them as mere ideologically-conditioned reflexes). But a closely-related process is at work in Arnold's comments on Greek and Roman culture, and is *not* at work in the "wisdom" of Johnson. Arnold's involvement is inextricably bound up with his unique and often profound reaction to the temper of his own times; another reason why that involvement cannot be treated as a mere saving fantasy, which served only to immure the Greek classics "in god-like calm, like the statues under glass cases of which the Victorians were so fond."

Henry Ebel

FOOTNOTES

[1] "Pater and Arnold," *Essays in Criticism,* II (April 1952), 219–221.

[2] "Arnold and the Classical Tradition," *Arion,* I (Autumn, 1962), 89–97.

[3] "Matthew Arnold and Marcus Aurelius," *Studies in English Literature,* III (Autumn, 1963), 555–566.

[4] *The Complete Prose Works of Matthew Arnold,* ed. R. H. Super, Vol. I: *On the Classical Tradition* (Ann Arbor, 1960), 58–59.

[5] *Ibid.,* p. 1.

[6] *Ibid.,* pp. 28–37.

[7] *Unpublished Letters of Matthew Arnold,* ed. Arnold Whitridge (New Haven, 1923), pp. 44–45.

[8] Matthew Arnold, "Marcus Aurelius," *The Victoria Magazine,* II (November, 1863), 7.

[9] *Complete Prose Works, op. cit.,* p. 101.

[10] *Ibid.,* pp. 101–102.

Robert Fitzgerald

T HE VERSION OF THE AENEID THAT WE
might have had in English poetry was never written. By this I do
not mean merely that there is no complete Aeneid in English as
good as Gavin Douglas' *Eneados* in Scots of the Early 16th
Century; I mean that during two periods, very roughly from 1570
to 1650 and from 1800 to 1880, someone might have done justice
to the poem, and no one did. It is easy to conceive an *Aeneid* by
Keats, who had read Virgil in school and whose power over
language resembled Virgil's, or by the Tennyson of *Milton* and
Ulysses. From these poets and their century, however, we do not
even have any partial attempts that are really memorable. From
Tudor times we do; an English *Aeneid* of the 16th Century exists
in fragments so to speak, or potentially. It can be so present to the
imagination that we can almost reconstruct it, or make a com-
posite. There is the dignity and sonority of Surrey:

> O Queen, it is thy will
> I should renew a woe cannot be told,
> How that the Greeks did spoil and overthrow
> The Phrygian wealth and wailful realm of Troy ...

and there is the motley splendor and kick of Stanyhurst:

> Now manhood and garbroyles I chaunt, and martial horror.
> I blaze that captayne first from Troy cittye repairing
> Like wandering pilgrim too famosed Italie trudging
> And coast of Lavyn; soust with tempestuus hurlwynd ...

And the élan of Marlowe:

> Not moved at all, but smiling at his tears,
> This butcher whilst his hands were yet held up,
> Treading upon his breast, struck off his hands ...

Spenser, an avowed Virgilian, could have made an admirable
Aeneid. But the poet most nearly capable of the full Virgilian
range was probably John Milton. Suppose that after his return
from Italy around 1640 Milton had taken up Virgil and had spent
the next years not in controversy but in retirement, translating
the *Aeneid*. Our literature would have been handsomely—and
very usefully—enlarged. Just as Marvell wrote the one truly
Horatian ode in English, Milton might have written the one truly
Virgilian long poem.

It fell to John Dryden, however, to produce the English *Aeneid*,
and at the time he did so neither he nor any other Englishmen
could manage, except momentarily, the kind of poetry required.
They were too interested in improving on it. I do not say this
entirely in malice, but with sympathy for the criterion of "sense"
and with respect for the cultivated and sometimes noble energy of
Dryden's writing. If anyone then living could have done a great

Aeneid, Dryden could. He was not narrowly a man of his time in the way Rochester was, for example. He admired and drew upon Spenser, Shakespeare and Jonson. He appreciated Donne's Satires, and the "Metaphysical" poets contributed something to his style. But after the Restoration of 1660, urbanity and abstraction overcame English letters, and Dryden himself wanted an English Academy, on the order of the French, to "purify" the language of poetry. In the exploration of the physical world, the Royal Society, of which Dryden as Poet Laureate was a nominal member, had succeeded Raleigh and Drake. Likewise in poetry, discussion and wit now flourished at a certain remove from discovery and experience.

If we think only of prosody, it may appear that the blank verse masters, Shakespeare and Milton, had exhausted one great form for generations. It is certainly impressive and odd that long before the end of the 17th Century the rhymed couplet had swept the field in English verse. We might imagine that the couplet itself diminished the range of poetry, but in fact pentameter couplets had been used by Douglas for his *Eneados* and by Chapman for his *Odyssey.* An *Aeneid* in blank verse would not necessarily have been any better than in couplets like these:

> Buskins of shells all silvered usèd she,
> And brancht with blushing corall to the knee;
> Where sparrows pearcht, of hollow pearl and gold,
> Such as the world would wonder to behold . . .

or these:

> When Evening grey doth rise, I fetch my round
> Over the mount, and all this hallow'd ground,
> And early ere the odorous breath of morn
> Awakes the slumbring leaves, or tassel'd horn
> Shakes the high thicket, haste I all about,
> Number my ranks, and visit every sprout
> With puissant words, and murmurs made to bless,
> But else in deep of night when drowsiness
> Hath lockt up mortal sense, then listen I
> To the celestial Sirens harmony,
> That sit upon the nine enfolded sphears,
> And sing to those that hold the vital shears,
> And turn the adamantine spindle round,
> On which the fate of gods and men is wound.

Each of these examples could be called Virgilian, Marlowe's for the image and sound, and Milton's for the running syntax and resourceful diction, culminating in his adamantine spindle, quite superb.

Dryden's predicament, then, was not that of being enslaved to the rhymed couplet; it was the enslavement of the couplet itself to a certain style. The example of the French Alexandrine had had much to do with tidying and balancing the English couplet, though Dryden himself remarked on the variety that the alternation of masculine and feminine endings gave the French couplets, and on the lightness that made the French language fall easily into logical symmetries. He realized that the genius of his own language might be cramped by these, but they charmed him and his contemporaries, and in place of greater touchstones Dryden was fond of quoting Denham's lines on the Thames:

O could I flow like thee, and make thy stream
My great example, as it is my theme!
Though deep, yet clear, though gentle, yet not dull,
Strong without rage, without ore-flowing full.

He was also fond of alluding to Waller as the man who taught smoothness to English numbers, by which he meant rhyming without wrenching the natural order of words, disposed as in "the negligence of prose." It is perhaps a revealing phrase. Engaged as he was in breaking ground for English criticism and in developing English critical prose, Dryden in practice wanted the discursive merits, a little negligence included, in verse as well.

At any rate, a new realm of possibilities had opened for English poets to explore, and we know the refinement to which in due course Pope would bring the couplet. But now another fact comes in for consideration, and that is that before this couplet became "heroic" its chief triumph was in satire. Dryden wrote *Absalom and Achitophel* and *Mac Flecknoe* in his prime, years before he thought of translating the *Aeneid*. Another way of putting this is to say that his couplet was mock-heroic first. The satires owe their savor partly to a deliberate use of epic convention or allusion for topical burlesque. In *Mac Flecknoe*, for example, there are a number of lines that parody well-known passages in Virgil:

At his right hand our young Ascanius sate,
Rome's other hope, and pillar of the State.
His brows thick fogs, instead of glories, grace,
And lambent dullness played around his face . . .

The pleasure given by this sort of thing was about all anyone wanted of the heroic under Charles II, apart from theatrical heroics, another genre. Could a style so ingeniously employed in making fun of epic be effectively used for epic? The same sequence occurred, and the same question arises, a generation later in the case of Pope, who wrote *The Rape of the Lock* before he translated Homer.

Under William and Mary in 1689 Dryden, a Jacobite and a Catholic, lost his Laureateship and his income and faced relative adversity. Among various shifts to support himself, he gave thought again to writing a heroic poem, an enterprise that his former royal patrons had not encouraged. He must have realized that by this time it was beyond him; even for the translation of

Virgil, upon which at length he settled, he doubted his powers and his poetic means. Insofar as chief among these means was the couplet trained in verse satire, it is curious to see him dragging his favorite Virgil into a discourse on satire which in 1692 he prefaced to a book of translations of Persius and Juvenal. Noting Martial's remark that Virgil could have written better lyrics than Horace, Dryden went Martial one better. "Virgil," said he, "could have written sharper satires than either Horace or Juvenal, if he would have employed his talent that way." As evidence, he supplied a well-chosen quotation from the Third Eclogue. The notion of Virgil as a satirist has the elation of some great figure of speech, a sublime chiasmus, when proposed by the author of *Mac Flecknoe* just before he girds himself for *The Aeneid*.

The art of translation before Dryden had been a gentleman's diversion or a scribbler's piece work, but Dryden's Virgil was a business venture, a writing project of a distinctly modern kind. He arranged for it, and eventually signed a contract, with his Fleet Street Printer, Tonson, and in a letter of December 12th, 1693, he said: "I propose to do it by subscription, having an hundred and two brass cuts, with the coats of arms of the subscriber to each cut; and every subscriber to pay five guineas, half in hand, besides another inferior subscription of two guineas for the rest, whose names are only written in a catalogue printed with the book."

This may not have been the first publishing enterprise of the kind, but it was the most ambitious and successful ever until then carried out in England. One hundred and one subscribers were found for the "brass cuts"—deplorable engravings of neo-classic statuary—and three hundred fifty-one gentlemen paid two guineas to be enrolled in the "catalogue" or list. Thus the total amount subscribed appears to have been 1,229 pounds 8 shillings. Besides his share of this, whatever it was, Dryden received gifts from the three noble patrons to whom he dedicated, respectively, the *Pastorals*, the *Georgics*, and the *Aeneid*—"that no opportunity of profit might be lost," as Dr. Johnson observed more than eighty years later. According to a recent estimate,[1] the poet's income can be reckoned at about 1,600 pounds, or 400 pounds a year if divided equally among the four years—1694, 1695, 1696 and 1697 —spent on the labor.

It probably came down to little more than three working years, as he himself counted it, for besides time lost to affairs or illness he took two months off to do a prose version of du Fresnoy's Latin poem, *De Arte Graphica*, and a preface for it. If we suppose

[1] By William Frost, in *Dryden and the Art of Translation*, (Yale, 1955).

Dryden to have worked 1,000 full days on his Virgil, he must have turned out an average of at least sixteen lines, or eight couplets, a day, for his *Aeneid* alone runs to 13,700 lines (for 9,896 Latin lines), and the *Pastorals* and *Georgics,* some of which he had only to revise, come to 4,358 lines more.

It seems that all England, or at any rate all Englishmen who had paid their guineas, awaited the result with impatience, if not with anxiety; the poet later complained that some grew clamorous. According to Johnson, "the nation considered its honor as interested in the event." Since Dryden felt under great pressure of time, his friends and admirers helped him as they could. Noblemen invited him to work at their country houses, a young barrister made him a gift of the principal annotated editions of Virgil, Addison at twenty-four undertook to write the prose "arguments" for the various Books, and Congreve, at twenty-seven, did Dryden the considerable favor of checking his *Aeneid* against the Latin text.

At the end of these exertions Tonson was able to bring out, in July, 1697, in the pomp of folio, "The WORKS of VIRGIL: containing His PASTORALS, GEORGICS, AND AENEIS. Translated into English Verse; By Mr. DRYDEN / Adorn'd with a Hundred Sculptures," etc. A few corrections and changes were made, and a missing couplet supplied, in a second folio edition in 1698. Dryden had been sixty-two when he undertook the translation; he was sixty-six when it was published. It was the longest sustained labor of his life. His health suffered from application to it, by his own account, and in any case he had but three more years to live. Although he may for a time have felt some hopes of royal recognition by their Protestant Majesties, he had refused to seek King William's favor and had resigned himself to his position as a veteran of a repudiated party and a vanished court—a court with whose vices he felt unfairly associated. He renounced satire, "for who gives physic to the great when uncalled?" and produced his Virgil as a demonstration of his independence and a means of maintaining it. In his Postscript to the Reader, he wrote:

> What Virgil wrote in the vigor of his age, in plenty and at ease, I have undertaken to translate in my declining years: struggling with wants, oppressed with sickness, curbed in my genius, liable to be misconstrued in all I write; and my judges, if they are not very equitable, already prejudiced against me, by the lying character which has been given them of my morals. Yet steady to my principles, and not dispirited with my afflictions, I have, by the blessing of God on my endeavors, overcome all difficulties; and, in some measure, acquitted myself of the debt which I owed the public, when I undertook this work. In the first place therefore, I thankfully acknowledge to the Almighty Power, the

assistance he has given me in the beginning, the prosecution, and conclusion of my present studies, which are more happily performed than I could have promised to myself, when I labored under such discouragements. For, what I have done, imperfect as it is, for want of health and leisure to correct it, will be judged in after ages, and possibly in the present, to be no dishonor to my native country ...

He was quite right. Few subscribers were disappointed, and the 18th Century immensely appreciated Dryden's *Aeneid*. Pope called it "the most noble and spirited translation that I know in any language." There is no doubt that it gave Pope the idea for his own enterprise with the *Iliad* some fifteen years later. The heroic couplet had had the heroic thrust upon it by Dryden. We cannot call ourselves acquainted with English poetry in his age and in the next unless we have read his translation, and it is still fascinating to see his mind at play over his great original.

Whatever the incongruities between the two poets, between the shy perfectionist of Latin verse in his Parthenopean villa and the able Restoration wit in his coffee house, the fact remains that few English writers have ever known or admired Virgil as Dryden did. Amid the pages of flattery, interested pleading and neo-classic aesthetics in Dryden's prefaces, we come upon nothing more genuine—and nothing more perceptive within limits—than his frequent references to Virgil. To some extent, of course, it was an interest that he shared with the age itself. Writers for whom Latin was still a living language knew what it was to make Latin verses and in this sense knew what Virgil had been doing. Aspects of the Virgilian lingered in their imaginations and took life again even in their candlelit theatres: Racine's *Andromaque* was first performed in 1667 and Purcell's *Dido and Aeneas* in 1689. Still, Dryden's devotion was remarkable. It began early and lasted all his life.

During 1665 and 1666, when London was being visited first by plague and then by the Great Fire, Dryden worked in Wiltshire on his Dialogue *Essay of Dramatic Poesy* and on a long poem, *Annus Mirabilis*. In the Dialogue he touched on Virgil as the "pattern of elaborate writing" and as Ovid's superior in restraint. In his preface to *Annus Mirabilis* he declared that Virgil had been his master in this poem, as, in a sense, anyone could see from the fact that some thirty passages in it were direct imitations or echoes. For example:

All hands employed, the royal work grows warm,
    Like laboring bees on a long summer's day ...

It is a baroque poem in which Virgil as a pattern of elaborate writing served him only too well, but Dryden's critical remarks on Virgil are another matter. "We see the objects he presents us with in their native figures, in their proper motions; but so we see them, as our own eyes could never have beheld them so beautiful in themselves . . . the very sound of his words have often somewhat that is connatural to the subject . . ." Not only is this just, but the concluding remark is far from commonplace even now.

In his subsequent prose, Dryden refers often enough to Virgil to give us the impression that the text lay open on his table for thirty years. He praised "the divine Virgil" more frequently even than he did Waller's contribution to English numbers. His last insights appear to have come, naturally enough, during his work on the translation. One, a particularly valuable one, he found a place for in his preface to *De Arte Graphica* in 1695. "Virgil knew how to rise by degrees in his expressions; Statius was in his towering heights at the first stretch of his pinions." In the course of his long preface dedicatory of the *Aeneid* Dryden wrote with a craftsman's interest in Virgil's style. He had compared Virgil and Ovid years before, to Ovid's disadvantage, and now touched again on this subject. Speaking of French poets, he said: "The turn on thoughts and words is their chief talent, but the epic poem is too stately to receive those little ornaments . . . Virgil is never frequent in those turns, like Ovid, but much more sparing of them in his Aeneis than in his Pastorals and Georgics.

Ignoscenda quidem, scirent si ignoscere Manes.

That turn is beautiful indeed, but he employs it in the story of Orpheus and Eurydice, not in his great poem. I have used that license in his Aeneis sometimes; but I own it as my fault. 'Twas given to those who understand no better . . ."

As we read Dryden's *Aeneid* we may find this passage recurring to us fairly often; it becomes a nice question, in fact, how much weight to give to the last sentence. Another passage of special interest in the light of the translation itself is that in which he remarks on "the sober retrenchments of his [Virgil's] sense, which always leaves somewhat to gratify our imagination, on which it may enlarge at pleasure . . ."

Of formal criticism, analysis of Virgil's composition in the large, Dryden had little to offer beyond a discussion of standard topics of neo-classic criticism (the relative greatness of heroic poetry and tragedy, "piety" versus valor as the virtue of the epic hero, the behavior of Aeneas toward Dido, the debt of Virgil to Homer, the elapsed time of the main action, etc.) that no longer seem to us of the greatest interest. He did notice that extended "epic similes" were introduced by Virgil after, not before, the crest of an action, and took as his example the one in Book I in which Neptune is likened to a respected Roman official calming a mob. A modern critic would not fail to see something "thematic" in this first simile of the *Aeneid,* but notions of that sort could not occur to Dryden. He wondered, oddly enough, why Virgil allowed Aeneas to be wounded toward the end of the poem—an episode that is not only obviously dramatic but makes for epic symmetry: the just prince's disablement balanced against that of the cruel exile, Mezentius, as the death of Pallas is balanced by that of Lausus. We hear nothing from Dryden of Virgil's architectonics and depth of suggestion, nor of the quality of his imagination—so supreme and terrifying when the Fury in the form of a small bird beats around Turnus' head in the final combat, so forced and awkward when Aeneas' ships are transformed into sea-nymphs and we are troubled for a moment by an image of nereids on that scale.

As to Virgil's way with language, however, I do not know any happier descriptions than Dryden's. "His words are not only chosen, but the places in which he ranks them, for the sound. He who removes them from the station wherein their master set them spoils the harmony. What he says of the Sibyl's prophecies may be as properly applied to every word of his: they must be read in order as they lie; the least breath discomposes them; and somewhat of their divinity is lost . . . he is like ambergris, a rich perfume, but of so close and glutinous a body that it must be opened with inferior scents of musk or civet, or the sweetness will not be drawn out into another language . . .What modern language, or what poet, can express the majestic beauty of this one verse amongst a thousand others?

aude, hospes, contemnere opes, et te quoque dignum finge deo.

For my part, I am lost in the admiration of it: I contemn the world when I think on it, and myself when I translate it."

Conscious as he was of the inferiority of his "coarse English," Dryden strove undaunted to correct it so far as he could. "I have endeavored," he said, "to follow the example of my master: and am the first Englishman, perhaps, who made it his design to copy him in his numbers [metrical excellence], his choice of words, and his placing them for the sweetness of the sound. On this last consideration I have shunned the caesura [elision] . . . For where that is used, it gives a roughness to the verse, of which we can have little need, in a language which is over-stocked with consonants. Such is not the Latin, where the vowels and consonants are mixed in proportion to each other . . ." His tentative claim for himself may recall a wicked remark of Swift's to the effect that people would not have been so aware of Dryden's merit as a playwright if he had not told them so often in his prefaces. But it is true and highly pertinent that English is over-stocked with consonants, while in Latin vowels and consonants are better mixed.

With respect to diction, the translator knew from Horace that Virgil's secret lay in the placement of words and their subtle stress upon one another, a mutual energizing of words within a line or passage to achieve that "majesty in the midst of plainness" that Dryden so admired. The difficulty of rendering such effects is rather simplified in his account of it. In practice, he said, "I found the difficulty of translation growing on me in every succeeding Book. For Virgil, above all poets, had a stock, which I may call inexhaustible, of figurative, elegant, and sounding words . . . Virgil called upon me in every line for some new word: and I paid so long, that I was almost bankrupt. So that the latter end must needs be more burdensome than the beginning or the middle. And consequently the twelfth Aeneid cost me double the time of the first and second. What had become of me if Virgil had taxed me with another Book?"

Dryden's opinion of what a translation should be had already been expressed at some length in various essays, beginning with his preface to *Ovid's Epistles* in 1680. No part of Dryden's criticism seemed more important or more definitive to Pope and Johnson. It has been rejected by some later critics, to whom scientific scholarship and historical study have made differences of language and culture appear more nearly absolute, but it has continued to be the premise of poet-translators, of Ezra Pound, for one. ("The best trans. is into the language the author wd. have used had he been writing in the translator's language.") In his preface to the *Aeneid* Dryden re-stated it. "The way I have taken is not so strait as Metaphrase [word for word] nor so loose as Paraphrase: Some things too I have omitted, and sometimes have added of my own. Yet the omissions, I hope, are but of circumstances [incidentals] and such as would have no grace in English; and the additions, I also hope, are easily deduced from Virgil's sense . . . I have endeavored to make Virgil speak such English as he would himself have spoken, if he had been born in England, and in this present age . . ."

There was nothing wrong with Dryden's command of Latin. It was better than ours is likely to be, and has been well defended[1] against imputations of ignorance. He used the latest edition of Virgil prepared in 1675 by the French editor Charles de la Rue (Carolus Ruaeus) for the Dauphin of France (*in usum serenissimi Delphini*), one of a series referred to by Dryden as "the Dolphins." This presented to him on every page not only the best text available in his time but a Latin prose paraphrase, or *interpretatio*, and notes. Dryden generally stuck to Ruaeus' interpretation and followed it in many of his expansions, but occasionally he insisted on his own interpretation and at least once left untranslated a line that baffled him in Ruaeus—though he later found a better reading in an edition by the Dutch scholar Nicolas Heinsius.

[1] By J. McG. Bottkol in *Modern Philology*, 11(1943)241–254.

As he worked with all possible speed, Dryden used all possible aids to composition, including such previous translations as he could lay his hands on. He does not appear to have known the Scots translation by Gavin Douglas; he made no reference to Surrey's version (1574) of Books I and II nor to Stanyhurst's version (1582) of Books I through IV. He had the Italian translation by Caro (1581) and the French translation by Segrais (1668); he had Denham's version (1636) of Book II, Waller and Godolphin's version (1658) of Book IV, and Ogilby's version (1649) of the whole poem. He also received from Paris in manuscript a translation by the Jacobite Earl of Lauderdale, completed before his death in 1695 but unpublished until 1718. Dryden drew on all of these for rhymes, phrases, and even for lines. He took five lines of Denham and acknowledged taking one; from Lauderdale he plundered freely, taking about 800 lines with improvements or at least minor changes and about 200 lines without change and without acknowledgment. We would call this plagiarism, but an ambiguous reference to Lauderdale in Dryden's preface may indicate that that nobleman had consented to it, perhaps because on another occasion he had printed a great many lines of Dryden as his own. Dryden admitted his debt somewhat disingenuously by saying that "having his manuscript in my hands, I consulted it as often as I doubted of my author's sense."

It is plain from Dryden's own remarks that he felt the inadequacy of his verse and his diction. To break the monotony of his couplets he resorted to triplets and Alexandrines, often in combination. This provided what might be called momentary relief, but did not suffice in the long run. In certain Books, III for example, the habit of the closed couplet so hobbled the movement of his narrative that he himself seems to have become bored with it, and in the following Books we find him trying more successfully to make verse paragraphs beginning within one couplet and ending within a later one.

He tried, likewise, to extend his resources of language. The effort was not constant enough to save him from the curse of a number of poeticisms that were even then clichés. Reiteration does not convince us that shades were so frequently dusky, bosoms manly, seas briny, gore purple, night sable, skies vaulted and rent by shrieks, to name only a few. One recourse from this sort of thing would have been to look again at shades, bosoms, seas, gore, night, skies etc., but this would have been asking too much not only of Dryden but of the age. The role of vocabulary in poetry can be slightly misconceived, and Dryden slightly misconceived it. The "store of words" he found so inexhaustible in Virgil was first of all *copia* of imagination and feeling, and Dryden matched it best—as on occasion he did match it—from the same sources, not by sticking in new words and Latinisms.

"He was no lover of labor," observed Johnson. "What he

thought sufficient, he did not stop to make better; and allowed himself to leave many parts unfinished, in confidence that the good lines would overbalance the bad." This would be fair enough if it took account of Dryden's haste, probably as much to blame for his faults as aversion to labor. A number of his bad lines were doubly bad in that they introduced literal absurdities into Virgil's narrative. In Book I, 302 ff, we hear that after the intervention of Mercury

> ponunt ferocia Poeni   ⚬
> corda volente deo; in primis regina quietum
> accipit in Teucros animum et mentem benignam ...   ⚬

The Carthaginians and their queen, so the Latin says, were put in a benignant mood toward the approaching Trojans. In Dryden, 414 ff,

> The surly murmurs of the people cease,
> And, as the Fates required, they give the peace.
> The Queen herself suspends the rigid laws ...

But at that point the Queen took no such action, and when, later, the Trojans appeared, they petitioned her to do so. In Book II, 52–3, a spear is hurled at the Wooden Horse:

> stetit illa tremens, uteroque recusso
> insonuere cavae gemitumque dedere cavernae ...

it stuck trembling, and from the blow in the belly the hollow interior gave a resounding groan. In Dryden, 68–9:

> The sides transpierced return a rattling sound
> And groans of Greeks inclosed come issuing through the
>   wound.

Apart from the padded "come issuing," this misrepresents the situation to the point of farce. If any Greek had been heard groaning, the Horse would have had a short career. Again in Book II, 541 ff, Priam rebukes Pyrrhus by recalling Achilles' mercy:

> sed iura fidemque
> supplicis erubuit corpusque exsangue sepulcro
> reddidit Hectoreum meque in mea regna remisit,

that is to say, Achilles showed compunction at a suppliant's trust, restored Hector's dead body for burial and sent me back to my kingdom. In Dryden, 738 ff,

> He cheered my sorrows, and for sums of gold
> The bloodless carcass of my Hector sold ...

But Priam had said nothing of "sums of gold," and it would have cheapened his whole appeal if he had; nor is it true that in the *Iliad*, alluded to in this passage, Achilles "sold" Hector's body to

[271]

⚬ for 'ponunt'] *read* 'ponuntque'
⚬ for 'et mentem'] *read* 'mentemque'

his father. The translator was merely rhyming a poor couplet. So it goes, too frequently, throughout the poem.

Faults of this kind were not necessary, and it may seem to us that they could have been corrected by a moment's thought. They betray the haste of the translator. But more than this, they suggest that Dryden did not really value fidelity in such particulars as we do. Though in theory he understood that his task was to do so, and liked to think that he had, he did not consistently enter into the mind of the original artist to the point of seeing, hearing and feeling the scenes that Virgil created. Most often he wished rather to make a literary artefact answering to another literary artefact, and this satisfied the taste of his contemporaries. Up to a point, of course, they were right. The *Aeneid* is not a realistic work of art. Nevertheless, Dryden himself had noted of Virgil that "we see the objects he presents us with," and this therefore was one of the qualities of Virgil that he must have hoped to emulate. If his failures mattered less to his own age than they do to ours, so much the worse for his age.

Minor effects of haste are occasional eccentricities like "herds of wolves" in VII, 21, or tangled syntax, as in VII, 92:

> This plant, Latinus, when his town he walled
> Then found, and from the tree Laurentum called . . .

or X, 752:

> The holy coward fell: and forced to yield,
> The prince stood o'er the priest . . .

or fatal asyndeton, as in XII, 414:

> And struck the gentle youth, extended on the ground,

meaning that he hit and felled him. Again, we are inclined to ask why Dryden could not have reworked lines like these, if not for the first edition then for the second. Johnson appears to have been struck by the fact that he did not do so. "What he had once written, he dismissed from his thoughts; and I believe there is no example found of any correction or improvement made by him after publication."

Johnson may be excused for thinking so, but in fact he was wrong about this. Dryden "bestowed nine entire days" on corrections for the edition of 1698. These are usually of a spelling, a single word, sometimes of a phrase or a line, and hardly ever represent an attempt to re-write a passage or to revise it substantially. If, however, we look at certain parts of the *Aeneid* that Dryden had already done years before for a literary miscellany, *Sylvae* (1684), we find a few revisions of longer passages. At least one of these is worth close attention. For lines 459–61 of Book V, the earlier version had:

A lion's hide, amazing to behold,
Ponderous with bristles, and with paws of gold,
He gave the youth. . .

Ten years later Dryden wrote:

> . . . and from among the spoils he draws
> (Ponderous with shaggy mane, and golden paws)
> A lion's hide. . .

Here several admirable motives were at work: to abandon the
padding phrase, to let the syntax float and carry through the
couplet, and to strengthen the image and "feel" of the lion's hide.
The line in parenthesis is masterful and typical of Dryden at his
best. This revision shows what the poet might have done if he
had been able, or had wished, to take his whole translation as a
draft and to spend another three years overhauling it.

Dryden's good lines are often very good indeed, and they occur
frequently enough to keep the reader on the alert for the next one.
He was capable of lyric beauty:

With branches we the fanes adorn. . .

Not her own star confessed a light so clear. . .

And rent away with ease the lingering gold. . .

But more often his peculiar excellence lay in a whiplike power of
statement, swift and flexible but weighted:

His holy fillets the blue venom blots. . .

And on the shaded ocean rushed the night. . .

See Pallas, of her snaky buckler proud. . .

While the fierce riders clattered on their shields. . .

Lines like these may not "overbalance" the inferior ones, but they
check the effect of them and contribute enormously to the vigor
of the translation. So does Dryden's syntactical ingenuity within
the couplet. Those "turns" that he regarded as Ovidian are indeed
Ovidian in the sense that Ovid did them to death, but they are
not quite so sparse in Virgil as Dryden suggested; in fact they
occur here and there very naturally in the compact Latin (*nostro
doluisti saepe dolore* . . . . *una salus victis nullam sperare sa-
lutem*). Virgil was perhaps deliberately sparing of them, but
Dryden certainly was not. Often they, too, give an effect of swift-
ness and concision:

Through such a train of woes if I should run,
The day would sooner than the tale be done. . .

> . . . All combine to leave the state
> Who hate the tyrant, or who fear his hate . . .

[273]

The truth is that structure of this kind had already become an essential characteristic of the couplet style that Dryden bequeathed to Pope. Dryden probably could not have translated Virgil, or anyone else, without "that licence" that he owned as a fault. What he meant by saying "'Twas given to those who understand no better," I am not sure, unless this is a unique reflection on the taste of his readers—surely not those who got their coats of arms on the brass cuts? Every so often, no doubt, it is chiefly interesting as a trick, a rhetorician's amusement:

> Her cheeks the blood, her hand the web, forsakes . . .

There is this about it, too, that since Dryden's wit in his satires depends partly on the balanced, antithetical style, the more we find of that style in his Virgil the more we are reminded of the satires. We are reminded of them, anyway, by Dryden's gusto in many passages:

> . . . a thirsty soul,
> He took the challenge, and embraced the bowl . . .

> . . . the bleating lambs
> Securely swig the dug beneath the dams . . .

Then there are moments when we perceive a tone of decided burlesque, as in the episode of Hercules and Cacus in Book VIII, or in this couplet given to Turnus in Book IX (658–9) on the subject of human fortunes:

> Some, raised aloft, come tumbling down amain;
> Then fall so hard, they bound and rise again.

That, I think, was for the boys in school. In general, though, Dryden's touches of the satiric gave variety to his style and kept it from being unrelievedly high-flown. Certain couplets seem to have come straight out of *Absalom and Achitophel,* and are none the worse for that:

> But cautious in the field, he shunned the sword:
> A close-caballer and tongue-valiant lord.

In the altercation between Drances, so characterized, and Turnus in Book IX, Dryden was able to use the gift for verse debate that he had exercised for years in writing for the Restoration stage.

The attitude conveyed by Virgil's whole narrative of the war in Latium is cumulative and very complex. The way in which time and again violence gets out of hand, by malign force overcoming the will of peaceful leaders, makes us think that the iron of the Roman civil wars had entered into the poet. His laments for slain princes are overdone to the point of bathos. Slaughter interests him, of course, as a challenge to description, but he does not have Homer's even-handed and rather superhuman gaiety about battle.

Dryden could scarcely equal Virgil's massive effect of tragic ambiguity, but for all his heartiness he, who had lived through Cromwell's time and Monmouth's, looked with a reserve of his own on martial glory. In an occasional turn of phrase he implies it:

> The champion's chariot next is seen to roll,
> Besmeared with hostile blood, and honorably foul . . .

That is neither heroic nor Virgilian, but it has edge and character, and a sophisticated civilization stands behind it.

I hope I have made clear how Dryden's *Aeneid* suffered from being the rush job that it was, and yet how brilliantly he brought it off. No one else, with no matter how much leisure, has yet achieved a version as variously interesting and as true to the best style of a later age as his was to his own. He allowed himself a complacent sentence or two about it, but the final judgment expressed in his Dedication was severe:

"I have done great wrong to Virgil in the whole translation: want of time, the inferiority of our language, the inconvenience of rhyme, and all the other excuses I have made, may alleviate my fault, but cannot justify the boldness of my undertaking. What avails it me to acknowledge freely that I have been unable to do him right in any line?"

Too severe.